Holy Warriors

THE MIDDLE AGES SERIES

Ruth Mazo Karras, Series Editor

Edward Peters, Founding Editor

A complete list of books in the series is available from the publisher.

Holy Warrior

The Religious Ideology of Chivalry

Richard W. Kaeuper

PENN

University of Pennsylvania Press
Philadelphia

Copyright © 2009 University of Pennsylvania Press

Published by
University of Pennsylvania Press
Philadelphia, Pennsylvania 19104-4112

Printed in the United States of America on acid-free paper
10 9 8 7 6 5 4 3 2 1

Library of Congress Cataloging-in-Publication Data

Kaeuper, Richard W.
    Holy warriors : the religious ideology of chivalry / Richard W. Kaeuper.
       p.   cm. — (The Middle Ages series)
    ISBN 978-0-8122-4167-9 (alk. paper)
    Includes bibliographical references and index.
    1. Chivalry—Religious aspects. 2. Chivalry—Europe—History—To 1500.
3. Knights and knighthood—Europe—History—To 1500. 4. Chivalry in literature.
5. Civilization, Medieval. 6. Europe—Church history—600–1500. I. Title.
CR4519.K347   2009
940.1—dc22   2009004274

Frontispiece: An illustration of idealized knighthood in a righteous struggle against
sin and vice. From a thirteenth-century treatise on virtues and vices by William of
Peraldus, *Summa de vitiis*. British Library Harley Manuscript 3244, folios 27b, 28.
Copyright © British Library.

To Margaret

Wer ein solches Weib errungen

Stimm' in unsern Jubel ein!

CONTENTS

Holy Warriors

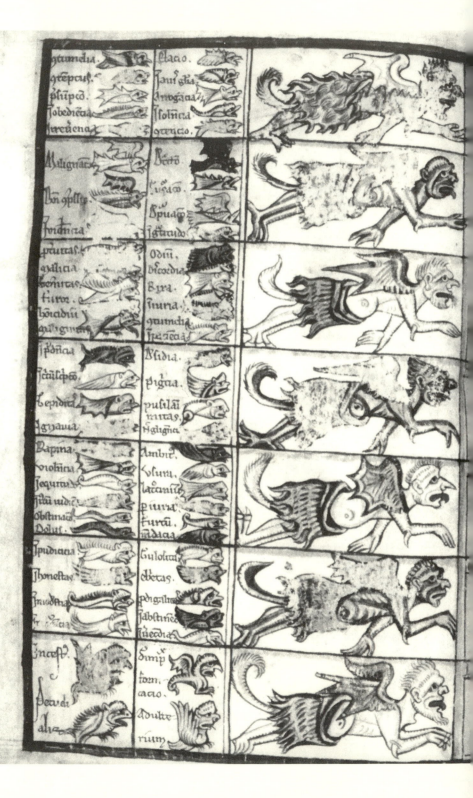

Spes tua ñ gaudii

Caritas

Xpiana religio.

Bona uolutas.

Disciplina

Humilitas

Violent Knights, Holy Knights

COMING UNEXPECTEDLY UPON the splendid manuscript painting in British Library Harley 3244 (folios 27b, 28) provided one of those moments that richly reward scholarly work in archives. This striking mid-thirteenth-century illumination vividly portrays knighthood in a righteous struggle against sin and vice.[1] It could easily have been missed, for the obviously visual part of this volume features an engaging bestiary (an illustrated, moralized "book of beasts" at folios 36–71b); this menagerie of animals so suddenly and colorfully intruded among somber treatises on sin, confession, and penance that I half feared an outburst of trumpeting, howling, and braying that would disturb other readers in that wonderfully quiet Manuscript Room. The serene calm and serious religious tenor of the book was only reasserted when I leafed back to a partial copy of a thirteenth-century encyclopedic work on virtues and vices by a French Dominican named William of Peraldus (Guillaume Peyraut).[2] This is the book for which our stunning illustration now provides a frontispiece.

The painting can likewise serve to introduce the present book on the religion of knights. Carefully planned and beautifully drawn, the bifoliate illumination brings chivalry and religion into the same conceptual framework. Yet the right-hand page irresistibly draws the reader's eye first, for with much boldness and confidence it presents a mounted knight fully encased in mid-thirteenth-century armor, ready for rough action with lance and drawn sword. At the top of this page a Latin inscription (emphasized by being outlined and written in red ink) serves as caption for the full painting; it quotes a passage from the Book of Job (7:1): "Militia est vita hominis super terram (human life on earth is *militia*)."³ This small Latin noun, *militia*, bears large meanings: it can denote hard struggle, or fighting, or knighthood. All these meanings seem to merge in the illustration. The knight drawn so prominently symbolizes the heroic struggle asserted in the biblical quotation; we could even say he symbolizes the medieval Christian ideal for the profession of knighthood. And we cannot doubt that religious validity is asserted for his struggle, for each part of his equipment has been given a pious meaning. The terms do not simply reproduce those well known from St. Paul (in Ephesians 6), who exhorts the believer to put on the whole armor of God, specifying parts and meanings. Nor could they reproduce the symbols used by the most popular writer of a manual on chivalry, the former knight Ramon Llull. Though Llull provided religious meanings for all parts of a knight's armor and even that of his horse, he likely wrote his influential *Book of the Order of Chivalry* decades later.⁴ The influential *Prose Lancelot* appeared decades before this illumination, but presents an entirely different set of symbolic meanings for the knight's equipment.⁵ Evidently the religious labels in our illumination have been chosen by the writer or illustrator, if not selected by the patron. The knight is, for example, firmly seated in the Christian religion (*Christiana religio*), his saddle resting on a blanket of humility (*humilitas*). The sword he bears in one hand is the word of God (*verbum dei*) as in St. Paul, but his lance is labeled steadfastness or perseverance (*perseverantia*). On each corner of his shield the name of a member of the Christian Trinity appears, Father, Son, and Holy Spirit, the lines converging in the center of the shield as *Deus* (the Godhead).⁶ Even the parts of the horse are assigned religious meanings, the horse's rump unfortunately being termed good will. Overhead, an angel descends from stylized heaven bearing a crown. It is not a royal crown, but rather the crown of victory won by the knight in his determined struggle. Inscribed on the band held in the angel's left hand is a maxim which seems taken from St. Paul (2 Timothy 2:5) declaring that only he who fights the good fight wins a crown.⁷ Equally interesting, the angel holds in its right hand a set of seven scrolls that bear equally potent language; in short form they convey the Beatitudes, those transforming sayings of Christ in the Sermon on the Mount. Their presentation here is intriguing. In each case the heavenly blessing for the recipient is noted, though the requisite human activity or state, even if assumed, is omitted. Thus the banderoles simply promise the holy warriors that

Theirs is the kingdom of heaven (*ipsorum est regnum celorum*)
They shall inherit the kingdom (*ipsi possedebunt regnum*)
They shall be comforted (*ipsi consolabuntur*)
They shall be filled (*ipsi saturabuntur*)
They shall have mercy (*ipsi misericordiam consequentur*)
They shall see God (*ipsi deum videbunt*)
They shall be called sons of God (*ipsi filii dei vocabuntur*).

As if the symbolic knight's fight against evil is merit enough to earn such divine favor, the requirements for receiving each of these blessings are not specified. In other words, there is no stated injunction that the recipients are to be poor in spirit, meek, hungering and thirsting for righteousness, merciful, pure in heart, peacemakers, no stipulation that it is those who mourn who shall be comforted.[8] We might already sense tension between the martial words from Job and the spirit of the Beatitudes, between the determined knight, weapons at the ready, and these forgiving, pacific sentiments from the Sermon on the Mount, possibly even between the full import of the Beatitudes and their shortened form, reduced to benefits received, as they are quoted here. A battle-ready knight is about to be festooned with streamers at least recalling the virtues of mercy, peace, and forbearance, though they are not specified. The conjuncture of ideas seems jarring.

The martial theme in the illumination cannot be doubted. A desperate combat is about to erupt from the vellum pages, more desperate and noisy than the briefly threatened intrusion of the bestiary. The eye of the knight, clearly visible through the narrow slot in his great helm, is sternly set on what will soon assault him from the left page, for as noted, this composite illumination spreads impressively across two folio pages. From the left folio advance serried ranks of grotesque demons representing the seven deadly sins, each sin backed by a cluster of smaller figures of supporting vices in a wonderfully medieval hierarchical pattern. Avarice, a chief sin, is for example backed by a smaller demon labeled usury. The knight has allies too, the seven Gifts of the Holy Spirit pictured as doves ranked before him on his side of the illustration, facing the enemy. But these pale and pacific birds hardly inspire confidence as stout or effective coadjutors in the fight to come. Moreover, the forces of right are desperately outnumbered; the sides stand sixty-nine to eight. Yet the viewer need not fear the outcome, for the knight is surely an ideally stalwart fighter for the right, however rampant and numerous the menacing forces of evil marshaled against him. Exactly how this warrior fits into the world of Beatitudes remains an issue, perhaps even a paradox.

As a first step toward understanding this tension and how it was resolved, we need to recognize that our illustration, however splendid, is a piece of collusive propaganda. Its visual and verbal program portrays the ideal knight as both pious and fiercely martial, a combination more easily shown in ideal form (as a fight against evil) than could be achieved within the messy details of daily life. Clerics advanced this ideal for knighthood and knights might have been happy to accept it as a flattering and valorizing representation of their profession. Yet it is most emphatically not a realistic picture, not a description of what knights actually were or what they actually did in a world much troubled by the consequences of sin if not by visible demons. This illustration, in other words, is prescriptive rather than descriptive. Powerfully presented, it shows us what clerics ardently wanted knights to be, even how knights might have liked to see themselves portrayed. Yet it would be a great error to accept this idealized and wishful view as displaying the essence of chivalry; it belongs rather to an effort that flattered warrior sensibilities as it tried to engage warrior piety and direct warrior energies.

These considerable energies in the knights had to be fitted within a society working to create order in a great many dimensions of life: not only governmental, legal, and religious, but also socioeconomic, and intellectual. Broadly governmental or political frameworks were being established by lay authority just as guidelines of doctrine and governing ecclesiastical structure were being elaborated by clerics. Textbook accounts too often bring chivalry into this broad picture of governance and social order without ambiguity, as a unidirectional force for peace and order. Chivalry is so easily sketched as a straightforward internalization of restraint among the warriors, knocking off the rough edges and making them proto-gentlemen. Violence and war, in this view, would be less likely, or at least (to borrow the phrase of an American president) "kinder and gentler." In *Chivalry and Violence in Medieval Europe*, I argued a case for the uneasy fit of chivalry within the governmental framework produced by kings and royal and ecclesiastical administrations busily lengthening their effective reach. That book emerged from a decade of reading the literature knights regularly patronized and read, or heard (thousands of pages of *chanson de geste*, romance, chivalric biography, and vernacular manuals). The evidence of this chivalric literature convinced me to attempt to complicate the common view. I argued that chivalry, centered as it was in prowess as the key to honor—that inestimable good—actually contributed as much to the problem of violence as it provided a solution. Knighthood surely did some of both, and both sides of the equation are important: the knights were in many ways loyal sons of Holy Mother Church and stood by kings and great lords whose patronage they enjoyed, whose courts they attended, whose armies they joined. Yet chivalry was deeply, essentially complicit in problems of securing public order. If royal governments undoubtedly needed the armed force and administrative services of the knights, they worried over their unlicensed tournaments and fortifications, their private wars, and their love of hot-blooded vengeance; they likewise feared their disregard for, or overawing of, royal law-courts that were coming to be thicker on the ground. While kings were personally proud to be knights, the knights were trouble-somely inclined to think themselves kinglets. Chivalry did not constitute a direct and unblemished force for order in the political sphere, not, at least, from the standpoint of kings actively engaged in building early forms of the European state or churchmen striving for order. The knights were a para-doxical force: necessary, but dangerous, rather like fire. If, as I have argued, leading agents and agencies in Medieval Europe struggled to come to terms with violence, the problem was intensified because knightly violence was con-sidered noble and heroic and could be carried out by private right in quest of the unsurpassed goal of honor. The issue of order involved not simply crime in a modern sense, not even war in a modern sense, but rather privatized violence infused into the upper ranges of the social hierarchy by the collapse of effective large-scale political authority from the late Carolingian era. The medieval states that slowly emerged—it needs to be acknowledged—took on an ambivalent role themselves. If they moved slowly toward an interest in the control of violence within the realm (a goal Max Weber saw as characteristic of all states), sadly they and their descendants into modern times have taken fighting with their neighbors as another goal. Striving for internal peace and fomenting external war seem to form the broad pattern. It was bound to in-volve the knights in complex relationships with the governance of kings and the ideals of clerics.

Tension and Paradox in Ideas

Constructing an ideology that would fit chivalry within a religious frame-work—the subject of the present book—moved matters well beyond govern-ing authority to an engagement of basic ideas old and new, lay and clerical.

Analyses of clerical ideas have filled our library shelves with hefty tomes that naturally continue to attract scholarly study (underscoring their importance). And scholars readily agree that these ideas were so fundamental in all dimensions of medieval society that any lay pattern of life necessarily drew on undoubted piety and religious language; at minimum such a lay pattern had to make its peace with clerical claims and ideals, or find ways of rejecting or skirting around them short of anti-sacerdotal heresy. Yet, as R. W. Southern has cautioned, clerical patterns were neither absolutely dominant nor static, and "the theories and mechanisms of secular society also developed. The world did not stand still while the clerical ideal was realized."[9] The age in which chivalry emerged and matured saw burgeoning religious piety among the laity no less than the creation of new religious institutions and clarification of major doctrines. It was an age in which the laity asserted new independence, indeed an age not only of anticlericalism but of outbursts of heresy.[10] If the knights, in company with so many lay people, showed a tendency to form independent religious ideas in matters of great concern to them, even while they stood as stalwarts against heresy, how would they respond when insistent clerical claims of leadership and direction touched their own profession? Did knightly piety move in concert with the waves of new religious ideas and with the tidal surges of widespread and creative lay piety throughout the period?

The problem arose when religious ideas threatened to invert or negate chivalry as a fierce warrior code. For the medieval European elite—both lay and clerical—the central question such inversion raised was stark: What had the religion of Christ to do with the worship of the demigod prowess in chivalric ideology? What result obtains when prowess confronts Christian *caritas*? Could broadswords—even if directed by clerical voices—carve a rough world into the shape prescribed by the Beatitudes? If active force mirrored divine judgment, did not mercy reflect divine grace? Chivalric texts urged mercy for helpless, defeated opponents, yet vengeance, a particularly prickly sense of honor, and unrestrained joy in the skilled and vigorous use of edged weaponry animated chivalric ideology.[11] Prowess meant less an ethereal moral courage supporting abstract right than the very physical triumph of armored men wielding honed weapons—or blazing torches—as they fought for all the reasons for which men have always fought. In the twelfth century Bertran de Born's many poems enthusing over the joys of warfare, with its clash of arms and wounded men, seem the polar opposite of the Gospel of Matthew.[12] Girart de Vienne, hero of his own *chanson*, similarly praises the sights and sounds of war, declaring that he would surely contract some dread illness if deprived of its joys for a month.[13] As the war against the Romans looms in the late fourteenth-century *Alliterative Morte Arthure*, Duke Cador cries out, "Now war is upon us again, all praise to Christ! (Now wakenes the war! Worshipped be Crist!)"[14] Tension could not be avoided. In colors still bright, our manuscript illumination embodies that tension through symbols and powerfully sacred words.[15]

How did lay and clerical ideas meet and negotiate an ideology acceptable to the warrior class of medieval Europe? Confronting this large and important question calls for close investigation and fresh analysis. We must ask by what intellectual pathways, even by what specific language, those who were especially concerned about religion and about chivalry in this developing society could find their way through the hazardous borderlands where religion and warrior life met and overlapped. The subject is usually considered within a framework of developing crusading ideas and practices, and is often viewed from the perspective of clerical or specifically papal initiatives.[16] As a well-nurtured subfield of medieval history, crusade studies have generated a vast and informative body of scholarship that I will draw on with gratitude; but I will extend the scope of investigation to the ideology of chivalry in general and will look closely at ideas propagated for or even by the knights themselves as they sought to shape—and certainly to justify—their hard profession.[17] This book seeks to explain the process by analysis of the close, if highly selective, fitting of chivalry within developing and conflicting strands of thought on significant theological issues.[18] The set of issues is basic: precisely how Christ achieved human salvation, the nature of penance and confession, and ideas about ideal social organization and the value of human labor—all emerging within the context of an unusually ascetic culture animated by an intensified lay piety significantly blended with lay independence. This study seeks to understand the power of paradox in the formation of chivalric ideology; it insists on the knightly embrace of asceticism, and emphasizes the degree of independence seen in a highly selective borrowing of the theological ideas utilized in forming knightly ideology. These thematic lines differentiate the approach of this book from classic studies by such scholars as Carl Erdmann, Maurice Keen, and Jean Flori—though I will draw on their works with no less gratitude than I owe to historians of crusade.[19] My aim throughout is to document the paradoxes necessarily built into a religious ideology of chivalry and to explain how and why they worked so well.[20]

Finding evidence that will reveal the ideals of a group that long emphasized virtues other than literacy, and wrote much less than the clerics even when they became literate, is a daunting challenge. As in previous work, I will turn to a mix of sources, emphasizing works of imaginative literature along with narrative sources, chivalric biographies, and manuals. My case for the usefulness of this mix of sources has appeared already and will be amplified here.[21] In this work I have also found invaluable another source that has received less attention for knighthood than it deserves: the copious body of *exempla* (moral tales told in sermons and read in collections by the elite). Many of these tales portray and instruct the knighthood. What I have found impressive is the congruity of all this evidence. A remarkably consistent body of ideas for consideration and debate about chivalry appears in the entire corpus of evidence across the centuries and regions in which chivalry was forming.

Evidence could (and occasionally will) be found on the general themes of religion and warrior life well before the High Middle Ages (roughly the later eleventh century through the thirteenth century). Yet a new critical stage emerged then and continued through the later Middle Ages (fourteenth and fifteenth centuries). I will limit my study to Western Europe and can only hope that other scholars will broaden the picture by moving east from the lands along the Channel. The forces under investigation began to take more defined form in these regions and during the High Middle Ages: chivalry came to life and the medieval church took on its most characteristic forms and elaborated many of its most characteristic ideas, especially on such matters of concern here as crusade, a strongly centralized papal governance, a developed canon law, and especially a newly elaborated theology for the laity. In a society animated by such changes, the complex links between violence and religion inevitably took on new or newly clarified form.

Paradox spreads like a spider web over the formation of chivalric ideology. Yet the issue of perception and the danger of presentism cannot be ignored. Were the tensions and uncertainties troublesome to medieval people or are they merely the imposition of modern sensibilities? Framing the question clearly is essential: what is at issue is not whether medieval people accepted and valorized violence. We know that they did, laity and clergy alike—as most people in other times and places have done. Rather, the issue is whether they recognized the paradoxes involved—such as pacific forgiveness alongside hot-blooded vengeance—and took any steps toward resolution of issues in troubled minds. These are difficult but essential questions. Our investigation requires us to confront the paradox that so often remains the elephant in the room, willfully ignored; we must ask if paradox registered and was addressed by thoughtful folk in the High and Late Middle Ages. The search can inform historical inquiry if we explore genuinely medieval views about knighthood, violence, suffering, and vengeance in relationship to historically contemporary ideas about piety, penance, atonement, and the will of God. Debate on these issues obviously produced disagreements within the groups of clerics and knights and not just between these two groups. Not all knights or clerics shared the views of others within their groups. Yet dominant values of medieval Christianity stood at odds with dominant values of the warriors. Looking broadly at each group should thus be useful.

Paradox in Clerical Thought?

It would be possible to think no paradox existed at all in medieval views on chivalry. Had not sensible clerics pragmatically come to terms with any troublesome issues? Did they not simply view God as the bellicose Lord of Hosts, emphasizing those biblical passages and patristic writings that came to that sharp conclusion? And if there was, indeed, any problem at all, was not crusade ideology the encompassing answer?

Most clerics had indeed found it necessary to accept war and violence from early days in a Roman empire wrapped around the Mediterranean Sea. In the succeeding Carolingian Empire and again in High Medieval Europe, learned clerical opinion and directive so significantly sanctified violence that some historians speak convincingly of a Christianization of warfare.[22] Since the Carolingian period most major armies setting off on campaign under some king or great lord were accompanied by a smaller host of supportive clerics to commune, confess, and bless the warriors.[23] What army and its leaders did not loudly proclaim that their cause was just? Few failed to muster at least some clerical backing for the claim, their opponents busily doing the same.

Among the clerics themselves, moreover, many betrayed a bellicose stance, praying for the success of campaigns they had encouraged, when not leading them. Vigorous church reformers, trembling with the desire to produce "right order in the world," were notoriously willing to use armed force to attain ecclesiastical goals. From the end of the eleventh century, crusades preached by stern popes and soon by wild-eyed hermits sent mailed men of undoubted martial piety to the Holy Land, Spanish and Slavic lands, and eventually into heretical or troublesome regions of Western Europe itself. The seemingly inexorable expansion of Europe proceeded on three cardinal points of the compass by use of the sword as well as the plough—both under the aegis of the cross. The blessing of religion descended on all these uses of violence.

Clerical writers could justify their blessing of the work of knighthood in frankly pragmatic terms. Were not knightly swords needed to defend the homeland, preserve clerical property, hang robbers, and repress or burn heretics? The *Ordene de Chevalerie* (an early thirteenth-century continental text) makes the point explicitly. Speaking for clerics, it declares:

> knights, . . . whom everybody should honour . . . have us all to guard; and if it were not for knighthood, our lordship would be of little worth, for they defend Holy Church, and they uphold justice for us against those who would do us harm. . . . Our chalices would be stolen from before us at the table of God, and nothing would ever stop it. . . . The good would never be able to endure if the wicked did not fear knights, and if there were only Saracens, Albigensians, and barbarians, and people of evil faith who would do us wrong. . . . it is given to the knight . . . that if he has acted according to his order, he can go straight to Paradise.[24]

Such pragmatic justifications eased the clerical path to sanctified violence. Moreover, as great lords themselves, clerics were inextricably involved in the world of armies and knighthood. They held estates owing knight service to some superior lord or to the lord king. They knew knightly force was needed in a violent and dangerous world and willingly held lands that supported it. Even those without landed endowment necessarily drew on warrior force. That enthusiastic clerical writer Gerald of Wales at one point found his household entangled in a family feud and had to seek military help from a Welsh lord who was his relative.[25] Thomas Becket, while still chancellor to Henry II, had knighted Baldwin, Count of Guines, with his own hand.[26] Language of vassalage came naturally to the famous archbishop, even in his moment of mortal crisis. Minutes away from martyrdom in Canterbury Cathedral, Thomas caught one of his knightly assailants by the mail shirt and as he powerfully sent the man reeling shouted, "Unhand me, Reginald. You are my sworn vassal."[27] In theory prevented from personal violence by canon law, clerics can readily be found leading forces and sometimes even wielding weapons themselves. The late medieval English crown even attempted to array the clergy in arms as a form of home guard.[28]

At times the ecclesiastical atmosphere seems suffused with martial chant. Warlike psalms inspired knights or their clerical backers. How remarkably must God's instructions to the Hebrews to smite the Amalekites hip and thigh have resounded in clerics' ears, let alone in knightly ears. This tonality was scarcely softened in monasteries whose monks considered themselves fellow warriors maintaining martial bastions against the active hosts of invisible evil in the world. Some religious houses, of course, had been founded as memorials to victory in thoroughly worldly fighting, such as those established by William the Conqueror and Philip Augustus, who "stamped the imagery of secular authority and bellicose concerns upon institutions which represented the reforming church at its most withdrawn from lay preoccupations."[29] The church found no difficulty in recognizing a need for violence in proper causes, properly directed, in an imperfect world. As Karl Leyser has eloquently exclaimed,

> It is worthwhile to pause and gasp at the extent to which Christianity from St Augustine onwards and indeed much earlier had been able not only to live with the phenomenon of war which profoundly contradicted its imperatives of peace but even to endorse it, both for the punishment of the wicked and the coercion of heretics and in the secular spheres of kingdoms and peoples fighting to avenge wrongs. Aristotle's *Politics* here spoke with a louder voice than the passivity of the Gospels.[30]

Yet while recognizing the truth of this concise statement, we can also see that potential elements of tension, even of paradox, were built into medieval Christianity; they may have given it supple strength in a world ever resistant to rigidly straightforward or systematic explanation.[31] Leyser aptly characterized the medieval discussion on war as a moral debate. There was more than one opinion. Inconveniently, clerics did not speak with one voice on so complex and troubling a set of topics as war and violence. Canonists, scholastic theologians, crusade preachers, priests hearing confessions—all could sustain their own arguments based on deep principles or informed by pragmatism. What we so readily term "the church" scarcely represented a monolithic body of thought. Swirling eddies of clerical dissent flowed against mainstream ideas that carried forward much justification of violence. However far below the surface, clerical memory stored so many dissenting textual injunctions from biblical, liturgical, and patristic sources documenting the religion of the Prince of Peace. Worry over their clear duty to correct the sins of the laity could hinder endorsement of all war. And not every pragmatic line of thought led to justifications of fighting. Local wars, after all, generated thoroughly pragmatic fears about social order and the safety of clerical personnel and property.[32] The fear might, of course, become quite immediate. William of Malmesbury says that a group of bishops meeting under the direction of a papal legate (to discuss the crisis caused by King Stephen's arrest of the bishops of Salisbury and Lincoln) decided not to excommunicate the king. Their reasons were twofold: they needed the advice of the pope, and they heard and saw swords being drawn![33] In short, the undoubted Christianization of violence and war loaded one side of a balance; yet the other side carried a weight of continuing Christian doubt about war and surprisingly brisk denunciation of specific knights or even the knighthood in general. This duality of view was undoubtedly tilted in favor of sanctified violence, but even if the doubtful view was less emphasized, it persisted throughout the Middle Ages.[34] Tension and paradox were not ended by reform popes, learned canonists, peace movements, or the preaching of crusade. The evident lack of crusading success after the first great effort may have led to fairly widespread doubts about divine favor for the enterprise; some portion of the faithful seemed to believe only in defensive war against the Saracens.[35] Searching critiques of knightly violence continued alongside much sanctification of warfare. The clerical view was usually modulated according to the perpetrator of violence, the victim of the violence, and, above all, the authority justifying it.

Yet incompatible ideas stood side by side, century after century, and were selectively emphasized as occasion demanded. If violence in the abstract was not an issue for most of the clergy, the practice of some particular violence was often very much at issue. And in cases where clerical rights, bodies, and property were at risk, or some larger sense of the internal peace and well-being of the commonwealth of Christianity loomed, the all but buried pacific ideas readily came out of cold storage into what might become the hot rhetoric needed in that hour.

In mid-eleventh century, Leo IX (1048–53), traditionally the first of a series of "Gregorian" reform popes, denounced the Norman knights so troublesome in Italy as acting "with an ungodliness worse than that of the pagans."[36] In desperation, he raised an army against them and led it in person. Leo was defeated and captured at Civitate in 1053. Some clerics condemned his undertaking such military leadership; others defended his action by claiming that his slain knights "rejoiced forever in heaven . . . united in glory with the holy martyrs."[37] Gregory VII (1073–85), the towering figure who gave his name to the reform era, at first proclaimed that knighthood was a profession that "can scarcely be performed without sin" and declared that a knight doing penance would normally have to set aside his arms while he atoned (though he might fight in specified good causes after consulting bishops).[38] His view implies that true penance was impossible while acting as a self-directed warrior who would be engaged, as H. E. J. Cowdrey explains, in "the sins inherent in his everyday manner of life."[39] This view came to be widely cited and it lived on in the influential manual of canon law, the *Decretum* of Gratian, and the standard textbook of Peter Lombard.[40] Though Gregory later modified this theoretical position (drawn from his intense concern for true penitence), his shifting views finally owed much to stark necessity, especially in his great quarrel with Emperor Henry IV. Cowdrey, the pope's modern biographer, carefully notes "the tentativeness and even inner contradiction of his thought and legislation about the bearing of arms by Christian laymen," and concludes that "Gregory the man of action outran Gregory the man of ideas."[41] Gregory's willingness to use force on a local or grand scale, his idea for a *militia sancti Petri* (armed force of St. Peter) drawn from the loyal knighthood of Europe, made him "the most warlike pope who had ever sat in St Peter's chair."[42] Clerical opponents (from the imperial camp) denounced him as a man of blood. His support for William of Normandy's invasion of England likewise brought an outcry. Gregory later wrote to William that he had received criticism "for the pains I took over such a bloodletting."[43]

The mass of issues remained unsettled and debated even after the beginnings of crusade. Clerical authors could rake the entire body of ordinary knights over rhetorical coals, excepting only a chosen few. St. Bernard set a high standard for such denunciation of the sins of ordinary knighthood doing its usual work. In his early twelfth-century treatise for the new order of the Knights Templar he was as vigorous in excoriating the generality of worldly knights as he was lavish in praising and assuring the select subset of monk-knights who fought under the new order. To the majority of knights he pointedly asked,

> What then, O knights, is this monstrous error and what this unbearable urge which bids you fight with such pomp and labor, and all to no purpose except death and sin. You cover your horses with silk, and

plume your armor with I know not what sort of rags; you paint your shields and your saddles; you adorn your bits and spurs with gold and silver and precious stones, and then in all this glory you rush to your ruin with fearful wrath and fearless folly.[44]

The rhetoric of other monastics might not achieve the vitriolic level of St. Bernard's prose, but the sentiment came from many pens.

Moreover, denunciations did not resound solely from cloisters. Robert of Flamborough, one of the circle of influential theologians clustered around Peter Cantor in Paris in the early thirteenth century, wrote a penitential, a book to guide priests in examining their flock during confession and assigning them proper penance. His treatise instructed these confessors to raise significant questions about warfare. The confessor is to ask if the warrior extorted any money or collected illicit exactions (*talliam injustam*), whether he killed anyone and under what circumstances or with what motives. The warriors must know that they cannot avoid confessing and doing penance for sins committed by arguing that they were just following the orders of their leader. Those who kill for avarice are as bad as idolaters. Warriors must not follow their worldly lord and contemn their heavenly lord.[45]

Another famous scholar, Alan of Lille, repeatedly thundered at later twelfth-century knighthood for its violence and greed. On one occasion his classroom was suddenly entered by knights who demanded that he settle for them the issue as to what formed the highest degree of courtesy. Alan not only answered their question (asserting that generous giving is the highest courtesy), he continued, archly, by saying that the highest degree of villainy was living by looting the poor, as they did. This sharp retort was still getting wide currency generations later through its inclusion in collections of thirteenth- and fourteenth-century sermon *exempla*.[46] Moreover, Alan had broadcast his message of warning against knightly theft and violence in his own book on the *Ars predicandi* (*Art of Preaching*), which told any aspiring preacher who read it how to address the knights:

Let him urge them to be content with their own wages [this from Luke 3:14] and not to threaten strangers; let them exact nothing by force, terrify no-one with violence; let them be defenders of their homeland, guardians of widows and orphans. So let them bear the outward arms of the world that they may be armed inwardly with the hauberk of faith.[47]

These thoughts, conjuring up so censorious a picture of the actual daily work of the knights, become much more explicit in his model sermon *Ad Milites*, directed specifically to the elite warriors. Alan included it in his preaching manual. He softens the bite of his critique somewhat by initially assuring knights that they have a high calling: "For this especially were soldiers ordained that they should defend their native land and that they should repel the attacks of the violent upon the church."[48] Undoubtedly this praise is sincere and emerges from genuine belief in their role. He soon shifts gears, however, and excoriates the knighthood in general, as he had verbally slashed at those who intruded on the sanctity of his classroom:

> but now soldiers have been made the leaders of pillaging bands; they have become cattle-thieves. Now they engage not in soldiering, but in plundering, and under the guise of soldiers, they take on the cruel nature of marauders. Nor do they fight against their enemies so much as victimize the poor, and those whom they should guard with the shield of knightly protection, they hound with the sword of savagery. Nowadays they prostitute their knighthood, they fight for gain, they take up arms to plunder. Nowadays they are not soldiers but thieves and robbers; not defenders, but invaders. Into the bosom of Mother Church they plunge their swords, and the force which they should expend against the enemy, they expend against their own people. They cease to attack their enemies—either out of idleness or out of cowardice—and against the peaceful household of Christ they wreak havoc with their swords.[49]

Even beloved chivalric honor might be merely a cause for destruction, he wrote:

> Where is vanity if not in worldly honors? They show their favor to a man only so that they may destroy him. They lift him up only to cast him down. They raise him up only to throw him the more heavily to the ground. In these is the vanity of vanities, for there is in honor an unbearable burden, and in the burden a valueless honor.[50]

Another sermon authority writing somewhat later, Humbert of Romans, reminded preachers that all lay nobility in the world—carnal as opposed to spiritual nobility—was founded on great evils as well as good. "For they often commit thefts, murders, sacrileges, and all manner of vicious evils (Nam raptores, homicidae, sacrilegi, et omni genere vitiorum scelerati, hanc habent frequenter)."[51]

Sermon stories delivered from pulpits across Christendom occasionally questioned even the fundamental chivalric urge for vengeance (so often effected through homicide). Vengeful attacks and killing—or at least killing fellow Christians—was not always countenanced with ease. One cluster of remarkable moral tales or *exempla*, told repeatedly, praises the ideal of the merciful knight who spares even his most vile opponent; instead of taking vengeance by attacking or inflicting a death richly deserved by common chivalric standards, he pardons the enemy in honor of Christ (in an action that often takes place symbolically on Good Friday). The former mortal foes proceed to church together, where the figure on the cross miraculously bows in stunning honor of his knight who chose charitable forgiveness over prowess-driven vengeance. Variants of this miracle story appear in numerous collections from the late thirteenth century through the early fifteenth century.[52] How they balanced charity and mild forbearance with hot-blooded vengeance and worldly victory remains a question. Clerical authors sometimes praised knights swinging their swords, even against fellow Christians, as agents of divine wrath; at other times they urged *caritas*. Bloody vengeance stands opposed to mild forbearance.

Our evidence (barely sampled here) shows that clerics held divided views on basic aspects of a warrior code and that it troubled the more thoughtful among them. Alongside valorization, a serious clerical critique of knighthood as a violent profession extended from the twelfth century into the later Middle Ages. We come almost full circle in the work of Richard Rolle, the most influential fourteenth-century English mystic, who denounced the violence of knighthood in search of vain, worldly honor with rhetorical exuberance almost the equal of St. Bernard's withering blast two centuries earlier. Rolle's attack targeted both the battlefield and the tourney ground. Here are his stern words from *Against the Lovers of the World* (*Contra Amatores Mundi*):

> Do not call such persons bold who when they tear the garments of others are rewarded with a bad death. With shining armor and gaily-decked horses they rush to battle; and before they strike a blow, they die inwardly. While they pierce the hearts of men, they themselves are struck to the quick by the devils' spears. Let us say to them, "Where is your God?" . . . Surely it is not our God, for they have made a god of

whatever they love most. Some make proud vanity or empty honor their god, for the sake of which they exalt themselves, endure hardships, undergo need, give and take wounds, kill and are killed.[53]

This hard-hitting critique charges that fundamental chivalric ideals lead to idolatry, to the virtual worship of another god.[54]

The contested views of churchmen pinned them ineluctably to paradox. They could scarcely show consistency on troubling issues of such deep concern to the chivalry no less than to themselves. What confronted them was not merely the issue of homicide in licit wars between kings and great lords, but the challenge of defining the very role of an *ordo* of laymen who were as necessary as they could be dangerous, both morally and socially. If clerics willingly accepted the claim of knighthood to an inherent right to practice violence, they also funneled intense critiques at the warriors along with claims to a directive moral superiority. In a world of much petty warfare and punitive raiding as well as major campaigns, and in a time of powerful and frightening Muslim advances, determined heretics, and plentiful bandits, the clerics could not doubt they needed a source of righteous force. Yet they could not forget that their safety lay in dangerous and acquisitive hands and that they must try to control and direct this force, prescribing its role and denouncing its dangerous sins. They could likewise never forget that they were followers of the Prince of Peace no less than the Lord of Hosts; they were bound to question much of the violence that marked knightly life, to thunder against vengeance, feud, pride, looting of the poor and the churches, and the host of sins inherent in tournament. They knew there was a peace that passed human understanding and they ardently wanted a more peaceful society, at least within Europe. If they were to do God's work a certain level of peace was an obvious requirement. The problem was how to direct the sacred *ordo* of knighthood while chipping away at a range of ideas and practices knights cherished as foundation stones of their profession, true building blocks of prowess yielding honor.

Paradox in Knightly Ideas?

Did the knights themselves worry about their own profession and actions? Did they sense the potential gap separating foundational principles of their religion from their fearsome and much-honored work with edged weaponry and all-consuming fire? And if they perceived disparity did they suffer any fear of divine displeasure and wrath? Exploring such questions for the knights is obviously harder than for the literate and loquacious clerics who made the full range of their views abundantly known. Knights in significant numbers acquired literacy late in our period; we must generally wait for at least the thirteenth or even fourteenth century to be certain that we hear their thoughts in relatively unmediated form. We must initially employ a combination of approaches, considering statements by the literate clergy who directed reforming words at the knights and who also wrote on behalf of the knights, celebrating the warriors' own thoughts and values in charters, chronicles, and, above all, imaginative literature.[55]

Clerics certainly made truly vigorous efforts to induce a healthy fear for sin and its consequences in the knights. As a reasonable baseline for our effort we might say that virtually all lay Christians in the Middle Ages trembled at the thought of death and what followed. They busied themselves in finding ways of obtaining what Eamon Duffy (no foe of the medieval church) frankly termed "post-mortem fire insurance."[56] Duffy believes the late medieval parishioners he studies were overwhelmingly preoccupied with "the safe transition of their souls from this world to the next, above all with the shortening and easing of their stay in Purgatory."[57] Some clerics liked to insist that prospects were bleak. A set of religious tales written in the mid-fifteenth century specifies that of 30,000 who died on one day in the twelfth century, only St. Bernard of Clairvaux and the Dean of Langres went directly to heaven, three others were sent to be cleansed in the sulfurous fires of purgatory, and the remaining 29,995 went straight to hell.[58] Equally sobering, all medieval folk knew that the punishment awaiting them on the far side of the grave was worse than anything endured on earth—the least pain of purgatory was commonly said to be more severe than the greatest earthly suffering[59]—and the unspeakable torments awaiting many in the fires of hell would, they knew, never end: "For sawle may neuer for pyne deye (for the soul may never die from pain)" is the grim and thought-provoking warning of a Middle English manual.[60] In the thirteenth century Étienne de Bourbon recalled a Dominican who tried repeatedly to convert the son of a count to "contempt of the world and entry into a religious order (ad contemptum mundi et introitus ordinis)." Finally this cleric managed the conversion by telling the man he thought it a great shame that his beautiful body would become fuel for eternal flames (pabulum incendi eterni).[61] "Medieval theology was not a jocund art,"

Eileen Power dryly observed, "and the thought of that perpetual damnation, which all but the few had merited, was forever before its eyes."[62]

Uncertainty and fear within knightly minds could be generated even when theologians, canonists, and confessors played the role of analytical scholar and helpful guide rather than sternly warning preacher. Simply trying to find a way through the dark maze of licit killing and plundering produced disagreements among clerics; such debates could easily sow uncertainties among any attentive warriors. Was all plundering licit? What if it involved despoiling the poor and churches—and what if the "defenseless" had fought back vigorously? Must a vassal follow his lord into a fight he thought illicit? How could one with certainty judge a licit war and the need for restitution? Were crossbows sinful weapons? Could Christians justly kill erring Christians? Some clerical solutions to such issues were so tortured in their reasoning that they could scarcely serve as practical guides, and must only have deepened any uncertainty lying heavily in the hearts of lay hearers or readers. Not much assurance could have come from the idea, for example, that a knight must follow his lord into any campaign, even one he considered unjust, but with the caveat that he not shed blood or take loot if the war were illicit. Manuals to be used by priests in confession sometimes specify criteria that would leave arms-bearers with glazed eyes and puzzled countenances. Many of the issues would, of course, resurface as soon as focus shifted to those sporting wars, the tournament.[63] Perhaps more than clerical warning stands behind the miracle story of the knight who became a monk, but remained spiritually troubled by his prior life. He found reassurance, finally, only by a dream in which the Blessed Virgin appeared to remind him that he had her help, having always bowed at the mention of her name.[64]

Even lists of basic virtues and vices that may have been more familiar to them could generate tension. Wrath provides a fine case in point. As one of the seven deadly sins—the very evils our ideal knight confronted in the Harley manuscript—wrath is regularly associated in Old French and Middle English sermons with lust for vengeance. Yet vengeance is a cornerstone of the chivalric ethos, the harsh repayment justly given for any diminution of precious honor. In the *Story of Merlin*, Bors's sword, the agency of the prowess earning his honor, is tellingly named Wrathful.[65] Contrary to ecclesiastical teaching, human wrath in this Arthurian text is the highly valued motive force behind a great and pious knight's characteristic weapon; his vengeance is a sacred duty and a self-evident good. Did the knightly recognize, to take another example, that pride was one of the seven deadly sins, but that this same quality appears as virtuous in great knights praised in chivalric literature?[66]

How such thoughts resonated in the minds of most knights is not easily estimated. In one sense, knights were simply lay Christians for whom all the expectations applied and all the set paths to piety lay open. In another sense they formed a highly particular and powerful subset of the laity.[67] There can be no thought that as a group they suffered a level of fear that utterly corroded belief in their own status and sanctified *ordo*; the macro evidence of centuries of knighthood vigorously practiced and joyously celebrated stands as witness.[68] It would be no more accurate to conceive of piety emanating solely from clerics who struggled to overwhelm determined knightly secularism. The knighthood in general, we may safely assume, was pious on its own terms.[69] Yet knightly piety asserted that securing honor in the world through vigorous prowess could not be hateful in the sight of God. In fact, their literature shows how often they simply assumed the merit of their actions and clothed them with religious terminology, even if it may seem to us ill-fitting.[70] What remained at issue were the precise forms that won divine approval and, when pressed, the directive authority claimed by the clergy.

We might thus doubt if knights trembled as demonstrably as others at the thought of the afterlife, despite clerical warnings of the morally risky nature of their activities. Undoubtedly the high status of the knights and their sense of personal service to the Lord of Hosts insulated them somewhat from even the most searching questions or assaults. Already in the twelfth century, their status was beginning the rise that would take them into the nobility and offered useful armor against intrusive moral pangs. Whatever religious professionals say by way of warning, the powerful in any age attempt to co-opt religion as justification for their lives, their characteristic work, and their social dominance. They find a degree of comforting reassurance in the belief that divine will has elevated them above others. Surely the God who gave them capacity and dominance in this world cannot desire their damnation in the next. Medieval barons, captains, and knights may share this comforting line of thought with more modern robber barons and captains of industry. Religion is the ultimate valorizing force in the world—or at least it was in the old world, before virtual deification of the market. What the divine has ordained must be right; and the powerful can so often convince themselves and others that the blessing of heaven has descended upon their status and all that supports it.[71] There was much to bolster this sort of confidence among the medieval knighthood. Did not the clerics sing their praises regularly and see a divine mission for them? As "those who fought" they constituted a particular *ordo*, one of the *ordines*, the "orders," prescribed for society by God.[72] With quite tolerable effort the knightly could block out much of the carping clerical criticism and listen contentedly to the glowing celebration of their necessary role in an ideal world.

Yet the critiques came insistently and it is hard to escape the sense that knightly bravado was sometimes a covering for fear, in effect whistling past the graveyard. Perhaps those whose hands carry out the killing and destroying in any society suffer late night thoughts about widespread destruction and the shedding of human blood, about retribution and final justice. Indeed, even proud, self-assured knights sometimes reveal that they harbored doubts and fears about their role. Men who proudly and self-consciously proclaimed that they lived by the sword might well have experienced some mental caution and agitation—if they were at all thoughtful—upon reading or hearing a sermon on the sixth commandment, a homily on the Sermon on the Mount, or on Christ's stern words to Peter in the Garden of Gethsemane about the fate of those who live by the sword.[73] We would like to know how Sir Thomas Malory reacted if he heard or read the characterization of pride in a late fourteenth-century manual on penance as "of owne hyness overgrete love (excessive love of one's own greatness)," especially if he heard these words soon after writing one of his passages of fulsome praise for the "worshyppe" owed great men whose hands carried out stunning acts of prowess.[74] We do know that the prominent mid-fourteenth-century knight Geoffroi de Charny wrote clearly, if briefly, about the "dark side of the force." In his treatise on chivalry (analyzed in the following chapter) he denounces vile arms-bearers who use their might without control, who break truces, attack without formal warnings, and the like. We can almost sense his shudder as he disposes of them as quickly as possible and hurries back to praise the good knights, those who use their great prowess in a broad range of recognized causes. He is hastily papering over a deep crevice in knighthood that few warriors wished to recognize: the prowess they liked to consider a chief virtue might simply reduce to morally neutral force.[75]

Consider so basic an issue as their understanding the meaning of the potent symbol of the crucifix at the core of their religion. The solemn drama on Calvary could only create a vortex of tension and paradox within the warrior elite. On the cross the incarnate Son of God placated the just wrath of an angry God the Father who would take fearsome vengeance—the word is regularly used—for human sin.[76] Through his grievous sufferings and his violent death, the Son paid the vast debt for sin that lost humanity owed the Father. With a focus on the Son the message is one of surpassing and self-sacrificing love; even from the cruel cross he asked forgiveness for his enemies. But the paradoxical insinuates itself by the clear inference that the vengeance of God the Father is averted and his wrath mollified only by terrible suffering.[77] In the divine view, meritorious suffering by the supremely righteous God/man is good; it atones for sin through the violence of whip, nails, thorns, cross, and spear thrust. Yet this shameful and violent treatment, causing the death of the Son of God, is also wrong beyond telling. Should not God's enemies then and now become the objects of suitable vengeance as God himself took vengeance for sin? A warrior society based on honor and prowess struggled with these troubling, surging ideas of meritorious suffering, vengeance, and forgiveness—a theme on which Alan Frantzen has written perceptively.[78] They were willing to suffer. Intoned tirelessly, the maxim among the warriors becomes, "Christ died for his men; we knights must die for our men."[79] Yet since vengeance no less than suffering had divine precedents, the warriors were also eager to take vengeance on enemies who wronged them. They knew that divine wrath was bought off by sacrifice and suffering, by that of his Son above all (on Calvary and repeatedly on the altar in the mass), and by the constant, mimetic suffering of all sinners in this world and in the afterworld. Thus any pacific meaning to the Passion of Christ is significantly and dramatically inverted. The message is shifted away from humble self-sacrifice by the divine in human form, away from a view of Calvary as the climax to a fully heroic but nonviolent life. The act of Christ ceases to be considered an end to cycles of vengeance and is twisted into a powerful stimulus for more vengeful violence. The late twelfth-century *Chanson d'Aspremont* mentions in passing the story of Christ on the cross forgiving Longinus, the centurian whose spear thrust he received. Yet the message drawn out is that if knights want to share in such divine forgiveness for sin they must show their faith by slaughtering the enemies of their faith.[80] With similarly breath-taking inversion of forgiveness, the Anglo-Norman poem narrating the late twelfth-century invasion of Ireland at one point pictures the invaders charging their foes stirred by their leader's cry, "Strike in the name of the cross! (Ferez al nun de la croiz!)"[81] In the *Chanson Aymeri de Narbonne*, Charlemagne intones a wish that God who forgave Longinus will grant victory to the hero Aymeri over his enemies.[82] God himself, in the early thirteenth-century *History of the Holy Grail*, uses the crucifixion lance as a tool of his inscrutable vengeance; through this holy lance that drips Christ's blood and is associated with the Grail, God promises vengeance to come.[83] Mingled ideas of righteous suffering and just vengeance echoed across medieval centuries and informed much thought about how to conduct a pious heroic life.

Charters recording donations of land may explain the motives clerics only hoped were at work; yet lay donors were at least unlikely to have objected strongly to what was said formally in their names on the eternal record of parchment. Their motives as set down in such records may frankly be fear. Early in the eleventh century when Duke Richard II of Normandy provided a landed gift to the Benedictines of Mont St. Michel, he avowed—in the straightforward words attributed to him in the charter—that he was "seeking to escape the pains of hell and obtain the joys of paradise, after the death of his body."[84] William of Newburg was certain that William the Conqueror founded Battle Abbey as atonement for all the Christian blood he spilled in his conquest of England.[85] Words given to Henry, Count of Namur and Luxemburg, in a late twelfth-century ratification of a vassal's gift, meditated on power and the need for its careful and pious use. "Because all power is from the all-powerful God, who, although he is powerful, does not throw down the powerful," the count begins in hopeful tones (as one of the powerful), "it is necessary that whoever desires to use in a healthy way, the power granted by God should strive both to serve the Lord of lords in fear and conserve faithfully those serving him." The result is his ratification of a grant to the church of St. Mary in Floreffe made by a man setting off on crusade; two types of service are prominent here: service in arms against enemies of the faith, and service with the purse by giving certain rights over to God's other servants.[86] In the early thirteenth century, Guy d'Arblincourt "wished to correct [his] excesses," and so, before setting forth on crusade, confirmed rights in a particular estate to the church of Chauny "for my soul and the souls of my ancestors."[87] Deathbed speeches of great lords were often penned by monastic chroniclers. A classic case of the genre comes from the twelfth-century chronicler Orderic Vitalis, who imagined William the Conqueror trembling at the end of his vigorous life, weighed down by sins and dreading the awful divine judgment to come. Concern for killing is prominent: "I was brought up in arms from childhood, and am deeply stained with all the blood I have shed (In armis enim ab infantia nutritus sum et multi sanguinia effusione admodum pollutus sum)."[88] While no scholar believes that these are William's actual last words, the idea of fears and doubts on his deathbed may not be pure invention; at minimum such accounts show the fears that clerics tirelessly tried to inculcate in knights. The modern dictum "no atheist in a foxhole" may find its medieval predecessor in "no obdurate knight on the deathbed." Indeed, the medieval dictum might well be extended to the eve or even the moment before battle when all warriors craved spiritual assurance.[89]

Did knights worry whether all their deeds of prowess throughout a long life in arms registered in the mind of God as righteous? Such doubts were sown by clerical declarations that prowess was, after all, a morally neutral quality.[90]

Recorded behavior of knights supports such interpretation. In his chronicle, Richard of Hexham noted that some English knights refused to continue a campaign against the Scots in the reign of Stephen. The reason was partly that the king of Scots was refusing to give battle, but also that Lent was beginning and they were evidently reluctant to use their arms in that sacred season.[91] A northern Italian saint named Obizio (d. 1204) began life as a knight but was so badly wounded in a fight at a bridge over the river Oglio that he was left for dead. Though he was carried to safety by a friend, while lying near death he experienced a terrifying vision of hell that led him to give up military life and become a helper of the poor and, eventually, a lay brother in the monastery of Santa Giula in Brescia; symbolically, at his own expense he rebuilt the bridge at which he had been so grievously wounded while a knight.[92] Simon de Montfort, who would become the ardent crusader against the Albigensians, would not join with most of the army on the Fourth Crusade in sacking the Christian city of Zara, but left the main host and went on to fulfill his vow in the Holy Land. He was not alone.[93] Contemporaries at least debated whether Edward III and his army worried about divine displeasure over their campaigning after a terrifying storm with lightning and huge hailstones struck the host near Chartres on "Black Monday" (April 14, 1360).[94] At the end of their lives many thought it prudent to exchange armor for a monastic habit. In mid-twelfth century a knight appropriately called Peter the Aged (Petrus cognomento Vetula) fearing death during a grave illness entered the cloister at Hombliéres, bringing appropriate landed gifts with him.[95] Caesarius of Heisterbach tells approvingly of the knight Waleran who even rode fully armed on his great charger down the aisle of the monastic church to the altar and there gave up his armor for the modest Cistercian robe.[96] Better-known figures underscore the point. The great knight William Marshal died under a Templar's robe;[97] King John of England was buried in a Benedictine monk's cowl.[98] Not all late converts could feel perfect confidence, however. Moral tales in medieval collections sometimes show former

knights worried about their military lives even after committing to the cloister.[99] Of course, knights were warned that counting on a salvific eleventh-
hour conversion might backfire, as one great lord in another of Caesarius of
Heisterbach's exemplary moral stories learned. This noble end-of-life gambler
planned to be safely wrapped in the monastic habit just after his death, but
Caesarius assured his readers a demon had already taken possession of his
hopelessly sinful body a year before his physical death, and he was most assuredly damned.[100] It was a well-known trick of wily devils, in fact, to convince
knights to postpone—until death overtook them—even a final confession;
suddenly it was too late.[101]

We can move a step closer to a secure sense of knightly views with the
imaginative chivalric literature we know they read or heard and patronized.
It is again helpful to remember that this is a literature of debate and reform.
There is much confident assertion in these works, of course, but fears hover
and sometimes dominate. A few cases must again stand for a massive body
of evidence. Among the eponymous heroes of *chansons*, Raoul de Cambrai
comes quickly to mind as, in fact, a complex mixture of what is admired and
even more feared. The leitmotif of his story is that a man out of measure cannot come to a good end. Raoul does not. Having, against his pious mother's
specific admonition, waged war with ravaging of the poor and burning of
churches—even a nunnery, with its nuns—he may well be considered an
antihero. Yet the text shows enough ineradicable admiration for pure heroic
prowess to satisfy a sense that it is not simply a clerical screed hostile to chivalric ideas, but is opening them to debate in an awareness of incompatibility.[102] Galehaut, one of the dominant and most admired figures in the early
thirteenth-century romance *Lancelot*, tries to convince a wise man to reveal
to him the moment of his death. He wants to be prepared, he says, "since I
have committed many wrongs in my life, destroying cities, killing people,
dispossessing and banishing people (car molt ai fet mals en ma vie, que de
viles destruire, que de gens occire et deseriter et essilier)." Master Elias, the
wise man, agrees that this must be true, "for any man who has conquered as
much as you have must have a heavy burden of sins, and it's no wonder (kar
nus hom qui tant ai conquis com vos avés ne porroit estre sans trop grant
charge de pechiés: et ce n'est pas merveille)."[103]

Bernier, a major figure in the long *Chanson Raoul de Cambrai* (the second part of which was written at roughly the same time as the *Lancelot*), expresses similar worries about sin, killing, and atonement. He, too, seeks wise
advice—in this case from a select group of his courtiers:

Advise me, barons . . . for God's sake. I am frightened at the thought of the sins I have committed, and alarmed at the number of people I have killed. Raoul [his lord] was among them, and that weighs on me indeed. I intend to go to Saint-Gilles at once and pray to the saint to intercede on my behalf with God our lord and king.[104]

In the Middle English *Awntyrs off Arthur*, Gawain and Guenevere, straying from their hunting party, confront a terrifying apparition (Guenevere's deceased mother, we learn) that suddenly rises from the nether world to warn the queen of sins at court. Gawain, the model knight, takes the opportunity to ask this spirit a question troubling his mind:

"What will happen to us," asked the knight, "who strive to fight, / and so trample down folk in many king's lands, / And ride over realms without any right. / To win worship in war through prowess of hands?"

The chilling answer from the otherworldly messenger combines a warning against greed, with a prediction of the fall of the Round Table as Fortune's wheel turns.[105]

Tension and paradox are central to romance literature, most of it written, as general scholarly agreement holds, by clerics of one stripe or another. As a literature not merely of affirmation and valorization, but of insistent debate and reform, romance amply documents the uncertainties we are seeking to establish. Clearly some clerical critics found truly hateful in the sight of God what many of their fellows, authors of romance, considered legitimate elements of the warrior code of chivalry. The tension and paradox appear within individual works no less than between works. A case of the former is evident in the sad puzzlement of Queen Guenevere, speaking to the hero Galahaut in the great prose romance, *Lancelot*: the queen laments that "it is too bad Our Lord pays no heed to our courtly ways, and a person whom the world sees as good is wicked to God."[106] At work behind her puzzlement were arguments such as the warning given by Alan of Lille (quoting Luke 16:15) that "What is valued highly among men is an abomination in the sight of God."[107] Did the chivalric life build upon laudable prowess and licit loot or was it a practice of grievous sin?

We might consider portrayals of the ideal last day for a knight as imagined by two sets of clerics. In sermon stories told from pulpits and repeated in one manuscript collection after another a pious crusader dies willingly on the Mount of Olives, or in a final, pious, suicidal rush into battle against pagans, thinking he could leave this earth in no better way.[108] By contrast, in the great Vulgate Cycle of prose Arthurian romance knights sometimes say after a particularly successful day of vigorously cutting down their enemies—fellow Christians, not Muslims—that they would be satisfied if God would give them death: for they will never again have such a grand day.[109]

Or we could turn to the radically differing moral evaluations of the results of chivalric prowess on the human body. Robert Mannyng of Brunne's *Handlyng Synne* warns that a tourneyer may wound an opponent or be himself wounded so badly that he never can thrive afterward.[110] Authors of chivalric texts turn the sentiment upside down. The capacity to kill an opponent, or at least to leave him seriously crippled, proves a knight's prowess and earns him imperishable honor. Sir Tryamour in his Middle English romance hits an enemy so hard that "He was nevyr aftur sownde (He was never healthy thereafter)."[111] Another hero, Lybeaus Desconus, breaks an opponent's thigh so badly he is ever after lame.[112] These authors accept what is clearly the point of view of the knights. One of the accolades Malory bestows on Lancelot is that many of the men he strikes "never throoff aftir (never thrive afterward)."[113] Another knightly author, the standard bearer to the great Spanish knight Don Pero Niño, similarly assures readers that his hero wounded an opponent so badly that he remained crippled for many days after their contest.[114] What is feared by some clerics is praised by others (and aligns their views with those of knightly authors). Centuries earlier Pope Gregory VII had worried over such tensions, saying that "although such men say with their lips 'Mea culpa' for the killing of many, in their hearts they nevertheless rejoice for the increase of their supposed honour, and they do not wish that they had not done what they have done; nor do they grieve that they have driven their brothers to hell."[115] This is, of course, why they wore the best armor available. If, on the spiritual side, their corporal suffering was meritorious, on the more worldly side, survival to enjoy victory was so very enjoyable. Enemies would assure a full measure of meritorious suffering; there was no need to boost such vigorous efforts by shedding defensive armor in order to maximize the result.

Chronicle evidence supports that from literature. Matthew Paris reports in mid-thirteenth century that Christ himself taught a prominent English lord a lesson about knightly wrongdoing on campaign. Christ appeared in a dream to Hubert de Burgh, a leading royal minister of the late reign of John and minority of Henry III. Burgh was conducting a campaign of devastation against the king's enemies and in the process was despoiling churches. In his vision, Christ from the cross instructed Hubert that when next he saw a crucifix he must spare the crucified and worship his image. As the devastation proceeded in the cold light of the next day, a priest approached Hubert, thrusting into his field of vision a large crucifix, remarkably like that in his dream. In obedience to the divine command, Hubert dismounted, fell to the ground in order to worship the crucifix, and restored the plundered ecclesiastical goods to the priest. He was later convinced that this faithfulness to Christ's command had won him a much-needed restoration to royal favor. Whether the incident moved him to a general lessening of his pillaging campaign is another matter, though the dramatic scene retains its value as evidence.[116]

A crusade chronicle from a century earlier may bring us equally close to knightly sentiments. At a crucial point during the crusading expedition that captured Lisbon in 1147 "a portent appeared among the Flemings."[117] It was the practice for a priest, after the completion of mass, to distribute blessed bread to the warriors. But on this Sunday

> the blessed bread was bloody, and when [the priest] directed that it be purged with a knife, it was found to be as permeated with blood as flesh which can never be cut without bleeding (sacerdos panem benedictum vidit sanguineum, quem dum cultello purgare iuberet, inventus est adeo cum sanguine permixtus, ut caro que numquam sine sanguine potest incidi).[118]

To a modern historian what is more remarkable is the moral drawn from the incident by the writer of this chronicle, a cleric who appears to have been quite close to the men at arms he served and, in fact, a spokesman for their views:

> And some, interpreting it, said that this fierce and indomitable people, covetous of the goods of others, although at the moment under the guise of a pilgrimage and religion, had not yet put away the thirst for human blood.[119]

Issues involving looting are significant throughout this chronicle. Sensitivity to the issue may have been heightened by Muslim taunts hurled at the crusaders in debate. "Labeling your ambition zeal for righteousness," they charge, "you misrepresent vices as virtues (ambitionem vestram rectitudinis zelum dicentes, pro virtutibus vitia mentimini)."[120] Are the Muslims here being

allowed to speak some of the inner fears that troubled the crusaders themselves? Even the priest's own sermon to the crusaders probed similar issues:
he reminded the warriors that since they have followed Christ and accepted
poverty, they must not trust in oppression or become vain in robbery.[121]

Other chronicles supply evidence to suggest tensions between warrior
vocation and religious ideals. The chronicle of Ralph of Caen—the author
was himself a Norman knight—records the vocational uncertainties of Tancred, one of the famous Norman adventurers active in southern Italy. The
issue troubling Tancred in the late eleventh century was clearly war, vengeance, and killing, especially as set against Christ's precept of turning the
other cheek. His uncertainties were disabling in a warrior: "the contradiction
lessened the daring of the wise man whenever he had opportunity to reflect
quietly." Tancred's mind was torn, Ralph says, between ideas of the gospel
and those of the world. But all his fears ceased once he had heard the message
of the crusade sermon of Urban II which "granted a remission of all sins (peccatorum omnium remissionem ascripsit)" to those setting out on the great expedition. With his natural vigor freed of spiritual doubts, Tancred went forth
a vigorous crusader.[122] The doubts he left behind provide splendid evidence.

Even the early Templars felt troubling doubts. Such uncertainties would
not be expected from the Templars who joined to the venerable and idealized
vocation of monk that of ideal Christian warrior. To some Christians, however, the compound seemed false and unworkable; outside voices had raised
serious objections to the very idea of such a combined vocation. Even more
interesting, fears had surfaced in members within the group. A remarkable
letter on the subject written c. 1128 by a man calling himself Hugh the Sinner (Hugh Peccator) has survived in a French municipal archive; Hugh may
have been one of the founders of the order, Hugh de Payns.[123] He writes to
his fellow Templars:

> we have heard that certain of your number have been troubled by
> people of no wisdom, as though your profession, by which you have
> dedicated your life to carrying arms against the enemies of the faith
> and peace in defense of Christians, as though, I say, that profession
> were illicit or harmful, that is, either a sin or an obstacle to greater
> advancement.[124]

Hugh finds the origin of such disparagement in the devil, who is tempt-
ing the knights of the order "with anger and hatred when you kill, with

greed when you strip your victim (suggerit odium et furorem dum occiditis et suggerit cupiditatem dum spoliatis)." His letter assures the brothers that they do not hate sinfully in killing nor covet dishonestly in their just looting, and he caps the case with the rhetorical question "should not payment be made to the man who lays down his life for the protection of his neighbours' lives (homini pro seruanda vita proximorum animam suam ponenti merces non debetur?)" In case his own words do not convince, he imagines Christ speaking to them: "You want to sit and to rest with Christ ruling but you do not want to work and be exhausted with Christ fighting (sedere uultis et quiescere cum regnante, sed laborare non uultis et fatigari cum pugnante)." In words that recall our Harley manuscript illumination, Christ is made to say "he who wishes to reign should not shirk work; he who seeks the crown should not avoid the fight (qui querit coronam non subterfugiat pugnam)." Christ himself toiled, Hugh reminds his brethren; it is the unavoidable price of peace and quiet. "Take note, brothers: if peace and quiet were to be sought in the manner you say, there would be no order left in the church of God (Videte, fraters: si hoc modo, ut uos dicitis, requies et pax querenda esset, nullus in Esslesia Dei ordo subsisteret)." Echoes of an ancient debate over the active and contemplative life rumble like distant thunder. But Hugh hammers his main point home again:

> the devil . . . now tells the knights of Christ to lay down their arms,
> not to wage war, to flee tumults, to seek out the wilderness, so
> that when he shows the appearance of humility he takes away true
> humility. What is pride if not to disobey what God has imposed on
> one? (diabolus . . . nunc militibus Christi dicit ut arma deponent, bella
> non gerant, tumultam fugiant, secretum petant, ut dum humilitatis
> pretendit speciem, ueram tollat humilitatem. Quid est enim superbum
> esse, nisi in eo quod a Deo iniunctum est non obedire?)

He enjoins the knight of Christ to "offer the sacrifice of your labour to God (vestri laboris sacrificium Deo offerte)." From the intensity of the case made we can only conclude that the doubts and fears that provoked so much rebuttal must have been serious, indeed.[125]

The impact of such evidence is redoubled by Jean Leclercq's argument that doubts of the sort Hugh was combating stand behind the more elaborate treatise St. Bernard wrote for the Templars six or seven years later, *In Praise of the New Knighthood* (*De Laude Novae Militiae*).[126] In that treatise Bernard, too, carefully assures the Templars that their fighting is licit and even praise-worthy in the eyes of God, that they kill evil, rather than men, and can, themselves, die in full confidence of paradise. If Leclercq is right, we can be sure that doubts persisted for years and that doubters may have needed to hear from a more authoritative and eloquent voice than Hugh's.[127]

Occasionally we can hear knights speak their fears directly. David Crouch has used early twelfth-century letters from the circle of Henry I of England to show that "these men who lived and worked in Henry's service were very conscious of the moral compromises they had made."[128] Other knights spoke directly to a particular unease over killing their fellow Christians. Joinville (the chronicler of the mid-thirteenth-century crusade of St. Louis) tells that Josserand de Brancion came away with the prize for valor in each of thirty-six battles and skirmishes in which he had taken part. Yet after one Franco-German fight that took place on a Good Friday, he entered a church he had saved from destruction, fell dramatically upon his knees before the altar and prayed aloud in Joinville's presence:

> Lord . . . I pray Thee to have mercy on me, and take me out of these wars among Christians in which I have spent a great part of my life; and grant that I may die in Thy service, and so come to enjoy Thy kingdom in paradise.[129]

The scene is real and immediate. We can almost hear the armor clank as the worried knight falls to his knees in anguished prayer; we certainly hear his own words.

A fourteenth-century miracle story praising St. Martial gives similarly valuable evidence. In the campaigning of the Hundred Years War, an English squire went out plundering (pro depredando per patriam) with his men in the region of Limoges, but was unexpectedly thrown into the raging Dordogne River when his horse harness suddenly snapped. Sinking to certain death beneath the rushing water, he made two quick promises: first, he would offer a certain weight of wax for himself and his horse when St. Martial's head was displayed in its sanctuary (ad ejus capitis ostentionem); second, he would never take up arms again against any Christian (nunquam adversum chris-tianum aliquem de cetero sumeret arma). At once, he sensed that a man led him, followed by his fortunate horse, safely out of the water.[130] Man and beast were saved by the squire's pious votive vow and by the promise to circum-scribe his participation in warfare that had not pleased God.

If more restrained, at least a similar sentiment appears in a remarkable account of deeds done by the great Spanish knight Don Pero Niño, written by his standard bearer in the early decades of the fifteenth century. The author admits what a pity it was that the great hero had to burn Christian dwellings during a raid on the isle of Jersey in the English Channel. The account even records a moving plea from these folk, asking that he spare their lives and homes: they argued that he should not have the killing of noncombatants, including children, on his conscience.[131] The moving scene and the arguments of the noncombatants made an impression on the writer: they are not suppressed, as the biographer could easily have done in his triumphal account of his hero's life.

Our evidence is diverse and only gradually escapes the taint of clerical mediation; but it is collectively impressive and moves in a direction suggesting that thoughtful knights sensed paradoxical elements in their relationship with their religion. Other knights, perhaps even a majority, might have been only vaguely aware of such tensions which, like old wounds, were so familiar and habitually suppressed that they seldom came to the level of consciousness, causing pain only when probed. Yet our sample of evidence suggests that many knights suffered troubling thoughts at some time in their lives, sensing incompatible elements of piety and prowess. Clerics worked hard to induce such awareness, but it seems likely that knightly piety in itself generated tensions. Bridging the gap was especially important to thoughtful knights and may well have had some importance to all. How the gap was bridged is the subject of this book.

A Roadmap

Each of the following chapters will examine evidence on these vexed issues. We begin in Chapter 2 with a pair of treatises written late in the development we are studying—in mid-fourteenth century—by highly thoughtful practicing knights from opposite sides of the Channel, Henry of Lancaster and Geoffroi de Charny. These works present developed ideas of heroic, meritorious atonement for sin through the hardships of knightly life. They show the tough knightly profession selectively incorporating religious ideas within a warrior framework, demonstrating significant lay independence.

Chapter 3 elaborates two broad topics that form the essential environment within which ideas of chivalry took shape. It first briefly considers the importance of clerical reform coming in two great surges: the famous Gregorian effort to establish clerical leadership and independence and the later movement gathering force from the later twelfth century. This later phase of reform sought to create a working theology to guide the laity. Emphasizing a penitential system with a focus on priestly counseling and individual confession, it recognized the variety of occupations of the laity and the need for spiritual guidance within the practice of each. One such occupational group, of course, was the knighthood. To establish a second essential element of context (much less generally investigated), the chapter emphasizes the atmosphere of asceticism that so powerfully marked High and Late Medieval culture. Chivalry grew within a remarkably ascetic environment that emphasized corporal suffering as an important source of spiritual merits.

A third crucial contextual element requires separate treatment. Chapter 4 analyzes the combination of piety and religious independence that characterized chivalric thought. This fusion informs all aspects of the knightly approach to a religious undergirding of their profession. Tournament and crusade, foundational elements of the knightly life, provide especially informative cases in point. How did knights respond to clerical strictures on tournament? How did they hear and incorporate elements from crusade preaching into their own undoubted piety? Their combination of piety and independence was crucially important: it allowed for a highly selective borrowing of ideas from both sides of current theological discussion. Ideas that benefited chivalry could be absorbed; those considered troublesome could be confidently ignored. Chivalry cannot be labeled either clerical or secular in inspiration, for it drew on each to produce the mighty alloy that gave it such strength.

Chapter 5 emphasizes the role of imaginative chivalric literature in the creation and dissemination of chivalric ideology. Evidence for three basic themes is outlined (though these elements sinuously intertwined in practice). The first established the sheer suffering inherent in the knightly life; the second asserted that spiritual merit, a counterweight to the heavy burden of sin, was earned in that hard life; and the third extended the valorization that was forged for crusaders to all knights—their entire vocation generated spiritual merit, not merely crusading against enemies of the faith. The religion of knights was not simply produced by clerics for crusaders. Knights had ideas of their own and they determinedly proclaimed the validity and penitential value of their demanding professional life in arms, even though some of its principles and ineradicable practices sorely troubled ecclesiastics.

The next set of chapters (6, 7, and 8) show how in three major instances religious ideas were selectively drawn from clerical discussions and infused into a tough warrior ethos. High medieval clerics loved order and rationality and they were attempting to fashion a distinct pastoral theology for the laity. Basic questions readily arose in their discussion. Exactly how had Christ achieved salvation for lost humanity? How might mere humans imitate his model in their own lives? What was the divine social and professional template for Christian society? That is, what social groups and labor were divinely planned? Did human labor incorporate spiritual value or was it merely a form of punishment for sin? What means provided the best hope for cleansing the general populace of sin? Thoughtful writers who spoke about chivalry (clerics and knights alike) borrowed skillfully from conflicting opinions in these debates, incorporating some lines of thought and confidently neglecting others. Theirs was a tightrope performance. They had to justify and sanctify knighthood by claiming it merited the blessing of God; yet they also had to avoid contrary ideas of the sort that filled the Sermon on the Mount. If the process seems logically contradictory or paradoxical, it was socially and culturally powerful.

Chapter 6 examines the fundamental case of differing ideas on exactly how Christ achieved the redemption of sinful humanity. The issue was central to medieval religion and raised the significant question of how sinful mortals should follow or imitate their Savior. One view emphasized that Christ enacted the classic warrior virtue of heroic victory over the devil and evil; the other stressed his meritorious suffering in expiation of human sin. Knighthood enthusiastically claimed both roles. Victory bravely won and victimhood willingly suffered were both built solidly into knightly religion. We will find Christ described as a victorious knight no less than a suffering servant and will witness the *milites* proclaiming that they exactly and devotedly follow his divine example.

Chapter 7 takes up the division of society into "orders" (*ordines*) with an appropriate labor envisaged for each. Since each *ordo* represented a particular social and professional group (required in the divine plan for an ideal society), each contributed its characteristic labor. Such work had to be related to individual salvation no less than to social utility. Again, two theological positions appeared side by side: work in any *ordo* could be considered merely penitential, or it could be seen more positively as approved by God, a pathway toward salvation. Knighthood, one of the *ordines*, had its ideal labor to perform. Was this labor of fighting merely a sad and usually sinful—though necessary—species of work, or might it be considered sanctified? Knightly ideology secured benefits from both theological points of view, combining the penitential with the meritorious. How forcefully such ideas of hard and meritorious labor (and suffering) were at work in society appears in the competition among *ordines* on the basis of their ascetic merit. Who suffered more and earned more of God's forgiving love?

Chapter 8 considers the clerical elaboration of ideas on sin, confession, and penance, asking how knights participated in an economy of salvation. Was physical suffering necessary for penance to be genuine? Should confession and penance take place once—heroically—for some great sin, or often, for quotidian sins?[132] Or was inner contrition the key? Once again knightly ideology drew characteristically on all sources of strength. A sense of the heroic stature of acts of penance was favored, but so, in effect, was the concept of repeatable penance. The hard knightly life of campaign and meritorious combat came to be viewed as a form of penance in itself. It remains doubtful how fully the knights cooperated with the ecclesiastical ideal of individual confession to their parish priest. They showed resistance; and they could claim that their own sanctified vocation, replete with righteous suffering, provided at least an attractive additional option—if not an alternative—for performing effective penance.

Knights were pious members of their society. Their ideology based itself on powerful religious as well as warrior ideas; in fact the veritable fusion helps to explain how long the ideals dominated and animated the lay elite. What ended its centuries-long innings? The final chapter (9) considers why this ethos of chivalry began to die out as the traditional medieval era was transformed in the fifteenth and sixteenth centuries and beyond. Monolithic explanations—gunpowder or military revolution eliminating the knights (and their supporting ideals), the transformative force of humanistic ideals, or of radical religious reform—are discounted in favor of a more modulated mix of forces. What seems especially crucial was rapidly growing state power, supported by changing ideas about noble formation, the kingdom as *respublica*, the duties of citizenship and—as ever—religious blessing on the process.

This book makes no claim that knights practiced a specific chivalric piety that excluded all other ideas and practices of lay piety. Knights surely followed standard forms of religious practice common to lay folk in general. That they believed strongly in founding religious institutions is manifest. The case is rather that knights could at will practice the pious forms of their fellow laymen (alms, pilgrimage, fasting, and religious foundation); but to the degree that it was useful, they could follow their own exclusive and carefully crafted channel of piety, one highly compatible with their violent ideal of prowess winning honor. A specifically knightly ideology blended major and sometimes competing strands of changing theology with the chivalric worship of the demigod prowess. They squared the circle and incorporated in their *ordo* the most ascetic tenets of their religion and the most bloodthirsty and vengeful standards of their professional code. Watching this process unfold is useful, even if it leads to sobering reflections. Its relevance to understanding religiously valorized violence that daily stains our newspaper accounts with blood scarcely requires comment.

CHAPTER 2

Two Model Knight/Authors as Guides

HENRY OF LANCASTER (c. 1310–61) and Geoffroi de Charny (c. 1306–56) were vigorous warriors involved in the constant, hard campaigning and diplomacy of the first phase of the Hundred Years War. Although they may never have crossed swords in any engagement, they were often present in the same theaters of war and did meet as envoys for a series of negotiations to secure a truce in 1347.[1] Each had high chivalric standing emphasized by being chosen an original member of his sovereign's knightly order, Lancaster becoming a knight of the Garter, Charny of the Star. The piety of each was dramatically registered by a valued sacred possession: Henry cherished a thorn from Christ's crown of thorns; Geoffroi owned what we now know as the Shroud of Turin.[2] The piety of each likewise took the standard form of endowment: Lancaster reendowed a collegiate foundation at Leicester; Charny a church at Lirey.[3] Both men reveal a puritanical streak that would have a long future among warriors in the West, an early form of that mentalité that would later form the minds of Cromwellians and Ignatius of Loyola.[4]

They were also both authors of extensive treatises that intimately explore the religious mentalité of chivalry. As prominent and pious chivalric figures whose books present more than a narrowly personal statement, they can speak for knighthood in their own times. Their books demand close attention in our inquiry.

Lancaster's *Livre de seyntz medicines*

Henry, first duke of Lancaster, wrote the *Livre de seyntz medicines* (The Book of Holy Remedies) in 1354, as he tells us in its final paragraph.[5] The book was meant to be read by his friends and was later owned by other prominent, strenuous knights, namely, Sir John de Grailly, Captal de Buch, and Humphrey, Duke of Gloucester, famous as the founder of the library within the Bodleian which still bears his name. The book came to Gloucester as a gift from "the baron of Carew"; apparently this is Thomas de Carew, a vigorous knight and diplomat.[6] Buch and Gloucester added their coats of arms to a copy still preserved.[7] These proud marks of ownership underscore our sense that the book presents a statement highly valued in eminent chivalric circles.

Lancaster's *Livre* takes an extremely physical approach to its subject and relies heavily on imagery from the author's knightly profession. It pictures his body as a castle and the soul as the treasure within its walls, beset by enemies which are sins. Since his ears, eyes, nose, mouth, hands, feet, and heart are each attacked by all seven of the deadly sins, the scheme allows for enough combinations and permutations to delight any scholastic.[8] E. J. Arnould, the mid-twentieth-century editor of the text, suggests that it was written in segments, day by day, right through Lent.[9] M. Dominica Legge suggested to Arnould that the work may have been produced as a form of penance.[10] I fear that some readers who struggle through its turgid prose and allegory gone to seed—244 pages in Anglo-Norman French—may think it penance to read. William Pantin, kind among historians, refers to the book as "a work of great freshness and simplicity" and agrees with Froissart that its author is "imaginative."[11] Yet Lancaster's biographer, Kenneth Fowler, in a classic understatement declares the book "not remarkable as a work of literature."[12] Even its editor, who tries to like it, declares the work "laborious," "long-winded and repetitive."[13] But it is vastly informative for our inquiry into religion and chivalry. Any reader who persists could not doubt that it was written by a knight writing with his profession in mind, even if we lacked Henry's announcement of authorship (his name written backwards in a final gesture of abject humility) at the conclusion of the work. The text crackles with chivalric or feudal terminology of wounds, war, courts, castles, siege, prison, ransom, vassalage, treason, safe-conduct, and the like.[14] In a telling military phrase, Lancaster even asserts that because of his sins he is at war with God. The daily kisses he gives to God at mass are intended to be signs of peace and truce between them, though he confesses that he constantly and traitorously breaks these suspensions of hostilities.[15]

Only a few pages into the text, Lancaster addresses our issues, in a passage worthy of full quotation:

> I pray you, Lord for the love in which you took on human form, pardon my sins and watch over me, dearest Lord, that henceforth I be able to resemble you in some ways, if wretched food for worms such as I can resemble so noble a king as the king of heaven, earth, sea, and all that is therein. And if, dearest Lord, I have in this life any persecution for you touching body, possessions, or companions, or of any other sort, I pray, dearest Lord, that I may endure willingly for love of you, and since you, Lord, so willingly suffered such pains for me on earth, I pray, Lord, that I may resemble you insofar as I can find in my hard heart to suffer willingly for you such afflictions, labors, pains, as you choose and not merely to win a prize [guerdon] nor to offset my sins, but purely for love of you as you, Lord, have done for love of me.[16]

Here we encounter a model knight declaring his willingness to suffer *in imitatione Christi*. He wants, ideally, to suffer out of pure, mimetic love, but the specific denial that his goal is merely to offset sins through suffering is informative, and likely reveals the actual link between suffering and spiritual merit in his mind. Any reader will quickly learn that the leitmotif of this text is suffering: together, the noun "suffering" and the verb "to suffer" appear in this text more than sixty times. The nouns "pain" and "travail" likewise appear repeatedly.[17] At the top of the scale Christ's suffering redeems humanity. The descriptions of Christ's torments during his passion, to a modern eye, pass the bounds of propriety and stand like a signpost pointing toward late medieval crucifixes from which many modern folk will want to avert their gaze. The sufferings of the Blessed Virgin are also imaginatively reproduced and fill whole pages; her tears, shed at each indignity visited upon her son, like warm white wine, cleanse the sinner's wounds and prepare them for the most efficacious healing ointment—Christ's sacrificial blood.[18] The sufferings of saints, and especially the martyrs, get at least honorable if rather generic mention. Their sufferings and martyrdom serve as added counterweights to Lancaster's sins on the divine scales of eternal justice.[19] But at the bottom of this hierarchy even human suffering, when endured in good causes and motivated by the right intent, yields some measure of satisfaction for the unmanageable debt owed for sin.

Sir Henry wants to suffer for the Lord he sometimes calls "Sire Dieu." He senses his guilt intensely. Mirroring relationships as lively as his bonds with his tenants, and images as venerable as the theological treatises two and a half centuries earlier,[20] Duke Henry calls himself "a foul and evil traitor, the chief cause of my good lord's villainous death (cheitif et malveis traitre, q'est la principale cause de la vileyne mort de son bon seignur)."[21] We have already noted his sense of making war against his Lord. Wishing to avoid pride, he says he would henceforth serve not worldly inconsequentials or worse, but God "en perils et en peyne."[22] For his great sins, he declares "I would put myself in pain and in perils so that I might find some way to please you, sweetest Lord (moy mettre en peyne qe jeo puisse ascune chose faire a la plesance de vous, tresdouz Sires)."[23] As this wish suggests, his suffering must in some infinitesimal measure not only resemble but repay Christ's own suffering, as he recognizes:

> I pray you, Lord . . . that I might so suffer all pains and sorrows
> patiently for love of You, sweet Lord, to repay you some part of what
> I owe for the most horrendous griefs, pains and vilanies that you
> suffered, sweet Lord, so graciously for wretched me.[24]

Or, again, he prays,

> That I can understand that through the slight pain I endure on earth
> I am quit of the great pains of hell. This is a good deal as for a little
> suffering in this world, which is nothing to endure, one can escape
> the pains of hell, which are so terrible and joyless: and a man certainly
> cannot earn more by well enduring your gift of suffering than to have
> by this a reduction of the pains of purgatory.[25]

These sentiments come from the pen of a man who refers regularly to "my wretched body (cheitif corps), and who says that his body deserves literally to be boiled, fried, and roasted in hell (en enfern boiller, roster et frire)."[26]

The pious, atoning sentiment could not be clearer; but is there any chivalric connection here? Is it likely that any knight, a joyful practitioner of prowess—as proudly physical a creed as can be imagined—would sincerely denigrate the body and long for its sufferings? Do such sentiments not emanate from clerics rather than knights and is not Henry of Lancaster merely aping such language as his confessor might use and impose? Even that would be evidence of interest, of course, but I want to suggest that much more is at work. In the first place the imaginative context that he has constructed for his work must be kept in mind. The sites of sin for which cures are needed he describes as wounds (not fevers to be cured or boils to be lanced) and wounds come from weapons. Sometimes wounded limbs, he knows (with his mind likely on the aftermath of battle) must be removed at the joint.[27] Henry sometimes also speaks of fractures (viles brisures)[28] which I am sure he did not imagine resulting from an unfortunate tumble down a newel staircase. The context of combat in this treatise directs our reading. His use of the terminology of pain and labor echoes the language many works of chivalric literature use to describe campaign and battle, as we will see. This likelihood is strengthened by his admission of fear when he hears tales of battle; his fears focus on being shamed or suffering sudden death without a chance for confession.[29] For other lay groups these terms might have more general meaning; for knights the backdrop for thought is campaign and battle.

Moreover, Duke Henry sometimes wonderfully reveals his train of thought, if indirectly. In discussing how the tears shed by the Blessed Virgin will wash the wounds of his own wretched body he comes to nasal wounds, a topic which puts the realist in him in mind of the blows that struck Christ's nose during his scourging. He comments, in all piety, that Christ's nose must have looked like that of a habitual tourneyer, and that his mouth must have been discolored and beaten out of shape. Here he writes with the voice of experience. Warming to his topic, he says that indeed Christ did fight in a tournament—and won it, securing life for humanity.[30] As a strenuous knight, his conception of imitating Christ readily turns to this martial version of the savior and his role.[31]

It seems to me not too much to claim, then, that Henry of Lancaster conceives of the strenuous knightly life itself as meritorious suffering, as a form of penance acceptable, even pleasing, in God's eyes as satisfaction for sin. In its own way, *militia* is a form of *imitatio Christi*.[32] We should note, above all, that Henry of Lancaster is not talking about crusade. Although he had personally gone on more than one crusading venture, and although he does mention pilgrimage with some regularity, never in his treatise does he specify fighting unbelievers; his references to pilgrimage seem to indicate travel to sacred places, not the armed pilgrimage that was crusade. When he declares that the great gift of divine salvation is a bargain, given the modest level of human suffering required in return, he may draw on a venerable theme of crusade sermons; but he is putting all suffering of knights into the balance pan, not specifically that suffering endured as a crusader. He thinks that the hard life and the hard blows that knights endure repay some of their vast debt to God, even, we must assume, if that means the campaigning of what we would call the Hundred Years War, rather than any crusade in the Mediterranean or in company with the knights of the Teutonic order. It is knighthood in general that represents for him a life of expiatory suffering; this includes crusade but does not inhere in crusade solely. Through suffering in heroic atonement he imitates Christ and in some small way repays the debt for sin.

Charny's *Livre de chevalerie*

This point of view emerges even more clearly in the second treatise, that written by Henry's contemporary, Geoffroi de Charny, the leading French knight of the age and author of a highly informative *Livre de chevalerie*. Charny was in the fullest sense a strenuous knight who apparently wrote this treatise for what was intended to be a grand new royal chivalric society, the Order of the Star founded by King John of France. Only the utter failure of this order under the repeated hammer blows of defeat suffered by French knighthood in this phase of the Hundred Years War, I believe, condemned Charny's treatise to obscurity in its own time. However, in company with Lancaster's book, it has much to tell us.[33]

If Henry of Lancaster wrote a religious treatise for which chivalry functions as a subtext, Geoffroi de Charny wrote a chivalric treatise with intensely religious overtones. Thus in analyzing knightly religion in Charny we can reverse the process by which we approached Henry's *Livre*. There we looked for religiously significant suffering and then found a link with knighthood. With the *Livre de chevalerie* we must first examine Charny's emphasis on suffering endured in the profession of knighthood, and then turn to find the linkage with religious expiation.

In company with Lancaster, Charny undoubtedly thinks physical suffering is spiritually good, the mere body is nothing. In fact, he refers regularly to the wretched body (*chetiz* or *chetifs corps*), using the very phrase beloved by Lancaster.[34] They could sing harmonious duets on the dangers of sloth, although for formally distinct goals. Charny's part would include truly vigorous denunciations of self-indulgent concern over choice dishes, fine wines, the best sauces; he can denounce soft beds, white linens, and sleeping late, in language that would do credit to a crusty monastic reformer.[35] Lancaster, we should note, would add his voice especially against the vice of gluttony; he was a noted gourmet, though he denounces this delight as a sin, and was suffering from gout when he wrote his treatise. "Too great a desire to cosset the body is against all good," is Charny's summary statement covering all forms of bodily indulgence.[36]

Instead, Charny finds the obvious goal in life to be vigorous military effort, disciplining the body, taking the endless risks and suffering that campaigning entails without fear or complaint. Charny even advocates embracing the dangers and pains with joy at the opportunity for doing deeds that will secure a man the immortality of human memory. It will also, he says pointedly, secure a man the sighs and admiration of soft ladies.[37]

Yet the emphasis is on masculine physical effort, struggle, and heroic suffering. The very process of getting to the scene of serious military action is worthy; as long as one travels to fight:

> For indeed no one can travel so far without being many times in
> physical danger. We should for this reason honor such men-at-arms
> who at great expense, hardship, and grave peril undertake to travel.[38]

Although he warns that "The practice of arms is hard, stressful and perilous to endure (le mestiers d'armes soit durs et penibles et perilleux a l'endurer)," he insists that for good men "strength of purpose and cheerfulness of heart make it possible to bear all these things gladly and confidently, and all this painful effort seems nothing to them (bonne volenté et gayeté de cuer font toutes ces choses passer seurement et liement, et tout ce travail ne leur semble nient)."[39]

To some extent bodily suffering and effort represent goods in themselves; but they must be seen as the necessary accompaniments of what I have argued is the greatest chivalric quality in Charny's mind, prowess. Skillful, courageous, hands-on violence, the bloody and sweaty work of fighting superbly at close quarters with edged weapons is the glorious means of securing honor, which Charny (in company with all professional fighting men in all ages) knows is well worth purchasing at the price of mere pain, mutilation, or even death.[40] Prowess and honor as a linked pair represent the highest human achievement to Geoffroi de Charny. Suffering is good because it is bonded to the prowess that secures honor. At the very opening of his book he constructs an ascending scale of the several modes of fighting. All are worthy since they demonstrate prowess and yield honor; but some are more worthy than others: Individual encounters in jousting are good, tourney (involving groups of combatants) is better, war is clearly best. Tournament, for example, is better than individual jousting, not only because it involves more equipment and expenditure but because it also entails "physical hardship (travail de corps), crushing and wounding and sometimes danger of death."[41] Obviously, real warfare involves even more effort and greater danger of death. Charny says concisely, "By good battles good bodies are proved (par les bonnes journees sont esprouvez les bons corps)."[42]

These good men who prove their worth with their bodies in combat bear a heavy burden as models for the rest, a burden carried only with "great effort and endurance, in fearful danger and with great diligence (a grant peine et travail, en grant paour et peril, en grant soing a s'entente mise)."[43] Their great deeds of prowess have been accomplished

> through suffering great hardship, making strenuous efforts, and
> enduring fearful physical perils and the loss of friends whose deaths
> they have witnessed in many great battles in which they have taken
> part; these experiences have often filled their hearts with great distress
> and strong emotion.[44]

We can usefully recall here Henry of Lancaster's willingness to suffer "persecucioun de corps, d'avoir ou d'amys."[45]

Charny laments that he can hardly tell fully of the lives of such good men, "hard as they have been and still are (si dures come elles ont esté et sont encores)."[46] But men of worth "do not care what suffering they have to endure." Charny lives so fully within this code that he cannot understand men who fail to realize the need for prowess, suffering, and honor. How vexing and shameful it must be, he muses, to reach old age without doing great deeds.[47]

Near the end of his treatise he provides a capsule statement one more time, in the hopes of reaching his audience with a message that seems to him not only vitally important but self-evident:

> And if you want to continue to achieve great deeds, exert yourself, take
> up arms, fight as you should, go everywhere across both land and sea
> and through many different countries, without fearing any peril and

without sparing your wretched body, which you should hold to be of little account, caring only for your soul and for living an honourable life.[48]

Here, as elsewhere, he pairs the soul with honor, raising in specific form our general question of the relationship between basic questions of religious belief and the putatively secular triad of prowess, honor, and military suffering. What is the connection in Charny's view?

Of course Charny is convinced, in the first place, that God is the source of a knight's prowess. As every good and perfect gift, it comes from above. "You can see clearly and understand that you on your own can achieve nothing except what God grants you," Charny intones, going on to ask, "And does not God confer great honor when He allows you of His Mercy to defeat your enemies?"[49] Possessing the qualities of a great man-at-arms has nothing to do with fickle fortune. For,

> if you have the reputation of a good man at arms, through which you are exalted and honored, and you have deserved this by your great exertions, by the perils you have faced and by your courage, and Our Lord has in his mercy allowed you to perform the deeds from which you have gained such a reputation, such benefits are not benefits of fortune but . . . by right should last.[50]

The pious response, as Charny insists tirelessly, must be to thank God heartily for the great gift and to use it well.[51]

But are the hard life and valorous suffering of a knight spiritually meritorious? Do they enter into the calculations that figure so prominently in the medieval economy of salvation by the fourteenth century? With a vengeance, Charny asserts that the knightly life truly qualifies.[52] He first approaches this topic when opening a discussion of the various orders in society. He will analyze not the three *ordines* of conservative theologians adumbrated by Georges Duby, but his own set of four: the married, monks, priests, and knights. The several specifically religious orders, he grants, pray for themselves and others and disdain the world and the flesh appropriately. Yet "they are spared the physical danger and the strenuous effort of going out onto the field of battle to take up arms, and are also spared the threat of death (et sanz nul peril de leurs corps ne a grant travail d'aler aval les champs pour eulz armer ne en doubte d'estre tuez)."[53] After wandering off topic to describe the knighting ceremony, he returns to this theme and declares knighthood to be the most rigorous order of all, especially for those who keep it well ("la bonne ordre de chevalerie qui entre toutes autres ordres pourroit l'en et devroit tenir la plus dure ordre de toutes, espeuciament a ceulz qui bien la tiennent"). Though tough regulations constrain eating and sleeping and require vigils of the religious,

> this is all nothing in comparison with the suffering to be endured in the order of knighthood. For whoever might want to consider the hardships, pains, discomforts, fears, perils, broken bones, and wounds which the good knights who uphold the order of knighthood as they should endure and have to suffer frequently, there is no religious order in which as much is suffered as has to be endured by these good knights who go in search of deeds of arms in the right way.[54]

Like the regular clergy, the knights on campaign suffer severe restrictions on eating and sleeping, but "when they would be secure from danger they will be beset by great terrors, and when they would defeat their enemies, sometimes they may be defeated or killed or captured and wounded and struggling to recover (quant il cuident estre asseur, lors leur viennent il de grans paours, et quant il cuident desconfire leurs enemis, aucune fois se treuvent desconfitures ou mors ou pris et bleciez et en la paine de garir),"[55] and to this daunting list must be added the perils of travel, shipwreck, and robbers. "And where are the orders which could suffer as much (Et ou sont les ordres qui tant pourroient souffrir)?" Charny asks rhetorically and in triumph. "Indeed," he says, capping his argument, "in this order of knighthood one can well save the soul and bring honour to the body (Certes en ceste ordre de chevalerie peut l'on tres bien les aumes sauver et les corps tres bien honorer)."[56]

Charny completes his case by denouncing "those who perform deeds of arms more for glory in the world than for the salvation of the soul (qui fait les faiz d'armes plus pour la gloire de ce monde que pour l'ame sauver)," and praises "those who perform deeds of arms more to gain God's grace and for the salvation of the soul than for glory in this world (qui fait les faiz d'armes plus pour avoir la grace de Dieu et pour les ames sauver que pour la gloire de ce monde)." "Their noble souls," he is convinced, "will be set in paradise to all eternity, and their persons will be forever honored (les ames dignes sont mises en paradis et sanz fin et les corps touzjours mais honorez et ramenteuz en touz biens)."[57] The parallelism between salvation and honor achieved by prowess is complete. By working the body, by hazarding the body in deeds of prowess, the merely physical is transcended, in one direction to achieve glorious and imperishable honor, in another direction to help conduct the soul through purgatory to join its glorified body in paradise. Henry of Lancaster termed this the safe-conduct which leads to joy "sans fyn."[58]

Like Lancaster, Charny is thinking about the knightly life in general, not about crusading. Again, like Lancaster, who went as a crusader against Moors in Spain and in North Africa, and (during a lull in the European war) against Slavs in Prussia, Charny went on crusade to Anatolia in 1345 (again, during a slow time in the Hundred Years War), and termed such fighting "righteous, holy, certain and sure (droite, sainte, seure et ferme)."[59] But in no way does either knightly writer privilege crusade. Charny is, in fact, careful to assure his readers that they can fight in all proper wars without danger to their souls. This insistence in both of our fourteenth-century knights is significant. Crusade ideology as developed by clerics traditionally distinguished between the often sinful fighting of knights at home and their redemptive and meritorious battles with enemies of the faith. To the contrary, all their arduous travel, all their privations, all the dangers and suffering in fights with worthy opponents in licit causes seemed to Lancaster and Charny to prove their love for God, and to repay some portion of their debt for sin which had necessitated his sacrificial love.

The convergence of thought in our two authors is all the more remarkable when we recall the different personal agendas evidently standing behind each treatise. Lancaster wrote an intensely personal and pious penitential work, likely day by day through Lent; Charny wrote a tract for the French royal chivalric order, intending to buck up the warriors of the kingdom at a low point in their martial success against English invaders. It can come as no surprise to find a differing tonality in the two works: Lancaster can scarcely pen a page without thinking of penitence and hell; Charny mentions the afterlife without specifically naming either hell or purgatory and does so only in reference to the bad men-at-arms whom he discusses briefly and with patent distaste.[60] Yet in the argument of both books the heroic, ascetic suffering of righteous knighthood merits divine forgiveness. Whatever their differences in tonality, Lancaster and Charny share a fundamental sense that through their hard lives knights do penance for their inevitable sins.

The Power of Paradox

To modern sensibilities, this line of thought, which seems so logical and necessary to Charny and Lancaster, will not represent religiously meritorious practices. In fact, it did not seem so to some medieval writers. In the twelfth century Ralph Niger, for example, objected. He asserted that "the shedding of human blood is in no way a fitting atonement for sins."[61] His view, of course, represents a dissent from what he knows is majority opinion. Most medieval scholars and theologians held views on warfare and the will of God that modern people may find difficult.

Adopting analytical neutrality we must take note of the remarkable benefits this line of thought guaranteed the knightly order in medieval society. The asceticism which so marked this society usually involved giving up something truly important: clerics (in theory) gave up sex; women (as Caroline Bynum has taught us) sometimes gave up food; all religious folk thought piety involved doing something unpleasant or giving up something pleasant.[62] But the knights can have it both ways with regard to suffering and violence. William James writes in *The Varieties of Religious Experience* that "the impulse to sacrifice" may be "the main religious phenomenon" and he describes "the undiluted ascetic spirit" as "the passion of self-contempt wreaking itself on the poor flesh."[63] What chivalric ideology did with sacrifice and the poor flesh is surely a remarkable case in point. Knights acquire turf on both sides of a great divide; they work both sides of a basic contradiction; and this yields power. Are they not at once victors and victims, self-exalters and self-abasers? They can praise hands-on prowess as the glorious practice of their beautiful bodies, which, of course, ensures their status as it wins them foaming praise and glittering loot. They can groan over their sufferings in hard campaigns and battles in which their bodies may be deprived of comforts, bruised, cut, and broken. Yet they can even more obviously gloat over the triumphs that secure their dominance. The very exercise of their professional labor thus helps to secure pardon for its inseparable wrongs. God himself has given them the great physical strength and spirited capacity by which their dominance in the world is secured. Yet he is also mollified when they suffer willingly, meritoriously, in a good cause, as did his son. Thus bodily superiority proved sword in hand is celebrated in epic and romantic literature and chivalric biography with pride and style; it stands alongside the sacrifice and suffering of hazarding the body, risking all, being on the receiving end of all that edged weaponry.[64] This is why

Roland, dying in his great *chanson*, can offer up his glove (symbolic of his knightly life) to a willing God, "for all his sins."[65]

The chivalrous are laying claim to participate in the dominant religious paradigm, based on suffering and bodily atonement, which is essentially clerical and specifically monastic in origin. At the same time they are enthusiastic practitioners of a chivalric paradigm based on prowess, honor, and bodily exaltation (which seems to be the eternal warrior code and specifically that originating in the Germanic West).[66] Lancaster says he wants his service to be for God, not for worldly causes worth nothing ("en chosez moundeynes de nient").[67] Charny carefully distinguishes the good men-at-arms from the sadly reprobate.[68]

Yet these model knights also demonstrate a spirit of decided independence within their piety. Each calibrates the scale himself; each decides, in effect, what God will approve on the basis of ideas largely drawn from non-theological principles and practices.[69] On the crucial matter of setting standards for good knightly life and work, our authors reach their own conclusions. Against all clerical strictures Lancaster was an avid tourneyer, who seems to have delighted in the colorful spectacle of the sport as well as its violence. A royal grant from Edward III authorized Lancaster and a group of knights of which he was captain to hold annual tournaments at Lincoln.[70] He is described in the grant as one "who delights in acts of war."[71] It is not surprising that in the midst of all his pious contrition on all other topics he manages to say that knightly pleasures such as tournament and dancing are not evil in themselves.[72] Aptly pouring salt into a wound, Lancaster even managed a string of puns that reverses the common clerical word play on tournament as torment. Picturing Christ as a victorious tourneyer for humanity, he says "Le turnoy estoit pur nous quant il par turment tourna nostre dolour en joie (the tourney was for us when he by his torments turned our sorrow into joy)."[73] Charny, too, accepts tournaments without a second thought and is even more blunt. Two rungs on his ladder of chivalric perfection, as we saw, involve individual jousting or the more active and thus more virtuous *mêlée*.[74] He approves discrete love affairs on the grounds that they will improve a man and make him more *preux*. No language or thoughts of fornication or adultery enter his text; perhaps they did not enter his mind. A cloud of such issues floated over knighthood: what causes are worthy and involve meritorious suffering? When is killing allowable, even meritorious, despite the sixth commandment? When is vengeance, so often linked by clerics with wrath— one of the seven deadly sins—actually just and meritorious?

Charny approves most of the *guerres* of his day, including what the lawyers would term private war, raiding, and counter-raiding, as well as grand campaigns often termed public war and led by kings and blessed by bishops or the bishop of Rome. As long as he follows the rules requiring formal defiance of an enemy, as long as he is himself a true *cheftain de guerre* or follows such a man, as long as he fights in defense of honor, a knight's hard campaigning and cutting will win untroubled accolades from Charny and Lancaster.[75] They consider all good knightly fighting to be religiously meritorious—or at least all that was carried out bravely by good men.

The lines of thought seem contradictory, yet they in fact merge, for chivalry in its religious dimension becomes knightly practice in what were considered good causes, suffering in atonement for sin and thanking God for the strength to do it all. And doing all that chivalry entails seems truly glorious to the knights, whatever the qualifications necessitated by any pacific line of religious sentiment. Surely Henry of Lancaster did not truly believe he was in essence a worm, however clearly he confessed to that state. Many a religious order stood ready to accept into their cloister a noble ex-worm, classically when age and infirmity had largely closed a vigorous chivalric career. Most knights, however, clearly remained in their status and worked out their relationship with God along professional lines. Henry of Lancaster's piety must have been real and his emotions surely focused powerfully in a religious vein. No disrespect is offered in insisting that he wanted to have it both ways: to be a powerful lord who can (as he confesses) stretch out his beautiful legs in the stirrups of his great horse on the tourney field or the battlefield; and also to relate the sufferings he endures as a knight to the passion of Christ.[76] He could scarcely imagine his piety foreign to his chivalry. Geoffroi de Charny, I believe, is so convinced of the religious rectitude of his chivalric life, so happy God has given it to him, so sure his own sufferings are meritorious, that with characteristic vigor he mentally fills in the gap rather than bridging it.[77]

Heroic prowess, meritorious suffering, lay independence (within a framework of lay piety), and highly selective appropriation of useful theological ideas—all formed a great amalgam in the thinking of Henry of Lancaster and Geoffroi de Charny. The crucial question thus arises whether this set of ideas had significant ancestry or is only a late or idiosyncratic development in the long lifespan of chivalry. The question will lead us back into twelfth-century sources, that is into the very era when chivalry was developing characteristic form. Do sources of this vintage link the hard chivalric life with religious atonement? Finding such links would suggest a long ancestry: the pattern in Lancaster and Charny began to form centuries earlier.[78] Thus we must search for elements of a developing ideology. Such a search cannot be a mere hand-picking of ideas that accord with views we have seen in Lancaster and Charny. Any emerging ideas that could narrow the gap between warrior values and religion must be considered significant. What ideas dominated the discussion? Did they anticipate structural elements in Lancaster and Charny? What ideas seem to have been acceptable to the knights (rather than coming solely from clerical strictures)?

Such a body of ideas can, in fact, be found. Key elements of this amalgam were at least two centuries old when Lancaster and Charny wrote, as each chapter of this book will argue. To understand how basic constituents of this chivalric religious ideology combined, we must first examine their setting, beginning with church reform, lay piety and a developed theology to guide it, along with the phenomenon of asceticism. These elements, staples of historical analysis on their own, must be seen afresh within the context of a developing chivalric ethos. Chapter 3 launches this effort.

CHAPTER 3

The Religious Context for Chivalric Ideology

A BROAD SET of ideas about the medieval warrior profession would necessarily be framed in terms of a religious no less than a military ethos. Powerful religious movements of the age thus form an essential backdrop to an emerging ideology that could justify and elevate knighthood. Three of these elements demand special notice because of their undoubted importance: church reform, the widespread culture of asceticism, and lay initiative and independence. Though they may be of equal importance, they do not require equal scrutiny in this study, since some have enjoyed more scholarly attention than others. Church reform, the first topic, is in particular a venerable staple of medieval historiography. The goal here is not to explicate so well-developed a historical theme but to establish its significant connections with ideas about knighthood. This is not the usual focus of investigation, and historians have not always linked surges of reform with the emergence of a special strand of lay theology for the knighthood in general. The second element of the religious framework requires more attention. All who study the middle ages encounter the dense atmosphere of asceticism in those centuries; they so regularly breathe this atmosphere that it may come to be taken for granted. Yet it deserves close analysis and can be seen as a crucial environment for the emergence of the chivalric ethos. The third factor, a remarkable degree of independence within genuine knightly piety, is important enough to merit separate treatment in the following chapter. Another theme (nurtured in the atmosphere of asceticism analyzed in the current chapter) will be repeatedly considered in later chapters and especially in Chapter 5: knightly meritorious suffering.

The Effects of Church Reform

Church reformers labored to effect their plans in every medieval era: but efforts with great impact on chivalric ideas came in two particular phases. General scholarly attention has focused on the earlier phase. From the second half of the eleventh century, clerics strongly advanced claims to superior status and a directive role within Christian society generally. Major figures of this Gregorian Reform drew upon and moved into the upper ranks of the secular clergy, becoming bishops and even popes. Their most pressing goal was to create right order in the church itself, closely conceived as a body of clerics; continuing renewal would then come through the purifying outreach of a hierarchical elite into the church as Christian society. The clerics would purify lives and religious practices, shaping and encouraging piety and sometimes disciplining its excessive enthusiasms in a dynamic social world. For no group was this goal more crucial than the knights.

Elaborating and enforcing this lay theology could not proceed at the desired speed. To produce right order in church and world, the reformers quickly found they required centralizing measures of governance and law. They were certain that institution-building and law-making centered on Rome would surely yield broad moral reform, the ultimate goal. Yet the immediate, if largely unanticipated, results were legalism, an emphasis on finance, institutionalization, and political conflict, most famously though not solely with the German emperors who had their own ideas about the proper ordering of society. So did many other powerful laymen. As kings, dukes, lay "advocates" of monastic houses—or simple local strongmen—powerful lay lords had secured an iron grip on much church property and often over clerical elections. Concerned churchmen understandably feared these laymen could block reform and delay or prevent the creation of an ideal religious society. Surely Christian society was to be guided by clerics marshaled solidly behind an effective papacy, rather than warlords acting under various titles.

Over generations, the institutional as well as theological implications of this program produced the Papal Monarchy so familiar to students of medieval history. Layers of officials, courts, and law slowly emerged, with one compass point of their expanding reach set firmly in Rome. Of course, the reformers encouraged and helped to provide acceptable outlets for lay folk who wanted to participate more fully in religious life and practices. The most enthusiastic of the laity could simply be encouraged to leave the world and enter some religious order, especially in an age fertile in new orders. Yet that option did not satisfy all and clearly could satisfy only a minority of knights who left the world near the end of their careers. Many faithful folk, the knights among them, wished to live fully religious lives without leaving the world for the cloister.[1]

As the violent storms of political struggle over investiture abated, serious thought could focus again on a clearer and more elaborate theological framework to guide the lives of lay folk trying to find firm moral ground in a world stirred by unsettling social and economic changes. New groups of reformers applied their talents and labor to just such efforts in the twelfth and early thirteenth centuries. In effect they launched a second important phase of clerical reform, seeking to develop a more elaborate lay theology as a framework for the religious life and practices of the great body of nonclerics.[2] The earlier phase of reform—that led by the Gregorians in the last quarter of the eleventh century—had given clerics a needed measure of independence and had secured papal leadership within the church. Movement toward a needed second phase came in the early twelfth century with a group of theologians in Laon (under the leadership of Master Anselm). As Alexander Murray has argued, these men "were in fact the principle re-founders, after the Carolingians, of systematic evangelical study."[3] By the late twelfth century a circle of learned theologians at Paris—whose ideas linked them to views of other leading theologians and canonists—were doing the hard work required on this second advance, elaborating a theology that was specifically crafted for the laity. Their task was to construct what Daniel Bornstein aptly termed "the definition of a form of Christian life that is neither sacerdotal nor monastic, but distinctively lay."[4]

Guided by Peter the Chanter or Cantor (d. 1197), as John Baldwin has shown, the group of theologians in Paris was especially vigorous in taking up the daunting goal of adapting religious thought for the brave new world of High Medieval Europe; they wrote, preached, and lobbied the powerful. The influential legislation of the Fourth Lateran Council of 1215 shows some results of their work.[5] Churchmen confronted a world of more money and all the vexing issues that money entails (especially issues of usury), of changing forms of war and the financing of war, of more directive power vested in kings and their courts. The circle of theologians in Paris included some of the most influential clerical writers and administrators of the next generation, Robert of Courson, Thomas of Cobham, Jacques de Vitry, Stephen Langton, Gerald of Wales, Geoffrey of Poitiers, Peter of Poitiers of St. Victor, Foulques de Neuilly, Gilles de Corbeilles, and Raoul Ardent. Although they gathered as

Parisian academics, they resolutely addressed pressing social issues, wrote co-piously, held councils, went on preaching tours, entered papal service, gained the support of so vigorous a pope as Innocent III and so powerful a king of France as Philip II. Under their guidance a more developed theology for the laity began to emerge.

Two major sets of ideas in their reform program are especially significant for our themes. First, they discussed the proper role and constructive labor of ideal social groups—socio-professional sets of people known by various names such as *ordo, status gradus, honor, dignitas, officium*—that constituted the building blocks of society and whose necessary labor animated the world within the divine plan. They were certain that usury was not licit and they worried about the spiritual consequences of warfare as well as commerce, vigorous labor in each being a potent source of sin.[6] Second, they worked at developing the theology of confession and penance as the means for dealing with sin which sadly distorted God's plan for human society. These ideas are so fundamental to chivalric ideology that two later chapters will examine the issues in detail. Chapter 7 will focus on a society of orders, each carrying out the labor proper to it, including the hard labor of knighthood. Chapter 8 ex-amines developing ideas of contrition, confession, and penance as the frame-work for dealing with the dread results of sin on individuals and society.

Far from solely a top-down impulse, burgeoning piety among laity as well as clergy animated a religious society seeking a wide variety of new spiritual outlets and pious practices. New church buildings in gleaming white stone arose in the green countryside, endowed often by pious lay gifts; pilgrims from all levels and professions flocked to visit a growing list of sacred destina-tions near and far; lay folk (along with the clerics) enthusiastically embraced the cult of relics, seeking (through the merit of the associated saint) health and grace from God; lay guilds and confraternities began to flourish.[7] The knighthood would take part in and be affected by this flourishing piety in its rich variety of forms. They endowed churches and monasteries if income permitted, or gave as generously as they could to existing houses; they read-ily went on pilgrimage and most notably on crusade; they formed their own professional, pious "order" and they venerated or avidly collected relics.[8]

Lay enthusiasm was laudable in clerical eyes, but it likewise entailed dangers. Tensions easily arose over the proper role for the laity in this vi-brant religious society undergoing change along so many significant lines. The question posed in stark terms—who was to be in charge of spirituality in this society?—was swiftly answered by the orthodox majority in favor of the clergy. Yet, put in only slightly less stark terms—how fully was the clerical elite to be in charge?—the issue of independence stubbornly persisted.[9]

Scholars for generations have emphasized anticlericalism and heresy among the laity in general; more recently some have not only stressed piety, but have insisted on loyalty and enthusiastic orthodoxy at the parish level up to—and even beyond—the Reformation. With regard to the knights, both views are extreme and the combination of piety and independence requires emphasis instead.[10] Deep spirituality can be sensed in some knights; nearly all were dutiful participants in the sacramental system that mediated fallible humanity's relationship with divinity. These warriors, whose literature emphasized hands-on violence, respected the work done by the priests' own hands at the altar or beside the deathbed. The knights followed most of the standard religious forms prescribed for lay people. They opposed heresy with strong voice and even stronger sword-arms. As both Henry of Lancaster and Geoffroi de Charny have shown us (in Chapter 2), they could be immensely and even verbosely pious.

But certain modes of thought and professional practice were crucial to them, and on such issues they required accommodation—or at least tacit noninterference—from the church. On such issues I am convinced that their attitudes were far from irreverent and were in fact founded on confidence that God was on their side and would understand. He was, of course, the bellicose Lord of Hosts, whose vengeance was a wonder to behold and a thrill to hear described (when directed against others). The knights imagined that their relationship with *Dominus Deus* (the Lord God) was ideally like that which should obtain with *dominus rex* (the Lord King). Sadly, both heavenly and earthly sovereigns had, in their own fashion, created troublesome ranks of official mediators (often compounding the problem by elevating men of no great social rank) who stood between the good knights and their good lord. The clergy and all those fussy royal bureaucrats were forever getting in the way, both sets armed with endless parchment books or rolls scribbled with crabbed Latin, outlining a restrictive world of do's and don'ts. Of course, ideas upholding knighthood could never uncompromisingly contravene the essential rites conducted by a specialist core of clerics (nor the need for monarchy). Yet late in an evening (perhaps after considerable wine had flowed), the knights might reflect that the ways of the Lord—as carried out by clerics—were frustratingly inscrutable. If the world were truly right, the knights could, when necessary, simply outflank all these intrusive intermediaries; on matters of chivalry essential to them they should relate to the Lord

God (or to the Lord King) directly and personally, on the basis of their good and hard service. Their concept of right order in the world differed from that of clerical reformers who claimed the same high goal.

Prudence intermixed with sincere belief led the knights to cooperate as much as possible with the religious and administrative intermediaries— their nephews, cousins, and uncles, of course. These worlds of thought overlapped and were congruent in significant fashion. But wherever ecclesiastical restraints (or royal bureaucrats) cut into chivalric flesh, the knights simply refused to comply; indeed, by and large refused to believe that they should comply, and this refusal was backed by that fundamental, proud sense of a personal understanding with the Lord of Hosts, the giver of their great prowess and ordainer of all victories.

Yet they knew that God expected meritorious suffering. We must understand the sheer power of asceticism in medieval religion in general in order to recognize its specific link with knighthood. All the knightly conceptions and debates under consideration in this study flourished and took distinctive form in an atmosphere of intensely held beliefs about meritorious corporal suffering. The cultural commitment to asceticism might easily be overlooked in the constellation of religious forces; how it operated within the ideological frame for chivalry merits a closer look.

Gloria Passionis, the Glory of Suffering

Both prowess and asceticism claim central spaces in chivalric thinking. They dominated the thought of our model knight/authors Henry of Lancaster and Geoffroi de Charny. While both sets of ideas may cause some queasiness to modern sensibilities, prowess is undoubtedly better known and appreciated than asceticism. A surviving academic insistence, however threatened, on reading classic works such as the *Iliad, Beowulf,* or the *Song of Roland* in introductory courses on history and literature teaches modern students fundamentals of the fierce ethos animating men who fought other men in hand-to-hand combat. It is a virtue, moreover, clearly considered timeless and relevant, as popular films and endless television shows amply demonstrate. Since the very idea of ascetic self-discipline is disavowed by arbiters of thought and practice in modern life, however, almost nothing of the literature of asceticism is still known to any but specialist scholars. The basic notion will surely seem puzzling if not repugnant to many today. Yet the motive force of this impulse within High and Late Medieval religion must be kept in mind if we are to make sense of men who could have taken Henry of Lancaster and Geoffroi de Charny as models. For them there was obviously a *gloria passionis*, a glory of suffering or endurance.

Of course an ascetic tradition is ancient and ubiquitous, not unique to medieval Christianity, nor totally new in the twelfth century. As Clifford Geertz observed, "there are few if any religious traditions, 'great' or 'little,' in which the proposition that life hurts is not strenuously affirmed and in some it is virtually glorified."[11] Furthermore, "In one way or another," as Eric Auerbach similarly observed, the Stoic idea of *passio* (suffering, enduring), "has played a part in almost every system of morality since the Stoics."[12] If early Christian thought was influenced by the Stoic ideal of standing aloof from the world with its unreasoning restlessness and strife, it significantly transformed the means to achieve this goal. As Auerbach explains, "The aim of Christian hostility to the world is not a passionless existence outside of the world, but counter-suffering, a passionate suffering in the world and hence also in opposition to it; and to the flesh."[13] In the New Testament, Christ's words (in Matthew 16:24) were taken as giving divine sanction to such a view: "If any man would come after me, let him deny himself and take up his cross and follow me." Here the two potent ideas of *passio* and *imitatio Christi* join: one follows or imitates Christ less by works of charity and love than through suffering that in some small measure joins with his sacrificial and redemptive passion. The emphasis evoked a comment from St. Bernard who, in writing for the Knights Templar, described the Holy Sepulcher as holding pride of place among all holy and wondrous sites recalling the life of Christ in the Holy Land. "I do not know why people feel a greater devotion at the place where he lay while dead than at the places where he did things while alive," Bernard muses.[14] He has already assured the Templars of the merits of suffering for God and especially dying for God: "Life is indeed fruitful and victory glorious, but more important than either is a holy death. If they are blessed who die in the Lord, how much more so are those who die for the Lord."[15] A long tradition informed this view. The general goal—especially prominent as the movement of monasticism gathered strength in the Late Antique and Early Medieval world—became spiritual warfare aimed at disciplining the body, and working past the merely temporal and physical to "open oneself to what God wants to give."[16] This will involve pain, as Richard Kieckhefer suggests:

The saints . . . viewed suffering as the specific means God has chosen both for Christ's redemptive work and for the sanctification of those who imitate Christ. Atonement came not from charitable works, nor from prayer, nor from enlightenment, but from pain. If God's wrath was appeased by suffering, this meant that suffering was somehow pleasing to God.[17]

If Christian asceticism draws on a tradition very much older than the twelfth century, there are still good reasons for stressing its impact in the period that interests us. We will see how the movement of ideas encouraged an ascetic culture in which the faithful increasingly earned religious merit through corporal suffering, deprivation, and pain. Such basic theological ideas have not always been brought into the story of chivalry, but they can help us to understand the infusion of Christian asceticism into the knightly ideology of heroism.

The medieval practice of asceticism could involve the closest calculation, a true economy of salvation. The hermit Dominic Lorica, as Peter Damian recorded, precisely worked out the spiritual effectiveness of his self-flagellation: efficiently using whips in both hands, he lashed his body through the reciting of three psalters of one hundred fifty psalms each; this yielded three thousand blows equaling one year of penance. He claimed credit for a total of one hundred years. Damian was himself a true believer in physical disciplining of the body, noting that those who used the discipline "believe they are partaking in the passions of our Redeemer."[18] By the High Middle Ages—and throughout the Later Middle Ages—both the practices and language used by medieval people in search of the *gloria passionis* will nearly disorient a modern investigator who uncovers them. For the people of this age, as André Vauchez has written, "Penance was a condition, virtually a way of life,"[19] and it was worked out on the body of the penitent. Jacques de Vitry told of a robber captain who, brought into a monastery and seeing the hard physical lives of the monks, asked what great crime they have committed to deserve such penance.[20]

The foundation for such views stood firmly upon innumerable stories that told of martyrs who went willingly, even joyfully, to unspeakable deaths as a witness to their faith. They are engaged in vicarious, meritorious acts of *imitatio Christi*. In the absence of convenient pagan oppressors in their own age, the successors of the original Christian martyrs—monks, nuns, and anchorites across centuries—devised creative methods of confining their own bodies or inflicting pain upon them.[21] Entry into cloistered life was compared to martyrdom; both seemed a second baptism, by which monks, nuns, and hermits were reborn into new life.[22] This impulse for glorious suffering and the language urging and praising it are obviously important to our investigation. St. Bernard's words on the ideal of the martyr, often quoted in the following generations, transport us directly into the High Medieval world of such thought. He says of the martyr,

> For he does not feel his own wounds when he contemplates those of Christ. The martyr stands rejoicing and triumphant, even though his body is torn to pieces; and when his side is ripped open by the sword, not only with courage but even with joy he sees the blood which he has consecrated to God gush forth from his body. But where now is the soul of the martyr? Truly in a safe place . . . in the bowels of Christ, where it has entered, indeed through his open wounds. . . . And this is the fruit of love, not of insensibility.[23]

This theme plays on and even intensifies in the Later Middle Ages. In his *Contra Amatores Mundi*, Richard Rolle (d. 1349) classically explained the need for suffering and struggle:

> Therefore it is to be affirmed that the fact that the persecutions of our enemies is useful and necessary for us has been demonstrated; lest, having no persecutor, we deserve no crown. Clearly, unless we fight, we do not conquer; and we shall not be crowned unless we conquer. Therefore soldiers are armed, victors are crowned, losers are killed. When they fight, they tarry in this world, when they conquer, they are taken up to heaven; and when they are conquered, they are thrust into hell.[24]

Such sentiments as Rolle's, if not quite such exuberant language, appear plentifully. Gerald of Wales had summed up this theme—indeed, the theme of asceticism generally—saying "The greater the struggle, the greater the crown."[25]

A variety of texts give us examples of lay people in search of personal morality often achieved through ascetic atonement.[26] From the thirteenth century, the Franciscans and Dominicans—in this regard heirs of St.

Bernard—urged lay men and women to engage in an affective piety that drew them imaginatively into the drama of Christ's suffering, graphically depicted for them in word and image. Just how far this might succeed appears in one of the letters of Catherine of Siena who urged, "Delight in Christ crucified; delight in suffering. Be a glutton for abuse—for Christ crucified. Let your heart and soul be grafted into the tree of the most holy cross—with Christ crucified. Make his wounds your home."[27]

By the late Middle Ages, as Mitchel Merback has argued, the crowds that pressed for a view around a site of public execution might—in addition to any purely voyeuristic motives—have interpreted what transpired before them in a religiously expiatory framework. They were about to see what all hoped would be a "good death." A condemned sinner (differing from them only in degree, or luck) would confess, suffer grievous bodily affliction in expiation for his or her sin, and go cleansed into the afterlife. So convinced were medieval people that suffering was meritorious that the criminal about to die might be considered a quasi-martyr, might offer to intercede for the crowd which, in turn, could be praying for him. The blood and body parts of the executed might be coveted for healing properties. Even the rope that hanged a criminal was likewise highly prized and credited with special powers.[28]

Could such attitudes pervade an entire society, or at least represent an elite cultural ideal, highly valued? Was High and Late Medieval society invested in pain and suffering in ways that set it apart from other societies in other times? Esther Cohen has advanced a broad and persuasive argument that the experience of pain in human history is not only culturally mediated but changeable over time, even within a given culture. In Medieval Europe from the twelfth century and increasingly in the later Middle Ages, the social and individual response to pain was not the utter rejection we take as a given in modern life, nor the impassivity (contemptuous disregard) or impassibility (transcendence) of some cultures. It was, rather, what she terms philopassianism, an actual embracing of physical anguish as useful. "Pain comprised both the penalty for original sin," she writes, "and the redemption of humanity." It was thus "from the very beginnings a central historical and cosmological force rather than an individual, evanescent experience."[29] This represents a sharp turn away from the reactions to pain found in the early medieval era. What replaced such views was a conception of pain and suffering as vehicles of grace, to be actively sought by believers who could thus imitate Christ. They would imitate his passion even more than his life and follow him in his newly emphasized suffering, some even in his death. At least to this degree they would be crucified with him, voluntarily choosing to suffer for him, as he had for them.[30] The pains they suffered on earth would indeed be salutary, for harsh as they might seem, they reduced the infinitely worse penalties awaiting them in the sulphurous flames and dark caverns of hell or purgatory. Pain and retribution were joined. During the early years of the Albigensian Crusade, Simon de Montfort was faced with a novice "heretic" who disavowed his beliefs after seeing the burning of his teacher, one of the *perfecti*. Cutting short all debate, Montfort ordered the fearful man burned also: if he was genuinely contrite, the flames would expiate his sin; if lying, he simply deserved the flames.[31] Cohen argues that belief in the usefulness of pain and suffering was socially widespread, not simply the high theory of a minority of ecclesiastical intellectuals: "philopassionism was an integral part of the common consciousness, an awareness so widespread and universal as to be considered axiomatic by contemporaries."[32] Scholars will certainly debate the exact nature and social spread of medieval ideas about meritorious pain. Few would want to argue that peasants in their fields or merchants in their counting houses were actively seeking corporal suffering on a daily basis. But all scholars will have encountered the pervasive element of philopassionism in the cultural evidence available on the society they study.[33] And all medieval folk seem enthusiastically to have admired the elite corps of saints, martyrs, hermits, and anchorites who represented the real specialists.

Religious intellectuals undoubtedly subscribed to ideas of redemptive suffering. The passion and crucifixion of Christ were ever in their minds, and they enthusiastically preached mimetic, personal, redemptive suffering to the laity. Devotional eyes turned increasingly to the agonies of Christ, with which the pious viewer was to identify. Although the identification was soulful, it sometimes also took the form of harsh ascetic practices carried out on the believer's body. Obviously, the vivid illustrations and descriptions of torments awaiting sinners in purgatory and hell reinforced the message, showing that corporal suffering could purge and release and would surely punish. The paintings would linger in the mind, as did descriptions of terrifying demons inflicting unspeakable tortures on those being painfully purged or those eternally damned. In one section of his collection of sermon stories devoted to fear of purgatory, Étienne de Bourbon presents a knight who clearly affirms that the pains he suffers there are like nothing on earth.[34] A late thirteenth-century set of stories includes an account of Lazarus, raised from the dead by Christ, but going through the remaining fifteen years of his earthly life unsmiling: he had seen the torments of sinners at first hand.[35] The technique is often used: in addition to the frighteningly specific paintings and descriptions, much might be left to a guilty sinner's fervid imagination, with only the magnitude of suffering in relation to anything known of earthly pain being specified. A ghost from a collection of *exempla* appears on earth to declare that to escape the pains he is suffering in hell he would walk a razor-sharp bridge from now until Doomsday.[36]

Ascetic heroes were held up for emulation, as surviving collections of sermon tales and moral manuals testify. One of Odo of Cheriton's set of moral tales written in the mid-thirteenth century presents a piously ascetic hermit who wept at the end of a year in which he has suffered no illness, for, he claims, God has forgotten him.[37] Another popular story pictured a hermit who discovered a new source of water conveniently closer to the cave that served as his home. He gave up any thought of shortening his walk for water when he noticed an angel counting the reduced number of steps that could make his life easier, but less meritorious.[38] A knight's daughter in a fourteenth-century collection of tales has already cut off her nose to escape an unsuitable marriage, preserve virginity, and remain wholly devoted to Christ. Living sparely in a peasant hut, she complains that God has given her no signs of love and rejoices when she is afflicted with skin disease, falling sickness, and leprosy.[39] In a similar collection of tales, a monk is saved in the afterlife by a display of the rods used to beat him for his sins in life.[40] A departing crusader is shown to align his family on the shore in order that his sailing should be the more wrenching.[41] The late medieval *Pricke of Conscience* informed English readers that suffering came from God as chastisement or test; taken well, it serves a believer as a substitute for penance: "and if he suffer it without complaint, it serves him in place of penance."[42] The same mental assumptions inform a thirteenth-century story told by Caesarius of Heisterbach of a monk who had once been a valorous knight (he had won fourteen warhorses in his first tournament). Afflicted with worms that continually swarmed from his body, causing a stench that his monastic brothers could not bear, for him, as Caesarius says, death and salvation approached as "the day of reward for so much endurance (dies adesset remunerationis pro tantae patientiae)."[43]

Knights absorbed and participated in this broad cultural investment in meritorious suffering and atonement. Although a general cultural value, asceticism was vigorously urged upon them in specific terms. A steady flow of miracle stories and sermon *exempla* that featured knights regularly linked their physical pain and suffering with divine forgiveness. Noting only a few examples from this abundant body of evidence must serve to establish the point. A late twelfth-century collection of miracles of the Blessed Virgin tells a story, often repeated in later collections, of three men-at-arms who have rashly killed a man in a church devoted to St. Mary. After all three subsequently fell victim to a disease the author calls "internal fire," they confessed to a priest, who imposed an unusual penance on them. They must wear the offending swords tightly bound to their bodies. We learn that the men willingly accepted this highly physical (and richly symbolic) penance; the author of the tale assures readers that they carried out the penance fully. He wants readers or hearers to accept the story as literally true and claims to have met one of the knights, even naming the house where the meeting took place, located at Amfreville-sur-Iton, between Rouen and Evreux. The writer testifies that the soldier's sword had gradually become embedded in his flesh.[44]

A more graphic account of horrific punishment inflicted by God on a knight in expiation of his sin was told by Master Boniface, Bishop of Lausanne, to Thomas of Cantimpré, who included it in his rich collection of stories and moralizing commentary, *Bonum universale de apibus* (*The Common Good from Bees*)—basically a set of stories for preachers written just after the mid-thirteenth century.[45] It concerns a noble knight from the bishop's diocese who went hunting with his pack of hounds in the Alps. Curious to find out what has set his dogs to furious barking, he comes into a beautiful grassy spot in the mountains. The scene there is anything but pastoral. He comes upon a large and courtly human-like figure (quasi hominem magnum et elegantem) who is in fact a dead knight sent back to earthly life in corporeal form as a timely warning to the noble hunter. While alive he had been, the spectral knight announces, a truly great sinner (peccator immanissimus) hard at work in the fighting between Richard Lion-heart and Philip Augustus; never did he confess or take the Eucharist. Only tears shed at the moment of his miserable death moved God to mercy. Yet divine mercy in his case is being decidedly tempered by ascetic atonement, for the knight is in continual, dreadful torment; two great iron nails are affixed so that they constantly wound his eyes and will continue to press into them until the Day of Judgment. Immediately after he has provided this explanation of his punishment the knight vanished; but the impact on the noble hunter remained, Thomas assured his readers. No longer would he live an evil life and ravage the poor. In fact he took it upon himself to give other knightly sinners the message of harsh penance he had seen inflicted, to encourage better lives in them. Along with the warning, of course, went the message that such torment in purgatory would finally save the knight at the Day of Judgment.

Though the physical details of this story are disconcerting, what surely must rank as the most ferocious story of knightly lay asceticism follows immediately in the *Bonum universale de apibus*.[46] A German knight who had led a life of evil (multis rapinis et caedibus per patriam debacchatus) was finally brought to justice and condemned to a merited decapitation. Far from disputing the sentence, he asked only time to make sufficient penance for his grievous sins. Simple decapitation would not be enough to wipe clean his slate. With the assistance of a relative he obtained an iron mechanical device revealingly called a dentrix—it clearly had teeth. With this device he urged the court to chop off, in order, his hands, elbows, arms up to the shoulder (vsque ad humeros), feet, lower and upper legs, then his genitals, ears, eyes, nose, lips, and finally the head. Although with sorrow, the court complied. When the grisly work had so far progressed that only the sinner's trunk and head remained, he said, cheerfully (hilari vultu), "If only this little torment I have suffered because of my sins, could be done to my miserable body again and even a third time, and in this way I could be crucified for the longest time."[47] Then, the tale says, his tears began to flow, he begged for prayers from the awed onlookers, and bowed his head for the last chop.[48] This hyperbolic story, we should recognize, is a mini-sermon on penitential suffering, not an account of horrendous judicial punishment.

At least a kinder story, also told by Thomas of Cantimpré, concerns the wise man and vigorous knight Count Louis of Looz (Lossensis).[49] This noble knight prostrated himself before a most holy woman, the Blessed Christina, tearfully confessing all his sins. He did not ask for an indulgence, which he knew she could not give (quam dare non potuit), but simply sought her prayers. Christina graciously petitioned God that she might take the count's sins upon her own body (vero in meo corpore) and this was allowed, by divine grace. Pleasant as it is to move away from the dentrix, we should note the common message here: sins are visited upon a knight's suffering body—unless he can find a saintly substitute.[50] God is mollified and the scales of judgment are tipped toward salvation by corporal suffering willingly endured, even on behalf of another.

The ascetic emphasis we have found in Lancaster and Charny reflects an old and established tradition. Knights' piety readily took ascetic form: their ideology incorporated meritorious suffering that came to them from pulpit, paintings, and sacred writings. Yet the measure of chivalric independence remained real, as the next chapter argues.

CHAPTER 4

Independence in Knightly Piety

FINDING THE BALANCE between piety and independence challenged knight-hood and all medieval writers who were certain they should speak to the chi-valric ethos.[1] Likewise, all modern investigators know that the presence and power of piety in chivalric life can never be doubted or downplayed. Yet we need to take into account the degree of independence (only briefly noted in the last chapter); its force shaped and complicated knightly piety. Much modern thinking and teaching about chivalry still tips the balance heavily toward the side of an uncomplicated piety among the knights, picturing them as unfail-ingly obedient sons of Holy Mother Church.[2] We cannot understand chivalry if knightly independence within that framework of piety is not emphasized. Like buttresses relieving the overarching vaults of a great church, these elements of independence supported essential chivalric ideals, taking on the unavoid-able strains. Interaction between piety and independence presents an exquisite balance of forces. We can initially see this balancing in a brief look at attitudes to tournament. A second case, requiring more discussion of the evidence, will focus on the knightly reception and reaction to crusade propaganda.

Tournament Triumphant

No scholar doubts that tournament was the quintessential knightly sport, cherished as one of the very elements inherent in chivalric self-definition.[3] Chivalric insistence on tournament—heedless of clerical disapproval—thus provides significant evidence of knightly independence. Clerical opposition is likewise a well-established historical fact; the clerks had loathed and challenged tournament from the time they became aware of its existence as a form of mock warfare dangerous to its participants and so often to others who simply happened to be in the way of wide-ranging fighting. Caesarius of Heisterbach's spokesman in his *Dialogue on Miracles* unhesitatingly announced that "of those who fall in tourneys, there is no question that they go to hell, if they have not been helped by the benefit of contrition."[4] As it developed, tournament had acquired a reputation for social and sexual opportunities that could only provoke clerical wrath; a festering source of all seven deadly sins, some of them claimed.[5] They continued to denounce it as an occasion for injury, death, and social disruption long after there was any real hope of eliminating so cherished an elite sport. We know who won this quarrel, but it is instructive to consider with what vigor and in what language the sides argued.

Thomas of Cantimpré can speak forcefully for the clerical side. An Augustinian and later a Dominican who studied with Albert the Great, around mid-thirteenth century he wrote a book with the wonderful title *Bonum universale de apibus* (*The Common Good from Bees*).[6] A book of confession stories told by sinners to friar-confessors, it was probably written for the edification (as well as the amusement) of fellow confessors. So much for the "seal of the confessional."[7] One story came to Thomas from a fellow Dominican to whom the widow of the offending knight had made sorrowful confession.[8] This powerful German knight, devoted to tournament, apparently had died in one; at least, Thomas says, "he died as miserably as he had lived (mortuus est autem miserabiliter sicut vixit)." His holy and devout widow, with much weeping (de rigeur for confession stories), told her spiritual father of a vision given her of her departed husband after his death. His exact location was not specified, but he was surrounded by a great gathering of demons who were performing a devilish version of the arming ceremony. They first outfitted him with *caligas*, heavy soldier's shoes—using spikes that penetrated from the soles of his feet to his head. Next came the knightly hauberk, secured to his body again with spikes that pierced him through, this time front to back and back to front. His great helmet was then nailed to his head, with spikes tearing through his body all the way to his feet. The shield they hung from his neck had a weight sufficient to shatter all his limbs. Apparently after tourneying, the knight had been accustomed to relax with a soothing bath, followed by recreational sex with some willing young woman. The demons in the vision dunk him in a tub of flames and then stretch him out on an incandescent iron bed where the sexual partner provided was a horrible toad (buffonis illius horribilis).⁹ His widow told her confessor that she was never quit of the terrifying vision.¹⁰

This story and many more like it thundered down upon the faithful from many pulpits; they were, of course, meant to be terrifying. Thick collections of surviving sermon *exempla* regularly provided preachers with ammunition for the war on knightly tournament, often characterized as accursed meetings and the spawning ground for sin.¹¹ Sometimes in a typically clerical fashion, the writer plays with words to assert that tourneyers should better be called tormentors. These arguments roll on as late as the fifteenth and sixteenth centuries. John Bromyard, a classic source, denounced tournaments in his great *Summa Praedicantium* (the Summation of Preaching, a manual mined for principles of religion and sermon stories, originally written by this English Dominican in the later fourteenth century). So much frivolous expense is involved, he writes, that "torneamentum est pauperorum tormentum (the tournament is the torment of the poor)." Many men are killed, and they become, he declares in a telling phrase, "martyrs of the devil (martyres dyaboli)."¹²

Of course by then the campaign was long a failure. Clerics had clearly lost the fight by the time of our two pious knightly authors, Lancaster and Charny, both of whom easily assume in their pious writings that tournament is a licit part of the chivalric life. Clerics may have clung to standard denunciations in manuals for sermons, but the knights had prevailed.

Crusade Ideology and Chivalric Ideology

Evidence on crusading propaganda and knighthood redoubles that from the determined chivalric continuance of tournament. The warriors selectively absorbed those ideas that fit within a framework of chivalric sensibilities. Of course it is easier to find clerical views outlined in theological and legal works. Yet we can recover the knights' views from crusade chronicles and can see their reflections in harsh strictures against them penned by clerics in sermons, confession manuals, and collections of miracle stories.

What Was Promised

Priceless spiritual benefits awaited the prospective recruit. Historians of crusade might quickly and justly point out that a carefully framed theology of penance was distorted in the lavish and unconditional promises which knights often heard in crusade propaganda. The canonically correct idea held that crusaders won only remission of temporal punishment (*poena*) for confessed sins, not the elimination of more basic guilt (*culpa*) for all sin. Yet as crusade preaching spread its message, as Carl Erdmann commented pointedly, "the world took no account of this distinction. Not one of the contemporary reporters of Urban's sermon at the Council of Clermont in 1095 reproduced the official terminology. What predominated instead was the general belief that the crusade procured forgiveness of sins and the soul's salvation."[13] Sermons generally offered crusaders just what they surely needed to hear and wanted to possess: unambiguous assurance of sins forgiven in this world and a safe passage through devilish perils to glory in the next. As James Brundage wisely cautioned,

> The nature and meaning of the spiritual merits that soldiers could earn
> by participating in a holy war, as well as the theological implications
> of this idea, remained unclear for a very long time, both to those who
> held out promises of such merit and, even more, I suspect, to those who
> acted on these promises.[14]

The valiant fighters in the *Song of Aspremont* are assured, for example, that those who die fighting infidels will sit at God's right hand, their sins forgiven without confession.[15] Writing of the crusaders marshaled against the Cathars, the chronicler William of Tudela said tersely, "once they knew that their sins would be forgiven, men took the cross in France and all over the kingdom."[16] Peter of les Vaux-de-Cernay in his chronicle of Simon de Montfort's effort against the Cathars could record equally summary promises: at the siege of Castelnaudry the bishop of Cahors and a Cistercian monk promise the crusaders that if they were to fall in this glorious struggle on behalf of the Christian faith they would be given remission of all their sins, would be instantly crowned with glory and honor, and would thus receive a reward for their labors.[17]

Peter sometimes records more circumspect promises, as he does when narrating the beginning of the crusade: all those who, inspired by zeal for the true faith, took up arms for this task of piety would receive indulgence for all their sins from God and his vicar, so long as they were penitent and made confession. No more need be said. The promise of indulgence was published in France; a great multitude of the faithful took up arms under the sign of the cross.[18]

In his extended description of the decisive battle of Muret (1213), he seems more careful, but his blessing bishop almost enacts a cleric drawn from a *chanson de geste*. The bishop of Comminges recognized that his colleague, the bishop of Toulouse, would fatally delay the crusading army by providing individual blessing with a wooden crucifix. He thus seized the crucifix and blessed the body of warriors en masse with the words:

> Go forth in the name of Jesus Christ! I am your witness, and will stand as surety on the Day of Judgment, that whosoever shall fall in this glorious battle will instantly gain his eternal reward and the glory of martyrdom, free of the punishment of purgatory, so long as he is repentant and has made confession, or at least has the firm intention of presenting himself to a priest as soon as the battle is over for absolution from any sins he has not yet confessed.[19]

It is easy to imagine the bishop shouting out his personal warranty to the massed warriors from his spot of high ground; yet all the qualifications may well represent fine print to the contract, emerging from the precise mind of the clerical chronicler. Perhaps little clerical labor was ever directed to correcting any excessive promises or misconceptions. It seems too much to expect careful correction from battlefield preachers who were convinced that God required them to launch a fully triumphant crusade.[20]

As Erdmann noted, lavish promises appear in accounts of the foundational sermon Pope Urban II preached at Clermont in 1095, calling for a great armed pilgrimage to the East.[21] Reports of this sermon establish popularly perceived principles that lasted throughout the life span of crusading. We do not, in fact, know precisely what Urban said at Clermont. The accounts written in twelfth-century chronicles could scarcely have reproduced the actual words of the pope decades later.[22] Yet these accounts give us motive ideas from a formative stage of crusading ideology. Through the following centuries these themes appeared in countless sermons, with the *exempla* that animated them sometimes taking on lives of their own in collections of miracles and moral tales; and the stories lived on also in chivalric literary texts. Such materials reveal common conceptions of crusading benefits.

Three major and closely linked themes appeared in these calls to action and fulsome praise of valiant crusaders. First, a theme of authority: ecclesiastical authority stands behind warfare that is most clearly licit and blessed in the sight of God. Willing obedience to answer the call and recognize the rightful voice that sounds it is the knights' first merit. By taking the cross—a most public and visible action—they acknowledge that the call to sanctified warfare comes to them from God through the clergy. Second, knights hear—whatever actually was said—that such fighting can earn spiritual benefits often amounting to remission of sins. Specifically, they are told that the severe and trying suffering which they are to expect on crusade is the mechanism of religious expiation and atonement. A third theme, however, is restrictive and admonitory: these penitential benefits gained by meritorious fighting are restricted to the work of those blessed by clerical authority. Especially in early days, knights are told bluntly that their characteristic practice of warfare at home, far from earning them any religious merit, is hateful in the sight of God; only the proper work of the subset of obedient crusaders confers potent spiritual benefits. The message becomes rather more nuanced over time, as we will see, but crusade is always upheld to knighthood as the ideal form of warfare, an outlet for warrior energies superior to the common practice of fighting with their coreligionists in Europe.

Clerical Direction Asserted

Clerical authority to initiate and direct holy warfare had a venerable history by the time Urban II preached at Clermont, whatever the novelties of that dramatic occasion. The trail of precedents stretched from the Christian Roman Empire through episcopal blessings on military campaigns during the Carolingian era. Precisely how effective these blessings proved as causal agents in any body of armed men could be debated by specialists, but most scholars might agree that a powerful valorization descended on the warriors.[23] Although Pope Urban's famous crusade message of 1095 directed crusaders against a foe considered infidels, interesting earlier evidence comes from the Norman campaign to conquer Anglo-Saxon England. Whether or not William the Bastard actually received a papal banner from Alexander II (1061–73) as a sign of divine favor for his invasion in 1066, he does seem to have enjoyed papal backing.[24] Yet William's fighting, if meritorious, was not considered penitential and did not enter into the economy of salvation for those engaged. After the conquest, a papal legate arranged a formal schedule of penance for those involved in the fighting in order to cleanse them of all sins committed on the campaign.[25] Equally interesting evidence appears in a letter sent from this same pope to Spanish clerics in 1064. Through these clerics the pope urged the warriors fighting Muslims in the *Reconquista* to confess their sins and accept the penance imposed by their bishop or spiritual father. By apostolic authority, however, he then lifted the penance from them and granted a remission of sins. One form of penance—fighting for the faith—it seems, was being substituted for more traditional forms.[26] This cumbersome process of assigning traditional penance only to replace it with meritorious crusade fighting is instructive. It was not, of course, the only pattern followed. Not many years earlier, Leo IX had led forces against troublesome Normans in Italy, and after this campaign some clerics asserted that those from the papal side who were slain had earned blessed martyrdom. When allied with the papacy, Norman forces in southern Italy and Sicily often fought under papal banners, or received them after victories.[27] His even more prominent successor Gregory VII had famously thought of summoning the warriors of Europe into papal service as a *militia Sancti Petri*.[28] If the relationship of divinely approved warfare to meritorious suffering as penance was at this point still in flux, behind the experimentation stands the assertion of clerical authority to speak for God in authorizing and directing warfare.

Close directive authority by clerics waned over the centuries. Subtleties and complexities of interpretation are best left to crusade specialists, but the general tendency for increasing control of the actual conduct of crusading by laymen seems clear. If clerical leadership under Innocent III directed the Fifth Crusade (1213–21), even that powerful pope had lost control of the Fourth Crusade; and another masterful pope, Gregory IX, could not steer the Barons' Crusade as he wished.[29] And kings had their own ideas and priorities, as Philip II of France had demonstrated by his departure from the Third Crusade, as Louis IX in his piety demonstrated in the crusades that he directed. Sounding the call for crusading and providing the money demonstrate continuing clerical influence; conducting the warfare and setting goals increasingly reveal lay directive force.

Spiritual Benefits Won

Meritorious suffering in crusade warfare generated significant benefits, often discussed. Surviving crusade sermons quote the fundamental biblical passage on Christian asceticism, relating Christ's words closely to crusading: "If anyone wants to come after me, let him renounce himself and take up his cross and follow me."[30] The chivalric form of following Christ certainly called on knightly prowess and required endurance. Though other forms of pilgrimage were meritorious, the crusade was superior because of the greater sufferings it imposed—a point that Geoffroi de Charny would have appreciated. Humbert of Romans forcibly insisted that if all humanity makes the pilgrimage represented by life, crusade represented the outstanding form of pilgrimage. He based his claim, of course, on the greater asceticism involved in the armed pilgrimage of crusade. If other pilgrims expose themselves to hardships, the crusaders "expose themselves to death, and this in many instances."[31] Gilbert of Tournai details that crusaders praise God with heart, mouth, and works; and the works he has in mind involve "the labours of satisfaction (labores satisfactionem)."[32] Through their suffering, as an able historian of crusading sermons observes, the knights "conformed" to Christ and enacted an extreme form of penance.[33] In the vivid language Jacques de Vitry addressed to crusaders, "God the Father signed [Christ], to whose flesh the cross, that is fixed with a soft thread to your coats, was fixed with iron nails.[34] "For," as Eudes of Châteauroux insisted, "he who wants to catch the Lord needs to expose himself to every danger and labour."[35] And Eudes specifies that it is crusading knights who best follow Christ into danger and physical labor: "today, who but the knights more aptly and more evidently trust that Christ is their lord? They follow the Lord's call like noble birds and they form his army and his cavalry."[36]

In stirring and pointed words imaginatively given to Urban II by the chronicler Fulcher of Chartres, the pope pledges unqualified spiritual benefits to the crusaders:

> I address those present; I proclaim it to those absent; moreover Christ commands it. For all those going thither there will be remission of sins if they come to the end of this fettered life while either marching by land or crossing by sea, or in fighting the pagans. This I grant to all who go, through the power vested in me by God.[37]

In the words supplied for Urban's sermon by Robert the Monk, the pope urges the knights in a similar if somewhat more comprehensive vein: "Embrace this undertaking for the remission of your sins, certain of the unfading glory of the kingdom of heaven."[38] Among those who reconstructed Urban's crusade sermon, Gilbert of Tournai used the most elaborate image:

> Just as small fish hide beneath rocks, so they escape the storm and are not swept away by the current, so crusaders are saved, so to speak,

hiding in a foreign and unknown land, whereas lovers of this world are swept away, while playing in the many eddies of worldly things, and die in their own country.[39]

William of Malmesbury may be the most eloquent reporter of words from Pope Urban II on this theme. His report pictures the pope urging his listeners to:

> Devote a little exertion to the Turks, and your effort will be rewarded by the anchorage of everlasting salvation. . . . The motive force of your toils will be charity, that following the Lord's commands you may lay down your lives for your brethren; the reward of charity will be God's favour, and God's favour will be followed by eternal life.[40]

The crusaders can expect, after death in such service, "the compensation of a blessed martyrdom (habituri post obsitum felicis martirii commertium)." "Those whose lot it is to die," he specifies, "will enter the halls of Heaven (Morituri caeli intrabunt triclinium)."[41] In telling the crusaders they must follow a narrow way, Urban says, in William's version of his words,

> It may well be that the path to be traveled is constricted, full of death in many forms, and overcast with perils; but this same road will lead you to the fatherland that you have lost, for indeed "We must through much tribulation enter into the kingdom of God." Dwell, therefore on the crosses that await you, if you are captured; dwell on the chains and in a word all the torments that can be inflicted on you; await for the strengthening of your faith these horrible punishments, so that, if it should prove necessary, you may procure by the loss of your bodies the salvation of your souls. Do you fear death, men of great courage as you are, and of outstanding fortitude and daring? Nothing that human wickedness can invent to use against you can outweigh the glories on high, for "the sufferings of this present time are not worthy to be compared with the glory which shall be revealed in us." . . . Thus our souls, set free by death, are either regaled with joys beyond all their hopes, or profit by punishment, than which they have nothing worse to fear.[42]

Jacques de Vitry pictured Urban preaching unambiguously that crusaders received "the remission of all sins with regard to punishment and guilt, and in addition eternal life."[43] Those who came to the aid of God now could be assured of "full remission of sins (omnium peccatorum integram remissionem)" and for the future "eternal life (vero vitam eternam)"[44] The theologian in him insisted only on one qualification: contrition and confession of sins as the necessary first steps, to be followed by the penance of hard campaigning. In his terms, this hard service on the crusade became the penance that follows contrition and confession:

> Those crusaders who prepare themselves for the service of God, truly
> confessed and contrite, are considered true martyrs while they are
> in the service of Christ, freed from venial and also mortal sins, from
> all the penance enjoined on them for their sins in this world and the
> punishment of purgatory in the next, safe from the tortures of hell, in
> the glory and honour of being crowned in eternal beatitude.[45]

Echoing an argument of St. Bernard, Jacques de Vitry proposed that the all-powerful God could, of course, have simply freed "his" land by a single shattering divine utterance. But he chose instead to honor his faithful men with the opportunity to join the cause, in the process saving many who would otherwise have been lost eternally.[46]

Crusade propaganda recognized—if only rarely—that ideal asceticism was not always fully in evidence among crusaders. A song written before the third crusade frankly tied romantic motives closely to crusading, proclaiming that through this fighting the knights great and small won not only paradise and honor, but also the love of their lady.[47] Sometimes even clerics felt a need to prop up the waning ascetic sense of the crusaders. The author of the *Chronicle of the Third Crusade*, for example, claimed that a discouragingly hard fight at Arsuf was actually a "glorious day" on which crusaders were simply sorely tested. He mused judgmentally over the great sins the warriors must have committed to suffer such bitter misery and require a "great fire of tribulation to purify them." Unsparingly, he grumbled that they might have accepted the harsh day "with pious longsuffering and without even a murmur of mental protest."[48]

But the argument usually assumes the warriors know that all of their hardships, deprivations, and, for many, martyrdom are the specific means of gaining needed religious merit. Even setting off for crusade could be an ascetic, penitential exercise. Jacques de Vitry pictures a knight about to embark on his crusade who has arranged for his much-loved little children to be brought before him "in order that his departure might be made more bitter and his merit increased."[49]

Encouraging stories show the crusading knights granted precious martyrdom at their request. A knight from the diocese of Utrecht, Caesarius of Heisterbach tells, "having vigorously served in war for the Saviour a whole year," was ready to return home when in a vision he saw his squire, who had been killed before his very eyes in combat with Saracens, entering heaven in the form of a dove. Reflecting that on returning home he would only fall into old sins, the knight returns to the fighting with even greater bravery. He falls in battle and is decapitated, the head carried about in triumph by the Saracens. But the Christians build a church over the spot where the brave man fell.[50] Another crusader, in a story told by Jacques de Vitry, even explains this great goal to his faithful black warhorse: "O black horse, good companion of mine, many a good day's work have I done mounting and riding you, but this day's work shall surpass all others, for today you shall carry me to eternal life." When he had said this, he slew many Saracens and at length fell himself, crowned with happy martyrdom.[51] Clearly even good warhorses understand the importance of what their masters are about. When a pious crusading knight hurries to the Mount of Olives, forgetting about practical details such as housing, his horse finds the best room and stands, blocking the door to secure lodgings for him.[52]

Of course good crusading service counted even if it fell short of happy martyrdom. One knight, snagged on hooks thrown over the walls of Jerusalem by crafty Saracens is left hanging there as a deterrent to missiles hurled against the walls. Although the captured man stoutly urges his comrades to continue casting stones so that he may win his martyr's crown, one stone hurled at the wall severs the ropes suspending the crusader and drops him to safety.[53] Whether or not they died, the crusaders—as the author of *The Chronicle of the Third Crusade* confidently declared—endured such terrible sufferings and losses that "Each of them should be acknowledged to have borne a sufficiently horrible martyrdom, although they did so in various ways."[54]

If the perils by land and sea were undoubted, the benefits were known and secure. Gilbert of Tournai provided a pleasing notion: just as the Knights Templar passed about without paying customary tolls, crusaders in general could walk through the high gate of paradise without any impediment (sine repulsa).[55] A recruiting song for what became the second crusade told French knights,

Whoever goes with Louis now,
Need never fear the devil's horde.
His soul will go to Paradise
With the angels of the Lord. . . .
Knights, please reflect upon this word,
You who in arms are most esteemed
Present your bodies to your Lord,
Who on the cross your life redeemed.[56]

Eudes of Châteauroux assured his hearers that a crusader "will be absolved from his sins instantly like the second thief on the cross."[57] Taking the sign of the cross effects this transformation by turning the recruit into God's mercenary, free from sin. The good men who stepped forward to be signed with the cross have undergone a veritable conversion. In the manner of monks (though not with their permanence or thoroughness), crusaders have escaped the world to become truly religious in the way that medieval people had long thought possible only to those who left ordinary secular life behind. Monks were sometimes thought to be barred from taking the crusading cross, since they have already undertaken a similar vow in pledging their lives to the cloister. Matthew Paris, for example, finds the abbot of St. Edmunds ludicrous for just such a misstep. "Forgetting that, with the cowl, he had undertaken perpetually to carry the cross of Christ, he assumed the ostensible sign of the cross to the derision of many."[58] Jacques de Vitry straightforwardly announced that he was preaching the crusade "to convert souls (propter animas convertendas),"[59] while Eudes of Châteauroux declared that his crusade preaching was intended to produce "the sinner's conversion to God (conversionem peccatoris ad Deum)," a conversion that—like St Paul's—required "nothing short of renouncing everything (nichil aliud fuit quam omnium derelictio)."[60] As both monks and knights, members of the order of the Knights Templar, of course, crossed the line between the lay and the religious status. God recognized their special order, one miracle story told: saying their liturgical hours in enemy territory, a group of Templars miraculously become invisible to attacking Saracens.[61]

An anonymous *Mirror of the Laity* (*Speculum Laicorum*) from fourteenth-century England—the story itself set in 1247—tells that a bishop of Ely advised a dying man to escape purgatory by taking the cross. After his death the man appeared to his brother in a dream and asked him to thank the bishop for such good advice. Correspondingly, any disbelief or interference with crusade preaching is dealt with sternly. This same text pictures a returned and disillusioned veteran of crusades actively discouraging recruitment; a dead comrade appears in a vision to reprove him, but in the conclusion of the story the naysayer falls from a height and bites off his own tongue.[62]

Equally important, the hard-won benefits were not limited to the crusader himself. Jacques de Vitry reminded crusaders that their sufferings can aid deceased parents who left their goods to them, if the crusading is undertaken in the intent of helping the relatives. Generalizing, he assures crusaders to

> have no doubt at all that this pilgrimage affords you not only the remission of sins and the reward of eternal life, but that whatever good you do on this journey on behalf of your spouses, children and parents, whether living or dead, will profit them greatly.[63]

Eudes of Châteauroux similarly promised the crusader that "he can also help his loved ones who are in purgatory if he takes up the cross and makes this pilgrimage for them."[64] And Matthew Paris reports a good case of the successful transmission of this message. The countess of Salisbury, who was also abbess of Lacock, was given a vision on the night her son William Longespee was killed on the crusade of Louis IX in the mid-thirteenth century. She witnessed a knight in full armor being received by glorifying angels into the halls of heaven and heard a voice assuring her that it is her son, whose heraldic device she had recognized. Learning much later of his death, she offered her thanks to God who has allowed her to give birth to so manifest a martyr. Significantly, she adds a hope that his merits as a martyr will swiftly elevate her to the heavenly kingdom upon her own death.[65]

Most crusaders could at least feel sure they were wiping clean a slate spotted by their own grievous sin. Matthew Paris tells that Earl Patrick of Dunbar, a most powerful Scots magnate who died on St. Louis's crusade had joined the expedition "in order to be reconciled with God and St. Oswin. For he had injustly harassed the monastery of Tynmouth, a cell of St. Albans."[66] For other knights the need arose from a lifetime of less specific but equally troublesome sinning. Richard Lion-Heart himself spoke for them—through the chronicler of his crusade—when, in a speech before the Battle of Joppa he proclaimed to his men: "We should receive our approaching martyrdom with a grateful heart . . . giving thanks to God that we have found in martyrdom the sort of death we were striving for. This is the wages for our labours."[67] The most dramatic case of such ascetic merit, however, appears in the *exemplum* that tells of the knight who suffers from a Saracen crossbow bolt lodged in his skull. Though his friends tell him they could find someone to extract it, the suffering knight insists that the enemy bolt that has penetrated his skull be left there "to serve him as a trophy on the Day of Judgment."[68]

Crusading Versus Warfare as Usual

If the clerics freely granted spiritual benefits to holy warriors, they broadly condemned fighting at home; their early crusade sermonizing was especially pointed, but even later messages promoted crusade as a higher form of fighting than knights generally waged. The contrast got a swift start: uncompromising denunciations of fighting as usual at home were regularly attributed to Urban's great sermon in its twelfth-century recreations.

Fulcher of Chartres imagined that Urban II admonished the knights in stark language:

> Until now you have waged wrongful wars, often hurling insane spears at each other, driven only by greed and pride, for which you have deserved only eternal death and damnation. Now we propose for you battles which offer the gift of glorious martyrdom, for which you will earn present and future praise.[69]

They must do better:

> Let those who are accustomed to wantonly wage private war against the faithful march upon the infidels in a war which should be begun now and be finished in victory. Let those who have long been robbers now be soldiers of Christ. Let those who once fought against brothers and relatives now rightfully fight against barbarians. Let those who have been hirelings for a few pieces of silver now attain an eternal reward. Let those who have been exhausting themselves to the detriment of body and soul now labor for a double glory.[70]

In addition to castigating their sexual licentiousness, Pope Urban, as William of Malmesbury pictures him preaching at Clermont, also denounced knightly violence:

Let us call it excess of appetite if you have taken every opportunity to ensnare your brethren, redeemed as they were for the same great price as you, and shamefully stripped them of their resources. But now, as you head for shipwreck among these dangerous reefs of sin, a haven of peace opens before you—unless you neglect it.[71]

By contrast, ordinary knights who have not made the decision to wear the cross are reminded by Jacques de Vitry that "Those who wear just any coat, which is called 'pannuncel' in the French vernacular, are not really known as soldiers of Christ; they do not carry his arms."[72]

Eudes of Châteauroux is even more blunt—Urban insists no thieves need apply:

Those who have stolen other people's things and do not pay what they owe do not take the cross in the right manner; it is better for a man "to follow the naked Christ naked" than to follow the devil. . . . The Lord does not want people serving him with absconded or stolen goods or with other people's belongings.[73]

Even imaginative chivalric literature, well known to valorize crusading, sometimes delivers warnings that have received less scholarly attention. If only occasionally, explicit messages announce that the warriors must stop fighting each other at home and turn their swords on what were termed the enemies of God. In *Girart de Vienne* (written about 1180, though projected into the Carolingian past) an angel stops the long feud between Charlemagne and Duke Girart. The heavenly messenger flatters the warriors' vanity as it clearly orders them not to fight each other but to concentrate on Muslim foes:

My noble knights, you have been honored deeply!
This fight shall be no more;
Not one more blow must be exchanged,
For the Lord our God prohibits it.
Instead, in Spain against the race of heathens
Your fierce prowess shall yet be known and needed;
Men shall know well your valor there and see it
Conquering for the love of God.[74]

Significantly, this advice is followed in the next *laisse* by a standard promise of divine pardon and grace earned by so pious a form of fighting.

Such specific warnings may wane somewhat in later centuries. The churchmen found themselves in a cruel dilemma over warfare at home. They needed to invoke divine blessing on kings who might secure necessary peace in Christendom. Yet under these monarchs, nascent states flexed every muscle in mutual warfare among Christians. Even rulers successful in reducing disruptive internal strife fought external opponents with equal vigor and claimed blessing and legitimacy for their fighting. Boniface VIII faced the classic dilemma when he tried to intervene in the warfare between Edward I of England and Philip IV of France.[75] As standard policy, church leaders thus continued to stress crusade as a vastly superior form of warfare; they relentlessly urged kings and emperors and their powerful subordinates to abandon internecine strife and to move forward in unity against a common, non-Christian foe. The very existence of the goal, stretching back across centuries, is significant; but the failure of this hope for more peace at home is writ large in later European history. Of course, ecclesiastical leaders had long vastly complicated hopes for crusading as a vehicle of peace by preaching it against designated enemies of the faith within Europe. The warriors would fight and, whatever the circumstances or the enemy, they would claim that they fought the fight God blessed. And they could secure clerical support at some level to effect their claims.

Chivalric Reception and Independence

How did these powerful themes touch knightly audiences? Did they accept the claim of merit through crusading rather than through quotidian squabbles over vengeance, property, or the armed service owed to superior lord or king? Personal statements giving the response of crusading knights are scarce. Yet helpful evidence is not totally lacking. Several crusade chronicles that seem especially close to a knightly point of view can give invaluable insight into what messages reached the knights and how they were received.[76]

Lisbon Crusade

One of the most useful sources is a somewhat neglected mid-twelfth-century chronicle, *De Expugnatione Lyxbonensi*.[77] It tells the story of the siege of Lisbon during the summer and autumn of 1147 carried out by northern European crusaders who joined the king of Portugal, Alfonso I. These crusaders

were primarily Anglo-Normans, Flemish, and Rhinelanders, along with recruits from Brabant, Brittany, and Scotland. This was one of the five European expeditions that we usually collectively classify as the Second Crusade.
Giles Constable has aptly termed this chronicle "perhaps the most detailed
surviving record of any military expedition in the twelfth century" and recognized its value as a crusading narrative.[78] The author has been identified
as Raoul, a priest who likely accompanied the Anglo-Norman contingent in
the crusading force that took Lisbon—one of the few successes of the Second Crusade.[79] Our author proves to be an excellent guide, as we will see; if
he shows much familiarity with relevant ideas from canon law and from St.
Bernard and other prominent writers on crusade,[80] he is likewise close to the
men of war whose actions he chronicles, and especially to Hervey de Glanville, the East Anglian knight who led the Anglo-Norman force. Raoul can
understand their point of view and seems often to purvey it with clarity across
the centuries. We can hear clerical crusading arguments and propaganda in
this chronicle; we can hear crusader opinions, almost crusader voices. Jonathan Phillips argues that all speeches in the chronicle have been modified to
support a set of themes useful in generating a new crusade decades after the
overall Second Crusade proved a failure, especially ideas of unity and humility against divisive pride and greed. Yet the account remains invaluable; for,
as Phillips notes, it provides a "snapshot of the ideas of an active and successful crusader from the mid-twelfth century."[81] If we find disagreement or
disenchantment with crusading ideas in this source they can be considered
all the more telling.

The entire treatise reads as an account of twelfth-century bonding of
prowess with pious military asceticism. When a severe storm strikes the fleet
en route, the leitmotif of pious penance appears at once:

> How many there were who, becoming penitent and confessing their
> sins and short-comings with sorrow and groaning and atoning with a
> flood of tears for the perversion of their pilgrimage, however it had been
> begun, offered sacrifices to God upon the altar of a contrite heart.[82]

Landing safely at Oporto, the crusaders gathered in the cathedral to listen
to a sermon preached by Peter, bishop of Oporto. Though he spoke in Latin,
interpreters translated his words into the language of each crusader.[83] Raoul,
who could listen to the Latin (and may well have served as one interpreter),
gives a complete Latin text. We could scarcely expect him to reproduce the

bishop's message verbatim and can accept the case, already noted, for later modifications in the text; yet it remains a rare and precious account.[84] The crusaders hear that even the rich among them

> have exchanged all their honors and dignities for a blessed pilgrimage in order to obtain from God an eternal reward. The alluring affection of wives, the tender kisses of suckling infants at the breast, the even more delightful pledges of grown-up children, the much desired consolation of relatives and friends—all these they have left behind to follow Christ, retaining only the sweet but torturing memory of their native land.[85]

Crusade sermons often reminded the warriors that they were expressing their love for God and were receiving his love in turn. Maier writes, "The concept of the crusader experiencing the power of Christ's love at the moment of the passion was convenient for explaining the mechanism of the plenary indulgence promised to the crusader."[86] Even before a blow has been struck or received, the bishop of Oporto says, meritorious suffering has registered with God as they have come "through so many perils of lands and seas and bearing the expenses of a long journey."[87] Their "hardships and pain (laborem et penam)" have caused them to be "reborn of a new baptism of repentance (novo penitentie renati baptismate)." The image of new baptism is significant; monks and nuns were thought, as successors to the martyrs of the heroic age of Christian persecution under the Roman emperors, to have undergone a second baptism which brought them into a new life, cleansed and free of sin. Like the martyrs and the regular clergy, these crusaders are told that they have put on Christ by voluntarily taking on a mode of life that entails corporal suffering and deprivation.[88] They have undergone a conversion experience bringing them into a new life.[89]

When the actual fighting begins, the bishop assures them, their violence will not count against them: "for in law it happens that whatever anyone does in self-defense is held to have been done lawfully."[90] Apparently one criterion for just warfare, however, is that they have given up their violence at home "by which the property of others is laid waste (quibus rapiuntur aliena)," and are taking up arms now to punish the impious, a duty which the righteous can perform with good "conscience" (bono animo).[91] "Indeed there is no cruelty where piety towards God is concerned (Non est vero crudelitas pro Deo pietas)," says the bishop, quoting St. Jerome to the arms-bearers before him. He similarly marshals evidence from the Hebrew scriptures, from St.

Augustine, and from other Church Fathers to prove the righteousness of the fighting about to begin. God has graciously allowed these men to cease their pillage and misdeeds at home—"concerning which there is no need now to speak in detail (de quibus non est modo dicendum per singula)"[92]—and has given them not new acts, but a new purpose; for their sin lies not in waging war but in the misguided goal of plunder. How this distinction does not disqualify the "pilgrims" whose lust for loot provides a mini-theme of the text is not made perfectly clear. The bishop ends his sermon, however, with assurances that money will be supplied in so far as the resources of the King of Portugal's treasury permit.[93] This reported language of a crusade sermon delivered in mid-twelfth-century Portugal dramatically recalls the words and themes at least attributed by twelfth-century chroniclers to Urban II at Clermont, in 1095, and repeated by all his successors as crusade preachers.[94]

As if to underscore divine approval for the episcopal message, a hopeful sign appears during the voyage down the coast to Lisbon. The crusaders see great white clouds coming down from the region of the Gauls (a Galliarum partibus) which encounter foul, black clouds over the Iberian mainland. They identify the white clouds with their own expedition, of course, and see a representation of the enemy in the dark and dirty cloud formation. From the decks of their ships the fascinated crusaders watch the "battle" in the sky and rejoice as the bespattered dark clouds move "in flight" toward the city. "Behold, our cloud has conquered! Behold, God is with us" they shout in relief and triumph.[95]

A second sermon reported by Raoul explicitly blesses their cause at a critical moment in the campaign: the crusaders' great siege tower, enveloped in prayers and sprinkled with holy water, is about to be pushed forward against the walls of Lisbon. The speaker was "a certain priest" who was almost certainly the author of the treatise.[96] If the sermon is indeed his, the full text provided may come even closer than the account of the bishop of Oporto's sermon to the meaning conveyed in 1147, even if it does not give words actually spoken. He begins reassuringly, telling the warriors that each has a guardian angel, whose special care can prudently be regained, if it has been lost, through penance. But the message soon turns more theoretical, to basic issues of the role of Christ in redemption. Christ became man, he reminds his martial audience, so that through patient human suffering he might provide salvation for humanity. Either unaware of Anselm's argument of a generation earlier (discussed in Chapter 6) or consciously turning aside from its analysis, he addresses the argument made by their Moorish enemies that other options for salvation existed, so that Christ did not have to become human and suffer as a man. God is free in his actions, Raoul asserts, but chose to enter human form and take on human suffering. "But the Son of God, according to the belief and worship of the universal church, became man in order that as such he might endure human sufferings (ut in eo humana pateretur)." And he continues (in a passage that would have warmed the heart of Henry of Lancaster, had he known it, two centuries later), Christ's coming and passion

> is a medicine for men of such strength that its potency passeth understanding. Oh, medicine that healeth all sickness, reducing swellings, restoring corruptions, cutting away the superfluous, preserving the necessary, repairing losses, correcting distortions.[97]

The preacher tells his beloved brethren "who have followed Christ as voluntary exiles and have willingly accepted poverty" that they must understand that "the prize is promised to those who start but is given to those who persevere."[98] They must "put on Christ once more (reinduite Christum)" and "cleansed by the new baptism of repentance (novo penitentie abluti baptismate)" advance on the city. It is, he tells them after all "through the inspiration of the Spirit that we have invaded this suburb in which we still remain (impetu Spiritus ducentis suburbium hoc in quo manemus invasimus)."[99] Coming to his peroration, the preacher urges his brothers: "at last arouse yourselves and grasp your arms (Expergiscimini aliquando, fratres, et capescite arma)." Dramatically, he elevates the piece of the True Cross that he holds in his hand. He assures them,

> if it should happen that anyone signed with this cross should die, we do not believe that life has been taken from him, for we have no doubt that he is changed into something better. Here, therefore, to live is glory and to die is gain.[100]

He promises his hearers that he will himself share in their trials and labors (in tribulationibus et laboribus vestris particeps) and hopes for a share in their rewards (premiorumque vestrorum). He closes with a prayer that the God of peace and love will direct them. In response, the crusaders fell upon their faces with groans and tears and rose to be signed with the cross. "And so, at last, with a loud voice, calling on God for aid, they moved the [siege] engine forwards . . . towards the wall."[101]

One need not doubt the piety. The tears and groans were undoubtedly heartfelt. Yet the emphasis in the minds of the crusading warriors may have moved along rather different lines, without their denying any word spoken in sermons by the bishop or now by their priest. Evidence of this knightly line of thought appears in the narrator's report of a speech given by one of the leaders, the knight who is clearly the narrator's hero, Hervey de Glanville. He reports that Glanville spoke "somewhat as follows" to his fellow Anglo-Normans. The issue he stresses is unity of purpose and action among the crusaders, drawn as they were from so many lands and moving toward more than one goal. Glanville reminds his fellows that "so great a diversity of peoples is bound with us under the law of a sworn association." They must therefore act together "in order that in the future no stain of disgrace shall adhere to us who are members of the same stock and blood." Warming to his subject, he asks,

> Who does not know that the race of the Normans declines no labor in
> the practice of continuous valor?—the Normans, that is to say, whose
> military spirit ever tempered by experience of the greatest hardships,
> is not quickly subverted in adversity, and in prosperity, which is beset
> by so many difficulties, cannot be overcome by slothful idleness;
> for it has learned how with activity always to frustrate the vice of
> idleness. . . . Brothers, take heed, and attend to the reform of your
> morals.[102]

These morals, it emerges, are faithfulness to sworn obligation in a time of crisis threatening unity. Through the "sin of a violated association" they will become "the objects of universal infamy and shame."[103]

Their pilgrimage is not founded, as it should be, on love (karitate), he warns, in a passage that begins to sound more theological. But the love to which he refers is the steady comradeship of warriors bound together in a sworn cause, anxious to win honor and determined to avoid shame. "Spare shame to your race. Yield to the counsels of honor. (Parcite generis infamie vestri. Assentite consiliis honoris vestri." He ended his peroration by humbling himself at the feet of the leaders of the knights. All wept with joy and cried out "God help us! (Deus, adiuva nos)." The reunited crusaders negotiate with the king of Portugal, whose charter promises them that only after the city "has been ransacked to their full satisfaction (ad eorum voluntatem perscrutatem)" need it be handed over to the king and his officers.[104] The vigor praised in the speech as the opposite of dread idleness will yield much profit.

It is obvious that the crusaders think of their hard service as ultimately blessed by God. But without denying the piety, it seems equally obvious that in the pressure of the moment their vocabulary is more likely to turn to shame and honor, to the "sin" of disloyalty to sworn obligation, than to more abstractly theological arguments or terminology. We cannot, however, think of their religion as merely a cover for truer motives. It is also important to remember how readily they seem to have listened to the intense argument of Raoul who did indeed wax theological, and how readily, and in tears, they were signed by the cross as the priest held in his hand a piece of the instrument of Christ's ultimate meritorious suffering.

It is likewise interesting that our author reports the debate between Christian and Muslim representatives as the fate of the city hangs in the balance. Unlike Muslims in some *chansons de geste*, in which they are reduced to cartoon-like figures, these foes seem worthy and smart. They put their finger on the sore spot and charge against the crusaders a massive self-deception. "Labeling your ambition zeal for righteousness, you misrepresent vices as virtues."[105]

The speeches and sermons Raoul provides help us to understand how malleable language is made to serve purposes that— at least from the perspective of a modern reader—differ significantly from an original spiritual content and intent. Here "poor pilgrims" declare that they are following Christ in suffering and poverty, by sustaining the hard labors of travel and the harder labors of conquering and acquiring loot—all reckoned as acts of spiritually meritorious penance earning divine love. For the historian, this use of pious language is significant, even if our reaction to it is unavoidably modern.

St. Louis's Crusade in Egypt

If the Lisbon chronicle is unusually informative, thankfully, it is not unique. A century later another crusade inspired an equally informative account. Jean de Joinville's biography of Louis IX (*Vie de Saint Louis*) devotes most of its pages to insightful and hair-raising stories of that king's crusade in Egypt in 1248–54.[106] He reports Louis's opinion that human greed is so common that "very few take thought for the salvation of their souls, or the claims of personal honour."[107] This seemingly casual statement by the king captures two of the major values at stake in this biography: achieving salvation and retaining honor. Despite his frank doubts about the motives of most men, Joinville thinks that in the mind of the king the two values are intertwined (as they were in the thinking of Geoffroi de Charny a century later).[108] They recall ideas of meritorious suffering leading to salvation and of chivalric warfare as the key to honor. Although these ideas could work well together in knightly minds, we will see that spiritual values do not easily share space with the proud and touchy self-assertion central to knightly identity.

Joinville leaves us in no doubt that as an aid to achieving salvation, crusading is ideally a form of quasi-martyrdom enacted through suffering *in imitatione Christi*.[109] He continually refers to the "trials and troubles (persecucions et tribulacions),"[110] of the crusaders, the suffering and the fear that make them "sick at heart (en grant melaise de cuer),"[111] even the martyrdom achieved by many, "which caused great mourning in this world, and great rejoicing in paradise (que maint grant duel en furent en cest monde, et maintes grans joies en sont en paradis)."[112] One of the most telling moments comes when, in captivity and in constant fear of death, the crusaders are addressed by an ancient man with hair as white as snow. Joinville says he

> asked us if we believed in a God who had been taken prisoner for our sake, wounded and put to death for us, and who on the third day had risen again.[113]

Receiving the positive answer he expected, the venerable man delivers his message:

> Then he told us we ought not to be disheartened if we had suffered these persecutions for His sake: "For," said he, "you have not yet died for Him, as He died for you."[114]

In the very preface to his book, Joinville has not only already announced that he will relate Louis's "great deeds of chivalry and his great feats of arms (ses granz chevaleries et de sez granz faiz d'armes),"[115] but adds that the king's chivalric striving and suffering ranks him among the martyrs:

> It seems to me that those who omitted to place King Louis among the martyrs have paid him insufficient honour, in view of the great

sufferings he endured in the six years I was with him on crusade, and more particularly because he followed the example of Our Lord in taking the cross. For if Christ died on the cross, why, so to speak did he, for it was as a crusader wearing that holy sign that he passed away in Tunis [on his second crusade, 1270].[116]

Joinville repeats the sentiment in opening his book proper, noting that "as our Lord died for the love he bore His people, even so King Louis put his own life in danger . . . danger that he might have avoided."[117] We learn that the Queen Mother, Blanche of Castile, mourned her son as dead from the moment she learned he had taken the cross.[118] Louis himself not only fought and endured the rigors of campaign, when supervising the refortification of Jaffa, he humbly carried hods full of earth, Joinville reports, "so as to gain the promised indulgence (pour avoir le pardon)."[119]

Joinville himself suffered alongside the king, beginning at his moment of departure from his home, as he set off along a route that would take him to shrines with holy relics on the way to the coast. Leaving home and family at his castle of Joinville was an agony for him, as our twelfth-century preacher had recognized it was for the Lisbon crusaders:

all the way to Blécourt and Saint-Urbain I never once let my eyes turn back towards Joinville, for fear my heart might be filled with longing at the thought of my lovely castle and the two children I had left behind.[120]

Even the prospect of sailing the Mediterranean, as he reflected on reaching the coast, had its own perils: "For what voyager can tell, when he goes to sleep at night, whether or not he may be lying at the bottom of the sea the next morning."[121]

No one who follows Joinville's vivid narrative of the harrowing events during the crusade in Egypt can question his identification of the crusade with bodily discipline, suffering, and mortification of the most extreme form. Alongside heroic images of Louis, resplendent in armor, masterfully leading the way,[122] he gives realistic descriptions of Louis suffering so unceasingly from dysentery that his underclothes must be cut away, of crusaders dying of grievous wounds, of the anguished cries of men having their swollen, diseased gums cut away so that they can chew food, of his own inability, in captivity, to listen with care to a fellow crusader hurriedly confessing his sins to him in terror as their enemies approach with huge axes, ready to decapitate them.[123]

Yet the knightly honor also emphasized in Louis's statement, quoted above, must be kept in mind. It can serve not only as a relief from the flood of realistic scenes of suffering, but as a key to the knightly approach to religion. At about this same time, the author of the *Song of the Cathar Wars*, William of Tudela, reported the prayer he thought was on each man's lips before battle: "Ah, Lord God of Glory, by your most holy law keep us from shame, do not let us be disgraced."[124] The independent set of standards, noted in Henry of Lancaster and Geoffroi de Charny, and in the Lisbon crusade chronicle, appears again here in the steady importance attributed to a chivalric ethos and the inclination to shape even pious practice to its requirements.[125] Honor must be preserved, come what may.

Joinville himself and, through his witness, many others constantly speak of the imperatives of honor, the need to follow a course of action that will avoid shame and disgrace. More than once King Louis or Joinville must settle disputes about prickly points of honor that could lead to French knights fighting among themselves, even with the enemy plentifully at hand to threaten them.[126] When, for example, one of the king's sergeants merely pushed a knight in Joinville's service, complaint of this dishonor was made to the king, who at first tried to laugh it off. Joinville threatened to leave the king's service (and thus quit the crusade) if justice were not done. As a result, on royal orders the offending sergeant appeared in Joinville's quarters barefoot and wearing only a shirt and drawers, holding a naked sword in his hand. Kneeling before the offended knight, he offered him the sword for use in chopping off the guilty hand at the wrist, if he so pleased. Joinville formally asked the standing knight to forgive the offense, he agreed, and the ceremony was complete.[127] But even if the sergeant's hand was never in serious danger, we should not miss the point that, given a less wise or flexible monarch, offended honor could have taken the Sire de Joinville and his men out of the crusading campaign.[128] Even the high and spiritually beneficial goal of fighting God's enemies could not be pursued if honor were sullied. It seems worthy of note that Joinville not only refused to join Louis's second crusade but in the process inverted the standard argument that as Christ had died for the knights, they must be willing to die for him. Joinville says his people at home are so oppressed by officials that, Christ-like, he must stay home to defend them and would, in fact, offend God if he became a crusader. Pressed by the King of

France and the King of Navarre to join the second crusade proposed by Louis
IX he responded:

> To this I replied that while I was in the service of God and of the king
> overseas [in Louis's first crusade], and since I have returned home,
> his Majesty's serjeants and the King of Navarre's had so ruined and
> impoverished my people that there would never be a time when they
> and I could possibly be worse off. I told them that if I wished to do
> what was pleasing to God I would remain here to help and defend the
> people on my estates. For if, while seeing quite clearly that it would
> be to their detriment, I put my life in danger by venturing on this
> pilgrimage of the Cross, I should anger our Lord who gave His own life
> to save His people. I considered that all those who had advised the king
> to go on this expedition committed mortal sin.[129]

Even if we can guess that Joinville had experienced quite enough of crusading on his first "pilgrimage," we need to recognize how much more his
statement reveals. An independent and self-reliant sense of piety appears in
sharp relief. No matter who says the contrary, another crusade is not a pious
undertaking.[130] Most strikingly, the usual formula about Christ and his men
is turned upside down. Joinville will follow Christ not by taking the cross
but by staying away from crusade and tending to injustices troubling his own
people at home. This is scarcely a line of argument that would have appealed
to Jacques de Vitry or any other preacher of the crusade.

His narrative of the fighting in Egypt also shows that the prowess which
secures honor is so admired that even clerics are praised for acting as men of
valor, whatever the ecclesiastical prohibitions against their shedding blood.
Did the knights have the famous Archbishop Turpin of the *chansons* in
mind?[131] As the crusaders retreated toward Damietta, the bishop of Soissons
realized that he felt no desire to return home, but only a great desire to be
with God. The story could come from a sermon *exemplum* or an epic. "So
he made haste to be with God, by spurring on his horse and rushing to attack the Turks single-handed. They . . . cut him down with their swords, and
thus sent him to be in God's company among the number of the martyrs."[132]
Earlier, a priest in Joinville's service had won his secular lord's fulsome praise
by arming himself and single-handedly driving off eight Saracens, piercing
one through the body with his lance. As Joinville reports with pride, "From

that time onwards my priest was very well known throughout the army, and one man or another would point him out and say: 'Look, that's my Lord of Joinville's priest, who got the better of eight Saracens.'"[133]

If they did not fight with their own hands, those clerics closely in tune with knightly standards could at least clear the way for the lay warriors. At a critical moment in the expedition to Jaffa, knowing that Gautier, Comte de Brienne and Comte de Jaffa, was under sentence of excommunication by the Patriarch of Jerusalem (the issue being ownership of a tower in Jaffa), the bishop of Ramleh took charge, declaring, in a scene that, again, could have been lifted from a *chanson de geste*:

> Don't let your conscience worry you because the patriarch won't absolve you, for he's in the wrong, and you're in the right. I myself absolve you in the name of the Father, the Son and the Holy Spirit. And now let's at them![134]

The result was that "they dug their spurs into their horses (ferirent des esperons)" and attacked.

In an even more tense moment, as Joinville and his knights realize that they will be captured by their enemies and are only debating to which party of Saracens to yield, a cellarer in his employ suggests that they not surrender at all. "We should all," he counsels, with words that, once again, could have been drawn from a sermon or miracle story, "let ourselves be slain, for thus we shall go to paradise (Je suis d'avis que nous nous laissions nous tuer; ainsi nous irons tous en paradis)." Tersely, Joinville comments, "But we none of us heeded his advice (Mais nous ne le creumes pas)."[135]

The value of this evidence from the Lisbon and Egyptian crusades is heightened by its congruence with evidence from *chansons de geste*.[136] As pictured in the *Couronnement de Louis*, the *Chanson de Guillaume*, the *Chanson de Roland*, the *Charroi de Nîmes*, knights showed a remarkable independence of spirit. They interpreted the hard campaigning and warfare of their profession, even when carried out against non-Christian enemies, in terms more compatible with lay aristocratic social norms than with clerical treatises and sermons. They thought of themselves as serving their lords or the lord king as guarantor of the order of their world rather than the pope. They defended a region, a realm, a homeland, more than a religion or moral ideal. If fighting the enemies of the faith was laudable, they insisted on the worth of chivalric combat per se. Such views reveal, as Jean Flori says,

une chevalerie plus aristocratique et laïque que les clercs l'auraient
voulue . . . une chevalerie que ne concerne pas nécessairement la
croisade telle que l'envisageait le pape . . . une chevalerie qui prend
conscience de son existence et de sa force et qui se forge une idéologie
qui ne se confond pas totalement avec celle que tentait de lui inculquer
l'Eglise.[137]

In the astute view of Matthew Strickland, "in the majority of warfare,
the knights seem to have paid scant heed to the Church's strictures on
conduct."[138]

The literature that they patronized—works better conveying chivalric
ideas than any other source—thus stands alongside chronicles particularly
close to the knights. Both present a picture of knighthood absorbing crusading exhortations through a distinctly lay, aristocratic filter. The result was
bound to be ideas shaped by significant chivalric independence no less than
undoubted piety. Crusade was surely the most pious form of knightly labor;
but in the minds of warriors it was not the sole licit form of that labor. Far
from having a unique quality or standing as the stark opposite to most of
their fighting, it graced one end of a continuum of their hard, pious labor in
good causes. Understanding that all honorable fighting of the good knights
constituted their true labor, we will not be surprised at the Lisbon Chronicle,
at Joinville's narrative, at Geoffroi de Charny's matter-of-fact comments on
crusade or Thomas Malory's respectful narration of the Grail quest as one of
the really special episodes in the history of knighthood that he relates before
going on with his story.

This degree of knightly independence is worth emphasizing because it
performed such major social or cultural work. Without it, how would the
spokesmen for chivalry (and this must be a mixed set of clerics and knights)
have managed to square the circle? How could they have manipulated the
malleable language of religious imagery or imagined that the hard work of
campaigning, the discipline and the risks of hands-on cutting and thrusting, could be a form of *imitatio Christi*, even when both sides in a fight were
Christian?

CHAPTER 5

Knightly Ideology Developed and Disseminated

IF KNIGHTHOOD RECEIVED essential support from an interlinked body of ideas, how did this ideology emerge and how was it diffused? The state of our evidence leaves such questions fraught with difficulties. We cannot know who talked with whom at each tournament or what was said about honor and atonement as the wine flowed and the candles burned low late at night in castle halls. Many voices were heard and many pens scratched on parchment and specific authors cannot be assigned for each idea. Our evidence has, however, strongly indicated that, however pious, ideals for chivalry were not simply generated by clerics and dutifully absorbed by knights. Not only did the warriors insist on certain lines of professional virtue, they selectively chose theological views and adapted them to fit within their framework of heroic and courtly norms. If this creative process involved paradox and generated sparks, it produced powerful valorizing results evident in the treatises of Henry of Lancaster and Geoffroi de Charny, in the appropriation and generalization of crusading propaganda.

This chapter emphasizes the role of chivalric literature as the great agency of creation and diffusion. In all its forms, this literature selectively absorbed heroic, religious, and courtly influences from elite society and channeled them, suitably trimmed, reinforced, or amplified, into the cultural sphere of knighthood. Like a transformer receiving electric current, this massive body of writing sent along the fusion of ideas at higher voltage to animate numerous receptors. Chivalric literature provided a feature of courtly society with its communal readings and numbers of private readers rising with increasing literacy. Authors remembered (or imagined) stirring words attributed to innovative popes of the stature of Urban II and harangues of monks with the charismatic force of Bernard of Clairvaux. They drew upon deeds and sayings of historical figures such as Godfrey of Bouillon, William Marshal, Geoffroi de Charny, and "le roi-chevalier" Richard Lion-Heart.[1] Above all, they created chivalric heroes by the dozen for readers and hearers whose appetite could scarcely be sated. In the process, they shaped ideals and contended with other writers taking on the same task. The result was a fascinating and complex dialogue between the exigencies of vigorous knightly life and the ideals embedded in a vast body of memories and literary invention. Tensions and paradox were not flattened or eliminated, but a mere chaos of clashing views was surmounted. Whatever the continuing debates, knighthood achieved an acceptable valorizing framework.[2]

Linked Ideas

Three broad concepts found throughout chivalric literature (*chansons de geste*, chronicles, romances, biographies, and vernacular manuals) convey the core of this framework. We have encountered these ideas in focused lines of inquiry and with specific evidence; it is important to bring them together here and to take account of the abundant literary evidence in support of their broad role. Unsurprisingly, these overarching chivalric ideas overlap with specific elements of crusading propaganda already analyzed: chivalric ideology no less than crusade propaganda emphasized knightly suffering and its spiritual merit; but, as we will see, a broad chivalric ideology stands sharply opposed to crusade thinking on strict clerical authority to legitimize fighting and on the extension of spiritual benefits to non crusaders engaged in licit warfare.

(1) A first emphasis falls on the sheer corporal suffering knights undergo in the exercise of arms throughout a lifetime in their tough profession. (2) A second clearly establishes the spiritually meritorious nature of that labor and suffering. Hard knightly labor is the licit work of their *ordo*, blessed by God who endows knightly prowess. As closely as earthly labor can, these tough and virtuous labors actually parallel the meritorious suffering and heroic labor of Christ. (3) Finally, this hard work and religious merit sanctifies all virtuous warriors, not solely crusaders. Even hard combat of Christian against (misguided) Christian brings merit. The labor of crusaders is not a contrast and a rebuke to ordinary knighthood, but simply ranks as its most obviously pious form. The principles, in short, announce that the hard campaigning

and fighting of knights is their licit work assigned to them by the Lord of Hosts; doing it well necessitates suffering that brings religious merit to those engaged in any good fighting for right causes, whether on crusade or not.

Though these thematic elements interlock in heroic knightly atonement, seldom will any single text lay out the entire set of ideas, neatly assembled. We must cast a wider net for the components, rather like recognizing the existence and grandeur of the entire Lancelot-Grail cycle, which seldom appears in single manuscripts, but must be pieced together from many overlapping sources. It seems characteristic of the way social or cultural ideologies grow and spread that they are likely to advance piecemeal, one set of links being established at a time: a single text may connect the first and second themes; another, the second and third; yet another, the first and third. Only in overview can we see the complete pattern.

(1) Knighthood Means Suffering

Suffering as atonement is not the topos one immediately associates with the proud and dominant chivalric layer in society. Yet, knighthood took form and did its work—as we have seen—in an intensely ascetic culture which paid great spiritual dividends to those who suffered. An emphasis on knightly suffering appears throughout the life span of chivalry and in all the types of evidence that present it to us. Abundant evidence shows that suffering and hardship, pain, toil, and endurance formed fundamental elements in the self-perception of knightly life.[3]

Twelfth-century *chansons* provide the *locus classicus*. Old Duke Girart cries out in the midst of fierce battle in the *Song of Aspremont* that his men must be prepared for suffering and can confidently expect all heavenly rewards offered to martyrs if they die.[4] Seven hundred doomed warriors ride across the battlefield of the Archamp in *The Song of William*, with bodies so grievously wounded their bowels drag between their feet and their brains spill out of their mouths.[5] "Saint Stephen and the other martyrs," as this *chanson* pointedly insists, "were no better than all of those who died for God in the Archamp."[6] The model warrior Vivien in this epic has not taken food for three days, is bleeding profusely from mouth and side wounds, and in his great thirst can find only the salt water of the Mediterranean or muddy water running across the battlefield, now mixed with blood and brains. The sea water he prefers to force down comes up involuntarily through his mouth and nose as the Saracens surround him and so severely increase his wounds with spears and javelins that his entrails fall to the ground.[7] He calls on Christ who suffered to preserve his courage and faith during his own suffering.[8] Later in this text William's nephew Guy, only fifteen years old, is thought too young to be able to endure the rigors of campaign and battle. William's wife Guibourg cautions Guy: "You could not undergo the hardships, watching by night and fasting by day, nor endure and suffer the fierce fighting."[9] *Raoul de Cambrai*, a text with no quasi-crusading theme at all, stresses how knights must endure great hardships, the death of kin and friends. They "suffer and endure (sosfrir et endurer)" the seemingly endless hacking and thrusting of combat that fills one *laisse* after another.[10]

Does this emphasis on knightly suffering in epic continue in later works? Thirteenth-century romance may depict the rigors of campaign and battle less graphically, yet the basic theme of chivalric suffering undoubtedly prospers. In the *Perlesvaus* (a romance written probably fairly early in the thirteenth century) the opening lines refer to "painne e travaill (suffering and hard work)." Thomas Kelly suggests that this theme "constitutes a main thread in the fabric of the narrative."[11] The hero, says the author near the end of his romance, "was never free of toil and hardship all his days as a knight (ne fu sanz travail e sanz paine en tant com il vesqui chevaliers)" and soon repeats that "his life was never free of hardship and toil (ne puet vivre sanz paine e sanz travaill)."[12] Likewise, the romances composing the great Vulgate or Lancelot-Grail cycle are insistent on suffering as a condition of knighthood, though one or two instances must stand for many in the vast expanse of that cycle. The hermit to whom Lancelot confesses in the *Quest of the Holy Grail* commends him for *soffrance*, suggesting fortitude or patience in suffering.[13] When the veteran Gawain instructs the young knight Melias about the rigors of chivalry early in this same text, the new knight replies that "God willing, he would endure any amount of suffering to preserve the honor of knighthood; nothing could keep him from it."[14] Praising another young hero, Claudin, Gawain describes him as "one of the best knights in the world whom I have seen endure most labor at arms and most pain and suffering in mortal battles."[15] Sir Gawain, of course, knew the suffering of knighthood first hand; after a single combat in *The Story of Merlin*, he "had already been so badly battered that he suffered from it forever thereafter."[16] In the Post-Vulgate *Merlin Continuation*, King Lot's brave suffering is extolled as exemplary:

The battle was cruel and pitiless; it began at tierce and lasted until vespers. If King Lot had not been such a good knight, his men would have been defeated sooner. But all alone he bore the burden of the battle, so that all those who watched him crossed themselves in wonder that he could endure half of what he suffered. He did great deeds and struck great blows.[17]

The *History of the Holy Grail* that begins the cycle had predicted just such pain and toil for knights. Anticipating the Grail quest, it announced that "the good . . . will undertake to suffer the difficult burden of earthly exploits of chivalry in order to learn about the marvels of the Holy Grail and the lance."[18] In the Post-Vulgate *Quest of the Holy Grail*, Gawain again praises the young Claudin, here in even more significant terms: "I know that he was a good knight by what I see he has suffered."[19]

The biography of the great knight William Marshal, written at about the same time, regularly calls to mind the suffering of knighthood. John Marshal, the hero's father, had endured severe hardships while fighting to support Queen Matilda,[20] and William himself later declared to Richard I that "all men of good birth / should suffer hardship and great pain / for their rightful lord,"[21] a principle recalling (perhaps even drawing on) the oft-quoted maxim from the *Song of Roland*:

We know our duty: to stand here for our King.
One must suffer hardships for one's lord,
And endure great heat and great cold,
One must lose hide and hair.
Now let each see to it that he employ great blows,
So that no taunting song be sung about us![22]

Marshal's biographer frequently points out how William and other knights suffered in battle,[23] in tournament,[24] and during captivity.[25]

Fourteenth-century authors busily inscribed similar sentiments. As Andrea Hopkins suggests in her study of a particular group of Middle English works, "the object of the quest is not necessarily 'love' and in a sense is not relevant, so long as it is not ignoble. It is the period of exile, of suffering and isolation which the hero must undergo in striving to attain his goal, to embody the ideal, which strikes the crucial note and expresses the essence of the romance spirit."[26]

Scenes described in the fourteenth-century Middle English romance *Alliterative Morte Arthure* closely recall much older *chansons de geste*, with fighters graphically plying weapons and suffering in gruesome detail. In one relatively minor fight,

> There at the front of the forest, where the road went forth,
> Fifty thousand fierce men were unhorsed at once.
> When those two armies came crashing together, knights
> Were wounded sore enough on either side;
>   . . .
> They cut down in that company shielded knights,
> Pierced those princes despite all the pride of their mail,
> Through chain-linked byrnies stabbed to the white of their chests,
> Burst asunder the brilliantly burnished braces;
> They chopped through bloody shields and bloody horses
> With their swords of gleaming steel.[27]

There can be little cause for wonder that, as in earlier epic, men are cut so severely that the filth from their bowels splashes on the ground beneath their horses' hooves or that Arthur reports from a significant dream a frightful vision in which "great, loathsome lions licked their teeth / As they lapped up the glowing blood of my loyal knights."[28]

The Middle English *Prose Merlin* (written in the mid-fifteenth century) may be less sanguine, but it uses pain as both a noun and as a reflexive verb. Knights "pain themselves" to accomplish their feats; they suffer great pain as they fight. The language used to describe the rescue of two kings during the barons' revolt against young King Arthur shows the cast of mind:

> The knyghts that were with Kynge Ventres *peyned hem sore* [painfully worked] to socoure their lorde, and so did the knyghts of King Loth. And Arthur's knyghts *peyned hem sore* to helpe Arthur, and to take and holde these other two kynges. . . . But *with grete payn* were these two kynges rescowed and horsed agein.[29]

Later King Leodogan hopes to find "a worthi man of armes that myght wele endure peyne and travayle to meyntene my were." To such a man he would willingly give his daughter, Guenevere.[30] Another late medieval English author, John Lydgate, similarly uses the word *pain* to represent the hard labor of fighting. In his *Troy Book* (written in the early fifteenth century) when Achilles "ne wolde lenger don his peyne (will no longer undergo his pain)" we know that he is, for the time being, withdrawing from the fighting.[31] Clearly the modern phrase to "take pains" represents only a pale survival of a once more vigorous meaning.

Our texts from different eras and regions, written in several languages, all agree. Grievous bodily suffering is the inevitable fate of stalwart men who campaign and engage in close personal combat with edged weapons. This emphasis is important. Acknowledging such pain and suffering could have been suppressed; insistent voices could sing solely of power and victory. Instead, far from being ignored or downplayed, the pain and suffering are emphasized by graphic depiction and tireless repetition. The knightly mentality is so often do or die, and the requirement so often is to suffer horribly and then to die. This ideological stance remains significant; whatever the body counts on historical battlefields, knights thought of themselves as truly suffering in their hard profession.

(2) Knightly Suffering Is Meritorious

The second theme helps, of course, to explain the first. Many texts picture knights suffering in defense of Christianity and so draw upon that potent line of valorization. To establish spiritual merit, authors of *chansons* repeatedly invoke crusade-like settings, projecting aspects of their own age back into the Carolingian era of their poems' settings. Blood-stained virtue cloaks the warriors as they heroically triumph over heathen foes or manfully and willingly die in the valiant effort. Whether these heathen "Saracens" are imagined as invaders of Italy (in epics such as in the *Crowning of Louis* or in epics such as the *Song of Aspremont*) or as Saxons invading England (as in Geoffrey of Monmouth's *Historia Regum Britanniae* or later in the *Alliterative Morte Arthure*), the vigorous knightly practice of arms and the dire knightly suffering easily acquire religious virtue. In effect, the authors of chronicle and epic anachronistically make the knights crusaders before there were crusades; as if dispensing a sacrament to the sound of martial chant, they provide glowing crusading justification for hard fighting.

Perhaps to state the case more accurately, they provide the blessing knights truly wanted, one that often is even broader and richer than that offered by bishops, popes, and canon lawyers known to historical knights. In the works of literature they patronized, the ahistorical chronology and the suprahistorical crusade benefits mix powerfully in a blessing descending on the grateful chivalric *ordo*, rather like the crown descending from heaven in angelic hands in the manuscript illumination with which this book began. The message is delivered repeatedly, as in the classic speech by the pope himself in the *Song of Aspremont*:

> I am a man who does not deal in lies;
> He who goes now against this foe to fight
> And for God's sake should lose his mortal life,
> God waits already for him in Paradise
> With crowns and laurels for the soldier of Christ;
> He shall sit us at his own right-hand side;
> Without confession, all the sins of your lives
> On God's behalf I now collect and shrive;
> Your penance is to fight with all your might![32]

The knights in the audience must especially have appreciated the pope's dispensing with any troublesome need for confession as he announced that fierce fighting counted as complete penance. They would likewise have listened approvingly to the speech by the archbishop near the end of *The Song of Girart of Vienne*. He tells Christian forces, locked in conflict,

> Barons, my lords, give ear to me and listen:
> I stand for God, Who made the world we live in,
> And for St. Peter, His regent in Rome city,
> To whom He gave the power of forgiveness
> To any sinners for any sins committed;
> I tell you now that any man who's willing
> To go with Charles, keeper of the French kingdom,
> Shall be forgiven for a lifetime of sinning
> In Lord God's name, Who made the world we live in."
> The French all say: "How high a pardon this is!"[33]

In fact the plan has come direct from highest heaven, carried by an angel who pointedly tells feuding Christians to stop internecine conflict and go to "Spain" where their "fierce prowess" is needed "in service of God's love."[34] However reluctant they might be to give up the joys and opportunities of fighting and feud—an obvious clerical goal for them—knights in *chansons* know the basic exchange: their suffering brings merit. In the *Song of Aspremont* none will go as messenger to seek aid from Charlemagne early in the great fight against the pagans, for to leave the fighting would seem cowardly in the worldly frame and a loss of penitential opportunity in the spiritual frame. As the knight Godfroi explains tersely, swearing by his faith, "Why should I not strike mighty blows for Jesus / and pay to God the debt of all believers?"[35] Later the pope has the same problem in finding a knight to carry even the standard that contains a piece of the true cross. Though the knights revere this potent relic from Calvary, they know they win God's grace by fighting weapons in hand and if necessary by dying in the fight.[36] Hope of gaining the reward of faithful battlefield service unto death is intoned by one knight after another who refuses to leave the active fighting. They cherish the quality of their hard-won reward. Amauri, one of the determined knights, imagines the reward: "On flowers in Paradise tonight I'll sleep / with all God's saints to keep me company."[37]

Some passages comfortingly assert that a warrior need not make the supreme sacrifice to gain desired spiritual benefits, though dying in battle remained the surest route to a honored place in paradise. Pope Milon in the *Song of Aspremont* tells knights that they are lucky to have the opportunity of winning salvation through their fighting. Though born in sin and deserving damnation, they can be absolved by striking great blows against the enemies of their religion.[38] Meritorious fighting and suffering short of death here seem sufficient. Other passages clearly state that crusading, with all its deprivation and dangers, is a form of martyrdom for all who suffer, not merely for those who die. This is the stance taken, for example, in *The Crusade of Richard Lion-Heart*.[39]

The romances so popular from the late twelfth century carry forward the theme we have found in *chansons* and point toward our third theme, the valorization of all licit fighting (to be considered shortly). Virtually all romances present fighting and suffering as meritorious and often locate the action in a world beyond that of crusading.[40] Romance settings represent the violence of the courtly world through lonely knightly quest rather than the warfare of panoramic crusade-like battlefields.

Their role in establishing knightly ideology thus stands out prominently. Without the quests so prominent in romance, a valorizing mythology extended to all licit knightly fighting seems much less likely. Romances likewise manage to be pious, or at least what the Victorians would have termed "improving," without living under complete intellectual control by clerics; they scarcely come unaltered from the pages of ecclesiastical doctrine. In short, questing in romance and the knightly mythology created by romance writers remind us again that knightly lay piety viewed its ideas through a powerful lens of lay independence.

Repeatedly in these stories a knight sets out from a courtly center on some quest that will significantly test his valor and endurance, a process that ideally forges him into a better man. So often the task set the questing knight is righting a particular wrong that troubles some member of elite society— classically a wounded knight or a threatened lady—who has sought help at a renowned court. Knightly prowess must be brought to bear against a local tyrant, or against the inhabitants of a castle who practice an odious custom in place of the straightforward hospitality endlessly recounted and praised. The hero's stunning deeds of prowess exalt knightly bodies performing hard and meritorious labor, suffering, and achievement. Undertaking lonely wanderings in wild and fearsome settings, knights encounter fierce foes and endure a succession of grueling all-day battles which leave the ground brightly littered with shattered mail rings and darkly stained with pools of chivalric blood. Yet they steadfastly persevere to conclude these worthy enterprises.

At minimum, the quests in even the most pedestrian romances show knights gaining honor through suffering and tough physical exertions. Such suffering can only entail merit with spiritual underpinning, given their cultural milieu. This tendency to assume the religious behind the lay is not surprising in a world that knew few other registers for the supremely important. Those who turned treason and cowardice into sins and paralleled the immortal soul with imperishable honor would see hard-won knightly merit as redemptive.

If even third-rate romances show knighthood proved at high personal cost, the most thoughtful and ambitious romances show knighthood truly transformed by hard, noble service. Carl Schmidt and Nicholas Jacobs argue—in significant language—that any romance hero must "go through a purgatory of 'loneliness and pain.'"[41] The most sophisticated stories, such as those of Chrétien de Troyes (even before his final romance, *Perceval*), show the young hero radically transformed by his quest. Jean Frappier sees the hero in Chrétien's *Yvain* so thoroughly reformed that he has become "a true chivalric saint (une veritable saint de chevalerie)."[42]

If only briefly, we should note, finally, that the considerable import of this second theme is boosted by a special intensifier: the knights think they are following or imitating Christ through meritorious, even redemptive suffering in licit fighting, as we will see in Chapter 6. This mimetic idea takes on powerful meaning for them, forming a potent bond with Christ seen as a divine warrior who suffered as they must suffer and who triumphs as they hope to triumph.

(3) All Good Fighting Counts

Chivalric texts readily blur or even eliminate the distinction between crusade and non-crusade.[43] Warriors did not consider crusade to be the sole licit form of military enterprise. If crusade (as most agreed) was the most pious form of fighting, it did not generally stand as the polar opposite to their quotidian combats at home, but merely graced one end of a continuum of their hard, pious, and meritorious labor in good causes. Writers resolutely grasp the mantle of divine blessing provided crusaders and stretch it to cover all knights fighting in good causes. Evidence appears in the several forms of imaginative chivalric literature, as well as in papal pronouncements, chronicles, and political propaganda.

Their fighting was readily sacrilized. Demonized "enemies of God" and foes denounced as "worse than Saracens"—even though Christian—have a way of turning up to play their ideological role, even on battlefields where we might not readily expect them. The goal is clear: if the enemy a knight faces is worse than a pagan, he will find it much easier to consider his warfare as meritorious as that of a crusader. He can destroy or kill with moral certainty; he can suffer with a sense of spiritual merit earned. The tradition was as venerable as the reform papacy of mid-eleventh century, half a century before the famous sermon that launched the First Crusade. Faced with the dire threat of Norman warriors in Italy, Pope Leo IX (d. 1054) tried to neutralize them with military force of his own; in the process he declared that his enemies "had shown an ungodliness worse than that of the pagans." His contemporary biographer provided the other side of this ideological coin by announcing that those who died in combat against the Normans were known to be "united in heavenly glory with the holy martyrs."[44]

By the early twelfth century, royal warfare targeted excommunicated Christians in France and was blessed by clerical authority. Guibert of Nogent writes that bishops and archbishops preached in support of the campaign of the French king Louis VI (Louis the Fat) against the notorious Thomas of

Marle. Although Thomas had served valiantly on the first crusade, he now was under excommunication by a papal legate. The case made against Thomas by Abbot Suger (Louis's admiring biographer) combines the charge of tyranny with an accusation that at home Thomas is "a plague to God and men alike."[45] The king's fight was to overcome—even to kill—misguided nominal Christians. In describing royal military vigor against Thomas and other minions of evil, Suger twice states that Louis "piously slaughtered the impious." The slain were, of course, Christian.[46] Before going into battle, the king's forces were absolved of their sins and assured of the salvation of their souls. A miraculous change from inclement to fine weather—needed for an assault on Thomas's stronghold—is taken as sign of divine favor for their martial work. In fact, a bishop's prayer had sought this particular blessing.[47] Abbot Suger had earlier in his account of Louis's deeds written that when responding to a threatened German invasion, the French host was convinced to set an ambush; the plan proposed against the invaders would "overthrow and slaughter them without mercy as if they were Saracens. The unburied bodies of the barbarians would then be abandoned to wolves and ravens."[48]

Across the Channel, Richard of Hexham, in his chronicle (written before 1164) describes the Scots invading the north of England as "more odious than the whole race of pagans" and quotes Psalm 79: "O God, the heathen are come into thine inheritance." He assures readers that the vengeance of God overtook the Scots. What makes them worse than pagans, it is worth noting in this case as in others, is not belief but behavior. They "spread desolation over the whole province, and murdered everywhere persons of both sexes, of every age and rank, and devastated towns, churches, and houses." This is a criterion for paganism that many Christians could readily find in their enemies, though not, of course, in themselves.[49]

Crusade propaganda and further papal directives could be cited in the same vein by the late twelfth and early thirteenth centuries.[50] A frustrated Pope Celestine III had in 1196 excommunicated the Spanish king Alfonso IX of León; in effect he even pronounced a crusade against him, though the step achieved little result.[51] With more effect, Innocent III in 1199 promised benefits the equivalent of those given crusaders to men willing to fight against his Hohenstaufen opponent in southern Italy, Markward of Anweiler, "in effect," as John C. Moore writes, "proclaiming a crusade against a Christian prince as Celestine III had done against the king of León."[52] Innocent branded Markward "another Saladin (alius Saladinus)" who was leading Muslim allies among his troops (quibusdam Saracenis confoederatus).[53] This same train of thought is likewise attributed to Richard Lion-Heart in Ambroise's *Estoire de la guerre sainte*, written in the closing years of the twelfth century. In telling the story of the warrior-king's crusade, Ambroise asserts that in the fighting on Cyprus against Greek Christians—those "perfidious Greeks"—the king "had no desire to hunt out Saracens worse than these."[54] That Christians could fight Christians without loss of sanctity became obvious. Boniface VIII (acting simply as Benedict Gaëtani to spare royalist sensitivities among the French) blessed both sides of the Anglo-French war conducted by Edward I and Philip IV. To borrow uncompromising words from Abraham Lincoln's Second Inaugural, "both [parties] read the same Bible and pray to the same God and each invokes his aid against the other." Earlier, in the well-known "political crusades" of the thirteenth century, clerics blessed warfare against Christians. During the troubled Fourth Crusade, the Christian city of Zara was infamously sacked and the Christian capital of Constantinople seized by a crusading army, despite, for a time, their excommunication by Innocent III. The pope could scarcely disavow all the work of a crusading army, raised by such great efforts and on which so many hopes were focused. Control of spiritually valorized warfare was patently slipping from the directing hands of clerics.[55]

Papal authority famously blessed the crusade against the Cathars (and their orthodox supporters) in the French Midi. The elder Simon de Montfort, who had left the Fourth Crusade as it attacked Christians, led the armed struggle for orthodoxy in southern France. Yet, as in the fighting in England during the early minority of Henry III, both sides in this conflict asserted religious valorization for their work. Opposing forces never simply aligned themselves on strictly religious lines. Northern orthodox Christian knights often fought southerners who, though Catholic, stoutly defended their region against invasion. If the invading forces were wrapped in the official blessing of the Roman church, those resisting the crusade might respond in kind. The *Song of the Cathar Wars* describes the scene as Provençal forces build a protective wall during their siege of Beaucaire Castle, held by crusaders called and blessed by the papacy. Despite this high clerical valorization of their opponents, the besiegers are sure that their fighting will bring spiritual benefits, even against papal-sponsored crusaders. As their chaplain advised, " 'My lords, in the name of God and the count [Raymond VI of Toulouse] I tell you that everyone who helps to build this dry-stone wall will be richly rewarded by God and by Count Raymond. Upon my holy orders, I promise each one of you salvation.' All together they shouted, 'To the pardon of all of us!' "[56]

The Barons' Crusade was preached by Gregory IX in 1234 as a classic expedition to the Holy Land and a step toward active Christian unity: but the call was redirected, without great success, to the Latin empire of Constantinople late in 1235, and complex local political interests rather than unity prevailed among the crusaders.[57]

Demonizing enemies as Saracens took various forms. Even cowardly allies might be treated as Saracens: in one *chanson* the French threaten Lombard knights placed in their front ranks against Saracen foes that if they flinch they will be decapitated as if they were themselves Saracens.[58] A knight in Chrétien de Troyes's *Lancelot: The Knight of the Cart* describes the inhabitants of the Land of Gore as "worse than Saracens";[59] the *Romance of the Rose* condemns Hohenstaufen leaders (Manfred, Henry, and Conradin) as having acted worse than Saracens when they started a war against their Holy Mother Church.[60] We cannot be surprised to find that early thirteenth-century crusaders are told to attack Cathars "more fearlessly even than the Saracens," that a French crusading knight who turned over a captured *castrum* to pro-Cathar forces was "worse than any infidel," that the citizens of Toulouse, resisting the crusaders and violating promises to men they had captured, were "worse than infidels," or that a massacre at Beziers is considered worse than anything since the time of the Saracens.[61] Eustache Deschamps used this same phrase against those misguided folk who sacked St. Germain in Paris in 1381;[62] Philippe de Mezières used the terms in denouncing pillaging arms-bearers who in his day were "worse in the eyes of God than Saracens."[63]

Spiritual valorization of pious warriors might take broader, more subtle and indirect forms. We have already encountered twelfth-century *chansons* picturing faithful knights playing the crusader in historical settings from Carolingian times. Yet not all epics mimic crusade; some portray the fighting of Christian against Christian in conflicts over land tenure and lord/vassal relationships with no loss of spiritual blessings descending on the warriors: some heroes of *chanson* move easily from fighting enemies of the Lord as proto-crusaders to fighting Christian enemies of the lord king as faithful vassals. The idea that all good fighting wins spiritual merit is reinforced in each case.

Loyal martial service to a legitimate lord could fuse with fighting against enemies of the faith. The author of the *Chanson d'Aspremont* describes a great proto-crusading battle of Christians against Muslims, but significantly adds the element of spiritual blessings earned by loyal service to the French crown. Early in the *chanson*, Duke Girart's wife, Emmeline,[64] admonishes

her recalcitrant husband not only to do his duty and serve his overlord, Charlemagne, but to fight for him against the enemies of the faith as an act of
penance:

> Now you indeed with such black sins are blemished.
> Who have burned churches and murdered men so many,
> Such awful sins, Girart, you've steeped yourself in,
> So now to Charles and with your sword do penance.[65]

Significant ideas cross boundaries as if by cultural osmosis. The venerable
belief that holy fighting helps repay the debt for sins is leaching into spiritual
merit for those who support royal action. Was not good kingship in its own
way holy? As Marsent, mother of the much aggrieved vassal Bernier, tells him
in the great *chanson Raoul de Cambrai*, "Serve your lord and God will be your
reward."[66] Crusade valorization blends into thoughts about other modes of
fighting, even into fighting against Christian opponents of a monarch who
is doing the work of God as the crowned and anointed head of a Christian
kingdom. The next step in this movement of ideas is to consider hard fighting
and suffering in any licit cause a means of knightly penance.

Some *chansons* drop the ideological framework of holy war against pagans in whole sections of text and treat all virtuous fighting as spiritually
meritorious, even in episodes without a single non-Christian enemy in sight.
The *Crowning of Louis*, one of the cycle of popular epics centering on William of Orange, is a classic case.[67] This *chanson* begins at the French court but
quickly shifts the scene of action to Italy threatened by Saracen invasion; it
thus creates the standard proto-crusade story frame for the early portion of the
chanson. William victoriously combats the invading Muslims who threaten
Rome, to which he has gone on a pilgrimage. He of course defeats Corsolt,
the fearsome pagan champion, in heroic single combat, closely described.
With this victory achieved, however, the scene shifts again and the action
returns to France and to William's fight to defend the inept but legitimate
monarch against his enemies, Christians though they be. William is following the advice given him by the pope, himself. "I should like to advise you,"
the pope has told him, "to go to the rescue of your lord, Louis as a penance"
or even "in act of penance (En peneance vos vueil ge comander / Que Loïis
vo seignor secorez)."[68] William's penitential sufferings and self-denial are real.
There may even be an unspoken intensifier to this proposed act of penance.

For when William took this advice, he walked away from his own wedding. Beside him at the altar stood a beautiful and rich lady, whom he never saw again once he left to do his duty to his lord. In any case, the central message is redoubled in this text, for near the end of the epic, we learn just how severe William's service has been, how much a penance he has actually suffered on behalf of his lord the king:

> for three whole years there was not a single day, however high and holy, that William did not have his burnished helm laced on and his sword girt at his side, riding fully armed on his charger. There was not a feastday when men should go to worship, not even Christmas Day which should be set above all others, that he was not dressed in his hauberk and armed. The knight suffered a great penance to support and aid his lord (Grant peneance sufri li chevaliers / Por son seignor maintenir et aidier).[69]

William even endures a spiritual penance added to his physical suffering. No easy option is open to him. He must fight unceasingly for Louis, even on prohibited holy days. This fighting is at once wrong and will be remembered to his cost at the final judgment; yet he must not cease to act vigorously. The message is hard, even paradoxical, and it is underscored by being repeated in the next *laisse*:

> For three whole years William the warrior was in Poitou, conquering that province. There was not a single day, however great an occasion, not even Easter Day or Christmas or the feast of All Saints that should be kept most solemnly, that he had not his burnished helm in place and his sword girt at his side, riding fully armed on his horse. The young knight suffered a great penance to protect and defend his lord (Grant peneance sofri li bachelers / Por son seignor guarantir et tenser).[70]

William's fighting, his self-denial, counts as a penance.[71] The message is clear and important: it is not only crusading that earns knights divine forgiveness; fighting the good fight for the monarch likewise reduces the debt owed for sin, even if this means crossing swords with rebels who are fellow Christians, even if it means a technical violation of holy days when one should ideally not fight at all. This valorization avoids any pretense of crusade against actual enemies of the faith. On the great balance beam that weighs good and evil to determine the fate of a knight's soul, William's stalwart fighting in the licit cause of his king counts heavily and positively.[72]

The phenomenal literary output of romance gives further reason to think such ideas were active in knightly minds and speech. Nowhere is this more evident than in the core story of the rise of Arthur and his kingdom. These works, so evidently popular among the elite, powerfully reinforced the trend to broaden the reach of ideas of redemptive warrior suffering. In romance all good chivalric fighting eases the knight's progress toward salvation; it is not limited to combat on vast proto-crusading battlefields strewn with pagan and Christian corpses.

In his great campaign against the Christian Roman Emperor Lucius, Arthur can defeat and kill his enemies with moral confidence because they have brought in hordes of outright pagans from "the East" to stand against him. This sleight of hand appears somewhat obliquely in the founder of this chronicle-like Arthurian story, Geoffrey of Monmouth (c. 1138), and quite explicitly in his successors Wace, perhaps two decades later, and Lawman (c. 1200).[73] In the crisis of Arthur's reign, when he must return to fight for his throne and wife in Britain, his archenemy Mordred has not only broken Christian law by taking the queen as his wife, he has likewise called in the pagans to fill the ranks of his army, as the texts sharply point out.[74] Such a man, by implication, is as bad as his allies.

In the *Perceval* attributed to Robert de Boron (the third romance in this late twelfth- or early thirteenth-century cycle), Arthur's Roman campaign pits him against not only the inconveniently Christian Romans, but against the conveniently pagan allies the emperor has called to his side—the king of Muslim Spain and the sultan (this king's brother), followed by their hordes of vigorous unbelievers.[75] And the end of this romance repeats the pattern we saw in Geoffrey of Monmouth's history. When Arthur returns to fight traitorous enemies at home, he learns that the archtraitor Mordred has not only recalled pagan Saxons, he has forbidden the singing of masses or matins within Britain. Each sword blow of Arthur and his men is justified as if on crusade.[76]

In the fourteenth-century *Alliterative Morte Arthure*, Arthur's warfare has pious intentions that must be forced upon impious enemies.[77] Christ is repeatedly praised for the outbreak of war in the council Arthur convenes to answer Roman ambassadors demanding tribute. As in the cycle of romances attributed to Robert de Boron, the Romans draw not only on Christian forces, but call in exotic—and pagan—eastern and African allies. Some witches and warlocks are even enrolled among enemy forces, for good measure.[78] That the poet has in mind his own age, and likely the contemporary fighting of the Hundred Years' War, appears in the references to Parliaments, English archers, Spanish foes, and even some named prominent families from the fourteenth century (such as the Montagues) who appear as supporters of Arthur. Yet through the intrusion of mythical "Saracens" the author plays his best ideological card for valorizing vigorous knightly war. The arch-traitor Mordred, like the Romans, has again enlisted pagan allies, so that as Arthur's forces effect a landing on the shores of England, Gawain can call out that they are surrounded by Saracens:

> We'll work like loyal men for the court of Christ,
> And for yonder Saracens, I swear on my oath,
> We'll sup with our Savior in ceremony, in heaven,
> In the presence of the King of Kings and Prince of all the others.[79]

After all in this force have bravely fought and died, Arthur swoons as he comes upon Gawain's dead body. He kisses the bloody corpse, and intones:

> "O righteous, almighty God, look down at this sorrow!
> This royal blood running out over the earth!
> Such blood would be worthy to take and enshrine in gold,
> For it's guiltless of any sin, as my Lord may save me!"
> And he caught it up reverently with his two clean hands,
> And he stored it in his helmet, and covered it fairly.[80]

Arthur's battle helmet becomes a chivalric reliquary, almost a chalice. Continuing the fight, the king again links good work with potent spiritual merit gained by fighting God's enemies:

> They are Saracens in that army; may we see them dead!
> Set on them with fury, for the sake of our Lord.
> If it is our destiny to die today,
> We'll be raised to the gates of heaven before we're half cold.[81]

Over a late Roman era campaign, studded with realistic late fourteenth-century details of secular warfare, the poet has drawn the richly opaque veil of crusading justification. If Malory, taking up the story again at the end of his vast book, eliminates the Saracens and witches, he does write Mordred into excommunicated state and shows him defying and threatening to de-capitate the "Bysshop of Caunturbyry" who had cursed him with bell, book, and candle.[82] Enemies such as these make the fight against them a spiritual exercise no less than a heroic pleasure.

Once again, the valorization may be more subtle. In the complex early thirteenth-century romance *Perlesvaus* (*Haut livre du graal: Perlesvaus*), Thomas Kelly finds that "Perlesvaus and the knights of the Round Table must be brought through adversity to the grace of salvation."[83] He notes that "ex-piatory action is not limited to deeds performed in direct service of advancing the New Law [Christianity]."[84] Stalwart fighting in licit courtly causes in this romance helps lead the knights to salvation. As we have seen, a century and a half later, Geoffroi de Charny fully agreed.[85]

At times, however, romance can become self-conscious about its message. At one point in the *Quest of the Holy Grail*, the heroes Galahad, Perceval, and Bors face attack by hostile knights at the Castle Carcelois. They swiftly kill their attackers and massacre even those fleeing "like so many dumb beasts." As fighting ardor cools, the heroes fall to debating whether they have enacted God's will with their swords. Galahad resists easy assumptions that they have done the right thing. At that very moment a white-robed priest suddenly appears—he even bears the Eucharistic host in a chalice. Fearful at first, looking at the bloody detritus of the slaughter, he soon assures the Grail he-roes that they have in fact carried out sacred work: "never did knights labor to better purpose; if you lived until the end of time I do not think you could perform a work of mercy to compare with this." The dead lying in bloody heaps before them, "in their treachery . . . had made the inhabitants of the castle behave worse than Saracens. All their actions went against God and the Holy Church . . . the Saracens themselves would not have behaved worse."[86] The killing is thus as meritorious as any accomplished on crusade, for the en-emies were even "worse than Saracens." Galahad is assured by the cleric that he has "done the finest deed a knight has ever done."[87]

Such valorized fighting in courtly causes appears even more explicitly in both the *Lancelot do Lac* and the even larger *Lancelot* within the Vulgate Cycle. Returning to the theme we saw plainly inserted in the *Crowning of Louis*, the heroic knight Pharian explains to his fellow warriors the spiritual virtue of hard service to a legitimate lord. They must fight to the death for their liege lords, the young Bors and Lionel, for

if we die for them it will be to our honor in the world and to our
renown as warriors, because for the sake of rescuing his liege lord from
death a man is duty-bound to put his own life ungrudgingly at risk. If
anyone then dies, he dies as sure of salvation as if he were slain fighting
the Saracens, the enemies of our Lord Jesus Christ![88]

Moreover, the point is restated in even broader terms later in these two
Lancelot texts. A former knight who has entered monastic life explains to
Gawain why he must abandon his monk's habit, leave the cloister, and return
to warfare in the world. His higher duty is to aid his son:

is he who destroys life without justification not worse than a Saracen?
If I went overseas to fight against the destroyers of Christendom, it
would be judged praiseworthy, for I must do all in my power to avenge
the death of Jesus Christ, since I am a Christian. Therefore I'll go to
avenge my son, who is a Christian, and help him against those who are
in the place of the unbelievers.[89]

For spiritual blessing, not even the vow to live as a monk trumps use of
arms in a good cause. Knightly ideology thus bonded meritorious suffering
to all licit, loyal service to kin and lord, even when the enemy was Christian.
How many knights would not have viewed all their hard fighting in European quarrels as sanctified? It was all, in fact, being sanctified by such arguments, whatever the abstract merits. Were not the enemies troubling their
own lives and realms worse than infidels?

Such speculation about knightly attitudes is not idle. Medieval armies
often claimed religious justification for their fighting. The English barons
opposed to King John in the struggle for Magna Carta, for example, called
themselves the Army of God, even though at the time they were under condemnation by Innocent III.[90] When the pope excommunicated by name
some of these baronial opponents of his ideal for right order in England, he of
course charged that these very men were "worse than Saracens."[91]

The most telling insight into chivalric thought processes may come from
accounts of three speeches to royalist troops in England in this period. Each
was made in 1217 by the great knight William Marshal: he addressed his men
twice in the campaign that led to their decisive victory over the French invasion force (and their English allies) at Lincoln, and he spoke to them again
before the naval battle off Sandwich. Marshal first addressed his followers at

Northampton, calling them "you who keep faith with the king (qui al rei estes en fei)."[92] The message that followed fused lay political and chivalric justifications for the coming battle with an unhesitating assertion that God's will is in their work and that God's blessing would descend on those who achieve it. Honor gained through standing by the king and acting in defense of wives, children, and possessions, that is, fuses with redemption of their souls. They are fighting, he assures his troops in a classic assertion of meritorious and heroic atonement, to safeguard peace and Holy Church and "to gain redemption and pardon for all our sins" through "the burden of armed combat."[93] "God wills it (Dex le velt)" the Marshal cries, quoting—consciously or not—the famous response of warriors who heard the sermon that launched the First Crusade in 1095.[94] He wants his men to "give thanks to God, who has given us the opportunity to take our revenge."[95] The words put cheer into his men's hearts.[96] When the army reached Newark, the papal legate, "as was his duty,"

> absolved them with full remission
> of all the sins committed by them
> since the hour of their birth
> so that they might be free to receive
> salvation on Judgment Day.[97]

Completing the moral template, he then excommunicated the French invaders.[98]

Just before the battle, Marshal addressed his army a second time, using stirring words that again associated shame and cowardice with God's curse, while linking victory and honor with the gaining of paradise. Those who will die need have no fear:

> God who knows who are his loyal servants
> will place us today in paradise,
> of that I am completely certain.
> And, if we beat them, it is no lie to say
> that we will have won eternal glory
> for the rest of our lives,
> both for ourselves and for our kin.[99]

Their enemies, fighting a war against God and Holy Church, are excommunicated, and are on their swift way to hell. God has given them into the hands of the just royalists. The Marshal, his biography assures, spoke as a worthy, loyal, and wise knight.[100] He kept up this encouragement even as his force moved into battle against these enemies, assuring his men of God's guidance and support.[101] Riding behind him in the charge, the bishop of Winchester called out Marshal's war cry: "This way! God is with the Marshal! (Ça! Dex aïe al Mareschal!)"[102]

Marshal gave his final rallying speech on the seashore at Sandwich, where his warriors had hurried to reinforce a fleet setting out to block the new and dangerous French thrust coming from the Channel.[103] Though briefer than the previous speeches we have noted, major themes are repeated: God has already given them victory by land and now will do so by sea. Their opponents act against God's will, but the royalists are fighting with the aid of divine guidance and will conquer "the enemies of God (les enemi Deu)."[104] The great victory of the king's forces was just what God intended (fu fet comme Dex volt)."[105]

Innocent's outrage, whole shelves of epic and romance literature, Simon de Montfort's moral scruples, the contesting valorizations of opponents in the Albigensian Crusade, the Marshal's speeches—all show how actively men engaged in the process of justifying even war between Christians. They proclaimed the spiritual legitimacy of their fighting and repeatedly branded opponents "worse than Saracens." A knight who fought and suffered for his rights or for his lord (or lady) earned heavenly merit. Crusade justification is generalized to cover lay warfare in good causes.[106] All meritorious suffering and fighting brought knights the spiritual reward they needed and craved.

CHAPTER 6

The Hero and the Suffering Servant

ALTHOUGH MEDIEVAL DISCUSSION of the theology of salvation has received close scholarly scrutiny, such ideas have not generally been brought into analyses of chivalry. Yet explanations of precisely how God is seen to effect human redemption from sin—a subject technically known as soteriology— played a powerful if subterranean role in shaping the religious dimension of chivalry as it emerged in an ascetic culture. Christ's role as savior was actively discussed in the High and Late Middle Ages, with no single line of thought dominating. Differing theological views, vigorously asserted, were taken up by advocates of chivalry to strengthen an ideology of heroic asceticism among warriors. Characteristic ideals of knighthood did not adhere to a single explanation, but drew upon both sets of major ideas for a hybrid religious ideology.

This chapter first explores how debates over so basic a theological issue as soteriology provided rich materials for thinkers and writers constructing this ideology. Second, the chapter analyzes how writers could view Christ as a model for knighthood by drawing striking parallels between his role in salvation and that of the knightly profession in the world. As portrayed by medieval thinkers, Christ's own combination of warrior heroism and ascetic atonement was crucially important to the development of themes we have been following. Ideally, a chivalric career meant following a savior imaginatively transformed into one of their own, a magnificent warrior who triumphed over his dread enemies but who also suffered grievously and meritoriously in achieving his crucial victory. A potential paradox becomes a triumph of valorization.

Two Theories on Salvation

A view of long standing often termed the Devil's Rights theory confronted challenges from newly emphasized views of satisfaction or atonement theology. In the traditional view, the devil's rights came to him through the fall of Adam and Eve, who had willfully put themselves —and all their descendants—into his power.[1] Christ boldly broke this foul and deadly—if legal—contract of enslavement either (depending on the writer) by a master-stroke of strategy or by bold personal combat. Entering sinless into the world he outwitted the devil by provoking him into a crucial overstepping of his jurisdictional rights over sinful humanity. The blameless son of the Lord heroically rescued rebels and traitors who had utterly abandoned their true sovereign and entered the dominion of a vile master. As R. W. Southern comments, this view was deeply satisfying to its age, perhaps more for its emotional than for its logical or religious impact. Twelfth-century folk, he writes, could "easily associate the daily experiences of life with a cosmic battle between God and the Devil."[2] Though he must die in order to achieve victory, Christ has played the role of a triumphant master strategist and stout champion in this cosmic struggle for the very fate of humanity. He acts, Southern notes, as a "warrior Redeemer" and is a "warlike and resourceful God who had outwitted Satan." This view could certainly touch knightly imaginations powerfully. God's work is analogous to theirs; he chose the site for battle skillfully, fought in a great struggle for the right, and won heroically, at the cost of his own life, willingly lain down.[3]

A quite different theory had also long existed, although it had received less emphasis. Christ's death could be interpreted as a sacrificial offering rather than a strategic victory and an outmaneuvering of the devil who possessed licit rights. This view received a major new interpretation and emphasis in a book destined for fame, *Cur Deus Homo* (Why God Became Man), begun by Anselm of Canterbury between 1094 and 1097 and finished in 1098. Scholars generally see this treatise as the new foundation for a theology of satisfaction or atonement.[4] In effect, the devil is denied all rights and the suffering Christ is put in place of the triumphant and actively heroic Christ.

In his book, Anselm moves away from the dominant early medieval sense of cosmic struggle between God and the devil; brushing aside Satan and his supposed rights, he focuses instead on sin as offense to divine honor. It would require either punishment by God or satisfaction offered by humans to achieve reconciliation. Since finite humans cannot make satisfaction to an infinite God whose honor has been infinitely offended, the purely voluntary blood sacrifice of Christ, the incarnate God-man, became necessary. Anselm's "stern, proud, and uncompromising refusal of easy comforts and consolations, and his rejection of facile excuses for human frailty" reinforced his technical understanding of the full importance of a lord's honor.[5] His stance may, at least in this regard, put us in mind of the treatises of Lancaster and Charny written more than three centuries later. With a tough-minded insistence on the majesty of God and the irreducible human debt, Anselm concisely wrote regarding satisfaction for sin, "only God could do it," yet "only man should do it."[6] Anselm emphasized that the sacrifice had to be offered willingly.

The potential such ideas presented for a chivalric ideology appears in a double emphasis built into Anselm's treatise. He insists both that the sacrifice and sufferings of Christ were necessary and that they were laudable. "To be acceptable, it needed to be shown to be necessary and glorious"— R. W. Southern writes—"as the only way in which a central purpose of the Creation—man's salvation—could be achieved."[7] Though men who denied their service to God were hopeless, Southern continues, "for those who were prepared to suffer, the Incarnation had extended the limits of the original covenant to the extent of bringing them into the presence of God."[8]

However exceptional his intellect, as a man of his age Anselm associated rendering God the honor due him with the *servitium debitum*, the knight-service owed to a lord.[9] That Anselm's ideas, abstract and difficult though they were, could eventually reach at least elite laymen directly or indirectly is shown wonderfully in Jean de Joinville's casual account of a conversation he had with his king, Louis IX. The king asked Joinville to tell him his conception of God. "Your majesty," Joinville replied, "He is something so good that there cannot be anything better (Sire, ce est si bone chose que mieudre ne puet estre)." Louis liked this answer: "Indeed . . . you've given me a very good answer; for it's precisely the same as the definition given in this book I have here in my hand."[10] Not only is it evident that Louis possessed a copy of one of Anselm's books—in this case clearly the *Proslogion*, the treatise in which he establishes this definition—but that in his youth Joinville had been taught and now still retains this definition, no doubt without owning the book, likely without ever holding it in his hand as the saintly king was doing.

Anselm lived in a world obsessed with asceticism, as we have seen. Significantly, an emphasis on meritorious suffering comes to fill much space in the new attention given to the humanity of Christ. Soteriological thinking is here infused with the *gloria passionis* we examined in Chapter 3. It is easy for modern investigators to forget how very specific this interest in Christ's passion became. In her influential study of the Corpus Christi festival devoted to the body of Christ, Miri Rubin has noted that "Devotions to the wounds [of Christ] had developed in the monastic milieu in the eleventh and twelfth centuries, but spread more widely in the later Middle Ages."[11] She adds concisely, "Christ's wounds were hailed as the essence of Christ's humanity."[12] The impact of this devotion on a pious believer's imitation is clearly captured by David Aers:

> We can see how the dominant model of Christ's humanity encourages
> quite specific forms of imitation. They seem characterized by the freely
> chosen infliction of bodily pain, miraculously sustained by God so
> that the holy person can go on and on performing such activities,
> reiterations that themselves confirm and sacralize the model that
> informs them.[13]

Given two active sets of ideas about Christ's role in salvation, it would be reassuringly straightforward to imagine that Anselm's views—so important in the broad sweep of Christian history—cleanly came to dominate theories of salvation from the early twelfth century. In fact, we must recognize that ideas of both the devil's rights and the suffering servant continued side by side throughout the Middle Ages. Anselm's theory did not sweep away competing ideas. He did not create a school of close followers, and many clerical thinkers did not accept his line of argument.[14] If imitation of Christ's suffering was prominent in devotional literature and practice, many believers continued to emphasize Christ's heroic maneuver and combat against the devil. Two explanations of the cosmic struggle for human salvation continued to satisfy.[15]

However distinct their emphases, ideas of Christ's heroism and his sacrifice often blended in clerical and lay writing. An early thirteenth-century crusade sermon by Jacques de Vitry rehearses the Devil's Rights argument in the form of a confrontational dialogue between Christ and Satan. But in the end Christ realizes he must counterbalance the sins of mankind and so offers his own body using the cross as a new balance beam for weighing good and evil in souls.[16] The hero modulates into the suffering servant. In a similar vein, Middle English sermons of the next century regularly stress the bodily suffering of Christ as a counterbalance to the devil's rights, which continue to be recognized. One sermon says Christ "suffered for us so painful a death to deliver us from the pains of hell and out of the devil's power."[17] In another the preacher proclaims "I assert that every man was won in battle through the mighty death that Christ suffered on the Cross."[18]

Henry of Lancaster's *Livre de seyntz medicines* (as we have seen) draws classically on both major lines of redemptive theology, heroic combat and sacrifice.[19] Lancaster emphasizes the "villainous, shameful and supremely anguishing death (vileyne et hontous et tresanguisouse mort)" of Christ, the "pains and grievous torments (peynes et grief turmentz)" suffered by his "sweet and tender body (douce et tendre corps)."[20] Yet Christ appears not only as the suffering, sinless redeemer who washes away the stain of human wrong with his sacred blood, but also as the great warrior who victoriously battles the devil, who had gained rights over humans. After all, Lancaster says, humans broke the homage they made to God at the time of their baptism,[21] and chose to enter the foul service of the devil ("pur servire l'ord vil diable d'enfern").[22] Lancaster can conceive of Christ as the victorious tourneyer who rescued his undeserving and traitorous human vassals from "everlasting, hopeless prison (prisoun sanz fin et sanz nul remede)."[23] The image is entirely compatible with that used by Étienne de Bourbon a century earlier; in one of his sermon stories this cleric refers to "Christus pugil noster (Christ our boxer or fighter)."[24]

Christus-Miles: Imitatio Christi, Imitatio Militis

Chivalric ideology adopted close parallels between Christ and knighthood and developed them to a remarkable degree, working the mimetic connection in both directions. Not only is Christ pictured as a warrior, the knights are represented as his valiant imitators. Their *imitatio Christi* parallels Christ's *imitatio militis*.

Chansons de geste made a powerful contribution by stressing the heroic and ascetic parallels: if Christ suffered combat and laid down his life willingly, so do his warrior heroes.[25] The parallel continued: in a classic case a French preacher (in the late thirteenth or early fourteenth century) explicitly compared the death of Christ to that of the great warrior Roland: both acted as great heroes, both in their combats cry out in anguish and thirst.[26] A long procession of epic heroes intone a crucial line in the formula: Christ died for us, his men; we must be ready to die for him.[27] Duke Girart notes the cost entailed in this formula and then intones the ideal in the *Chanson d'Aspremont*:

In Your most holy name, O Lord God,
I came here, Sire, for You to the battlefield of Aspremont;
So many worthy men whom I had raised,
I committed to you yesterday morning;
And here is the only homily to be drawn;
You died for us, and we should die for your sake.[28]

Vivien, the martyred hero of the early part of the *Song of William*, elaborates the ideal in this twelfth-century *chanson*. He at first prays the Blessed Mary to help him avoid death at the hands of Saracens.[29] Yet he quickly repents of this prayer and explains why.

That was the thought of a stupid fool, thinking that I could save myself from death, when the Lord God Himself didn't do it, suffering death for us on the Holy Cross to redeem us from our mortal enemies. Respite from death, Lord, I may not pray for, since You would not spare Yourself from it.[30]

Earlier in this text, Vivien has stoutly maintained his willingness to suffer for his men in battle against countless pagans; he swears he will not fail them and employs a revealing oath: "And I vow to you by God, the mighty king and by the spirit He embodied when He suffered death for sinners, I shall not fail you however hard-pressed my person."[31]

The message is equally clear in chronicle. Geoffrey of Monmouth's *History of the Kings of Britain* pictures Bishop Dubricius admonishing Arthur's men before battle, expounding the meaning of the Scriptures by shouting out from a knoll serving as pulpit:

The Sacred text teaches that Christ laid down his soul at His enemy's feet for our sake: lay down your souls for Christ's limbs, which are being torn by the insanely motivated tyranny of the Saxon people. . . . To the just man death brings glory, to the sinner eternal punishment. . . . He who has fought the good fight will be given a crown in recompense. . . . Reverence is owed to martyrs along with Christ, Himself a martyr, to Whom be glory, power, and honour for all time.

Before the sound of his words has faded, the men seize their weapons, eager for the fray.[32] Sometimes this message is delivered in language that is less direct but no less powerful. Ambroise, who wrote a poem on the crusade of Richard Lion-Heart, parallels the sufferings undergone by crusaders on particular days during Holy Week with the events of Christ's passion on those days:

> 'Twas Wednesday of the Holy Week
> When God knew pain and travail bleak
> That we, for our part, suffered
> From vigils and from fear and dread.[33]

The idea appears in both Old French and Middle English romance. Perceval states the principle clearly, late in the *Perlesvaus*, using the potent language of bodily toil and pain:

> there are no knightly deeds so fine as those done for the advancement of the Law of God, and we should toil for Him more than for anyone; for just as He exposed His body to pain and suffering and destruction for us, so must every man risk his body for Him.[34]

A later English author wrote a similar sentiment into *The Siege of Milan*, though here stated as a curse hurled by Archbishop Turpin against Charlemagne who is temporarily reluctant to join battle with Saracens:

> Christ suffered more sorely for you, grievously wounded with a spear, and wore a crown of thorns. And now you dare not enter the battlefield for to fight for him. I tell you men will hereafter think your soul lost, since you falsely abandon your law, and will call you King of Scorn.[35]

This Christ-knight link was praised as embodied in the thoroughly historical leader, King Louis IX of France. In his moving account of this king's crusade, Joinville seems almost to lift the formula straight from the page of a *chanson*. He says, "as our Lord died for the love He bore His people, even so King Louis put his own life in danger . . . for the very same reason."[36] In the dedication of his book he is even more specific about the comparison between Louis and Christ. Joinville says his king should be placed among the martyrs: while wearing the crusader's cross Louis had not only suffered grievously, he had died in Tunis, following the example of Christ who died for his men."[37]

What is more, when Joinville says Louis put his life in danger, the phrase is "mist-il son cors en avanture," literally "he put his body into adventure," using the very term, *avanture*, that summed up the questing of knights in romance.[38] This usage seems all the more significant when we read on to find Joinville say he will tell of Louis's great "chevaleries," his great feats of chivalric prowess. Joinville interprets chivalric questing as *imitatio Christi*, fighting the good fight and suffering as Christ did for his people. While the king and his men were in Muslim captivity as this disastrous crusade collapsed, we should recall that an aged and white-haired man comes to them—as so often Joinville narrates striking events but gives no explanation—and says they must not be downhearted. "For you have not yet died for him as he died for you."[39] Such imagery, moreover, was not limited to crusade settings. Across the Channel, the image of a later king of England as *miles Christi* was proclaimed in the liturgy employed in public worship. Under the guiding hand of Archbishop Chichele, these rituals presented Henry V as the victorious warrior of God in ceremony and public processions arranged for the feast days of a roster of military saints, with St. George at the head of the list.[40]

The imagery even takes on tones of courtly love service, as Christ becomes not only a knight but a lover of his lady, the church, saving her, suffering for her.[41] An explicit presentation of the Christ-knight as courtly lover was written into the Middle English *Ancrene Wisse*, probably composed in the second quarter of the thirteenth century.[42] The author (who wrote for some anchoresses from privileged families in the English West Country) sets the stage for the story that interests us by asking a question that would have warmly pleased Geoffroi de Charny: "Is not he a foolish knight who seeks rest in the fight and ease in the place of battle?"[43] He then quotes from the Book of Job the line we first encountered (at the beginning of Chapter 1) in our Harley manuscript illumination, "Milicia est vita hominis super terram," which he renders in Middle English as "Al þis lif is a feht as Iob witneð (All this life is a fight, as Job testifies)."[44] The story itself takes a romance setting: a lady is besieged in her castle by enemies who have ravaged her lands and reduced her own estate to poverty. Though a powerful king offers help and sends gifts and embassies, she foolishly rejects his offers. When the king comes in person to show her his power, tell her of his kingdom, and offer to make her his queen, she still disdains him. With selfless love the king defeats her enemies, but suffers grievously in the fight and dies of his wounds. Only by a miracle does he rise again. The text explicitly draws out the obvious meaning as an allegory of Christ's work of salvation. He is said to have shown the lady "by his knightly prowess that he should be loved."[45] He has "engaged in a tournament, and

had, for his lady's love, his shield everywhere pierced in battle, like a valorous knight."[46] This shield is actually his body, which he willing offered in
suffering. The large theological question is then asked: could he not have
achieved this victory in some less difficult way? An answer is given: he chose
this means, to give humans no excuse for not loving one who had paid so dear
a price. His shield, like that of any victorious knight, is set up prominently in
the church—in his case, it is the rood screen uplifting the cross bearing his
body, the shield-image in the poem.

The text is doubly important. Though it conveys the earliest known English Christ-knight imagery,[47] it tells its story in a manner that suggests familiarity on the part of the hearers. This imagery is not being told for the first
time. Effortlessly, courtly elements have blended with a type of soteriological *exemplum*. Moreover, as Sister Marie le May perceptively noted, this text
quotes St. Bernard more than a dozen times and states outright that "hit is
almost Seint Beornardes Sentence."[48] This reference to Bernard's ideas puts at
least the roots of the Christ-knight image back into the middle decades of the
twelfth century. Le May plausibly suggests that St. Bernard's military imagery and thoughts of king, lover, and spouse gradually took on the specificity
of the word knight in texts like this one in the thirteenth century.[49]

Twelfth-century thoughts and images derived from St. Bernard and his
Cistercian followers, picturing Christ as a knight, were redoubled by Franciscan and Dominican friars in the thirteenth and fourteenth centuries. An
"Allegorical Romance on the Death of Christ"[50] has been convincingly attributed to Nicholas Bozon, "that prolific Franciscan" of the late thirteenth
and early fourteenth centuries.[51] In a casual aside of much interest for our
inquiry, the noted Anglo-Norman scholar Dominica Legge commented that
in Henry of Lancaster's *Livre* "there are many resemblances to the Contes of
the Franciscan Nicole Bozon."[52] Ideas flowed easily between elite members of
lay and clerical society.

Widely known thirteenth-century romances made their own significant
contribution to linking the image of a Christ-like knight with the work of
salvation, or at least conversion to true religion. The *High Book of the Grail,
or Perlesvaus*, probably written in the first decade of the thirteenth century,
spills over with symbolism complex enough to snare any who would interpret
it; yet it seems safe to assert that it enthusiastically and closely sets knighthood within the context of salvation: the task confronting the knights and
heroically performed by them is establishing and upholding the New Law of

Christianity, with the hero Perceval cast in a powerfully messianic role. His fellow knights Gawain and Lancelot, late in the romance, witness his bold entry into the Turning Castle, achieved by driving his sword deeply into the gate, frightening off the fierce guarding beasts and causing the castle to stop its miraculous revolutions. Though they are themselves warned off because of its many perils, Gawain and Lancelot are fully aware of Perceval's triumph and its results:

> They drew back straightway, and there in the castle they could hear the greatest rejoicing that ever a man had heard; many were saying that the knight who had come would save them in two ways: he would save their lives and save their souls, if it pleased God to let him conquer the knight who bore the devil's spirit.[53]

The point is driven home as firmly as Perceval's sword in the gate. Prophecy, the text informs its readers, held that all the people of that castle and of the other castles of which he was guardian would worship the Old Law until the coming of the Good Knight; that is why the people of the castle said as soon as he came that the knight had arrived who would save their souls and save them from death; for the moment that he appeared they all ran to be baptized, and firmly believed in the Trinity and adopted the New Law.[54]

Of course the mountain peak of Christ-knight images in romance appeared about a decade later, in the character of Galahad written into the romances of the Vulgate Cycle. Although the setting is that of a Round Table feast, the drama presented in the *Quest for the Holy Grail* soon incorporates elements from the biblical account of the meeting of the risen Christ with his disciples in the upper room, combined with aspects of Pentecost. As a prelude to Galahad's entrance, the doors and shutters close by themselves, without darkening the hall. A venerable man dressed in white miraculously appears, leading a knight in red armor (red and white being colors associated with Christ). The guide utters the characteristic blessing of the savior: "Peace be with you."[55] The knight is Galahad, whose salvific career and actions—including the performance of miracles—will unfold in the romance. His character and achievement explicitly counterbalance the role and function of Balain, the unfortunate knightly bearer of sin, whose story is outlined elsewhere in the cycle. Balain's career tells us much about Galahad. Merlin had spoken frankly to Balain in the *Merlin Continuation*, prophesying his

Dolorous Stroke that will maim the Grail keeper with the sacred Lance of Longinus, begin the frightening marvels of the Grail, and cause so much divine wrath and destruction:

> It is my opinion that in you we have recovered our mother Eve, for just as from her deeds there resulted the great sorrow and misery by which we all pay, suffering, from day to day, so the people of three kingdoms will be impoverished and devastated by the blow that you will strike. And just as there was a prohibition against eating the dolorous fruit, so there is a prohibition from the High Master himself against doing what you will do. This sorrow will come about, not because you aren't the best knight now in the world, but because you will break the commandment no one should break and wound the man most valiant in our Lord's sight at this time in the world.[56]

In short, Galahad, the perfect knight who achieves the Grail and heals its keeper, figures Christ, undoing the terrible wrong introduced into the Arthurian world by Balain. "Since by man came death, so by man came also the way of salvation," as St. Paul wrote (1 Corinthians 15:21). Writers of romance might reasonably be considered as borrowing and rephrasing in chivalric form these famous words. This parallelism was no heresy, for Balain is no Eve and Galahad no Christ. Yet one knight calls to mind "our mother" who brought sin into the world, while the other recalls our savior who redeemed the world. The most familiar story is told with chivalric figures in the key roles. We would miss the potency of this symbolism were we to ignore the religious figuration at work.

Striking images of the Christ-knight, often including the courtly lover theme, continued to appear in the early fourteenth century in much humbler works, such as an anonymous French poem, "Comment le fiz deu fu armé en la croyz (How God's Son Was Armed on the Cross)."[57] This work even begins with the address familiar to readers of chivalric romance: "Hear now, lords, about great chivalry (Seignours ore escotez haute chiualerye)."[58] Another intriguing poem (written about the same time) that develops the Christ-knight image with particular richness was appended to a manuscript of Peter of Langtoft's chronicle. Its language is worth noting, for this is another hybrid work, blending the aventure of romance with a mini-sermon on satisfaction theology.[59] The very title given the poem by its adept nineteenth-century English editor, Thomas Wright, accurately shows the fusion: "An Allegorical

Romance on the Death of Christ."[60] A knight/king seeks to revenge himself on the traitor who led away his lady. Though he could have come in full power with an overwhelming army of horse and foot, the king wills to win back his lady by himself, as he is well qualified to do. "His name was so renowned for prowess," we learn, "that the tyrant feared his chivalry."[61] Aware that the tyrant would never consent to fight if he recognized his opponent by his proper arms, the knight takes on the armor of one of his lowly bachelors, named Adam. Slipping into his lady's chamber, he is armed by her with "very strange armor (mut estraunge armure)." His aketon (padded undercoat), for example, was pure white flesh; his armor plates were bones, his helmet a skull. Thus armed, he freely offers himself (fraunchement se profrit) to do battle against the tyrant. The gentle knight takes "many a hard blow (Maint dure assout)" at the tyrant's hands, but "suffered it a little while (un poy de temps suffrit)."[62] When the disdainful tyrant demands homage and service, the knight tells him that no serf could use force to demand service from his lord. The tyrant then tries, and fails, to tempt the knight with great gifts of lordship, but is again defied. They set a date for a new battle; they will meet on a mount, on a Friday. There the knight—"completely by his own will (tout à son ayn degré)"—mounts a warhorse with a varied coat showing four elements: cyprus, cedar, olive, and palm. It was a painful mount (trop dure), but the king persevered.[63] He is alone, having prohibited his own army from coming to his aid, to show that he alone will regain the love of his lady. Surrounded by the tyrant's entire army the king displays his white shield, his blood-red helmet and hauberk, his sword forged of an iron nail, a lance of patience. The tyrant's fierce blow penetrates the shield and inflicts five wounds. Though the tyrant thinks he has won, the knight has actually defeated all his enemies "through his prowess (par sa pruesce)." He raises his lance, now called sufferince (qui suffraunce est dist) and cuts off one of the traitor's hands. When the tyrant rips off the king's assumed armor and realizes whom he confronts, he flees in confusion.[64] The knight rescues his lady and grants her the pardon she seeks, significantly adding, "you have cost me very dear today (Vos me avez costé mut chier huy ceo jour)." He has won her, he admonishes, "by blood and sweat (par saunk e suour)." She must recognize the cost: "Look at my face, how it is bruised; / Look at my body, how it is wounded for you (Regardez ma face com est demaglé / Regardez mon corps, cum est pur vous plaié)." He sets his love in a safe place, promising to return and marry her, taking her to his palace. The poem ends with a prayer to the noble knight who won the entire human race in battle (Qe conquist en bataille tot humayne ligné).[65] The admonition to look at Christ's body "wounded for you" seems almost drawn out of the liturgy of the mass.

This text intricately twines the two major lines of soteriological thought we have examined. The lance of suffering cuts off the devil's hand: heroism and satisfaction ideas merge in the thrust of a lance blade. The cross, site of suffering, becomes a warhorse. Christ's very human, sweaty labor in the fight recalls the French lords pointedly reminding clerics that warrior sweat had brought Christian France into being.[66] Christ's bruised face calls to mind Henry of Lancaster's blunt but pious meditation on the bruised face of the figure Langland named Iesus the Jouster.[67]

Indeed, the image of Christ as knight may be best known from Passus 18 of William Langland's *Piers Plowman* (written 1377–79), within a generation after our model knights Lancaster and Charny. Already in Passus 16 in the B text of that work, Langland has said that Christ must joust to settle "by judgment of arms whether Piers's fruit should be taken by the Devil or Christ."[68] Christ then "jousted in Jerusalem, a joy for us all."[69] Passus 18 specifies, in famous language, that Christ "will joust in Piers's armor / In his helmet and hauberk, human nature."[70] The fierceness of their fight will be registered in the natural world by earthquakes and unnatural darkness.

Heroic and sacrificial notions twist and intertwine like flourishing vines. Literary texts have provided one connection between such ideas and knighthood. Surviving sermons show another route by which ideas could reach many who never read them directly. A Latin sermon, very close in theme to Friar Bozon's poem, was written in the late thirteenth century by the Dominican Gui d'Evreux. A similar Latin sermon from the early fourteenth century was written by the Franciscan Albert of Metz.[71] One work in a collection of sermon tales by Odo of Cheriton from the mid-thirteenth century[72] again presents Christ as an armed knight who has engaged in what is once more specified as the hard, bloody work of knights; he has entered into battle and has emerged victorious. Yet he wins by suffering. His knightly lance is called both Patience and Sufferance (as in our in our opening Harley manuscript). Once again Devil's Right theology blends with satisfaction theory to form the amalgam that is so important to the ideology of chivalry.

The trail of known sermons leads in the direction of others long lost or obscure. One of a set compiled about mid-fourteenth century (preserved in Merton College, Oxford), and intended for popular consumption, familiarly refers to "that sermon about the round table (illo sermone de rotunda tabula)." At least five manuscripts refer to this theme.[73] The most complete example, copied in a fifteenth-century preacher's notebook, unmasks the meaning of this tantalizing reference. The preacher's aim is to explain an obscure theological point: why the Son, rather than the Father or Holy Spirit, was made incarnate for human salvation, a theme Anselm could have appreciated. All three persons of the Trinity, the text explains, "can be called knights of the Round Table, because all are equal in virtue and power." But the devil challenged the Son, like a knight at a festive joust called a round table, that is, a tournament in which one knight would touch the displayed shield of another to initiate combat.[74] "Therefore it was fitting that the Son descend and defend his shield and fight with the devil."[75] These Round Table sermons go off in a particular direction, explaining a somewhat esoteric theological question. Yet they significantly adopt practices of Arthurian chivalry in claiming that all persons of the Trinity could be compared to jousting knights.

Throughout the remainder of the Middle Ages evidence is abundant and unambiguous.[76] In the last quarter of the fourteenth century, a Middle English sermon meant for the laity pictures Christ as a knight conquering a giant (the devil) who has captured and imprisoned his father's servants (humanity). The preacher declares that sinful humans were won in battle by Christ's powerful death on the cross.[77]

Even the book of advice for his daughters written by a French knight in 1371, only about a decade after the deaths of Charny and Lancaster (and printed in English translation by Caxton in 1483) uses the same knightly imagery for Christ's passion. The author, the Chevalier de la Tour Landry, adds to a story about a knight selflessly saving an accused woman that he acted "As did the sweet Jesus Christ who fought for the pity of us and of all humanity."[78] A poisoned apple enters the story (perhaps borrowing from the Arthurian tradition of Queen Guenever), but there can be no doubt of the allegory. The Chevalier makes all plain. In Caxton's translation,

> And thus for compassion and nobility the gentle knight fought and suffered five mortal wounds, as the sweet Jesus Christ did, who fought out of pity for us and all humanity. He had great compassion lest they fall into the shadows of Hell; thus he alone suffered and fought the terribly hard and cruel battle on the tree of Holy Cross. His shirt of mail was broken and pierced in five places, namely his five grievous wounds received of his free will in his sweet body for pity of us and all humanity.[79]

Whatever the overlaps in soteriological ideas, the persistence of two major theories of salvation and their frequent fusion remain highly informative. Christ's prowess joins his suffering. Knightly imaginations could readily identify with each, for the warriors could picture themselves triumphing with the victorious savior as *milites Christi* and suffering like him in hard chivalric life that was a form of *imitatio Christi*. Their good work was modeled on Christ's salvific sufferings emphasized in satisfaction theology.

Painful awareness of distortions and paradoxes must have struck some thoughtful observers then as they will now. Cultural alternating current of high voltage easily leaped the gaps between opposed ideas. Movement was constant and rapid in both directions. If the knights piously performed *imitatio Christi*, their tendency was to clothe Christ in military dress. The model of the heroic, nonviolent life had lost its key qualifier. If the historical consequences can be debated, the benefits to knighthood were undoubted. This will be apparent, in the next chapter, in the notion of the chivalric as forming an *ordo*, with sacred work to perform in the divine plan.

CHAPTER 7

Knighthood and the New Lay Theology: *Ordines* and Labor

Knights' Tales: William Mauvoisin and Owen in Saint Patrick's Purgatory

Twelfth- and thirteenth-century European culture ordered, analyzed, and classified the social world, no less than the natural world, in an effort to align human society with the will of God. They wanted to identify ideal social categories and to define the proper labor to be performed by each. Given the social and cultural ferment of the time, such an effort could scarcely avoid contention. Given the social status and the particular labor performed by knighthood, the warriors would often stand near the center of this vigorous discussion. Two splendid stories from the twelfth century can take us directly into this search for order in society and meaning in labor.

One story was set down on parchment around 1133 by Benedictine monks who denounced the very profession of knighthood in the course of narrating a quarrel over property.[1] "How William Mauvoisin [literally William the Bad Neighbor] Became a Monk (De Guillelmo Malevicino monacho facto)" was a story the monks of Notre Dame of Coulombs (in the diocese of Chartres) obviously liked to tell. The written record would preserve their version of a series of events important to them.[2] It is a tale of an outstanding knight (miles optimus) who is grievously wounded in a war between two local lords.[3] Sharply spurred by the fear of death, William hurried to this monastic church where he offered himself as a monk, was accepted, and, so the monks reported, tirelessly engaged in pious discourse about the monastic life.[4] Significantly, he offered more than his personal conversion. If only God would allow him to recover from his wounds and give him time for penitence, William vowed he would found a chapel in the castle of Mantes in honor of another reformed sinner, St. Mary Magdalen. He cleared a path for the realization of this promise of a propertied gift by securing approval from lay and ecclesiastical authorities at every level: the king of France, the bishop of Chartres, and the canons of Mantes (canonicis ipsius villae). God was gracious, we learn, and William recovered. But then humans intervened: he was swiftly taken by relatives from the monastery to the city of Chartres on the pretext that he could get better medical care there ("sub occasione quod medicamina sibi necessaria apud Columbas invenire non possent, quae Carnoti copiosè invenirent"). In fact, he was "slipped out and seduced (ductus et seductus)" by them, says the monastic writer tersely and judgmentally. Won over by the entreaties of his worldly relatives, that is, William agreed that new arms and armor should be made for him. Throwing aside the shabby habit of a monk and resuming secular garb, he mounted a great warhorse and stretched out his hand to take once again his knightly shield. It was a mistake. At once divine wrath struck him with fire in the old wound that he had thought fully healed. Raving, William rushed back to the sanctity of the cloister, hurrying to the nearest monastery: but he could not avert divine judgment, even though he became a monk again—of St. Peter, Chartres, under profession of Notre Dame of Coulombs—and even though he showed sorrow and contrition in his bodily affliction. He died, our monastic author triumphantly insists, on the very day he gave up the profession of a monk and, forgetting spiritual warfare, returned to mere warfare in the world. William had been a powerful man in local society; he received the monastic burial he craved; but hopes for his fate in the afterworld cannot have been high. God is not easily deceived. Wishing to aid the departed soul as much as he could ("de ejus anima sollicitus, vel volens supplere, in quantum poterat"), Samson, William's brother (an important cleric—at that time provost of the church of Chartres and later archbishop of Reims), consulted with King Louis, Geoffrey, bishop of Chartres, and the canons, in order to secure the dedication of the church in Mantes to Mary Magdalen, thus fulfilling his brother's expiatory promise in this world. The goal, obviously, was to soften his punishment in the next.

We can see that the monks' interest in the tale was twofold. At the most apparent level it established the circumstances of a donation important to them; the church of St. Mary Magdalen at Mantes was to be a dependent of the monastery of Coulombs ("quae esset sub ditione Columbensis ecclesiae"). Yet the rich detail provided—especially divine wrath striking William just as he reaches out for the emblematic knightly shield—suggests that broadly ideological as well as propertied interests are being buttressed in this story. Not only is the sanctity of a vow to follow the monastic profession reinforced, the monastic life itself is once more shown to be superior to mere warfare in the world. Though he sadly lost sight of this after his initial fearful and temporary conversion, William, we must assume, fully realized the severe spiritual dangers inherent in his life as a knight by the time he died in terror, having perhaps too late returned to the cloister, "raving (desaeviente)." This little story makes a large point about the spiritual perils of knighthood, even as it speaks to the security and superiority of monastic life or the possession of a particular piece of property. The knightly shield William bore in this story decidedly carried no names of the trinity or of the Godhead, as in the idealized Harley manuscript illumination of the mid-thirteenth century examined at the opening of this book. Clerical ideas about knighthood and its characteristic labor could be more critical than idealistic and supportive.[5]

A second story gives insight into knightly views on these issues. It is a curious and highly popular tale from the late twelfth century, the *Tractatus de Purgatorio Sancti Patricii* (*Treatise on Saint Patrick's Purgatory*).[6] It is, of course, a clerical text in the sense that the original *Tractatus* was written in Latin, apparently by a Cistercian monk (a Henry or Hugh of Saltry), but we will see that it conveys strongly held knightly ideals—in fact, that it presents them with much confidence.[7] Mirroring the developing knightly ideology in general, this text combines exultation of their *ordo* with ideas of pious atonement through the hard practice of their characteristic labor. It was popular and widely read. Numerous Latin copies of the full account have survived and verbatim extracts or abbreviated accounts were copied into various Latin chronicles and collections of saints' lives and miracles.[8] Translations brought the story into many vernacular languages, including Old French and Middle English.[9] By the thirteenth century the story, at least as told in outline, had even been condensed into a sermon *exemplum* and thus found its way to a yet broader audience.[10] Especially interesting, the creative translation into French by Marie de France in the late twelfth century, *Espurgatoire Saint Patriz*, must have reached a wide lay readership. Thus we will consider two texts simultaneously (supplementing them with others as seems useful): Hugh's

Tractatus and Marie's *Espurgatoire*. They tell the story of the knight Owen (Owain, Owein) and explain his motivation with frankness in a story aptly characterized as an instant medieval bestseller.[11]

Of his own pious volition, Owen determined to carry out an enterprise at once heroically bold and piously atoning: he will enter the pit on Station Island in Lough Derg, County Donegal, Ireland, a place traditionally considered an earthly gateway into purgatory. In short, he would bravely enter purgatory while still alive. The monastic author claims that the story of this exploit came from Owen himself and that he got it through a single intermediary. The knight's visit to the dread site supposedly took place around mid-twelfth century. Marie's translation may have appeared around 1190, shortly after the composition of the Latin account.

This account can be taken in one sense as an extended *exemplum*, presenting clerical ideas about sin and purgation in general. Yet in another sense it represents a chivalric tale of *aventure*, that is, a tale of the sort of knightly adventurous questing that emerges from the tradition of romance writing—a tradition that always drew upon very human and physical brave deeds and endurance as much as any spiritual dimension.[12] We are given the significant information that Owen wished to atone for sins that troubled him and that had provoked clerical denunciation. The Middle English text suggests that the sins of this "tough and powerful young man (douhti man and swathe wight)" have been martial: "He knew much of battle and without doubt was quite sinful against his creator."[13] Marie says he had "labored against God with his great cruelty (kar mult aveit sovent ovré / cuntre Dieu en grant cruëlté)."[14] We are told in the Latin text that Owen "manfully (virilis animi)"[15] brushed aside the bishop's warnings of great dangers and entered the purgatory, "wishing to undertake a novel and unusual act of chivalry (nouam et inusitatam cupiens exercere militiam)."[16] In Marie's account, Owen makes this declaration as he rejects the traditional penance imposed by the bishop. He announces,

> Lord Bishop, I do not want
> To expiate my sins easily
> Nor endure such a penance.
> Too much have I transgressed against my Lord,
> And offended my Creator.
> Accordingly I would choose, by your leave,
> The most heavy penance.[17]

The motivation and even the language convey important ideas about chivalry, its labor, and penitence. Owen wants to expiate his wrongs by a physically heroic penance to match his very physical sins—his wrongful labors—of admitted cruelty. The bishop tries, instead, to get him to enter a monastery, Marie says, arguing that course to be "more certain (plus seürement)."[18] To this traditional solution, Owen answers stoutly that he "would not do that. / He would take no habit / Besides the one he had."[19] The language is worth noting. A habit marks an *ordo*; Owen is stating his determination to remain in the *ordo* of chivalry and to seek expiation and salvation through pious work as a knight. He knows, of course, that it will involve suffering (peine).[20] Though he confessed to the bishop in good form, he has chosen his own mode of penance against the bishop's advice, and he insured that it was truly and corporally heroic, as the account of his visit to purgatory will make terrifyingly plain.

As he prepares for this chivalric sortie into purgatory, wise and helpful religious men warn Owen that he must be vigorous and valorous: "you are perforce compelled to act manfully or else you will die body and soul because of your inaction."[21] Putting his body at risk as a knight will have determinative influence on the fate of his soul, no less than his body. He tells the clerics that in order to please God he would not "flinch from suffering, / Pain, and torment."[22] Owen, "who in the past had bravely fought men," is now instructed in what the clerics consider a new kind of chivalry ("ad novi generis militiam instructus") and is "now ready to give battle bravely to demons."[23] The Harley manuscript illumination (used to open this book) comes once again to mind, with its ranks of vile demons massing against the ideal knight, who is armed and ready for the fight. Only the specific spiritual meanings given to Owen's weaponry differ: he is armed with the breastplate of justice, the helmet of hope, the shield of faith, and grips the sword of the spirit.[24] Owen repeatedly invokes the name of Christ, as he has been admonished, to escape the torments that a host of howling demons will inflict on him. He is "Christ's knight (le chevaliers Ihesucrist)."[25] In this case, however, the designation decidedly does not mean entry into a religious order. We might even say that in place of doing the *opus Dei* of the monks in cloistered asceticism and prayer, he is doing the heroic work God demands of him as a knight.

The demons begin their dread work by dragging Owen with iron hooks back and forth through a huge, blazing bonfire built especially for his benefit. But he proves himself a true "soldier of Christ" and demonstrates "spiritual chivalry" as the fiends try to break his steadfast resistance with this and each succeeding torment. They show him the horrifically physical punishments being inflicted on sinners who have been consigned to their domain. He endures blasts of heat and numbing cold gales, sees sinners spiked to the ground, dunked in molten metal, turned on a great wheel blazing with fire, to which the fiends attach him, too. He must cross a perilous, narrow bridge over a stinking river teeming with demons trying to dislodge him. Persevering steadfastly, Owen finally comes to the Earthly Paradise beyond purgatory, sees the shining gateway to the Celestial Paradise from afar—a gateway he can hope to pass through after his death. He then manfully returns through purgatory to the beginning point, the pit opening onto earth. He has escaped with life and soul inviolate, and returned to human life. He becomes a crusader and a friend to Cistercians.

The clerical agenda is clear. This is a classic account of purgatory, drawing on many existing texts and traditions. Yet we cannot miss the references to his *ordo* and its labor, or the romance element in this wonderfully hybrid text, for all these emphasize the knight's adventure, his courage and steadfastness in suffering "manfully (viriliter)" as a stout knight who is told that he can thereby be "purified of his sins (ut a peccatis tuis purgeris)."[26] The statement that Owen fought as a crusader after his return to the world is appended as a brief coda to the main work; playing the crusader is the result of his penitential suffering as a brave knight, not its sole or even its primary exercise. He is secure in his own knightly *ordo*. Marie de France pictures the knight upon his return from purgatory asking his king if he should now enter a religious order.

But the king answered

> That he should remain as he was, a knight.
> He counseled him to retain this station
> So that he might serve God well
> And so he did for the rest of his life.[27]

Marie underscores this important point near the end of her poem. Gilbert, a prominent Cistercian, has come to Ireland and finds he needs a local translator; Owen fills that need, but would go no further, would not leave his *ordo*:

> He remained with Gilbert,
> And served him well.
> Yet he did not wish to change his station,

Becoming either a monk or lay brother:
He would die a knight,
And would never take any other habit.[28]

Owen will not play William Mauvoisin by seeking salvation within a cloister. The ideas imbedded in chivalric literature—in this instance a generation of epic and romance writing—have left their clear mark on the relationship of chivalry to satisfaction theology through the labor of its own *ordo*. The venerable genealogy of ideas we found in Henry of Lancaster and Geoffroi de Charny again manifests itself in sources nearly two centuries earlier. If he read or heard the account of Owen's bold, knightly deed, as seems likely, Geoffroi de Charny could only have approved so resolute an assertion of the knightly order, so fine a demonstration that its labor provides bodily repayment to God.

Sacred Social Orders and the Value of Labor

Medieval society never actually divided simply into those who pray, those who fight, and those who work, the *oratores*, *bellatores*, and *laboratores* beloved of conservative clerical writers in the Middle Ages.[29] It was not a schema accepted and used by all learned analysts. Clerics actually proposed a great variety of frameworks for conceptually organizing society, based on varying numbers of component groups and the labors proper to each. Yet behind all variety medieval thinkers generally pictured a social world rightly structured on categories reflecting a divine plan. They had long applied to certain vocations the term *ordo*, meaning a division of society that was sacred in that God desired its existence and had ordained its appropriate labor as essential for human society.[30] They also used other terms, such as *status, ministerium, officium*, sometimes as synonyms for *ordo*, sometimes to indicate a profession for whose existence and labor divine approval was more problematic.[31] Clerical opinion on the broad subject of identifying groups that properly constituted Christian society and labor was not monolithic or unvarying.

One powerful reason for the diversity is not far to seek: an increasingly complex High Medieval society required and generated a variety of ideas on social groups and labor. It is important to note both what changed and what remained unmoved. Two *ordines* from the trifunctional scheme—the *oratores* and the *bellatores*—continued to dominate the highest levels of the social pyramid, supported by assertions of divine approval. Medieval scholars never doubted that collectively (and in each of their many subdivisions) clerics formed an *ordo* (or a set of *ordines*), doing God's work on earth. Over time (and sometimes with weighty reservations) writers and thinkers made the same claim for the warriors—knighthood, too, was an *ordo* with an ideal labor intended in God's plan. As urban and mercantile elements in society grew rapidly in number and influence, the prominence of new lay groups demanded further analytical subdivision and much moral guidance. Clerics realized that they could not deal with an undifferentiated laity as merely a bloc of nonclerics, a lumpish *ordo* of *labores*, to use trifunctional terminology. Since lay folk lived their lives and did their work in a variety of social and professional groups, an effective pastoral theology would have to address these occupations as working components of the church.

Such analysis might theoretically elaborate a relatively new and positive view of worldly labor. Commenting on the Carolingian era, Carl Erdmann observed, "as yet, the ethical theories propounded by churchmen generally failed to take into account 'professional life,' whether that of a class of warriors or anyone else's."[32] The need was for a list of licit lay vocations and a vocational morality for each. At first the search would not yield neat or consistent results, even at the hands of medieval clerics accustomed to analytical subdivision of any issue confronting them. The list of *ordines*, *status*, and other licit socio-professional groups remained flexible, varying from one writer to another. Some thinkers kept the threefold idea, but divided humankind along the lines of sexuality—the virgins, the continent, and the married. Some mixed sacred and social categories, such as the division into nobles, clerics, laymen, husbandmen, and women; or into clerics, monks, peasants, paupers, and "all men."[33] The twelfth-century nun and visionary Elisabeth of Schönau (d.1164/65), pictured Christian society clustered as the married, the celibate, prelates, widows, hermits, and children.[34] Jacques de Vitry (d. 1240) thought in terms of clerics, priests, married people, widows, virgins, soldiers, merchants, peasants, craftsmen, and "other types of men."[35] At the end of the twelfth century, John of Freiburg listed questions for confession to be directed to fourteen lay and clerical *status*.[36] As we have seen (in Chapter 2), Geoffroi de Charny, one of our model knightly authors, borrowed either from the clerics or from his own imagination a set of four statuses: priests, monks, the married, and the knights.[37] In all this variety, all writers considered the knights to be one fundamentally constitutive social group.

Clerical intellectuals worried about the morality of labor performed within their designated social groups, at least where lay folk were concerned. Modern scholars have debated the result. Most have long argued that the twelfth and thirteenth centuries brought about a clear change in thought: some have even suggested a revolutionary change. They argue that earlier medieval views contrary to the dignity of human labor gave way to valorization.[38] If performed carefully, honestly, and humbly, in obedience to divine will, work was acceptable to God, even the work of lay men and women. They were not barred from salvation by their work and indeed might advance their spiritual state through labor. Admonition accompanied this cautious acceptance, of course. If clerics sanctified each ideal group and its role, they also castigated all its besetting sins. Especially after 1200, critiques were funneled through a standard type of sermon called *sermo ad status* or *sermo vulgaris* (a sermon addressed to lay occupational groups). Crafting such religious appeals and warnings to specific groups of people was widespread. In the early twelfth century, Honorius of Autun wrote sermons for various status groups: clerics, judges, the rich, the poor, *milites*, peasants, and married folk.[39] In the mid-thirteenth century, Humbert of Romans, master general of the Dominicans, published several collections of sermons, each containing a hundred models for use by preachers who wished to speak specifically to—or at least about—certain social groups and their activities. Local clerics preparing sermons could likewise mine those of Jacques de Vitry for their useful *exempla* relating to characteristic social groups and their labor.[40]

The clerical view does seem to be broadening and positive. Medieval university scholars who produced model sermons sometimes made elevated claims for ordinary work. Jacques de Vitry, for example, granted that those who work hard and honestly at their toil are valued by God as much as those who sing all day in church or keep watch throughout the night in prayer.[41] He thinks good work is a duty for all. Humbert of Romans added that work helps all—even the rich and the clerics—avoid the sin of idleness (*otium*).[42] Endured patiently in a licit cause, almost any suffering by medieval people could be thought to bring spiritual merit, redeeming the faults of the sinner.[43] At maximum, good lay folk in every profession could work toward salvation. As the twelfth-century writer Gerhoh of Reichersberg asserted, "every profession . . . has a rule adapted to its character, and under this rule it is possibly by striving properly to achieve the crown of glory."[44] We have already seen that Geffroi de Charny made this very claim for knighthood in his mid-fourteenth-century treatise.

This line of evaluation continued throughout the Middle Ages. An even more positive interest in human work of all sorts appears in a classic late medieval work. In Book 4 of John Gower's *Confessio Amantis*, written at the end of the fourteenth century, sloth, we learn, is prohibited by all law.[45] Moreover, Gower attributes to Solomon the Wise the idea of the naturalness of human labor: "As birds are made for flight, so is man for work."[46] Work is necessary for those who think "for to thryve,"[47] and present folk should recognize the splendid achievements of past labors, both manual and mental, which could scarcely be reproduced, Gower thinks, in the present. These feats came from human effort under divine blessing. The use of metals, for example, was found "Thurgh mannes wit and Goddes grace."[48] Gower provides a long list of discoverers and inventors that he finds worthy of remembrance.

A variety of forms of human work, scholarly tradition holds, were to some degree accepted by medieval ecclesiastics; clerics recognized that work was necessary for a well-ordered society; it was also useful for helping individuals to practice humility and avoid the snares of sin, baited by idleness. Some churchmen attractively saw human labor as generating wealth beyond subsistence needs, thus providing the wherewithal for charity.

This emphasis on the positive clerical evaluation of labor undoubtedly catches one important dimension of emerging clerical thought. Yet the emphasis has recently provoked sharp criticism. The revisionist work of a Dutch scholar, Birgit van den Hoven, stresses these cautions. She and other scholars argue for a divergence of ideas on this basic theological question.[49] In place of ready agreement and a linear progression of validating ideas, they find a significant ideological divide; medieval thinkers writing on labor showed no unanimity, sometimes even no consistency within single authors. George Ovitt, Jr., comments succinctly on these contradictions:

> God ennobled work by doing it himself; God punished postlapsarian man by making him earn his bread in the sweat of his brow. Nature was intended for man's use; nature is to be cared for and emulated by man. Monks must labor with their hands; monks must be preoccupied with the opus Dei (i.e., prayer and contemplation).[50]

The case made by revisionists commands attention. Any thought of ideas shifting in a single and progressive direction, of a revolutionary triumph for a positive theology of labor, should be viewed with caution. For work is, finally, valued by many medieval churchmen, not for itself or what it produced, but because it is considered penitential: it is hard enough and demands enough submission and sacrifice to entail suffering and thus become a form of penance. Labor not only produced a dampening effect on inherent human sinfulness but through suffering achieved a redemptive effect. The point is made concisely in a collection of Middle English homilies by John Mirk. One of these warns that, "whoever would escape the judgment at the Second Coming . . . must work his body in good works and supply his bodily needs with labor, and put away all idleness and sloth. For whoever will not work on earth with men, as St. Bernard says, will labor with the devils of hell."[51]

Labor is here a substitute, endured on earth, for the pains imposed in the afterlife for sin. Similarly, in Old French literature it is striking how often the verbs "travailler (to work)" and "pener (to suffer)" appear together.[52]

Another layer of caution is useful. The churchmen are, of course, far from any taint of genuine egalitarianism in their thinking on labor. They maintained an ideal hierarchy of occupations, with themselves naturally at the top and the others, with declining elements of spirituality, ranked in descending order.[53] Even John Gower, whose positive evaluation of human labor we have noted, ranked the work of the mind well above work of the hands:

> Labor with the hands is productive, such that in daily life and actions a man might be able to live. But he who for the sake of wisdom [doctrine causa] bears labors in the mind prevails further and obtains perpetual merit.[54]

Moreover, it is hard to extract even minimal acceptance from the ecclesiastics for some professions ineradicably embedded in society. They remained worried about the knights and were deeply concerned and censorious in particular about merchants, whom they denounce as "usurers" with a vigor we will discuss below.

It is interesting to speculate on how most lay folk would have understood the story of the fall of humanity in the Garden of Eden as told in Genesis. Whatever softening might come from progressive theologians, would not the more negative evaluation of ordinary labor linger as the message to be drawn from the punishment of Adam and Eve? It would be easy to miss the subtleties—God's good labor of creation, man's joyful prelapsarian labor—and concentrate on physical work imposed as a consequence of sin, even as a punishment for sin. This seems the message that would stand out dramatically. Adam and Eve are not only exiled from the Garden of Eden; Adam is also condemned to earn his bread by the sweat of his brow and Eve is to bear children in pain, as another species of penitential labor of the body.[55] During a theological discussion in the *Song of Aspremont*, for example, the expulsion from paradise and the need for human labor are linked to sin: of Adam the author says, "his paradise he lost and had to leave / and work to live."[56] Work always retained a certain penitential character in the thought of many medieval churchmen and many who listened to them.

Rather than a simple division into two clear analytical camps on the value of labor, there was likely a spectrum of views that clustered at opposite ends of a scale calibrating its value. Far from a new religious valorization of labor sweeping away an older sense of labor as penitence, we find sets of contending ideas that coexisted in clerical culture generally and may even have intermixed in single minds. Work could be valued for its social, charitable, and individual benefits; but it was often cherished as a cause of commendable personal hardship and suffering, even as a form of penance for wrongs committed. Perhaps this split is deeply rooted in human nature. The Latin noun *laborare*, after all, carries the meaning of both work and of suffering. The duality might be understood and appreciated even among dedicated modern professionals by five o'clock on a Friday afternoon. Yet asceticism marked medieval culture to a remarkable degree and left its heavy imprint on views of labor.

An ethical evaluation of the labor performed by the knightly order was an obviously crucial element of the much more general discussion of lay labor. In fact, it presented an undeniably special case for analysis. The knights' labor was fighting: essential and dangerous work, both morally and socially. The tools might seem unusual, the work sometimes glorious, sometimes distressing; yet work it was. As a medieval French proverb plainly asserted, "no good work could come from a knight without a sword, a clerk without a book, or a laborer without tools."[57] In their treatises (examined in Chapter 2) Lancaster and Charny repeatedly employ some form of the noun "work," or the verb "to work." As these authors suggest, knights work the body physically; they perform hard and perilous labor. Though wary of sin, they considered their labor pleasing to God. Such a view likely commanded general agreement among proud warriors. Clerics were necessarily of more than one mind and both defended and deplored the labor carried out by knights on campaign and battlefield. Debate over violence and war occupied many medieval minds.[58] The very existence of a moral debate rather than a single clerical position is important; and it worked within a context of continuing general discussion of accepted lay groups and labor.

The knights, as usual, got the best of two worlds. Most socio-professional groups involved in hard physical labor merited a lower level of regard in the minds and blueprints of scholars who unsurprisingly placed much greater value on intellectual work. Yet knightly ideology carried out one of its characteristic intellectual coups in securing high spiritual merit for the truly physical work done with their hands. In most clerical schemes such work, *opus manuum* (work done by hand), clearly suffers from this taint. The work of prayer and contemplation, the *opus Dei*, drawing on knowledge of Latin and liturgy, could be managed only by those of status who so often did no manual labor. The knights undoubtedly performed hands-on labor, but unlike most manual work it won them spiritual benefits, not to mention high praise and towering piles of loot. Exercising prowess was their highly valued *opus manuum*. Chivalric literature is full of specific, exulting references in which knights insist that they have won victories by cutting down opponents with their own hands; such work, they know, insures imperishable honor in this world and an appreciative reception in the next.[59] They will not accept that this manual work brings reduced merit. In his authorized biography of the great knight William Marshal, the author reflects at one point on the nobility of the work of chivalry in comparison with other labor:

> What is armed combat? Is it the same
> as working with a sieve or winnow,
> with an axe or mallet?
> Not at all, it is much nobler work,
> For he who undertakes these tasks is able to take a rest
> When he has worked for a while.
> What, then, is chivalry?
> Such a difficult, tough,
> And very costly thing to learn
> That no coward ventures to take it on.[60]

The inversion of the clerical view is striking. Far from encouraging humility as the antidote to swelling pride, the knights' particular form of work inflates a well-fed sense of their superiority and rectitude. The characteristic labor of their *ordo* establishes them at the top of lay society; it gives them a platform from which to compare their status even with that of the churchmen, as we saw so plainly in the treatise of Geoffroi de Charny.

Charny spoke for his *ordo* in declaring one of their clearest and most constant assertions: God has graciously granted their much-valued prowess and regularly ordains their victories. These claims for a blessed labor could scarcely be labeled extreme by critics. Did not the holy fathers address them as the order of *bellatores*? Did not clerical writers find the determinative agency of God on every battlefield? Charny's own piety intersected with a long clerical tradition to yield his intense belief that prowess is a divine gift for which the knight must be ever thankful.

Some works of imaginative literature even picture the very hand of God guiding and strengthening a knight's hand as his sword executes its valorous slashes.[61] And even the prosaic chronicler who told of the Anglo-Norman invasion of Ireland in the late twelfth century repeatedly assured readers that the victories of his heroes came by divine grace; he is certain that they left thousands of their enemies vanquished on one particular field "through the force and power that the good Jesus granted them."[62]

Yet abundant evidence also emphasizes that the knightly form of work was bitterly hard, involving undoubted deprivation on campaign and the possibility of injury or death in brutal close combat, with weapons honed to a good cutting edge. This suffering allows the knights to claim penitential merit, as we have seen. Their situation is utterly unlike others who work by their hands, as William Marshal's biographer emphasized. The patient farmer bent over his spade in cold muck and rain, like the humble cobbler bent over the torn shoe on his bench, must know he is doing God's will and accept that each physical ache and each hour of resignation will be toted up for the final spiritual accounting.[63] The knight on his great warhorse waiting to charge might feel anxiety, but could also experience the adrenalin rush of impending battle; if he wins, he is richer and more honored. If he suffers wounds or even death, he has repaid God a part of the debt for sin by his hard labor in a good cause. Chivalric ideology again takes on powerful form by drawing on complex theological ideas and shaping them to its profession.

The theological divide—or spectrum of view—over orders and their labor offered a golden opportunity in the use of the power of paradox. From a rich quarry, knightly ideology could extract rock-solid ideas that justified their particular status and work. Or, to use an image they might prefer, they planted a mailed foot firmly on each side of the line of debate in order to lay claim to benefits from each while carefully avoiding limitations of either.[64] This highly selective process would be repeated.

Knighthood as an *Ordo*

In 1114 a church council meeting at Beauvais deprived Thomas of Marle, an infamous evildoer, of his *cingulum militarem*, literally his belt of knight-hood.[65] A man difficult to constrain, he had to be condemned in absentia. Yet this symbolic deprivation retains significance, for it was meant publicly to exclude him from the military *ordo* which he was thought to have dis-graced by flagrant and rapacious behavior.[66] Linked more to past practices than future actions, this ecclesiastical censure recalls Carolingian precedents of several centuries earlier. Legislation enacted in synods and councils of the ninth century had declared that warriors guilty of grave crimes were to be deprived of military standing; these decrees apparently led to effective action. As Carl Leyser commented (in presenting this evidence), chivalry had "mani-fold roots," some of which reach back into the Carolingian past.[67]

Granting the likelihood of earlier roots, many scholars argue that chiv-alry emerged more clearly in the later twelfth century.[68] It is noteworthy that references to a knightly order multiply in surviving sources from the mid to late twelfth century. The danger lurks of mistaking the better survival of evi-dence for an increased sociocultural phenomenon, but the sheer number and variety of references finally cannot be gainsaid. Speaking of knighthood as an *ordo* becomes almost reflexive in the words uttered or written by knights no less than by clerical intellectuals. A few references can indicate this trend, though the goal must be to observe an important process unfold, rather than to isolate each datable reference.

If Guibert of Nogent referred (at roughly the same time as the condem-nation of Thomas of Marle) to crusaders, at least, as an *ordo equestris* (an order of mounted fighters), much more interesting is the self-description of English knights in 1138 as reported in a chronicle; they told a high cleric before a battle with the Scots to leave the fighting to them "as their ordo required (sicut il-lorum ordo exigebat)."[69] Only a few years later, Abbot Suger, in his account of the deeds of the French king Louis VI, referred easily to a young man as "well versed in the pursuits of the knightly order."[70]

By the second half of the twelfth century, the Geiger counter of relevant evidence begins to click more regularly. John of Salisbury, writing just after mid-century, considered knighthood—not merely Templars or crusaders—a licit profession intended in the divine plan.[71] Even an early administrative treatise, the *Dialogus de Scaccario*, written in 1179, recognizes that knighthood is characterized by a collective honor that sharply constrains royal officials in dealing with its individual members.[72] Though the first redaction of the *Moniage Guillaume* (William in the Monastery), from about 1150, has little to say about the knightly order, the second redaction of this *chanson*, written about 1180 (as we will see) devotes lengthy conversations to a highly favorable comparison of the knightly *ordo* with that of the monks.[73] We have already noted the view of the knight Owen (in the tale of St. Patrick's Purgatory) that the military order is fully sufficient for a pious warrior. Chrétien de Troyes in his *Perceval*, probably written before 1191, famously refers to chivalry as *le plus haut ordre* that God has ordained and made.[74] Considering the disorderly conduct of his knightly nephews, a contemporary cleric, Peter of Blois, bitterly complained, "The order of *milites* now is not to keep order."[75] Alan of Lille also weighed in on the critical clerical side in his sermon *Ad Milites*,[76] which refers to the belt of knighthood, the *cingulum*, as the outward sign of knighthood; he declares hopefully that it must be a symbol of a true, inner knighthood. At the same time the bishop of Rennes, Étienne de Fougeres, in his *Livre des Manieres* asserted the validity of the knightly order, but added warnings. The knight, he wrote,

> can save himself in his order
> If nothing is found to cause him remorse.
> But if he wants to murder traitorously
> Or deceitfully steal or kill,
> Then he must indeed be expelled from the order
> Have his sword removed, be harshly punished
> Spurs removed
> And be thrown out from among the knights.[77]

The bishop who penned these lines looked at knights with unblinkered vision. But it is worth noting that even the disqualifying sins are violations of the true form of lay "labor" within the order.

Through the early decades of the thirteenth century, references to the knightly order mount in the influential Vulgate or Lancelot-Grail Cycle of prose romances. The term appears only once or twice in the romance composed first, the *Lancelot* (c. 1215–20), and again just occasionally appears in the *Story of Merlin* (after 1230); but this vocabulary increases dramatically in the *Quest of the Holy Grail* (c. 1225–30), with about a dozen references, and in the *History of the Holy Grail* (after 1230), with more than two dozen references. The usage continues in continuations such as the Post-Vulgate *Merlin* and *Quest*.[78] Sometimes these texts even enthusiastically refer to chivalry as the noble order or the high order. By about 1220, a clerical treatise has appeared under the title *Ordene de chevalerie* (The Order of Chivalry); the treatise urged churchmen to recognize the merits of chivalry and the debts Christian society owed it.[79] Ramon Lull's highly popular treatise significantly entitled *The Book of the Order of Chivalry* appeared in about 1280. Henry of Lancaster and Geoffroi de Charny in mid-fourteenth century had no doubts that they were members of a sanctified *ordo*. Their fifteenth-century fellow knight and fellow author Thomas Malory could scarcely restrain his praise for what he repeatedly termed the "hyghe ordre of chivalry."

Ceremonial practice reinforces the evidence of terminology. At about the same time as *ordo* usage increased, a young man's formal entry into knighthood increasingly involved the formal rite of dubbing, as Jean Flori and Maurice Keen have emphasized.[80] Even if the strictly religious elements in the ceremony vary with time and location, a formal rite of entry into knighthood suggests that the new knight is joining a distinct body of men performing a specified labor.

Competitive Asceticism Among *Ordines*

A scheme of divinely sanctioned social orders would be important to all the groups in question. It is thus hardly surprising that though scholars composed an ideally harmonious social world in treatises, sharp competition among groups was common in the real world. As Caroline Bynum has argued, the twelfth century discovered not only the self but a plenitude of groups, each busily engaged in self-definition (no less than competition).[81] Competition could find expression through religious ideology no less than social status and economic acquisition. It played an integral part in shaping knightly ideology. How did the chivalric *ordo* rank vis-à-vis that other self-assured *ordo*, the body of clerics? How did both of the most privileged and valorized *ordines* view other social groups, and especially the only one that really mattered to them, the merchants? These debates opened another avenue for asserting chivalric independence, however pious the knights considered themselves. Chivalric assertiveness naturally produced sharp reactions within the ecclesiastical caste and stimulated claims (as old as the Gregorian Reform) for clerical superiority and leadership in the march toward salvation.[82]

Competition so often turned on the degree of asceticism practiced by those in each constitutive social body. Any group that successfully claimed to endure and suffer more than another could boast higher spiritual merits than its rival, earning more of God's good will. This competition was made all the more keen by the high expectations placed on valid social groupings in maintaining the sort of ordered world on which God would smile.

The clerics set the standard. They famously (and theoretically) abstained from sexuality as a form of bodily discipline and meritorious sacrifice. The tenor of their claims, evident from so many twelfth-century sources, can perhaps nowhere better be appreciated than in *The Jewel of the Church* (*Gemma Ecclesiastica*) by that most popular writer of the age, Gerald of Wales. His book, as he tells us with characteristic modesty, was warmly appreciated by no less an ecclesiastical figure than Pope Innocent III.[83] Gerald sounds the theme of celibacy tirelessly. Significantly, he discusses the struggle in military and highly ascetic language: "Resist the desires of the flesh manfully. Dry up the springs of lust through fervor of the spirit. The greater the struggle, the greater the crown."[84] He continues, "Know, then, that if a man does not punish himself, God will do so."[85] And he significantly adds, "No crown is given unless the struggle of a fierce battle has taken place."[86] This last statement appears prominently on the Harley manuscript illumination analyzed at the opening of this book. Gerald goes on in a vein that would suit that illumination perfectly. "We ought to fight continuously against the strong desires of the flesh; we must suffer [with Christ] if we are to reign with him."[87] Quoting the Book of Job, he intones that monks must recognize that "life on earth is a warfare and a continuous conflict with the enemy."[88] He summarizes for his brothers the teaching of St. Paul, using language that draws on potent *Christus-miles* parallels:

> As Christ offered the Father His entire body as a victim for us,
> generously exposing Himself to pains, to spittle, to stripes, to chains,
> to blows, to insults, and finally to the ignominious gibbet of the cross,
> so we should crucify our bodies to the world for His sake and willingly
> exposing ourselves to abstinences and insults and persecutions, devote
> our bodies completely to the service of God.[89]

A few lines later Gerald approvingly quotes St. Jerome, "You are effeminate soldiers if you desire to be crowned without a struggle, for no one will be crowned unless he fights manfully."[90] Within the cloister, even within the priesthood, life is interpreted as a species of spiritual warfare, with celibacy the key to ascetic discipline. "That a priest needs to be pure," Thomas of Cobham's *Summa Confessorum* declares in the early thirteenth century, "is so obvious that it hardly needs saying."[91] John Pecham in *Ignorantia Sacerdotium* (1281) states that although holy orders are a form of perfection, marriage is a sacrament for the imperfect. True heroic endurance, in other words, graces the celibates.[92] Clerics were expected to practice a genuine form of self-denial. The growing powers of the institutional church watched closely to be certain of their self-discipline, and assured them of God's favor won through the abstinence and suffering of their bodies.

Sometimes the clerics saw themselves standing apart from all lay people, whether of chivalric or mercantile stamp. In one sense, this is only an instance of the rivalry of all groups that some scholars have emphasized as an aspect of high medieval social thought no less than a fact of social interaction. From a highly theoretical perspective, clerics could lump knights and merchants together; both groups of lay folk were troublesome and their labors morally dangerous.[93] One of the standard *exempla* that appears in numerous collections asks the question, how many demons does it take to watch a certain site? The answer always specifies that many agents of the devil are required to keep watch over a monastery, filled with a multitude of true souls, but only one need watch some other site (the target of the story), since its inhabitants are already given over to the power of the devil. Significantly, though this targeted site may be a town gate or marketplace, it may also be a castle.[94] Both the knight's ruthless violence and the merchant's endless usury troubled society and offended divine order.

The competition began in youth, as clerics recognized. An early sense of their religious vocation, adult clerics often recall in later writings, produced animosity from brothers whose feet were set on the path to knighthood. Gerald of Wales says his brothers disturbed his early studies with their ready praise of the knightly life.[95] Guibert of Nogent, dressed even while a child for his adult career as a monk (though his father and brothers were knights), later said he considered the "rest of my race . . . in truth mere animals ignorant of God, or brutal fighters and murderers."[96] We have already encountered Peter of Blois bitterly complaining of young knights that "The order of milites now is not to keep order."[97]

Clerical controversialists clearly did not always accept the knightly claim to carry out the divine will with their swords. They jibed that the actual labor of knights was theft and rapine. Étienne de Bourbon in the mid-thirteenth century told a story handed down from early Dominican friars in Burgundy. They had encountered knights driving before them cattle and oxen plundered from the poor. The laymen asked the friars what they are and are asked the same question by the friars. Surprised, the laymen say that one can tell at once that they are knights ("Immo videtis quod milites sumus"). But with malice aforethought one of the friars answers that they surely are cattlemen, for one is identified by the animals one drives. Yet, the friar continued—twisting the blade already thrust home—rather than you leading the stolen cattle to your homes, the cattle are driving you to burn in hell ("Sed, ut dicam verius, ducunt vos dicta jumenta ad inferni patibulum pocius quam vos ipsa ad vestram domum").[98] In another of his sermon tales, Étienne de Bourbon presents a wicked provost seizing cattle in a war that pitted the bishop of Macon and his allied townsmen against the count of Macon and his knights. Noting one lone cow left behind, the provost loudly orders its seizure. God's judgment falls upon him precisely at that moment and for the rest of his life he is able to say nothing but "Seize the cow! (Tange vaccam!)"[99] Defending their own ascetic turf, clerics sniped at knightly claims with practiced skill and undisguised glee. The monks in particular enjoyed a good story showing that knights who thought themselves tough and worldly found life in the cloister unbearable. Caesarius of Heisterbach writes that an abbot told him that "a certain knight" who was the genuine article—"honourable and renowned in military service (honestum et in militia nominatum)"—tried to convince a comrade to enter a monastery as he had done. But the comrade replied "with a word of great cowardice": "I am really afraid of . . . the lice that infest your robes (Vere, amice, ego forte . . . timeo . . . vermiculi vestimentorum)." Caesarius adds proudly, "indeed the woolen cloth does harbour a quantity of vermin (pannus enim laneus multos vermiculos nutrit)." He even pictures the converted knight himself reviling his timid fellow: "Alack! What a valiant soldier! You whom swords could not terrify when fighting for the devil! Have you to be frightened by lice now that you are going to be a soldier of Christ?"[100] The vituperation works in this case and (as is usual in monastic stories) the cloistered life claims the soldier. But the underlying monastic assertion of superior meritorious suffering is obvious and informative.[101] Caesarius later makes the same point using the monastic diet. A "certain man still in the world (quidam ex saecularibus)" marvels that converted knights "so delicately brought up in the world, can live upon simple vegetables, peas and lentils."[102] Even priests, though they lacked the thoroughly heroic image of monks, could still claim a more demandingly ascetic life than the laity.

"Nothing in this life," William of Pagula wrote of the priestly vocation in the early fourteenth century, "is harder, more burdensome, or perilous than the office of bishop or priest; but nothing is holier in the sight of God if one soldiers on and does his duty in the way Christ commands."[103]

The clerical revulsion from blood pollution by the knights at all levels could be strongly felt and expressed. Abbot Suger in his *Deeds of Louis the Fat*,[104] quotes Pope Paschal II who declares that knights' hands are stained by blood from the sword. In describing the coronation of his hero as King of France, Suger significantly distinguished between the merely secular sword of knighthood and the ecclesiastical sword used righteously to correct evildoers. In the coronation ceremony, he insists, Louis exchanged one for the other.[105] Perhaps this loathing of blood pollution was again at work in the minds of Abbot Suger and of Gerald of Wales when (borrowing from the Roman author Lucan) they described the German Emperor and Richard Lion-Heart, respectively, as happy only when they could mark their triumphs by walking in the blood of their enemies.[106]

We can imagine how knightly blood pressure rose when satiric stories were told by chuckling clerics, busily advancing claims for the meritorious suffering of their *ordo*. Apologists for the knightly *ordo* did not let down their side in answering them. One of the popular epics of the cycle of William of Orange, the *Moniage Guillaume* (William in the Monastery) puts this conflict of *ordines* directly into the spotlight. An aged William retires to a monastery, leading to much discussion of the monastic and knightly orders, to the benefit of the *bellatores*. As already noted, not the first redaction of this text from about 1150, but the second of about 1180, shows this sharply competitive emphasis.[107] An angel guides William, aging and tired after his vigorous career in arms, to enter a monastery. He is changing his *ordo* under heavenly guidance, but he is not an easy convert to the monastic life. Though (reminding us of William Mauvicin) he hands over his shield symbolically to St. Julian, the heavenly patron of the house, he inserts an escape clause in his pledge: if needed by his king to combat pagans, he will return to the world of physical fighting, paying for the privilege. Yet William hears from the abbot that he must now suffer for his sin of killing so many men, as he accepts the tonsure and dons the robe of a monk (far too short for his vast frame). He proceeds to frighten the other monks by his strength and touchiness (and to beat them when provoked). Even worse, he nearly consumes their supplies of food. Jealousy and resentment lead them wickedly to plan a mission for him that can only be fatal, since they prohibit fighting against the robbers they know will attack him on the journey they propose. This plot device sets up humorous scenes—William progressively and piously giving his prized possessions to the robbers, but finally defending his pants—but it also produces fascinating conversations in the monastery about clerical and knightly *ordines* as William and the abbot spar verbally before he obediently sets forth. The abbot preaches a code that is the inversion of the knightly line: one must, as a form of penance, suffer evil without fighting back.[108] But William declares this code too cruel and condemns all those who created it to the devil who must be behind the order. He has no doubts about the superiority of the order of chivalry and responds to the monastic prohibition of violence with assurance:

> Master, he said, your order is too strict!
> Such a convent could come to a bad end.
> God should hinder whoever established it.
> The order of chivalry is worth a good deal more;
> It fights against Turks and pagans;
> For the love of God it suffers martyrdom,
> And is baptized in its own blood
> To establish right order.
> Monks do nothing but eat and drink
> Read and chant and sleep and snore.[109]

William drives his point home by repeatedly associating the monastic order with shame, the knight's greatest fear.[110] Soon he redoubles his point by repeating his entire defense of the chivalric *ordo*: it is the force needed to conqueror Saracen lands and to convert these unbelievers to true religion. Monks who send out knights into danger are meanwhile eating, drinking wine, and snoring in their cloisters.[111] He refers with sarcasm to monastic services that will be held over his dead body when he is killed by the robbers.[112] A historian blessed with a time machine might enjoy watching in the far corner of some hall as lay members of the audience react to the poem declaimed for their entertainment.

One of the short miracle tales by Caesarius of Heisterbach makes a similar point about the knightly *ordo* more concisely. A dying lord hears a commotion in the adjoining room.[113] Asking the cause, he learns that his nephew is trying to rape some woman there, and she is proving difficult. The dying knight is a lover of justice and unhesitatingly declares, "Hang him." The household knights only pretend to obey, fearing consequences after the old man's imminent death. But as he lingers, he catches a glimpse of his nephew very much alive. Calling the young man close to his bedside he plunges a fatal dagger into him. At the point of his own death, shortly thereafter, he is visited by a bishop come to hear his confession. Noting that in recounting his sins the great knight has omitted the killing of his nephew, the bishop refuses to give him the host, the consecrated bread transformed into the saving body of Christ, and walks toward the door. The old knight triumphantly tells the bishop to look within his pyx (the carrying box) for the host. The host is missing there, but lies on the knight's tongue. God has understood the knight's virtue and has given him the saving sacrament, even though the bishop did not. The story remarkably portrays God's valorization of direct and vigorous knightly action, even though it violates the usual religious norms enforced by the clergy.[114]

Occasionally we can hear the knights speak their minds, even in the twelfth century. Late in that century, Henry II of England expressed the characteristic knightly riposte, claiming superiority rooted in the very toughness of their lives as warriors. In words that would have warmed even the great heart of Geoffroi de Charny two centuries later, he contrasted knightly meritorious suffering with the easier, less hazardous lives of clerics. Gerald of Wales (always the best source of gossipy direct quotation) reports the king's words, spoken in response to an offer of the crown of the Kingdom of Jerusalem conveyed to him by the patriarch of Jerusalem. Henry archly told the patriarch, "The clergy can call us to arms and perils, since they themselves will receive no blow in the fight nor shoulder any burdens that they can avoid."[115] It comes as no surprise that a monk's vision in the early thirteenth century pictured Henry in fiery armor in the other world, perilously mounted on a stallion snorting sulphurous fumes.[116]

Ambroise's *Estoire de la guerre sainte* shows the continuing debate. Hugh de la Mare, a cleric, urges Richard I to withdraw out of danger during the fighting on Cyprus before the king reached the Holy Land: "Sir, get away, for they have hordes of people, beyond counting." Richard responded sharply: "Sir clerk, concern yourself with your writing and come out of the fighting; leave chivalry to us by God and Saint Mary."[117]

Later in the thirteenth century, elaborate remarks by historical French nobles are reported by the chronicler Matthew Paris in his *Chronica Majora* for the year 1247.[118] In the process of forming sworn associations against clerical financial exactions, these lords denounced the "superstitious clergy" who seem to have forgotten that "by the warfare and bloodshed of certain people in the time of Charlemagne and others, the kingdom of France was converted from the errors of the gentiles to the catholic faith." Such unappreciative clerics, the French lords insisted, "would place us in a worse condition than God wished even the gentiles to be in, when he said, "Render unto Caesar the things that are Caesar's and unto God the things that are God's." The secular lords know, to the contrary, "that the kingdom was neither acquired by written law nor by the arrogance of clerks, but by the sweat of war." Let the clerics, they say, return "to their condition in the early church and by living in contemplation, may, as becomes them, show to those of us leading the active life the miracles which have long since departed from the world." The thrusts are sharp, the independence and lay confidence are manifest. Knightly mentalité clearly endows strength sufficient to banish any disabling fears about the morality of its characteristic labor. As we have seen, Geoffroi de Charny (who favored fare and attire simple enough to warm the heart of even an uncompromising monastic reformer) came directly to the point by describing chivalric suffering and comparing it to the supposedly hard life of the clerics. He caps his case by asking, rhetorically, "and where are the orders which could suffer as much?"[119]

Other knights on the stage of history and their fellows on the pages of imaginative literature directly assert the rectitude of their own order against clerics who would play the warrior. This was trespassing on the preserve of the sacred labor of the knightly *ordo*. Just before the Battle of the Standard, fought between the English and the Scots in 1138, Archbishop Thurstan of York boldly announced that he and his parish priests bearing crucifixes would join the English fighters.[120] In a scene that parallels contemporary *chanson*, the archbishop solemnly gave the English forces, gathered before him in arms, God's blessing and forgiveness after they had accepted private penitence and a general three-day fast with alms.[121] Although the archbishop again declared his determination to join the army in battle, English barons firmly informed him that he should return to his prayers and religious duties and leave the fighting to them "as their order required."[122] A century and a half later, when on another northern field of battle the English and Scots again fought, another bishop was told to act within his *ordo*, by knights confident of their own. At Falkirk in 1298, Anthony Bek, bishop of Durham, actually commanded one division of the English army. Yet when he tried to restrain his fighters who were eager to advance, these proud warriors told him plainly, "It is not for you, bishop, to teach us about knightly matters, when you should be saying mass. Go and celebrate mass and leave us to get on with our military affairs."[123] The word *ordo* is missing, but the knights assert a strong sense of the proper function for clerics and for knights.

Some clerics were clearly sensitive to the basic knightly argument. Caesarius of Heisterbach tells of a fearful priest who carried a sword on a night journey. Encountering a hideous man whose figure suddenly grew to the height of the trees, he fled in terror, only to be told by lay brothers in a monastery what he should have known: the devil fears a psalm, not a sword. In other words, he was acting outside the principles of his *ordo*.[124] Richard de Templo, an Augustinian who incorporated the *Estoire* of Ambroise into his chronicle, at one point exclaims, "How distant, how different is the life of contemplation and meditation among the columns of the cloister from that dreadful exercise of war."[125]

That such conversations can likewise be found in romance shows their widespread dissemination. In the Middle English *Sultan of Babylon*, the warrior Ferumbras makes the point. While still a pagan (before his defeat by the hero Oliver converts him to Christianity), he unhorses a fighter leading a contingent out from Rome and is surprised to find the man is tonsured. The unhorsed man is, in fact, the pope. Ferumbras may be a pagan, but as a warrior he is given the knightly line of thought,

> Fye, priest, God give you sorrow!
> What are you doing armed in the field,
> Who should say matins tomorrow?
> I hoped you would be an emperor,
> Or a war-chief of this host,
> Or some worthy conqueror!
> Go home and stay in your choir.[126]

Mythology for the Knightly *Ordo*: Round Table and Grail

All these speakers stand firmly on the ground of a distinct chivalric *ordo* and the performance of its proper labor; all challenge the clerics and would restrict them to the work of their own *ordo*. Sometimes, more subtle tactics were employed, and indirect maneuver rather than frontal charge guided knightly strategy. This meant elaborating what Maurice Keen aptly termed the mythology of chivalry. Creating such a mythology powerfully buttressed the claims made for a chivalric *ordo*. While never openly anti-sacerdotal, elements of the mythology in fact often placed the knights in a close, direct relationship with God, the founder of their *ordo*. Such constructs might show disturbing tendencies to circumvent the clergy or at least to minimize their mediating role; they constituted flank attacks in the competitive struggles among the *ordines*.

One remarkable intellectual construct even elaborated a mythical genealogy of chivalric heroes. The *Quest of the Holy Grail* (c. 1225–30) traced the line of the great Lancelot (while criticizing his sinful liaison with Queen Guenevere) and introduced his yet greater (and sexually pure) son Galahad. Lancelot is declared to be descended from Christ, through generations of pious knights and Grail keepers.[127] His son Galahad, the perfection of spiritual knighthood, even takes on significant attributes of Christ. *Imitatio Christi* here is raised to a higher power.

Yet another succession of knights—in this case a line of heroes who were not imagined blood relatives—not only connected chivalry to Christ himself, but reached even further back in time to incidents and characters in Jewish sacred history. The famous Nine Worthies, three sets of three great heroes, were presented as founding pillars of chivalry. Great knights from any writer's own time might receive fulsome praise as worthy to be number ten in the series; no doubt all knights could try to see at least something of themselves in the Nine Worthies who gave chivalry so glorious a past.[128] Since the sets pictured three classical heroes (Hector, Alexander, and Julius Caesar), three Jewish (David, Josua, and Judas Macabeus) and three Christian (Arthur, Charlemagne, and Godfrey of Bouillon), the line of models for knighthood again extended chivalric history well back into a glorious past and combined historical figures with literary heroes. In fact, this cultural genealogy is obviously and significantly older than that of the church itself, since it predates the founder and all the early fathers and saintly martyrs. At the very least, chivalric literature created knights about whom the odor of sanctity hovered. In the best-known examples the knights recall Christ himself, as all scholars recognize in the events marking the death of Roland in his *chanson*, or the symbolism and deeds associated with Galahad in the great *Quest of the Holy Grail*. Humbler knights in works less renowned can show some of the traits of sanctity.[129]

The specific symbols of Round Table and Grail suggest a divine mission for chivalry. Robert de Boron achieved this in three romances on Merlin and the Grail written in the late twelfth or early thirteenth centuries. In effect he cross-pollinated the pseudo-historical chronology of Geoffrey of Monmouth with the potent religious symbolism of Chrétien de Troyes. This fusion was absorbed wholeheartedly in the chivalric literature that conveyed knightly ideology.[130] Christ could be thought of as a knight, as we have seen—as even his disciples might be (with a little more effort); and the fellowship of the Grail table was obviously knightly in the sense of a European court. By the mid-fourteenth century, monarchs on both sides of the Channel were, in effect, founding tables for their own royal chivalric orders—the Garter in England and the Star (or Noble Maison) in France.[131] Robert de Boron conceived of Arthur's Round Table as the third in a trinity of tables.

Grail and sacred table symbolism combined. At the First Table, Christ and his disciples gathered for the Last Supper, sitting around the vessel that became the Grail. It was later used by Joseph of Arimathea, to whom Pilate had entrusted Christ's body and to whom Christ entrusted the vessel to hold his sacred blood. Whatever Chrétien had intended by the mysterious *graal*, apparently a platter carried in sacred procession in his romance, *Perceval*, Robert's Grail has become eucharistic, the sacred chalice of the mass. Knighthood is linked with the central sacrament of the altar.[132] Other elements of the Last Supper become powerful chivalric symbols as well: the empty seat left by the guilty withdrawal of Judas would evolve, remarkably, into the famed Siege Perilous, a seat that would serve only the greatest knight in the world and destroy any lesser man who deigned to try.

Under divine instruction, Joseph of Arimathea created the Second Table, and gathered the faithful around it, with the Grail at its center for marvelous sacramental meals. Utherpendragon, Arthur's father, would of course produce the Third Table, directed by Merlin.[133] Through Robert's pen, one of the divine goals set for the knights of the Round Table in the time of Arthur is to find the Holy Grail now come to Britain where it rests in the care of the Fisher King, who is Perceval's uncle. Though this current Grail keeper is terribly ill, he cannot find release in pious death, Merlin foretells, "until a knight of the Round Table has performed enough feats of arms and chivalry—in tournaments and by seeking adventures—to become the most renowned knight in all the world."[134] The requirements are significant: prowess is bonded with piety.

In the third romance in Robert de Boron's trilogy, Perceval is destined to be this knight, to sit in the mysterious vacant seat at the Round Table, and finally to succeed in the quest for the Grail. No less impatient than destined, however, he sits prematurely in the vacant seat, encouraged by all his fellow knights who think his demonstrated prowess in a tournament has already earned him the right.[135] Perceval is spared divine wrath only by pure grace; the stone seat splits beneath him with a noise like the end of the world. The stern voice of God announces that the seat will never mend nor will healing come to the current keeper of the Grail—the maimed Fisher King—until, the text pointedly repeats, a great knight "has performed enough feats of arms and goodness and prowess."[136] The knight who achieves so much, the Voice assures, will be guided to the castle of the Fisher King where he must ask the right questions: What is the Grail? Who does it serve? Though Perceval first finds the Grail castle, he fails to ask the questions and is told he cannot have the Grail, "because you're not wise or worthy enough, and have done too few deeds of arms and prowess and too few acts of goodness."[137] Perceval, of course, eventually makes all right, with Merlin's help finds his uncle, asks the questions, heals the Grail keeper, and replaces him, retiring from chivalry. What seems so striking for our inquiry, however, is the strong link forged between good knightly prowess and the central relic in the story, the original Eucharistic vessel. The three tables and this vessel connect the *ordo* of chivalry, characterized by its demanding life of arms, to Christ himself and to the vessel that re-creates his sacrifice—and triumph—at the altar.

This ideal of knights searching for the Grail is more famously elaborated in the *Quest of the Holy Grail* in the Vulgate Cycle, a few decades after Robert de Boron completed his trilogy. As this romance blends clerical exhortation and chivalric independence, it shows the tensions that could crackle within a single work. Strong clerical visions for an order of knights surface unmistakably, but lay independence is equally clear, though perhaps not always recognized. The clerics, granted, tried determinedly to bend the moral direction of Grail quest to spiritual rather than worldly chivalry. Yet in the process, this meta-quest in fact brings the religious charge in romance to maximum valorizing potential. Though most knights fail, the finest, ideally exercising with their swords and their bodies the characteristic work of their *ordo* (as even the clerics envisioned it) achieve virtual union with God, who feeds them himself from the Grail. To Galahad, the finest of all, God even reveals himself. In much humbler passages along the way, the Quest makes major concessions to the realities of chivalric life as lived in the world. Tournament is accepted as licit without a murmur. The crucial virtue of prowess is largely accepted as a God-given talent, provided only it is well exercised and its ultimate origins acknowledged. Perceval hears talk of his *ordo* and its hard labors from "a man robed like a priest" speaking to him from the deck of a miraculous ship:

[God] would try you to determine whether you are indeed his faithful servant and true knight, even as the order of chivalry demands. For since you are come to such a high estate, no earthly fear of peril should cause your heart to quail. For the heart of a knight must be so hard and unrelenting towards his sovereign's foe that nothing in the world can soften it. And if he gives way to fear, he is not of the company of the knights and veritable champions, who would sooner meet death in battle than fail to uphold the quarrel of their lord.[138]

Would knights hearing such passages think only of spiritual struggles and the Lord God? Or might they think of their faithful service to a secular lord or—what seems more likely—of the hierarchical continuum of lords beginning on earth and reaching into heaven? Would the conception of hard service register as purely spiritual or would it have a strongly physical dimension in their minds?

One suspects that knights must commonly have read or heard all highly clerical themes in their own fashion, receiving the contents through a powerful chivalric filter, the same filter we have already encountered at work in the knightly reception of crusade preaching (in Chapter 4). At the end of the Middle Ages, Sir Thomas Malory certainly employed such a filter for his version of the Quest. In his *Morte Darthur* even the Grail Quest emerges as a wonderful adventure and a blessing descending on knighthood. Far from reading his source as a stern *sermon ad status* (to be taken to heart point by point as a practical guide to an *ordo* and a remedy for its many faults), he seems deliberately not to see the failure of most knights on the quest and even wipes from his hero, Lancelot, as much of the tarnish as is possible. Galahad glows with unearthly virtue and is admired at a distance by Malory; but Lancelot is the best of sinful knights, the sort of model a practicing warrior might conceivably emulate. Malory is devoted to a society led by the "moste Kynge" and the "moste knyght." Even as it slides inexorably toward the cliff edge, the society of the Round Table, Malory's Hyghe Ordre of Chyvalry, is glorious and grand in his sight, though its incurable ills must be painfully lodged in his heart.

Blessed Virgin, Ally of the Knightly *Ordo*

If the Grail quest is well known, one of the trump cards held by the knights is too often ignored. They buttressed their high *ordo* through a close relationship with the Blessed Virgin. The Queen of Heaven was their special patroness. Her protection confirmed their validity, perhaps even in some dimensions their superiority.[139] Her knights did her great honor and she responded, on occasion even being represented as magnanimously accepting gifts from their illicit loot.[140] Her protection is invaluable: the demon who has insinuated himself into a household is unable to work his evil on the knight who honors the Virgin daily.[141] A knight who has sold his soul to the devil by denying Christ, is saved when he stoutly refuses to deny the Virgin. She intervenes with her son in gratitude.[142] Repeatedly, she is shown coming to the aid of imprisoned knights, for whom she had a special affection.[143] As that pioneering medievalist Henry Adams noted, "On every battlefield of Europe for at least five hundred years Mary was present, leading both sides."[144] She generously arranges time desperately needed for confession leading to forgiveness of their sins. Her gracious generosity flows in response to even the most formal devotions or the most abbreviated verbal declarations on the point of death. Caught by his enemies, as one *exemplum* pictures, a "noble but crime-stained knight" pleaded for time to confess, a plea denied by his nervous captors, anxious to decapitate him. He had time only to state his intention to confess before the sword blow struck. Yet the Blessed Virgin intervened with her son and the knight's good intention saved him, says Caesarius of Heisterbach, who tells the miracle story.[145] Even more graphic is the tale of a Norman knight who was truly shameful and wicked and guilty of various killings and atrocities, as the Augustinian Thomas of Cantimpré tells. He was finally caught by his enemies in a pass and summarily beheaded. But as the severed head rolled down the slope it continually and horrifyingly called out (non paucis horis clamans horribiliter) to the Blessed Virgin Mary. Understandably frightened, the all but paralyzed killers endured continuous cries from the knight's grisly head hour after hour (incessante capite clamante). A quaking priest summoned from a nearby village at first would not come near the body and insisted that he would do nothing until the head was replaced atop the knight's corpse. As soon as this was done and the priest had miraculously heard the dead knight's confession, peace was restored, and all present marveled at the power and favor of God's Mother.[146] Though the loving power of Mary is the religious point the clerical author clearly wanted to establish, a knight might take special notice of the Virgin's favor to one of his order, even to one scarred by sin. She understands the problems and weakness of knights and forgives those devoted to her. In a sermon story, a robber-knight who says fifty Aves every day narrowly escapes capture by his enemies. He thanks the Blessed

Virgin who has saved him, but receives a timely warning in the form of a vision: Mary offers him dainty food in a foul dish, a symbol of his devotions offered her in the midst of his blemished life.[147] She could even forgive knights who trouble the clergy. A parish priest who has been harassed and plundered by a neighboring castellan finally loses patience and, holding a consecrated host in his hand, threatens the Virgin; he will not release her son until he is avenged on that knight. In a vision he sees his enemy hanging over the pit of hell, supported only by five golden cords. An angel with a drawn sword stands ready to cut the cords and plunge the sinful knight into the eternal blazing pit. The priest enthusiastically calls for that very action. But when the Virgin explains that these cords are the Aves said daily by the castellan, the priest desists. He explains the vision to the knight, converting him to a better life.[148] Yet life-changing repentance does not always seem to be required. A knight who buys a young girl from her parents while he is riding to a tournament spares the girl's virginity because he learns she is named Mary. Though he is killed in the tournament, his soul is saved, as this girl learns in a vision in which the Virgin Mary appears. Girls with other names, one fears, would have been well advised to avoid this knight.[149] Another knight has a vision of judgment with fierce demons coming to seize his soul. He manages to fight them off, using as he would a sword the taper he had once dedicated to the Blessed Virgin in a church.[150] Another knight, who lives openly by plunder, nonetheless adores the Virgin and though his heart has been pierced by an enemy weapon is miraculously saved from instant death in order to make confession and secure salvation.[151]

Knights must have deeply appreciated these stories told in sermons or savored in private reading. Joinville includes one at the point in his chronicle of the crusade of Louis IX where he relates his pilgrimage to the shrine of the Virgin at Tortosa: "it was there that the first altar was erected on earth in honour of the Mother of our Lord." Among the many great miracles he knows were accomplished by the Virgin there, the example he chooses to tell concerns a man possessed by the devil, whose friends pray for his health. But from within him the devil cries out in response, "Our Lady is not here. She is in Egypt giving help to the King of France and the Christians who will land this very day to fight on foot against the mounted forces of the heathen." Joinville assures his readers that the date was written down and given to the legate who gave the information to him in person. "I can assure you," Joinville testifies, "that Our Lady did indeed help us that day, and would have helped us still more if . . . we had not angered her and her Son."[152] It is a story

Henry Adams could appreciate: the Virgin helping out her knights on the field of battle.

Joinville's story is set on crusade, but the most famous story of the Virgin's aid concerns the mock battlefield of tourney. In versions retold endlessly across the Middle Ages, a knight on his way to a tournament stops to hear a mass sung in her honor in a church by the road. Lost in devotion, he forgets the tournament completely. Suddenly remembering his knightly goal, he hurries toward the tourney field, only to meet returning jousters who congratulate him on his victory, some even acknowledging that they are prisoners won by his admirable display of prowess. Momentarily astonished, he comes to understand that the Virgin has jousted for her faithful knight in his absence.[153]

This asserted assurance of help from St. Mary sets knights far apart from laymen in other socio-professional groups, and especially from the merchants. Can one imagine the Blessed Virgin counting out coins, working the scales, collecting interest, or selling goods in a marketplace, even for a merchant who had devotedly honored her? The explanation is not simply that the Queen of Heaven favored sinners of high social status. The Virgin was, in fact, known for the dramatic help she gave even to the humble. Eileen Power went so far as to claim that for all her chivalric friends, she liked common folk best.[154] Robbers of all ranks who showed her any devotion seem to have given her no pause. In a late twelfth-century story, another tale endlessly retold later, she supports a convicted thief on the gallows for three days, preventing his drop to sudden death and allowing him time for repentance and salvation.[155] Stories of her help for merchants or usurers, however, are conspicuously absent.[156]

Elite *Ordines* Versus the Merchants

Knights and clerics could readily agree on one point: both groups were certain that their respective *ordines* and labor vastly outshown that of merchants and their labor. Disdain for the merchant was, of course, one of their areas of solid agreement. Though often fearful and worried about the knights, the clerics showed a decidedly less favorable view of the merchants. One tale pictures a usurer, who has endowed a church and secured burial before the altar, rising suddenly from his grave to beat the monks with a candlestick snatched from the altar; even reburying his body outside the churchyard secures them no peace, for the man haunts the neighborhood. Finally the monks realize that they must purchase peace by returning his gifts, earned by foul usury.[157] An even more damning sermon story, provided by Jacques de Vitry, shows a deceased usurer refused burial in the church cemetery by the parish priest. When the usurer's friends protest, the priest puts the corpse on the back of an ass and suggests the will of God be done. Straightaway the beast carries its load to the gallows where robbers are hanged and shakes it off into a dunghill, where the priest leaves it.[158]

Knights warmly seconded this denigration. That both they and the churchmen needed the merchants' services and their liquid assets is obvious; that from a practical perspective they more or less came to terms with them can be demonstrated. Canon law creatively swung open the door of religious valorization just widely enough to prevent complete censure of the merchants' work, so crucial in the urban and economic boom medieval Europe experienced. Yet deep animosity remained and was frequently expressed. Attacks from the privileged *ordines* on usury and usurers—the category into which all men of trade were indiscriminately dumped—appear in a steady stream of vitriolic moral tales for private reflection and sermon preparation.

Why did knights and clerics combine in despising merchants? Social status comes first to mind. Whatever their own disputes and rivalries, knights and the upper clergy shared broad social layers: whether in youth they took up arms or served at the altar, they thought themselves marvelously superior to those who went into trade. Both elite groups enjoyed looking down privileged noses at bustling men of markets and finance. Yet so obvious an answer seems incomplete. Ideological as well as social criteria entered the equation. The knights, for all their faults, clearly could be better fitted than usurers within an ideal ecclesiastical plan for human society. Such ideas mattered.

One of a set of *exempla* collected in the fourteenth century makes the case concisely, using trifunctional terminology with the merchants censoriously appended:

> The three kinds of human that God made are the clerics, knights, and workers; but the fourth kind was thought up by the devil, namely the townsmen and usurers who are not clerics because they do not know letters, are not knights because they do not know how to bear arms, and are not workers because they do not engage in human labor and the devil works them. Likewise the merchants are among men like the drones among bees who do not make honey nor carry fruit, but do harm to the bees. Similarly the merchants oppress the clerics, outfit the

knights, and shake down the workers and because on no day do they serve, they suffer idleness and injure many. For this reason Solomon said that idleness begets all evils.[159]

If not good theology, this is powerfully revealing social commentary.

Clerical intellectuals widened the distance between merchants and the elite orders by their hatred of usury. Long suspect by the twelfth century, usury provoked newly intense condemnation, seen in the enactments of the Lateran councils of 1139 and 1179.[160] The Parisian circle of Peter the Chanter, especially concerned with issues of social ethics, played a prominent role through preaching campaigns and through influence in ecclesiastical legislation late in the twelfth century and through the early decades of the thirteenth century. In fact, they seem to have pioneered the use of vivid sermon *exempla* to castigate the usurers, often showing them in full evil in life and in final confusion upon their deathbeds.[161] The emergence of the several orders of friars not many years later ushered in the ideal set of enthusiastic preachers and confessors to broadcast the message and apply the technique to the widest possible audience.

Some of the intellectuals tried hard to accept the merchants. Jacques de Vitry included them in "the multiform types of men" who "have special rules and institutions differing from each other according to the different types of talents entrusted to them by the Lord, so that the one body of the church is put together under its head, Christ, out of people of differing conditions."[162] Yet he told of a cleric who wanted to "show to all how ignominious was the profession of usury, which no one would dare publicly to confess." He announced in his sermon, "I wish to absolve you according to the trades and professions of each (officium et ministerium singulorum)." Beginning with the smiths, he then called on all the men present to rise craft by craft; but when he asked for the usurers to rise to receive absolution, for shame no one dared stand up, "but all hid themselves for shame, and were derided, and put to confusion by the others for not daring to confess their profession."[163]

Eudes de Châteauroux (another in the Paris circle), contrasted townsmen and usurers with the good knights signing up for crusade. Unlike the knights who showed their thorough trust in God, these townsfolk do not want to join the movement, "and what is more they aim to deprive those who join up of their inheritance." Yet, Eudes exults, "the authority will always stay with the nobles, whether or not the usurers who devour them want it."[164]

Feelings ran deep, as the *exempla* show. One poor knight who asks a count for aid is rudely interupted by a rich bourgeois in the count's retinue, who declares his lord has nothing to give. The right-thinking count, however, gives the worthy knight this very bourgeois, to hold until ransomed.[165] Another knight turned monk, sent to sell asses on behalf of his religious house, proves constitutionally unable to play the lying merchant: he honestly explains the faults of the beasts.[166] When a usurer who has acquired the possessions of a knight dies, the knight marries his widow and together they enjoy the good life while the dead sinner roasts in hell.[167] Another knight while crossing a bridge in Paris hears a wealthy burgher blaspheming God. He punishes the man with a terrible blow to the mouth, breaking the offender's teeth. Brought before the king of France to answer for this action, the knight says that he would be unable to bear hearing his earthly king reviled, how much more should he revenge his heavenly king. The earthly king honors and releases him and ignores the burgher's claim.[168] On his wedding day a usurer passed beneath the portal of a church bearing a stone figure of a usurer. At just that moment the heavy stone purse clutched by the figure broke loose, and in its fall struck and killed the man.[169] It is hard to imagine a parallel story picturing a knight killed by a stone sword falling from a military statue on a church façade. Gifts from knights were accepted with honor and thanks, even by clerics who were not concerned to know if the source might be morally tainted. But the oats a usurer gave to a priest in an *exemplum* is found to be full of serpents. No wonder a usurer who insists on a third of his wealth being buried with him must suffer demons in the other world who grant his wish by stuffing his mouth with red-hot coins.[170]

End-of-life scenes usually offered a favorite stage for deprecating usurers. In the throes of death they lose speech, but recover only to ask about their money. Their bodies rest uneasily in consecrated ground and may have to be moved. One, whose dead body is examined, strangely has no heart; it is soon found, of course, in his money chest.[171] The story contrasts sharply with that reporting the examination of the heart of a pious knight who had died while on crusade—on the Mount of Olives, in fact: the heart was found to contain a golden crucifix.[172] Little wonder that a knight is reported to have shouted out in a crisis of the Cathar wars, "we are suffering worse torments than a money-lender's soul!"[173]

The disdain of elite *ordines* is obvious, and the likely ideological underpinning for it is significant. Supporting all these particular expressions of dislike is the utterly nonheroic profession of the merchants: the labor of their *ordo* involves no meritorious suffering. Clerics genuinely suffered in rejecting the allures of sexuality and thereby won high praise and divine approval. The hard lives of the knights similarly brought them spiritual merit. The merchants ran their hands lovingly through piles of polluting coin, but practiced no physical asceticism at all, and after being soundly excoriated on earth faced an uncertain future.

We must recognize that the knights in fact won the competition and got the best of both worlds. Though their labor involved acts of mutual blood pollution in armed combat, their sufferings in campaign and combat not only won them the loot and the praise that sustained their dominant position in society, it likewise bolstered their hopes of yet greater glory in the halls of heaven. Such conceptions of *ordo* and labor underscored their vigorous and self-confident mentalité.

Knightly conceptions of *ordo* and labor underscore their vigorous and self-confident mentalité. Though some fears may have crept in after midnight, or in a crisis, or on the deathbed, knights seem by and large to have thought they enjoyed a positive relationship with the divine. With their labor largely defined as they would wish, they could gladly accept membership in an *ordo* created by clerical intellectuals. Even on his deathbed the great William Marshal demonstrated this view with a confident assertion that certain clerical strictures on knightly life could not be true. Gawain walks in the same glow of confidence as an ideal chivalric heaven opens welcomingly and he is surrounded by throngs of grateful folk he has saved by arduous works of *caritas* on earth (the charity in this case achieved with his sword).[174]

This is not the heaven of the clerics, crowded with ranks of pacific saints and virgins intoning hymns. It recalls rather the great hall of Valhalla with the Christian God at last on the dais, wearing truly divine armor as he welcomes his fellow warriors as guests at the unending feast.

CHAPTER 8

Knighthood and the New Lay Theology:
Confession and Penance

A FEW YEARS after the victorious William the Conqueror had won the English crown, the Norman bishops composed (in 1067–70) an ordinance imposing penance on those men-of-war who had helped William gain his great prize. Their slate of sins had to be wiped clean of wartime wrongs. The ordinance laying out conditions was confirmed by the papal legate, Ermenfrid of Sion. The clerics, in effect, invert Geoffroi de Charny's scale of merit linked to increasing prowess: they produced a graded scale of penance according to the severity of military sin committed. In descending order of severity, penance was imposed for killing a known number of men, wounding a known number of men, killing or wounding an unknown number of men, etc. Motive was also addressed: fighting for gain entailed heavier penance than fighting "as in a public war." There were additional clauses for the further sins sure to occur in the wake of campaigning and conquest: adultery, rape, fornication, and violation of churches. Whether or not these penances were effectively carried out is unclear, but the direction of thought is significant.[1] Two earlier post-battle ordinances survive, though many may have been lost. Penitentials from the eighth and ninth centuries imposed fasting on warriors who killed in battle; but the evidence is confusing, as Sara Hamilton notes.[2] The Norman ordinance may have been, if not the last in a series, at least a late example in a long chain of formally imposed penances for battlefield killing and wartime misdeeds, stretching back several centuries into the Carolingian past.

Thoughts connecting warfare and warriors with confession and penance were in fact significantly shifting, as we can see by comparing this Norman ordinance with several roughly contemporary papal letters. Writing in 1063 to the clergy who would instruct warriors setting out from Italy to join the war against Muslims in Spain, Alexander II required the volunteers to confess their sins to a bishop and accept an assignment of penance; yet he then removed these same penances because of the campaign that they were about to fight. Their hard struggle would itself become a penance, and killing in warfare—here, of course, the killing of non-Christians—would not require the remedial steps imposed by Ermenfrid of Sion on the Norman conquerors. As the pope explained in another letter, killing was permitted when the aim was repressing crime or fighting enemies of the faith.[3] About twenty years later, Anselm of Lucca, the noted legist for the reform papacy, argued that the good warriors of Lucca fighting against imperial troops—Christians, of course—were gaining forgiveness through their hard service: a *remissio peccatorum*. The French jurist Ivo of Chartres, as David Bachrach has pointed out, recognized a case for post-battle penance, but relied heavily on views of such early Church Fathers as Augustine who saw a sinless role for soldiers when their motive was not booty.[4]

The timing of these changes in thought is interesting. H. E. J. Cowdrey takes the Norman promulgation of a penance for the Conquest as a sign of the conservatism of both the Norman bishops and the legate and suggests that the practice of assigning general scales of penance for military sin died out about the time of the crusades. Bernard Verkamp similarly concluded that imposition of such penances for campaign and battle ended as early crusading began. In Gratian's foundational canon law collection, the *Decretum* (c. 1140), as David Bachrach notes, these penances imposed on warriors after the fight have finally disappeared.[5] Ideas that will contribute to powerful currents in crusading thought and chivalric thought are just emerging at the end of the eleventh and beginning of the twelfth century.

Satisfaction for Sin: The Range of Views

Theologians knew that sin separates humans from God; as rebellion or treason against the highest Lord, it could provoke his dread wrath against individuals or entire groups of sinners. They were also certain that sin distorts and destroys proper human relationships and ruins the ideal social world intended in the divine plan. Life on earth, after all, should to some small degree anticipate the ordered bliss of heaven, rather than the grim turmoil and torments of hell to which sin leads. Confession and penance were the means of neutralizing the poison of sin in individuals and in society at large. In the process, of course, clerical agency was asserted and clerical primacy promoted. Confession and penance formed the most significant elements in the new theology being developed for the laity. Through a renewed emphasis on these remedies, clerics intended once again to enact reform, to make right order in the world and guide sinners to bliss in the next world.[6]

So basic a set of ideas generated differing views both among the medieval theologians struggling to make them effective and among modern medievalists trying to understand their use and effectiveness. To fit chivalry into the framework, we must examine the range in points of view, old and new.

Scholars have in fact long placed the processes for dealing with sin under their microscopes, trying to understand what the system was, when it began, and how it operated. Yet on basic issues inquiry is in considerable flux. Recent work charges that earlier scholars imagined the categories of confession to be more stable and the processes more systematic than was actually possible in the medieval world. Taking prescriptive treatises and clerical legislation as evidence of accomplished fact, some scholars—the critique asserts—have projected too precise a taxonomy and too unitary and orderly a chronology of change. In this revisionist work, sharp turning points vanish and lines of demarcation blur.[7]

Though generalization remains difficult, a broad traditional scholarly view can be identified; it posits several lines of significant change. Along one such line, it is suggested that mechanisms for confession and penance moved from public ceremonies involving entire groups to private meetings of individual sinner and supervising cleric. Another line of change involves a shift from these major and nonrepeatable cleansings to the regularly repeated meetings with a priest better known in later Catholic history. Along with these structural changes, content in confession and penance also has been seen to shift: exterior, often heroically physical acts of penance yielded to a greater concern for true inner contrition for sins. The decisive step is often thought to have arrived with the Fourth Lateran Council of 1215, which issued Constitution 21, *Omnis utriusque sexus*.[8] This decree required that each year all adult Christians make a private and individual confession to their parish priest before receiving the Eucharist. The goal was annual spiritual self-examination on the part of all the faithful, accomplished under clerical supervision. The sinner's own parish priest was to serve as confessor and spiritual guide; acting as a physician for the soul, he would pour the spiritual equivalent of oil and wine onto their wounds. To instruct and guide the priests, a steady stream of handbooks flowed from the pens of scholars. Some of the works may have been intended for literate lay folk themselves.[9] An unanticipated catalyst for the process appeared in the creation and rapid spread of the new orders of friars. Within a few decades their influence was felt throughout Christendom. They specialized not only in preaching to the laity but in hearing confession as well; the processes were, of course, considered complimentary. According to the Dominican Humbert of Romans, a friar who preached but refused to hear confessions was analogous to a farmer who sowed but did not reap.[10] The harvest of lay confessions was, in fact, plentiful. As is well known, the friars' vigorous confessional work led the parish clergy to feel their competition quite keenly.

If much evidence supports such elements of the traditional view, significant qualifications are emerging. Even if they grant significance to the legislation of 1215, some scholars argue for continuing influence of a much older tradition of ideas emphasizing contrition.[11] They also insist on a variety of forms of penance in actual practice, rather than a revolutionary shift after 1215 that replaced one paradigm of thought and practice with another. Close studies of evidence from 900–1050 in the German Reich by Sara Hamilton, and of thirteenth-century northern French documents by Mary Mansfield, in effect bracket the Fourth Lateran Council chronologically and make this revisionist case. Hamilton proposes continuities with the Carolingian past but sees a vital era of development in the tenth and eleventh centuries, well before the work of Innocent III and his colleagues; Mansfield finds that public penance was not dramatically edged out by repeatable private confession and penance but persisted as one acceptable form through the thirteenth century and, in some regions, well beyond. An exact taxonomy of types of penance, as both scholars argue persuasively, existed more in the formal treatises of scholastics than in the practices of confessors and parishioners. In fact, they argue that the very notions of public and private penance, often used in scholarly analysis, tended to blur in actuality.

Given these critiques, it seems especially unlikely that a straightforward timeline can now be accepted, with successive periods and discrete types of penance (as found in prescriptive documents) completely replacing their predecessors.[12] No doubt scholarly debates will be fruitful and multiply in years to come. In trying to understand chivalric piety, however, we can respectfully and prudently sidestep the particulars of scholarly debates and concentrate on a few features that are both relevant to the present inquiry and not in hot contention.

Our question is how knighthood could be fitted into the structure for dealing with sin. Prickly chivalric pride in their *ordo* and a firm belief in its licit and valorous labor could justify disruptive violence by pious, proudly independent knights. Could they be brought to accept structures of atonement and contrition for sin?

It is highly significant that once again a range of theological views—rather than straightforward agreement—persisted on ideas about confession and penance. Current scholarship, as we have seen, suggests that older and newer views could coexist, even in the same minds. This repeats a pattern we have encountered before with regard to other basic issues: the theology of Christ's role in redemption (in Chapter 6), and the theology of social orders, labor, and suffering (in Chapter 7). Where a range of religious ideas or practice coexisted, those who wrote about knighthood could draw selectively upon them all. Writers valorizing chivalry once more found it wonderfully useful to pick and choose, in the present case incorporating religious elements that gave a splendidly penitential stance to knighthood. New (or newly emphasized) ecclesiastical plans and practices could become not only compatible within the profession of knighthood, but indeed highly supportive of it. Chivalric ideology was fond of having the best of all possible worlds of thought.

A crucial question was whether the mechanism of atoning for sin should be considered heroic and intensely physical, or rather as a more spiritual and interior dialogue between the sinner and God. Is grievous bodily suffering, in other words, the potent solvent of sin, or does heartfelt contrition work that marvel?

Heroic atonement through intense or prolonged physical pain and suffering had many adherents.[13] Spectacular forms of heroic penance for notorious sins undoubtedly continued into the High Middle Ages and beyond. They might still be imposed on offenders for specific, heinous sins, as appears in both historical and imaginative literary accounts. Perhaps most famously, public beating with rods was accepted by Henry II of England after the murder of Archbishop Thomas Becket. In the pages of romance, well-known figures such as Sir Gowther, Robert the Devil, and Guy of Warwick (each recognizing himself guilty of heinous offenses) willingly endured harsh bodily suffering in recompense.[14] Readers of such texts knew that many of their contemporaries would have participated in imposed fasts, processions, and nonvoluntary pilgrimages, and would know that the truly heroic in their world (especially among the clergy) continued to subject their sinful bodies to even more creatively taxing penances. Heroic and physical forms of occasional penance continued to be considered efficacious for individuals and sometimes for entire groups and communities.

The tradition itself had venerable clerical roots, of course, reaching back to the heroic penance sometimes imposed in the early church. "One knows he is forgiven," Thomas Tentler explains of this view, "because he is willing to perform the overwhelming penitential exercises demanded by the church. The consolation of this system lies in its difficulty. . . . only the ascetic seemed efficacious."[15] It was a tough tradition. As the influential early theologian Tertullian wrote of heroic penance in the first centuries of Christianity,

> The harder the pains of this second and only penance, therefore, the more effective it is as a demonstration; so it should not be shown in the conscience alone, but should also be directed towards some external act. . . . The less you spare yourself, believe me, the more God will spare you.[16]

Medieval writers continued the chant. Gerald of Wales wrote, "Know, then, that if a man does not punish [himself], God will do so."[17] Or, as St. Bernard wrote, debts not paid on earth must be paid "in purgatorial places (in purgabilibis locis)."[18] By the fourteenth century, texts like the *Pricke of Conscience* concisely instructed that sins must be paid for in this life or the next. Having encountered the medieval obsession with asceticism, we cannot feel surprise at the central place physical suffering held in many minds worried about sin and atonement. The elaboration of a doctrine of purgatory in the High Middle Ages was an obviously powerful stimulus. Jacques Le Goff has argued for the birth of purgatory as a substantive in language and a place in cosmography by the end of the twelfth century, though ideas of interest were clearly in circulation well before then.[19] It may have given trembling sinners hope for an eventual release from the antechamber of hell and joyful entry into paradise; but it surely reinforced the idea that the debt of sin must be paid by grueling physical torment endured for years on end. All knew that the soul possessed a corporality that made the physical nature of suffering terrifyingly certain. Étienne de Bourbon straightforwardly asserted that any pain in purgatory was worse than any known on earth (excedit enim omnem penan quam unquam passus est aliquis in hac vita). He continued with a harrowing story of an evil official who declares half a day in purgatorial pain worse than his long-term illness while alive on earth.[20] Thomas of Cantimpré had joined the priesthood in order to improve the uncertain otherworldly fate of his father, a knight; he recorded terrifying dreams in which his father's face would appear to him, battered by the harsh, punishing blows he regularly received in purgatory. These dreams, Thomas assured his readers, brought home to him in the midst of his everyday concerns the physical reality of purgatorial punishment.[21] Popular views seldom doubted that bodily pain and suffering would be involved in atonement. John Bossy speaks to this point tersely:

> While the remission of sins was in the textbooks the effect of a threefold action of contrition, confession and satisfaction performed in private between individual sinner and an individual priest, it was in practice governed, like marriage, by an unwritten tradition that sin was a visible and social matter to be redeemed by acts as visible and social as the Passion of Christ.[22]

Luther noted disapprovingly in his Ninety-Five Theses (1517) that ordinary folk still believed that they must undergo painful penances in order to have forgiveness of sins.[23]

Since the process of physical atonement, as theologians emphasized, could begin in this world, it would behoove a sinner to get started on making the required satisfaction. Any punishment owed but not accounted for on earth would lengthen the time sinners experienced the refined tortures of purgatory, if the sins did not condemn them to eternity in hellfire. The living, as pictured in *exempla*, often receive visions of dead companions suffering horrifically in purgatory or hell for sins unexpurgated on earth. One of a pair of knightly friends, a sermon told its hearers, planned to do penance for three years for a great sin, but died before he could even begin. His troubled spirit appeared in a dream to his friend, who charitably took on the penance for him, and was rewarded by annual visions showing the dead sinner's blackened body cleansed and lightened by successive thirds.[24] A fourteenth-century pastoral handbook instructs the priest to inform his parishioners: "All the good things you will do and all the difficult things you will endure are your penance."[25] Lenten fasting and sexual abstinence, the physically difficult or even dangerous enterprise of pilgrimage—let alone the hidden hairshirts or the public flagellant movements—persisted in an age intensely aware of the example set by the suffering Christ and the early generations of his saintly martyrs. At the end of the Middle Ages, Martin Luther, while a young monk, would nearly ruin his health with harsh bodily discipline.

Some clerical voices continued to use the threat of harsh physical punishment to bolster their insistence on full restitution of stolen property. Jacques de Vitry records the vision focused on a virtuous knight who had fought as a crusader in the Holy Land and against the Cathars. Yet after his death, the hero suddenly appeared from otherworldly torment to seek a friend's help; he needed the living fellow knight to restore property he had stolen so he can be freed from dire punishment.[26] In another of his tales, a knight who died while on campaign with Charlemagne in Spain wanted a companion to give his valuable horse as alms. But the fellow fails to act and in a dream learns from the dead knight that his release from the terrors of purgatory is being delayed; the defaulting knight is warned that judgment will fall upon him, as well. It comes more swiftly than anticipated. The very next day the frightened companion dies miserably and in a highly uncertain spiritual state.[27] Clearly, clerics wanted knights to restore stolen goods; interestingly, they did not want them to become too confident in even the considerable benefits of crusading.

Yet strong though this tradition of physical atonement was, other ideas and practices led away from the corporal and heroic. Legislation from the highest ecclesiastical authority in 1215 required periodic interior reflection and emphasized contrition for sin; confessors were supported in this task by a steady flow of new preaching manuals and collections of tales that could animate sermons. Emphasis usually fell on the sinner's necessary contrition, which the priest, acting as physician of the soul, was to encourage through skilled and patient probing. Given this vital inner state of true contrition, and its necessary expression through the observable flow of tears, a sinner need not feel so very much worry over outer works of penance closely calibrated in units of suffering to match the severity of sin committed. The way was officially cleared, in fact, for penances to be lightened in weight as well as emphasis. Some thought it more a sign of acceptance of the necessary mediation of Holy Church than a painful payment to God through physical suffering. Contrition, these theologians argued, was the crucial element in reconciliation between sinful humans and the divine, though they never ceased to insist on the role of the priest and the actual performance of penance. Of course, a few clerics may have longed for sterner measures all around, such as the priest in an *exemplum* who, when troubled by a knight with an infirm leg, thinks not of medicinal confession and light penances but boldly prays that the other leg might be afflicted also, disabling the troublesome man.[28]

Increasingly, as most lay folk experienced it, the regimen of confession and penance was becoming nonheroic, repeatable, and local. Weberian sociologists might say that it was becoming routinized in the religious life of the majority. For them the sacrament increasingly meant that they periodically recalled their quotidian sins and showed their parish priest genuine contrition of heart; they then performed the light physical penance assigned, usually some task far from the heroic. Pragmatic theologians in fact encouraged confessors to assign lighter penance, hoping thus to encourage the laity to participate fully and effectively in the healing process of confession. Some of the numerous manuals written to help confessors actually suggest a process of bargaining to find a penance that the sinner will accept and perform. A steady flow of miracle stories shows this feature of negotiated penance, often brought into the process after resistance to the idea of confession and penance on the part of knights. Caesarius of Heisterbach tells of a knight who will perform no penance assigned. To the frustrated confessor's question as to what the knight could actually perform, the response is that he could refrain from eating sour apples from a horrid tree on his property. This becomes the set penance. Of course, the man quickly develops a craving for that very fruit, once it is prohibited. If the story reveals psychological insight, it likewise provides us with insight into pastoral practice.[29] A similar story is told about an English sheriff whose penance is not to eat cod, which he loathes.[30] An even bolder knight refuses penance, arrogantly insisting his servant will do it for him. The weary confessor tells the servant to remind his master of death ever approaching.[31] Some stories suggest confessors must exercise caution. A knight pictured in a fourteenth-century *exemplum* actually kills the confessor who tries to impose a pilgrimage to the Holy Land. The next confessor, a prudent man, insists only that the knight's servants remind him of his eventual death at every meal.[32] Much less harrowing still is the penance given to a knight who confesses, while in the Holy Land, that he has committed adultery under a tree in his garden at home in England. Moved by his wife's dream that he is being stabbed to the heart under that very tree, he finally confesses. His Franciscan confessor requires him simply to say five Aves. In a dream, his wife then sees a doctor healing the wound in his heart with five flowers.[33]

Those who valued contrition of heart over harsh physical penances also tended to favor frequency in the process of penance. The cleansing rite should be offered and experienced regularly in a regimen of spirituality that sustained the sinner through a lifetime—not once, or very infrequently, to expunge a great sin. With a focus on quotidian wrongs and the need for recurrent self-examination, the process should be repeated. Such thinkers parted company with practice in the early church: originally, penance for major sins was heroic, it took place once in life, and it changed that life, setting the sinner apart in a new social and religious category, the *ordo peni-tentialis*. Some clerics insisted that the old sinful lay life must be abandoned in order for a true penance. Some laymen shared their view. In his book on penance (1208–13) Robert of Flamborough pictures a sinner (who respect-fully calls his confessor "Lord") asking why confession and penance must be repeated. Would not once suffice? The questioning layman learns that on Judgment Day he will have to vomit up all his sins, and so would be well advised to confess regularly and receive the light penance (penitentiam minuas) assigned.[34]

Clerical thought was clearly moving along more than one line of devel-opment. Spiritualizing influences undoubtedly affected the practice of con-fession and penance. Yet the need of grievous bodily suffering remained a cultural component in the general populace throughout the Middle Ages and beyond. Vividly specific paintings of purgatory and hell in church murals are now faded, but must once have been more vivid in every sense; on church façades we can still see the stone sinners being thrust into the maw of hell by stone demons; stories told out in sermons by impassioned friars or read even by the laity in book collections and treatises can only have increased the sense of tension. Tireless emphasis on physical punishment in the afterlife contended with clearly interiorizing lines of thought. Purgatory and hell did not become spiritualized and nonphysical. Interior remorse moved by love of God and located more in the incorporeal human soul than in the body remained opposed by almost unspeakable corporal afflictions visited upon sinners who must endure them without any bodily dissipation as final release from torture. The question remained: is God mollified and divine justice satisfied primarily by intense physical suffering or by inner contrition and sorrow of heart? The theological impulse in the direction of spirituality and internality, so naturally attractive to modern investigators who emphasize it, scarcely commanded the entire range of theological views on sin and redemp-tion. Other and more vigorous ideas were still available.

Knights, Confession, and Penance

Evidence from miracle and sermon stories and from chronicles focuses our attention again on how knighthood could fit into the emerging theology designed to cleanse human society of besetting sin. Though the question is difficult and the evidence murky, several specific questions allow an approach: (1) Did knights know and care about this theology of atonement? (2) How thoroughly would they participate? (3) Would they willingly turn to their parish priest as confessor?

(1) Close scholarly investigations on both sides of the Channel help settle the question of knightly knowledge and concern.[35] In a significant study, David Crouch has made an interesting case that the early twelfth-century military aristocracy in England "shows signs of highly valuing the sacrament of penance" and that they aspired to regular, private confession. The English church was working to encourage a "penitential culture" among its laity that had even become "exciting and fashionable" among the lay elite. He draws evidence from the deathbed statements and the lives of a number of males and some females at the royal courts of Stephen and Henry I. This penitential tradition of interest reaches back into the 1120s and likely has even pre-Conquest roots.[36]

Evidence of a different sort suggests knightly awareness of the new emphasis on confession radiating from the Lateran Council of 1215. John Baldwin has studied a set of French romances written just before and just after the great council, considering these literary works at least an initial gauge of aristocratic awareness, since they were directed to courts filled with knights and ladies.[37] The two works predating the council were written by Jean Renart—*L'Escoufle* (1200–1202) and the *Roman de la Rose* (c. 1209). These, Baldwin argues, show an exteriorized and routinized sense of religion based on clerical performance of rituals; little or no interior sense of sin appears, but a generous sense of the importance of such lay values as honor and the preservation of good name is prominent. The two sample works written after the council, however—Gerbert of Montreuil's *Roman de la violette* (1227–29) and his Continuation to the *Conte du Graal* of Chrétien de Troyes (written about the same time) show a new interest in doctrine and especially focus on the sacrament of private penance. Heartfelt contrition is even emphasized in these later works as essential to a good confession.[38]

Undoubtedly, Gerbert of Montreuil was promoting the latest theological ideas about confession and penance to the knights who thronged the courts to which he sent these post-Lateran works. Such romances provided an important channel for the diffusion of chivalric ideas. Of course, this educational effort does not prove that these ideas were fully accepted. As Baldwin notes, the new ideas "competed with but did not entirely replace the exteriorized forms of the previous generation."[39] Clerical views, however, had clearly gained a hearing. These likely took hold over time. Jeremy Catto argues for close engagement of the later medieval English nobility:

> The development of the practice of personal confession, stimulated by the friars in the thirteenth century, is an obscure but probably fundamental aspect of later medieval religion. . . . It is likely that by drawing attention to the individual conscience, the practice of confession altered the whole scope of moral life. There is evidence that members of the high nobility took practical steps to examine their consciences systematically.[40]

Clerics certainly broadcast their message to the knights throughout the High and Later Middle Ages. In a starkly admonitory tale, William of Newburgh shows penance making the difference in the eternal fate of two twelfth-century English knights. His account could have been pressed into use as a sermon *exemplum*. Though both men attacked churches during the troubled reign of King Stephen (1135–54), and died on the same day, one came to everlasting bliss because he did penance; the other, who did not, roasted in eternal flames.[41]

How carefully clerics tried to fit the message to the knightly audience. They know the sensitivities they must address, illustrated by a knight who resists going to confession because he thought it would be a sign of cowardice.[42] Tellingly, one late fourteenth-century English manual attempted to reach the knightly by joining confession to chivalric ideals; the author provided a rather shaky list of ways in which making confession actually enhances that great chivalric quality of "worshype."[43] A Middle English *Gesta Romanorum* refers twice to penance as a kind of tournament: "the tournament of penance by which we may come to eternal joy."[44] The wise confessor in a story retold frequently draws on military customs used for ending quarrels; he tells a stubborn knight who will not make full peace with God through penance that he should at least declare a truce for a fortnight. He then extends the term gradually, finally getting an unlimited peace between God and the truculent knight.[45] A more blatant inducement for the warriors appears in a miracle story told by Caesarius of Heisterbach: he presents a knight who wins a judicial duel against a huge opponent through "the virtue of confession."[46]

All this evidence and scholarly analysis is helpful and important. We can likewise appreciate the need for caution, a need that may bear strengthening as we continue with our list of questions.

(2) The vexing issue, of course, is estimating how broadly or enthusiastically acceptance and participation spread among the knighthood. The great body of chivalric literature shows much borrowing of clerical ideas but also highly laicized forms of penance. Men who considered their profession heroic likely wanted penance to be heroic. In the early thirteenth-century *Lancelot*, the hero himself assigns such penance to a traitor that Lancelot (rather than God) would consider himself well repaid.[47] A knight in a story by Caesarius of Heisterbach takes the prize by assigning himself two thousand years in purgatory.[48] The notion of paying with swords and meritorious suffering would be an attractive alternative. A late medieval English book of homilies, Mirk's *Festial*, insists that a sinner must

> work his body in good deeds, and sustain his life with labor, and
> put away all idleness and sloth. For he who will not work on earth
> with men, as St. Bernard says, will indeed work with the fiend of
> Hell. . . . For just as a knight shows his wounds sustained in a battle to
> his great commendation, so all the sins for which a man has confessed
> and done penance can be shown much to his honor and to the great
> discomfort of the devil.[49]

After Gawain has accidentally killed a lady in the *Merlin Continuation*, his penance is assigned by ladies at court (as commanded by the male authority of Arthur and Merlin). This penance turns out to be practicing certain ideal chivalric values in his life: always serving and defending ladies—"unless it is against your honor"—and (as Arthur insists) ever granting mercy to a defeated knight.[50] In the terrible internecine killing that disrupts the Grail quest late in the Old French Lancelot-Grail cycle, Calogrenant, who knows he is about to die blameless under the sword of his brother Lionel, calls out:

> Dear Father, Jesus Christ, who allowed me to enter in Your service,
> though I was not as worthy as I should have been, take pity on my soul
> so that this pain which my body must endure because of the good and

kind deed I attempted [the rescue of a maiden while his brother was in great difficulty] may be counted as penance and relief to my soul.[51]

How ideal if penance could indeed consist—as much as possible—in the very practice of their hard lives as warriors. This book has argued repeatedly that such a view formed one major strand in chivalric ideology. We have found a steady stream of passages that openly assert (as Lancaster and Charny did) what is at least suggested in the death of Calogrenant—that the very vocation of chivalry is a form of penance. In his *Morte Darthur*, Sir Thomas Malory, another practicing knight, gives a telling speech to Gawain whom a hermit is trying to bring to penance in standard form for his "synne." Gawain asks what that penance would be, only to be told it must be what the hermit decides: "such as I woll gyff the." Gawain responds: "Nay, I may do no penaunce, for we knuyghtes adventures many times suffir grete woo and payne." No further penance is needed or can be tolerated, since the hard knightly life is in itself penitential. The good man can respond only with a resigned "Well," and hold his peace.[52] At times even a hermit must simply recognize knightly life and assumptions and factor knightly labor into the formula of penance.[53] After Gaheriet has confessed all the sins of which he thought he was guilty, the *Merlin Continuation* says a hermit "gave him such penance as he thought he could do along with his labor at arms."[54]

(3) Knights adopted penance into their vocabulary and mentalité: yet without discounting their piety, it seems fair to doubt that they were generally willing actors in the ritual of confession precisely as outlined in Canon 21 of Lateran IV and the handbooks for confessors. We must picture the actual process.[55] There were no medieval confessional boxes to assure genuine privacy. Confessing sinners knelt openly in a church at the knees of their priest, who inclined his body toward them with his hood providing the only screen to block their voices. The shame proud folk felt in making such a confession was in fact part of the penance, sometimes even the most important part, as was recognized by both theologians and writers of romance.[56] Even if the confession might be whispered into the hood of the priest's inclined head, so that it was largely inaudible to others waiting their turn, acts of satisfaction imposed could well reveal the nature of the sin. The principle that the punishment should fit the crime did not have to await the genius of Gilbert and Sullivan. Even the jurisdictional reservation to the bishop of certain classes of

sin (and a few to the pope) provided further clues to all interested observers in the community.

There was another worry to trouble knights. Did confessors tell tales, sober or in their cups? We know they talked to each other, as their books of *exempla* document.[57] Moral tales undoubtedly appreciated by the laity pictured dire consequences for those confessors who broke the formally imposed silence. In one, a knight who had secretly killed a man confessed his dire sin, only to learn that the priest revealed the murder to their ruler, hoping for a reward. Instead, the righteous ruler blinded the priest and cut out his tongue.[58]

It is hard to imagine knights confessing their sins individually in an open church while kneeling before the local priest, even if we picture them moving by right to the head of a queue of their fellow parishioners or even, more likely, if the church were cleared for them.[59] Questions that knights might be asked as guides to making their confession could require answers about pillage, extortion, injustice, oppression of tenants, violence against clerics, killing in war, participation in tournaments, urging a lord into unjust war, simony, and keeping a private chapel without license.[60] Insight into knightly reluctance appears indirectly but powerfully in the steady stream of admonitory *exempla* urging full participation. A pious knight, one such story relates, was ashamed to confess to his parish priest and so sought out the urban anonymity of London to confess in Westminster Abbey. There a clever devil disguised as a monk heard him tell his sins to no good spiritual effect. As he lay on his deathbed, only the powerful intervention of Saint Peter, the Virgin Mary, and Mary Magdalene saved him from eternal fire.[61] Were historical knights as unwilling as this fellow to participate along with all their social inferiors in a practice so tinged with shame and to carry out the patently nonheroic penance assigned?

Concern over possession of unlicensed private chapels (a question that we have seen could be asked of confessing knights) raises the likelihood of one solution: confession to a private chaplain in a congenial setting. The practice was likely widespread, especially after the appearance of orders of friars on the scene, though precise estimates are likely impossible, especially for those below the level of the very great. Philippe Contamine says that in France by the later Middle Ages they were "innumerable."[62] Jeremy Catto writes of the later medieval English nobility, "Perhaps by 1300, certainly by 1350, it had become customary for noble families to be advised by their own confessors, usually friars, who were trusted intimates of the household, and often executors of their wills."[63] In mid-fourteenth-century England, Henry of Lancaster, as we have seen, wrote his *Livre des seyntz medicines* at the advice of his own confessor; across the Channel, one of many privileges cherished by Geoffroi de Charny was a license to keep a private chapel. Scholars would like to know at what social rank (and in what numbers and by what time) the potentially troublesome aspects of confession were lessened by the privilege of recourse to a private confessor. If, as seems likely, a significant body of knights of lesser status than the great lords lacked this privilege, we are left asking what transpired in their minds as they heard that their salvation depended upon periodically acknowledging their faults to the local cleric. It seems significant for proud knights at any level and in any time that the act of confession and the penance that followed involved shame.[64]

Knights who confess in romance almost invariably tell their sins to a hermit or sometimes to a cleric of suitable standing: an abbot, a bishop, or even the pope, rather than the prescribed parish priest.[65] Caesarius of Heisterbach reports a lord in the habit of confessing to four abbots at once.[66] The choice of confessor in knightly literature is significant, for hermits (and even the bishops in romance) are much closer to the knights in spirit, in social status, even in vocation than any local priest. Regularly, romances specify that the hermit in question is a former knight who has given up the vigorous life in a more sedate old age. Romance hermits live at a convenient single day's ride from each other, their hermitages dotting the forest with little cells of accessible hospitality and holiness. Hermits understand knights and cater to their every need; their hermitages are congenial confessionals no less than plain hostelries. Living the heroic life in a spiritual mode (after a hard and heroic knightly career), they are close to the divine and can interpret dreams, sometimes predict future events, often guide the perplexed, and willingly hear confession. As the Post-Vulgate *Quest of the Holy Grail* explains,

> Know that at that time there were in the kingdom of Logres a great
> number of hermits everywhere, which was not without its amazing side,
> and there were few who were not knights or noblemen. At that time
> by God's grace, all the knights of that kingdom, after they had borne
> arms thirty or forty years, left their lands and their families and went
> to the mountains, to the most secluded place they could find and there
> performed penance for their sins.[67]

These are ideal clerics hot from the forge of knightly imagination. How real this image could be for practicing knights appears in the wonderful story told in the life of Saint Wulfric of Hazelbury, an English hermit of the mid-twelfth century. A vigorous knight gave this holy man his chain-mail hauberk "as to a stronger knight" and the hermit wore it until in old age it simply slipped off his withered shoulders.[68] The romance image of a solitary knight errant in a forest hermitage consulting with an old hermit on spiritual matters—and at least infrequently confessing tearfully to him—is one form of pious and independent response by chivalric ideology to the new lay theology.

In some of this literature, knights even dispense with the hermits, arranging penance for themselves without any clerical mediation, often after a clear message of warning comes to them directly from God. The degree of independence is striking. Once they receive the divine warning and survive the crisis it entails, the reformed sinners announce a new life. Yet they often do condign penance through the continued heroic exercise of their knightly labors, though now in a new mode. Here chivalric ideology is manifested in action rather than explicit statements of ideas. Guy of Warwick in the fourteenth-century English romance classically shows this point of view.[69] Through the first thematic half of the romance he tries to perform enough chivalric acts of prowess to win the love of Felice, the daughter of his lord. She has high standards in such matters and it takes thousands of lines of hard labor with lance, shield, and sword against able foes before she accepts Guy as a knight and finally as the best knight. Having won every fight and thus won his lady in marriage, Guy experiences an unexpected crisis. One night, musing over the night sky "thikke with sterre," his thoughts turn to the splendid honor God has done him by granting him victory always. What has he done for God in return? In all his fighting he has sought merely worldly fame and the hand of a prized lady. These thoughts bring a resolve to enter "goddis seruyse" (God's service). Felice, to whom he generously offers half the spiritual benefit he will earn, advises him instead to follow traditional aristocratic modes of repaying or pacifying God; Guy should found churches and monasteries.[70] Guy, however is thinking not of endowment but of heroic asceticism, carried out with his own body: "What I have done with my body / shall be paid for with my body / To free me of that wrong."[71] Though he bequeaths his sword to his unborn son (leaving instructions for his eventual knightly training) and sets off as a pilgrim, Guy is soon drawn back into a vigorous life of prowess. He atones for his earlier chivalric life, one heedless of God, with a new chivalric life of pious prowess "in God's service." This entails more fighting as a great knight, now without incurring the stain of vainglory. He fights for the rescue of friends and the restoration of their honor. In other words, his great prowess upholds the ideals of lay society through the valorous fighting that wins him spiritual merit. This highly popular romance pictures knightly conversion/atonement as carried out essentially on chivalric terms; a special interpretation of the economy of salvation rests on the understanding that links the good Lord and one of his good knights. Guy satisfies God throughout most of the remainder of his life not by walking pacifically as a barefoot pilgrim, staff in hand, visiting shrines, but by fighting bravely with weapons and suffering meritoriously. That he becomes a hermit near the close of his life hardly discounts the half lifetime of knightly atonement. Rather, it simply shows the aristocratic capacity to make use of all religious options, and to close a career with a kind of extended deathbed experience, the enacted equivalent of wearing a monastic or Templar robe at the end of life, after a rich career of heroic atonement through demanding deeds of prowess. Knightly ideology fused elements of current theological thinking on confession and penance in a manner best calculated to advance chivalry. It is no accident that a story in the *Gesta Romanorum* refers to Christ calling men to the "tournament of penance, by which we may come to everlasting joy."[72]

That knights are pointedly reminded how powerful and necessary confession and penance are seems telling, an indication that their views were not fully in accord with ecclesiastical precepts. The author of the Post-Vulgate *Quest of the Holy Grail* pictures even Bors, pious Grail knight that he is, reminded by a hermit "that if you were the best knight now in the world, your knighthood would only harm you until you were clean confessed and had received the body of God."[73] Readers of one miracle story learned that a knight who went to confession accompanied by a devil came out so changed by confession that the devil could no longer recognize him.[74] Models embodying clerical views appear in imaginative literary texts doing and saying what the clerics ardently preach. The thirteenth-century Post-Vulgate *Death of Arthur* presents a classic example. The archbishop of Canterbury, keeping company with the surviving Grail knights, exuberantly declares penance to be "better than all other worldly things," and promises to keep at it while life lasts; it is only slight suffering and it brings such disproportionate benefits.[75] A departed sinner in the *History of the Holy Grail* reports from an otherworld of flaming torment that all sinners can yet hope: God forgives them "as long as they do penance."[76] Gawain learns from a hermit during the *Quest of the Holy Grail*, that the seven brothers he killed for their evil custom at the Castle of Maidens could better have been allowed to do penance and thus reconcile themselves with God.[77] A hermit gives Lancelot even more specific advice in the post-Vulgate *Quest of the Holy Grail*, didactically specifying that atonement for his sin requires the three processes of contrition, confession, and penance, as stressed in current theology.[78]

Ideal knights may occasionally be shown obediently confessing and carrying out the penance assigned in at least an approximation of the approved manner. And most are prudent enough to know that at the end of life confession is a wise step. We can take Arthur, fearing imminent death early in the *Lancelot*, as crying out for all knighthood, "Oh God! Confession! The time has come!"[79] When he is actually dying from grievous wounds late in the *Alliterative Morte Arthure*, the king again calls out, this time in genuine need: "Call a confessor for me carrying Christ in his hands; whatever happens, I will be confessed quickly."[80] At least some of Malory's characters reinforce the point. A sorrowful Lancelot confesses to a hermit, and wears a hair shirt in the name of holy penance.[81] This proud knight, who has always returned a hostile blow with interest, now gladly takes a penitential beating ("the discipline") from his hermit/confessor.[82] Bors dons a rough tunic and changes his diet (to a regimen that will dampen lust) at a hermit's insistence.[83]

That the message could, indeed, reach receptive historical knights can be read in the treatise of Henry of Lancaster. Henry has interiorized the framework of contrition, confession, and penance: he writes repeatedly of confession of heart (contrite de coer), is sensible of the danger of sudden death, admits that he must make "satisfaction for sin with his body and goods according to the direction of his priest."[84]

The depth of piety in Lancaster's treatise is informative. Yet the great mass of chivalric evidence leaves the impression that moving many knights into an ideal clerical frame for atonement could be difficult.[85] Even the ultimately religious hero Perceval (in Robert de Boron's romance named for this knight and in Chrétien's more famous romance) comes to genuine confession only after many years of brashness and sin. His sister has warned Perceval that knights in the area would kill him simply for his horse, but that he must likewise be careful not to commit the great sin of killing a knight. He is also burdened by the sin of causing his mother's death by suddenly leaving home in search of the chivalric life. His sister wants him to confess and take penance from their uncle, who is a hermit. Almost as if baiting the hook, she adds that this holy uncle might be able to put him on the right track for the Fisher King (another uncle), who is keeper of the Grail. Though Perceval agrees, all that transpires in the hermitage is a polite conversation in which the hermit-uncle tells Perceval he should not kill knights but should rather "spare them and bear with them in all kinds of ways for the sake of your mother's soul."[86] If this is some quasi-penance, Perceval is unable to perform it, for he kills a knight immediately after leaving the hermitage (though he is sorry, and thinks the man brought it on himself).[87] He then wanders seven years without thinking of God at all. At the end of that time, he is seen by pilgrims on Good Friday, armed and ready for more fighting. Realization of his error sends him back to his hermit-uncle for what is stated to be confession and penance (the content of each left unspecified). Yet even after religious cleansing, he still breaks his chivalric vow not to sleep twice in one place until he finds the Fisher King and Grail. In his Grail quest, it is Merlin who rebukes him, but then shows the way to his goals.[88] Spiritual and chivalric conversions are evident here, both purchased at the cost of a hard life of prowess and goodness as required by Merlin and even by God. If all comes out as it should, the slow progress also registers.

Clerics recognized how demanding their task was, how tentative progress could be. Henry of Lancaster seems more pious and malleable than many of his fellow knights. Major knightly figures in the classic Vulgate Cycle of romance and in the great compendium of chivalry by Sir Thomas Malory show they have not fully absorbed the clerical guidance and warnings. Significantly, Malory, a practicing knight no less than an author of romance, mentions confession and penance scarcely at all, except in his retelling of the *Quest of the Holy Grail* which he largely borrowed from a highly clerical French source, where they were emphasized.[89]

Clerics clearly worried about this degree of knightly unwillingness to participate fully, as they continued to worry generally about the unsettling independence written into much of chivalric literature. A sizeable body of sermon stories, stretching across several centuries, documents their conviction that knights need regular correction and encouragement—even sharp if indirect threat—on issues of confession and penance. Many sermon *exempla* provided by Étienne de Bourbon begin with the phrase, "a certain infamous knight was unwilling to perform any penance at all."[90] In one of these stories even Pope Alexander III (1159–81), while in France, failed repeatedly to impose penance on a knight; he finally gave the sinner his valuable ring asking only that the knight think and talk of death whenever he glanced at it. This worked; the knight returned, requesting that a full penance be imposed for his wrongs.[91] Yet another knight will do no fasting, pilgrimage, or even prayers as penance. Told by an accommodating confessor to avoid the food he hates (a technique we have encountered before), he comes to crave it. Told to avoid manual work on Sunday, he feels strangely compelled to take over a peasant's plow in the fields. Finally, he gives in and asks for a real penance.[92]

Warnings to the obdurate could be dramatic, but only sometimes are said to have worked. Gerald of Wales assured readers of his *Jewel of the Church* that a young man from the army of Philip II of France was unable to enter a church whose doors stood wide open. Advised by a monk that some unconfessed sin blocked his entry, the man confessed to stealing wood from a poor widow, restored the value of what he had stolen, and accepted penance. The case was solved.[93] A heretical great lord (in a story from Caesarius of Heisterbach) unwisely scorned the church of Rome and, rejecting confession, died impenitent. Only one result could follow.[94] In another of his *exempla*, a certain Landgrave Ludwig (a notorious robber and tyrant, who had died two years before Caesar wrote) has rejected his confessor's urgings to repent: if he is one of the elect, the landgrave argues, he is saved; if not, no good deeds will help. Caesarius warned all readers that the man died under a great burden of sin.[95]

Timeliness was crucial. Pragmatic clerical voices tirelessly reminded knights that lives filled with much danger should be insured by regular confession; death came swiftly and unexpectedly. Why delay? The very repetition, of course, points to a continuing need to convince the doubtful. Such motives obviously inform the clerical tale in which Emperor Ferdinand III in the mid-thirteenth century was visited three times by the solicitous Virgin Mary, who warned him to make his confession. Though he unwisely ignored two warnings from even so powerful a source, her third visit at last moved him and he sought out a confessor. It was just in time. On the following day he was killed in battle by a stone.[96] The terrifying, spectral black knights who threaten Arthur and his fellows in the *Perlesvaus* are significantly identified as those who died without repentance; they must scour the woods at night and collect body parts of slain knights.[97] A grimly realistic tale by Caesarius of Heisterbach pictures a knight and his two sons fatally wounded by enemies. When Cistercian monks come to remove the bloody bodies and find the father still alive—though he at first feigns death, fearing they are the murderers returned—they provide him with the "oil of pity and the wine of repentance" through confession and last rites. This knight, Caesarius announces firmly, entered heaven.[98] Was not the reader or sermon listener first to admire the charitable Cistercians and then to ponder the fate of the others? One of the highly practical benefits a heavenly patron or (more commonly) patroness provided, in fact, was time for that final, all-important act of confession in *articulo mortis* (at the point of death).

In clerical stories, knights are regularly said to have neglected confession and to stand in great need of such aid. A knight devoted to St. Mary Magdalene is killed in battle, an *exemplum* tells, but through her merits revives long enough to take the crucial final act.[99] Historical figures who appear in the *History of the Albigensian Crusade* regularly and gleefully report that important men on the opposite side died without time for confession.[100] The Blessed Virgin regularly provides such services (as we have already seen in Chapter 7). Three brothers in an *exemplum* told repeatedly had plotted to kill a knight, but were foiled; two were captured and hanged. The third managed to escape and prayed to the Blessed Virgin that he might never die without making his confession. When the avenging relatives finally caught him and hacked his body to pieces, he was graciously given time to confess before he expired.[101] Even to a knight who openly lived by plunder, she provides the crucial time for confession as he lies dying with a lance through his heart. He has, after all, been her devotee.[102] She convinces another pillaging knight to use his gains to found, enter, and lead a monastery. Yet he still requires close attention; when he dies without confessing, she must approach her son to secure his salvation.[103] And delaying confession while counting on last minute help, or waiting until the death agony struck, was literally playing with fire. Delay costs seven additional years of torment in purgatory for one warrior.[104] Walter Map tells a strangely admonitory story about the knight Eudo, who has lost all possessions and makes a desperate compact with the devil for recovery. One of the most seductive devilish arguments convincing Eudo is that he need not fear hell, being assured "you have a long life before you, and ample time is left you. Moreover, before your death I will forearm you by three plain tokens . . . so that after each you may have time to repent."[105] Eudo and the devil set to work plundering at will. Of course, the knight repents only temporarily after the first two warning signs (a fall from his horse that breaks his leg, and a seeming chance arrow striking his eye), slipping quickly back into the sinful life of pleasure and plunder. Though truly repentant and fearful after the third sign (the death of his first son), Eudo confronts an angry and disbelieving bishop when he tries at last to confess; on the spur of the moment the angry bishop assigns Eudo the pen-ance of throwing himself into a blazing fire. Walter Map blames the bishop for such a penance, but relates that Eudo leaps joyfully into the flames, anx-ious to perform his penance, and is burned to ashes.

Clerics worried over one final knightly lapse: they might make a partial confession or they might not carry out the penance assigned. In more than one *exemplum*, a knight brought to confess willfully leaves some sins untold. One warning pictures a knight unwisely making an incomplete confession to his bishop. A monk observing him can see a symbolic black dog gripping the knight by the throat, even after the unwitting bishop has pronounced absolution. Only when the knight is brought back for full confession does the phantom dog loosen his grip and vanish.[106] Full performance of penance similarly freed a sinful knight from the torment of a lizard attached by sharp teeth and claws to his shoulder, in a story told earlier by Walter Map.[107]

Perhaps the most evocative evidence appears in a short and charming French romance, *Le Chevalier au barissel* (*The Knight with the Barrel*). The story is pious, and direct; in fact, it seems (like *Saint Patrick's Purgatory* dis-cussed in the previous chapter) a blend of extended *exemplum* and romance. Written in the late twelfth or early thirteenth century and reproduced many times, it suggests how hard it could be to get some knights to confess and how much harder to get them to understand contrition.[108] Even if he is "of great reputation (de grant renon)"—and handsome, rich, of good family, noble in appearance—the knight in question surely stands in dire need of confession. He is, in fact, false, disloyal, traitorous, fierce, prideful, and cruel. From a secure fortress that eliminates fear of lay authority at any level (king, prince, count, viscount), he has for thirty years sallied forth to ravage the district, sparing neither high nor low, males nor females, lay nor religious folk; all falling within his power are killed, robbed, or shamed. He has no more fear of God than of lay authority; he avoids all religious services, and ignores days set aside for pious fasting. As the story opens, he even demands a fine venison breakfast on Good Friday when all the faithful should reverently fast and, above all, avoid meat. His friends—obviously more pious knights—"si chevalier . . . qui plus de cuer a Dieu tendirent"—try to convince him to confess his sins to a holy hermit in the neighboring woods, adding that he should shed tears of repentance. "'Cry?' he exclaims. 'Is this some joke?'"[109] He roughly suggests they can cry while he laughs, for he surely will not shed tears.[110] His similar response to the idea of confession in general, a few lines later, is "Confess! A hundred devils!"[111]

Yet he finally goes with "those hypocrites (ces papelars)," asserting that he does this for their sake, rather than for God. He intends to make a phony confession like that of Renart (li confessions Regnart)—the wily and amoral fox in the popular animal stories of the day, who even tricked and ate his bird/ confessor.[112] To make such a faked confession, he crudely declares, is merely "to piss into the wind."[113] He certainly will not appear humble; he comes to the hermitage "more fierce than a mad dog or a werewolf."[114] Though his friends piously come before the holy man in confession, this proud knight resists, but possibly reveals a crack in his armor by asking, with regard to God, "Why should I pray to him when I do nothing for him?"[115]

A model of wise persuasion, the hermit meets the knight outside his chapel; speaking softly, respectfully, he welcomes the recalcitrant sinner, appeals to the gentle heart that, as a knight, he must possess, offers him his services as priest of Christ crucified for all sinners. This care is met with more rudeness: the knight announces that he has nothing to say to the priest, and nothing to receive from him; he would actually prefer a nice fat goose (cras oison) to anything the priest has on offer. Confessing, the holy man assures the knight, is done for God, not for his priest. But the knight declares the hermit would be too harsh an intermediary (trop fier plaidieu) and they, in effect, begin the bargaining process over penance often suggested as a technique in confessor's manuals. When the hermit assures the knight that he need found no religious houses (no maison et no capele et no couvent), the knight counters that he will cooperate on condition he is not even asked to give charitably or say prayers (que ja aumosne n'i ferai ne patrenostre n'i dirai). Assuring him he can leave if he is displeased, the hermit takes him sweetly by the hand into his chapel. The knight complains that the priest never stops and enters the chapel with ill grace. The hermit—again, sweetly (doucement)—leads him to the altar and there announces that the knight is his captive now (or estes vous en ma prison) but must consider it no insult to talk with him.[116] Unless he were to cut off his head, says the hermit, the prisoner could not escape by any act until he has "told his life (dite vostre vie)." Wrathfully, the knight refuses and—obviously considering himself formally a captive—demands his liberty. But the hermit now begins to speak specifically of sins, confession, and the penitence owed to God who died on the cross. As sweetly as before, he asks the knight (who has warned that he is close to killing him and freeing the world) to tell him just one sin.[117] It is Good Friday, the hermit implores, the day of Christ's great sacrifice. Finally moved, the knight-prisoner (li sires qui tous fu pris) finally experiences a sense of thorough shame (devint trestous honteus).

An important milestone has been reached, and yet the issue of penance remains. At first the hermit suggests fasting each Friday for seven years. Astonished, the knight says he could not manage even three years. Nor can he consider walking barefoot for a year, the next suggestion. Nor would he wear wool without underclothing; his flesh would be troubled and the vermin would be obnoxious. Nor would he discipline himself each morning with a switch; a "bad idea (pesme novele)," the knight thinks. He announces as a principle that he cannot think of striking or tearing his own flesh (Je ne poroie ce souffrir ne ma car romper ne ferir). Likewise he rejects pilgrimage to the Holy Land, or to Rome, or to Santiago, or even going annually to a local monastery, there to say specified prayers while kneeling. Finally, the hermit names a penance easily accepted: the knight must simply fill and return the hermit's water barrel. With a scornful laugh (de desdaing rist), the knight agrees. An apparently easy task, however, proves impossible: water will decidedly not flow into the barrel, whatever he tries. Outraged, he revisits the hermit and swears a great oath[118] to achieve the task set for him. The hermit sees divine anger for sin in the miracle; the knight feels only irritation and assures one and all that he does nothing for God.[119] He will find a stream to fill the barrel.

His penitential quest, such as it is, begins. For a year he searches, suffering much "paine et travaus."[120] Selling his clothes for food, he must wear garments that cover him with shame.[121] He wanders in all weather; he is forced to beg. After a hard year, his travels take him back to the hermitage on another Good Friday. There he hears that his penance has not been completed because it lacks repentance.[122] The hermit calls out for mercy to God and the Blessed Virgin, offering himself as the object for divine wrath while praying vicariously for the knight. Witnessing this selfless love from a man unconnected to him, holding nothing from him, the knight abandons his characteristic state of wrath and fierce independence. He prays for true repentance and senses his own responsibility for his sins. With "bele courtoisie" God recognizes his good intent and allows the knight's troubled heart to generate a single great tear from his eyes. This falls "like a crossbow shot (com on trait de boujon)"[123] straight into the barrel. The single tear fills the barrel to the breaking point. A joyful hermit pronounces the penance complete, the sinning knight saved from hell. He receives a final communion from the hermit and dies piously in his arms.[124]

This process leading to confession and penance is, of course, imaginary; the ending miraculous. At the edge of the stage hover pious knights pictured as accepting the penitential system of the church. All ends well. Yet the spotlight has relentlessly followed the recalcitrant knight in center stage and revealed (with theatric exaggeration) the elaborate, even devious, means a confessor might have to employ—even a hermit, the chivalric confessor of choice—to bring a proud warrior to recount his sins and accept the clerical scheme for their cleansing.

In a rich mix of ideas, clerics debated whether sin was neutralized by heroic, physical penances or by inner contrition, whether confession was essentially a public rite for cleansing a sinner once in a lifetime or was to be used repeatedly in a regular program of private sessions with a parish priest. As always, chivalric ideology drew on more than one strand of religious discussion—while ignoring or suppressing others—to construct the most supportive set of interlinked ideas. In effect, knightly ideas emphasized the heroic element in penance over contrition of the heart, but accepted the idea of repeatable penance; meritorious suffering of their profession stood alongside (perhaps, for some, in place of) a regimen of cleansings mediated by their local priest. The fusion of heroic with repeatable penance gave them maximum benefits and eliminated any disabilities or dread stain of shame. In tough cases and emergencies, pious shame might prove unavoidable, of course; a sense of guilt or at least political prudence might demand dramatic—even shaming—rites of a great knight/king: Henry II after the murder of Thomas Becket, Emperor Henry IV in the snow at Canossa. In general practice, however, knighthood at every level wanted no form of penance that would diminish their status or sacred honor. They compromised, but maintained a needed degree of independence. Those who were able turned to private confessors in their households. But the general belief in hard knightly labor and merit seems to have remained firm. They warmly asserted that they had a special arrangement with the Lord of Hosts, with the Christ-Knight, and with the gracious queen of the heavenly court. While never straying from piety, their view differed significantly from the model that clerics mandated for lay folk in general. Exactly how regularly this left most of them kneeling before the priest on the floor of their parish church remains unknowable.

Their stance brought splendid benefits to knighthood. By insisting on their own heroic, corporal penance they could claim they stood beneath the banner of religious conservatism: they followed—or rather modified for their own use—one of the ancient strands of penitential practice dating to the early Christian church and helped maintain it into the age of chivalry. Yet they firmly believed true penance was possible while continuing in a military profession. Performing penance through deeds of arms was the praiseworthy practice of their *ordo*. Physical suffering endured throughout a lifetime of campaign and battle for righteous causes counted when souls were weighed in the balance, closely watched by demons and angels.

CHAPTER 9

Writing the Death Certificate
for Chivalric Ideology

CHIVALRIC IDEOLOGY ENJOYED a remarkably long and influential life in early European history. Throughout the High and Later Middle Ages and for an uncertain run of years into the Early Modern era, chivalry formed the framework for thought and action among the nonclerical elite. Since many who merely hoped some day to join the elite—or who were actively taking on its coloration as fully as possible—likewise looked to chivalry as the guide to life and conduct, chivalric ideology may safely be considered the lay esprit de corps, the body of ideas by which laymen evaluated conduct, shaped thought, and launched aspiration.[1] Alternative frames of reference had not been much in evidence.

Yet nearly all scholars would insist that, somewhere in the borderlands between "late medieval" and "early modern," vigorous medieval chivalry died, or at least underwent radical transfiguration. Were it possible to draw up the required certificate, what words would we enter for cause of death? Justifiably, we might consider simple natural expiration in old age unlikely for so vigorous a body of ideas, and we may likewise rule out mere quiet euthanasia to relieve an aged sufferer. Prudently, we may leave the issue of the justifiability of alleged homicide to other inquests.

Like the reliable Captain Renault (as played memorably by Claude Raines) in the classic film *Casablanca*, we might first round up the usual suspects. The resulting lineup will obviously include some of the great motive forces of the age: (1) changing military professionalism, technology, and tactics; and the bureaucratic support of war (often considered a "military revolution," sometimes specifically narrowed to a "gunpowder revolution"); (2) the new learning represented by humanism as a challenge to a chivalric lay esprit de corps; (3) radical religious reform undercutting spiritually efficacious atonement secured through meritorious corporal suffering; and (4) growing state power.

If the list seems long, it shortens quickly. Could the technology associated with gunpowder simply blast the practice of chivalry—and its ideology—out of existence? Close investigations suggest that early gunpowder weapons were neither accurate enough, nor sufficiently lethal at long enough distances (especially against decent armor), to effect a revolution by themselves.[2] Was the force of a set of broader tactical and sociocultural changes (size of armies, infantry tactics, new fortifications), so sudden and sweeping that they—rather than sulfurous blasts of black powder—killed the chivalric ethos by rendering the men who practiced it superfluous? In the view of many scholars it has become increasingly hard to rank such agencies as prime suspects.[3] Granted, debate has been highly productive as well as contentious and continuous for more than a decade.[4] But however informative this body of scholarship on warfare and society in various periods, it has not produced any agreement as to timing and pace of change. With estimates of time of death varying over centuries (carrying into the seventeenth or even eighteenth centuries in some instances) and with precise agents still in doubt, this cluster of suspects can be exonerated as primary cause.[5]

Humanism and the Fate of Chivalry: Erasmus and More

Could new ways of thought powerfully at work in society prove sufficiently destructive of chivalry to warrant an entry on its formal death certificate? If chivalry functioned, as this book has argued, as the pattern for elite lay society, might not radically new ideas about the formation and nature of the elite ranks mount a disabling challenge?[6] Such questions draw our attention first to humanistic thought as a hallmark of the era. We will then turn to a second set of potentially challenging ideas, radical notions of religious reform.

Some of the most famous practitioners of humanism could champion an anti-heroic, anti-war, and anti-chivalric stance. How severely humanist scholarship could target the heroic ideal embodied in chivalry appears in the early sixteenth century in works of two leading Christian humanists active in England, Erasmus (who visited regularly at this time) and Thomas More. Though Henry VIII was acclaimed as an ideal ruler by many humanists, Erasmus and More expressed horror at the vigorous war policy the king embraced early in his reign.[7] Henry liked to be styled the Tenth Worthy (completing the medieval set of nine) and founded royal armories at Greenwich to provide plate for the "marcyall ffayts" that were his delight.[8] His humanist critics never endorsed pure pacifism (an anachronistic concept for the time), and showed the prudent indirection required whenever criticizing such a monarch; yet Erasmus and More vigorously attacked the chivalric ideal that animated his early foreign policy. Though his father had exercised frugal caution and had maintained a French alliance, Henry patterned himself instead on the warrior king Henry V and sought a great continental victory to shine alongside his medieval predecessor's triumph on the field of Agincourt.[9] With fantasies of showy victory in mind, the young Henry reportedly asserted

> that it behooved him to enter upon his first military experience in so important and difficult a war in order that he might . . . create such a fine opinion about his valour among all men that they would clearly understand that his ambition was not merely to equal but indeed to exceed the glorious deeds of his ancestors.[10]

To this end he assembled an army more than three times the size of the one Henry V had led in his earlier invasion of France. In this new force (or its adjuncts at sea or on the Scottish border) served thirty-six of the forty-two temporal peers of the realm or their representatives, contributing more than a third of Henry's army from their own retainers.[11] Royal policy had obviously gained aristocratic support.

Closely informed about the invasion, Erasmus lamented that behind the pomp, the blare of trumpets, and the blasts of guns there was "wholesale butchery, the cruel fate of the killers and the killed."[12] His Christian peacemaking, though not pacifism, was based on the Beatitudes, interpreted in a direction quite unlike that in the manuscript illustration with which this book began.[13] "A tragedy like that," Erasmus lamented, "contains such a mass of woes that a human heart can hardly bear to describe it."[14] His own heart had been wounded by news that Alexander Stewart, a dear friend and former pupil, had been killed at the recent battle of Flodden. To this lamented friend he rhetorically posed the question, "Tell me, what had you to do with Mars, the stupidest of the poets' gods, you who were consecrated to the Muses,

even to Christ?"[15] Constant human warfare has always meant brother killing brother, father killing son, he believed, even when all are Christians. "O
blindness of the human mind! No one is astonished, no one horrified." Custom determines all: "So true it is that nothing is too wicked or too cruel to
win approval, if it has the sanction of custom." He charges that the customary
practices of the heroic stance, of chivalry, have distorted the gospel. Young
men rush to war inflamed by exemplars held up for them by flatterers and the
foolish (including theologians); only slowly do they learn "to the suffering of
the whole world, that war is a thing to be avoided by every possible means."[16]
Erasmus even denounced the classical font of heroic literature: "Our Illiad
contains nothing, indeed, but the heated folly of stupid kings and peoples."[17]
Erasmus had opened his earlier treatise, *Enchiridion*, written to a practicing
soldier, with the passage from Job that headed the Harley manuscript illumination examined at the start of this book: "militia est vita hominis super terram" (the life of man on earth is warfare—or struggle, or a form of chivalry).
But his book interprets this maxim in a purely spiritual sense; undercutting
structural timbers of the chivalric ethos, he repeatedly denigrates mere physical capacity to overwhelm opponents, blasts hollow worldly honor, and warns
against the insatiable appetite for vengeance that makes the injurer worse
than the injured.[18] To those contemporary Christians who found justification
for warfare in accounts of divinely sanctioned conquest in the Hebrew Scriptures he wryly commented that yet these same people eat pork.[19]

Thomas More enthusiastically joined the attack on the heroic muse.
Though his first target presented less challenge to his pen than the great
Greek classic Erasmus had denounced, he did satirically deflate a contemporary poem written in high epic style about a slain French naval leader.[20] Yet
more potently, in his discussion of military affairs (de re militari) in Utopia,
he advocates a strictly pragmatic and clearly non-heroic approach to warfare.
His Utopians regard war with loathing "as an activity fit only for beasts."[21]
Contrary to the view of most people, "they count nothing so inglorious as
glory sought in war."[22] His telling inversion of chivalric values continues with
a claim that the best victory is won not by prowess but "by stratagem and
cunning," for even animals can win by brute force.[23] Avoiding danger is more
important than gaining fame.[24] Best of all is to sow dissention among the
enemy, assassinate their leaders, or encourage their unfriendly neighbors into
action so as to win without fighting at all. Picked troops of Utopian youth
must be readied to kill or capture enemy leaders on the field, if it comes to
a fight, but rough mercenaries (by which More evidently means the Swiss)

should do as much of the fighting as possible. Utopians do not ravage enemy territory, sack captured cities, or indeed take any booty at all. Even if it is inevitable, war should simply be fought efficiently and won quickly, without grand thoughts of honor. Such ideals stand much of chivalric thought on its head.[25]

The issues, of course, remain how widely the circle of ideas spread, how influential they proved to be, and how representative they were. As a frontal assault on a warrior ethos, the results can only register as failure. Had the critical point of view of these humane humanists won a flood of converts in high places, chivalric attitudes (and all their progeny)—the very antithesis of their views—might have been hurried at least a few significant paces toward the ash-heap of history.[26] Of course this did not happen. Erasmus believed that original sin worked through inherited social customs, and we have already noted his sad recognition that custom justifies even the wicked and the cruel. Whether or not the heroic ideal in its chivalric guise embodied wicked and cruel components, it could scarcely be dislodged from a central place in the thinking of leaders of the early sixteenth century by the honed critiques of humanists meditating on uncompromising gospel truths.

It seems likewise undeniable that the great figures of Erasmus and More did not represent the broad body of humanist thought. Other scholars easily came to see God's work progressing through actions of their particular godly prince; praising ideal governance in their lifetimes, they kept one eye on the ancient Roman *imperium* and its ideally dutiful soldiery.[27] The will of the powerful would safely continue to exercise its inherent rights; violence proudly performed by the elite was still gilded and sanctified by an ethos with roots far beyond any critic's uprooting grasp.

Humanist scholarship, in short, spoke with no unified voice on tangled issues of war, violence, and peace. Its techniques and sources could carry a writer toward more than one goal; its eloquent style and prestigious sources could serve more than one master. In this sense, humanism brought a method, an approach to learning, more than a set body of ideas. If certain currents of ideas were dangerous to a chivalric ethos, the thought and writing of other humanists could be highly supportive. So much in the corpus of ideas revived from antiquity could readily be coopted to adorn and buttress surviving elements of the chivalric code. There had always been, in fact, a strong courtly component within chivalry itself which provided open portals to the new ideas.[28] Sensitive and spiritual men such as Erasmus, More, and Colet agonized over the atrocities and sinful wastes of war; other writers drew on fashionable classical learning as they unstintingly lauded heroic deeds of bold warriors in their own age or any other. The path was cleared by a belief that warriors of the ancient world they so vastly admired were practicing ideal chivalry and were, in fact, its founders. Writers steeped in the classical view that the all-important quality of manly virtue (Latin *virtus*, Italian *virtu*) was a military attribute would have little difficulty in drawing on antique authors when writing about chivalry in their own time. In the fifteenth century, the Burgundian court especially acted as a fountainhead for disseminating such ideas. Striking evidence of humanistic praise for chivalric ideals persisting into the sixteenth century will be examined shortly (when we consider two adoring biographies of model French knights). More generally, the political and religious context shaping the entire later medieval and early modern era easily muffled voices severely questioning warfare and the need for martial heroism. It was truly difficult for religious critiques of war in the abstract to win hearts and minds in an age characterized by decisive religious conflict. Given crusades by Teutonic knights, Hussite wars in Bohemia, and eventually the invading Turkish armies reaching the gates of Vienna, justifications of heroic fighting were not hard to invent.[29] Such pressing problems ensured that a wide range of humanist opinion existed. This variety of ideas was significant. It enabled—for a brief time, at least—a successful continuance of an old technique: selective chivalric appropriation of current ideas.[30] The heroic ethos lived on, and warriors did not want for enthusiastic and learned supporters who could pen praise in the most up-to-date style.

Yet the relevant issue was so often authority rather than war itself. War could scarcely be dislodged from its invisible throne. Humanists sang the praises of martial glory even more than they reflected the glowing ideals of the Sermon on the Mount; but the authority to lead and regulate war at every level remained crucial. Their sources, no less than their patrons, inclined many humanist scholars to highly favorable views of authority that could promote a perceived public good. Ciceronian ideas of public well-being could be integrated with stress on great deeds of individual prowess.[31] In short, the new learning could strongly reinforce an older tradition of a public authority in whose service heroes fought.

Practitioners of the new learning could thus scarcely end the robust life of chivalric ideology. Yet they could undoubtedly play a highly important role as accomplices to that deed. Beloved classical sources gave scholars a new respect and potent new valorization for the idea of *respublica* as the common good or common weal that trumps individual honor. Medieval writers, rulers, and administrators had been no strangers to the idea of the common good; their statutes and proclamations extolled the *communitas regni*; and kings and their assemblies, estates, *parlements*, and parliaments self-consciously enacted new laws *pro bono publico*.[32] Yet the new emphasis on the common weal is significant. If the sociocultural context for chivalric ideas had always shown a highly individualistic coloration, the new emphasis reinforced emerging ideas on citizenship.

The broad trend seems to move toward elevating and instructing an elite corps of citizen-governors. This is famously the goal of Sir Thomas Elyot's *Book Named the Governor*, fulsomely dedicated to Henry VIII in 1531. The work was obviously popular, as its frequent reprinting shows. The volumes are filled with descriptions of classical virtues to be absorbed and vices to be eschewed by those who would help the much-admired sovereign govern what Elyot terms the public weal.[33] His self-designation as a knight on the title page is the only time that potent word appears in the entire work.[34] In the long run, this emphasis on citizenship would tell.

New patterns of education slowly created a climate of elite opinion that focused on the sovereign at the apex of a hierarchical commonwealth of citizens. Heroic ideas had to absorb new valorizations. Though humanist writing caused no sudden death, gradually and powerfully it helped bring chivalric ideology to its end by the support given to growing state power.

Radical Religious Reform and Chivalric Ideology

Changes in religious ideas—another potential agent in the demise of chivalric ideas— likewise need to be seen within a generous chronological framework. To borrow the apt phrase of David Potter, we should think of "a long-term organic regenerative movement within the church."[35] Perhaps scholars too long shared with inquisitors and magistrates from centuries they study a liking for labels, wanting to know if some individual or group in the early years of this reform movement was truly heretical or orthodox, "Lollard," eventually "Protestant," "Lutheran," or "Calvinist."[36] The impression has grown upon historians that many late medieval or early modern folk themselves would have been less sure about the analytical usefulness of these labels, particularly in an age when labels might serve merely pejorative ends or indeed might bring intended criminal liabilities. Ideas attractive to these folk might not clearly categorize them in boxes left from old inquiries. Pondering personal piety and church reform could lead to a great variety of conclusions.

Did changing currents of religious thought affect ideas of chivalry in the shadow-land between Medieval and Early Modern? We have seen that a well-documented past connected knightly piety and valorization with religious debate and (at least on their own terms) had allied them with waves of reforming energy within the Church.[37] Even more powerfully, reform tides gathered force once again. In simplest terms, the question becomes how a knightly ethos still very much alive in late fifteenth- and early sixteenth-century Europe would negotiate its way through this new terrain. Could the process by which chivalric ideology flourished continue in this brave new world? Could apologists for chivalry continue to appropriate religious ideas in active contention?

An unusually perceptive clerical observer in the early sixteenth century might have feared that radical, even shattering, religious reform was acceptable to those who held chivalric ideals. Might it not connect with their dangerous tendency to independence? Along important lines the knightly ideology had long moved in directions that, however pious, did not always reinforce clerical authority or lead to Rome. Was not the Protestant reform in effect a lay revolt against the highly clericalized church produced since the Gregorian Reform of nearly half a millennium earlier? If the sixteenth-century reform brought the revanche of the laity against the clerical caste, as is sometimes claimed, might not chivalry align itself with the new expression of lay autonomy? As the esprit de corps of the lay elite, chivalry had significantly staked out its own domain, at times standing against the high claims of the clerical caste so self-consciously elevated by the Gregorian Reform and so stoutly asserted and elaborated thereafter.

Yet our hypothetical observer's worst fears obviously did not materialize. Protecting its own prerogatives, knightly ideology came to terms with the religious world it found in fifteenth- and sixteenth-century Europe. Whatever individual consciences might dictate, the body of knighthood in any region came to accept the religion—and the religious blessing—that was on offer, though the process sometimes required time and bloodshed. An elite, chivalric ideology accepted either reformed or traditional religion and survived the late medieval turmoil and even the shattering of religious unity. The military elite, in short, retained religious valorization; knighthood remained the stout champion of piety, whether it was reformed or traditional.

Yet they could not work the old magic of drawing strength from opposing sides in theological debate, incorporating only what was wanted. Religious disputes now became fundamental as never before. In the High and Later Middle Ages, disagreements over religious ideas affecting knighthood, while given serious thought, could scarcely have threatened unity in the church. Rather they marked debates that emerged as the medieval church produced such unity as it achieved.[38] A maturing knightly ideology had readily borrowed any element from debates in which all voices were granted orthodoxy, even as individual writers expressed strong preferences.

Debates at the end of the Middle Ages opened gaps between opponents that proved to be unbridgeable. Book burnings, image smashing, bulls of solemn excommunication, graphic woodcuts showing the pope as Antichrist or the Roman Church as the Whore of Babylon—let alone the bitter and open warfare that soon broke out—did not open broad avenues for compromise or opportunities for selective knightly appropriation. Religious formulations may always at their core retain an individual character, but throughout the period in question institutional religion remained communal or regional.

Like all others in society, knights finally had to choose a side, or perhaps had rather to accept the side chosen for them. For no governing power could be indifferent to the valorizing force of religion. Good governance had long fused with true belief and practice, whatever the quarrels of kings or great lords with popes and bishops. Lay authority that had been building effective power throughout the High and Late Middle Ages now strode assertively into the center of the debate, claiming the sovereign's God-given power to protect true religion. *Cuius regio, eius religio* was the principle that triumphed—the one who reigns determines the religion.[39] It was a principle to roll Gregorian reformers in their ancient graves.

What is more, the knights themselves—and not merely our imagined clerical observer at the close of the Middle Ages—might have found much to generate caution in the new and radical ideas of religious reform. Some of these reform notions, had they been seriously carried into life, could indeed have had a devastating effect on essential elements of chivalry. We can plainly see the dangers posed by reform in a treatise written by a late fourteenth-century English knight, Sir John Clanvowe. His little book *The Two Ways* appeared more than a century and a quarter before Luther's 1520 treatise *On Christian Liberty*.[40] Its importance rests not in its broad historical force, which in fact was quickly dissipated, but in its witness to the potential gap between new religious ideas and a chivalric ideology by then centuries old.[41] Clan-vowe's starkly reformist and puritanical stance marks a great distance from more traditional modes of thought found in Henry of Lancaster and Geof-froi de Charny a generation earlier. Warning the faithful to avoid the "brood wey," that broad and worldly way of sin that leads to destruction, Clanvowe urges readers to follow instead the "nargh wey," the narrow and otherworldly path that will guide them to salvation. Simplistic though the formulation sounds, it completely inverts chivalric ideology—in effect standing a writer like Malory on his head—and severs the link to traditional religion forged over centuries. As Clanvowe asserts,

> To God all virtue is worship and all sin is shame. And in this world it is ever the reverse, for the world holds worshipful great warriors and fighters who destroy and win and lay waste many lands and gives much reward to those that have plenty and who spend outrageously in meat and drink, in clothing and building and living in ease, sloth and many other sins. And also the world worships them much that would proudly and spitefully be avenged for every wrong that is said or done to them. And of such folk men make books and songs and read and sing of them in order to hold the memory of their deeds the longer here upon earth, for that is a thing that worldly men desire greatly that their name might last long after them here upon earth.[42]

Clanvowe assures his readers that God as sovereign judge of truth sees mat-ters differently. In the presence of God and all the company of heaven,

> all sin is shame and non-worship. And also such folk that would like to live meekly in this world and avoid such aforesaid riot, noise, and strife and live simply, and eat and drink reasonably and clothe themselves meekly, and suffer patiently wrongs that other folk do and say to them and hold themselves satisfied with little of the goods of this world, and desire no great name or nor reward of this world, such folk the world scorns.

The world considers them "lolleris and looslis," foolish and shameful wretches. But God considers them to be very wise and worshipful.[43]

Not only does God prefer such unworldly—we might say non-chivalric—men, Christ gave mortals the great example; far from being a strenuous knight, he lived by values that required him with charitable patience to suffer scorn from worldly men:

> And all that he suffered patiently. And Saint Paul says that Christ suffered for us leaving us an example that we should do so following in his footsteps. And therefore we follow his steps and suffer patiently the scorns of the world as he did, and then he will give us grace to come in by the narrow way to the worshipful bliss in which he reigns.[44]

The message is shocking in the context of late fourteenth-century chivalric society. Displays of prowess—long touted as the essence of chivalry—lead not to imperishable honor but to unthinkable wrongs against a multitude of victims. Chivalric pride and display reinforcing crucial status wither in the face of the demand for utter simplicity and humility. If he makes no explicit attack on traditional religion, Clanvowe simply sidesteps the established and basic notion of an economy of salvation with so much penance neutralizing punishment for so much sin; he likewise ignores the mediation of the priesthood and even traditional reliance on the intercession of saints or the powerful aid of the Blessed Virgin. How he could hold to these views and this pattern of life and yet consider himself a member of the *ordo* of knighthood remains unclear. It would seem impossible. Chivalry as practiced by William Marshal, Henry of Lancaster, Geoffroi de Charny, and Thomas Malory cannot be contained or even understood within the covers of *The Two Ways*. Knighthood assuredly did not take the "nargh wey."

Most notably, Sir John conceives of Christ's suffering in terms of the worldly taunts and jeers hurled at one who refused to live by the false standards of society. Christ's true disciples must follow his "traces" and suffer for their own unconventional beliefs and lives. The *imitatio Christi* here is not corporally ascetic, not mimetic physical pain and anguish as parallels to the lash, the nails, and the cross, but the very different discipline of ignoring withering scorn and abuse from a conformist world smugly sure of all its standards, its hierarchy, and those who exercise dominance based on violence. So interior a view of the essentials of life with so little regard for great deeds performed heroically, edged weaponry in hand, is no code of chivalry. If the life of Christ is the ultimate heroic, nonviolent life, then the *imitatio Christi* is not the practice of chivalry.[45]

Yet Clanvowe's name will never appear on the death certificate of chivalry. That his radical ideas on reform could not realize their potential consequences in the world might simply seem self-evident. Implementing them would require the crumbling of social hierarchy in general, and within chivalric ideology would tear apart the connective tissue, destroy the carefully calibrated compromises, and break bridges between paradoxical borrowings from differing sets of religious ideas. The historical record on the fate of Lollard heresy in the upper reaches of society in England confirms this initial sense.

Lollard Knights

Scholars of late fourteenth-century England have long kept under surveillance "a prominent group of earnest, secular, intellectual knights who were interested in literature and religion."[46] Their interest in literature linked some of them to Chaucer, Christine de Pisan, and Eustace Deschamps.[47] Their interest in religious reform brought them under suspicion of heresy. They were contemporaries (though not direct followers) of John Wyclif, whose increasingly heretical ideas had found a home in at least one university and had traveled into city and countryside by means of books and preaching.[48] Heresy was in the air and, as Chaucer's Harry Bailey snorted, one might "smell a loller in the wind." Since K. B. McFarlane began the modern investigation, these famous "Lollard knights" (Sir John Clanvowe prominent among them) have stood at one epicenter of debates swirling around the native English heresy of Lollardy itself.[49] In the eyes of some scholars Lollardy ranks as the Reformation that almost was, but that failed by attempting radical change prematurely; to other scholars it is only a sideshow with no significant connection to the break in the church that finally happened, since the English Reformation was caused by political necessity rather than religious ferment.[50] Fitting the particular cluster of knights into the broader picture has, not surprisingly, proved difficult.

If the detailed beliefs of these knights elude us among the wisps of our evidence, exact labels may, once again, be less important than a general phenomenon. Most scholars agree that we are not confronted with a sect in the sixteenth-century sense of that word. Even a much more loosely uniform body of opinion and belief may be lacking.[51] Yet here are knights with a base in the royal household of Richard II allowed a fairly open range of experimental views on religious belief and reform. There may well, in fact, have been more of their sort than appear in the chroniclers' lists of suspects. McFarlane spoke of these pious knights as the insular form of the Devotio Moderna and as "not so much a distinct sect as a group of extremists," who reveal a broader (if less intense) trend in fourteenth-century religion.[52] The inward-turning piety and somewhat puritanical morality widespread among the elite could easily move sensitive souls in this direction. In fact, some of the qualities associated with Lollards, especially a species of Puritanism that led to a denigration of the mere body and a well-developed sense of personal unworthiness, were evident in the writing of Henry of Lancaster and Geoffroi de Charny a generation earlier.[53] As Jeremy Catto has argued,

> It is probable that sympathy for the ideals of the Lollards was spread among the nobility much more widely than their small clique of courtiers, and merged with their responses to the serious call to inner devotion and self-knowledge made by Richard Rolle and the other mystical writers of the age.[54]

Radical reformers in England seem to have pinned their hopes to pious leadership drawn from the lay elite and especially the commons in parliament, counting on them to launch a movement for reformation of the church. It proved to be a fatal mistake on several levels. Their very program, in the first place, though it contained material as well as spiritual enticements for the lay elite, also included elements that were absolutely incompatible with chivalric ideals. Urging disendowment of the church could always gain lay attention, that is, even among those lords and gentry largely deaf to spiritual formulations; but the pacifism that we saw in the treatise by Sir John Clanvowe would scarcely win over an elite with a highly military self-conception.[55] In the Twelve Conclusions posted at Westminster Hall during the meeting of Parliament in 1395 (and possibly on the doors of St. Paul's, where convocation was meeting), the tenth statement thoroughly denounced warfare and even crusading as incompatible with the Christian life:

> Manslaughter by battle or pretended law of righteousness for temporal or spiritual cause without special revelation [from God] is expressly contrary to the New Testament, which is a law of grace and full of mercy. This conclusion is openly proved by the example of Christ's preaching here in earth, which mainly taught love and to have mercy on his enemies, and not to slay them. The reason is that when most men fight, charity is lost after the first stroke, and whoever dies outside of charity takes the highway to hell. Furthermore we know well that

no cleric can show by scripture or reason lawful punishment of death for one deadly sin and not for another. But the law of mercy that is the New Testament forbade all manslaughter: "in the gospel it is said of old, you shall not kill (in evangelio dictum est antiques, Non occides)."

The corollary is equally radical: it is completely robbery of the poor when lords purchase indulgences "from pain and guilt"

> for those that serve in their hosts [for war] brought together to slay Christians in distant lands to win worldly goods, as we have seen. And knights that travel to heathen lands to earn a name in slaying men win much displeasure with the King of Peace; for our belief was advanced by meekness and sufferance and Jesus Christ hates and threatens fighters and man slayers. "He who lives by the sword, shall perish by the sword."[56]

Unfortunately for the reformers, their clarion calls did not easily shake a conviction that knighthood rightly fulfilled a necessary martial role within traditional society. As one writer (who may have been Thomas Hoccleve) charged,

> Hit is unkindly [unnatural] for a knight
> That schuld a kynges castel kepe
> To babble the Bibel day and night
> In resting time when he shuld slepe.[57]

Two significant historical events stood like brick walls to block the path that hopeful reformers envisioned for England. In 1381 the Great Rising sent shock waves through the propertied elite of England, jittery since the disquieting news of the brutal French Jacquerie had reached them several decades earlier. Since authorities tend to stand or fall together, the rising of 1381 caused nervous officials of church and state and the landholding elite in general to worry over connections between radical Wycliffite ideas about religious reform and dreaded social unrest. All doubt was removed when hope for radical religious reform led to outright treason in the next generation.[58] One of the "Lollard knights," Sir John Oldcastle, who had become Lord Cobham, diverted Lollard hopes from gradual persuasion through parliamentary reform into outright revolt. He had loyally served the future Henry V as a vigorous knight on campaign and enjoyed his friendship within the princely and then the royal household. Yet his open espousal of Lollard ideas and his hopes of radical religious reform—especially separating the clerics from the wealth that corrupted them—brought charges of heresy. He had apparently counted on effecting reform through his royal friend, but the new king saw himself as a defender of orthodoxy; once Oldcastle had been examined and condemned by the archbishop and bishops, royal friendship gained him only a grace period of forty days before he should suffer the terrifying death inflicted on an obdurate heretic. During that period of royal grace, Henry urged him to recant—at least in a formal sense—to defuse a crisis. Instead, he managed to escape from imprisonment in the Tower. Within a few months he planned to capture the king and tried to launch an armed rising. When, early in 1414, his active supporters gathered outside London, crown spies had given ample warning. The attempted coup generated only half-hearted support, failed miserably, and brought disastrous consequences for all hopes of radical reform. Heresy and sedition now were not only fused, they stood darkly shaded in evident failure. As J. A. F. Pollard dryly stated, the elite discovered they "were King's men first and religious radicals second."[59] The English church did not have to worry about disendowment for the next century. For perhaps as long a time, those who ordered their lives by the ideology of chivalry confronted no worries that their actions offended God as some radicals had implied. The real winner in the suppression of Oldcastle's revolt was, of course, the crown, which had preserved order, suppressed heresy, and proved how essential its role was in maintaining each goal.[60]

Martin Luther

Martin Luther may never have heard of Lollards or Sir John Clanvowe, though he surely would have found ideas of a plain, God-fearing life based on biblical principles highly attractive. Likewise, Luther probably spent little time thinking specifically about chivalry, though he could urge Christians to struggle as valiantly as knights against evil.[61] But he had assuredly heard of John Hus (a name his opponents would not let him forget) and at least through that Bohemian link had some connection with the reforming ideas proposed by John Wyclif a good century and a half earlier.[62] To members of the German elite, the very name of Hus brought fearsome associations of heresy backed by the armed force of rebellion, of both political and religious independence.[63]

Luther's enemies pressed him to recognize his relationship to Hus; his own experiences forced him to confront sin and forgiveness; hard realities of the political world in his lifetime brought the question of licit force to the fore. In his early religious life he undoubtedly obsessed over performance of good works and fearfully practiced harsh physical penance. The trend among learned theologians, however, pointed toward interiorizing the process of reconciling God and humanity. In time, Protestant reformers, as the astute historian of theology Berndt Hamm has emphasized, finally reduced the declining physical element to nothing.[64] Since forgiveness for sin had been totally achieved by the sacrifice of Christ, human effort was not necessary. *Solus Christus, sola gratia*, became the reform principle—salvation came from Christ alone, given simply through divine grace. Old ideas yielded grudgingly in practice, however, and Luther moved slowly toward denial of sacramental status to penance; he sometimes circled back to insist on its importance.[65]

The point may seem abstruse to modern non-theologians, but dramatic consequences could result from the trend to de-emphasize physical penance and especially from the Reformers' sharp closure eventually given to that trend. If personal asceticism ceased to be a means of atonement and was no longer considered spiritually meritorious, it was not the proper imitation of Christ, not the personal sharing of his bodily suffering as it had been enacted in hope and dread by believers for centuries. The venerable scales weighing good and evil deeds in an exacting economy of salvation—vividly and repeatedly pictured in miracle stories—were now broken and discarded as useless.

If this line of thought carried heavy consequences for European cultural history in general, its potentially shattering effect on chivalric ideology has gone almost unrecognized.[66] The religious underpinning of knighthood depended on the performance of specific and highly physical good works, on heroic, meritorious suffering. Warrior heroism had firmly bonded with traditional ascetic and transactional religion. If radical religious reformers' ideas were fully accepted, knighthood lost a major valorizing prop to its very reason for being.

As it appeared in print and sermon, Luther's early schema for a reformed religion indeed threatened to undercut chivalric ideology, however far this may have been from his conscious intent. In his treatise *Christian Liberty* of 1520, Luther classically outlined his argument for justification of sinners by faith alone, rather than by their own redeeming works. He accepts that "fastings, watchings, labors, and other reasonable discipline" might help to subject the recalcitrant body to the spirit,[67] but insisted that all such works are a consequence, not a means, of salvation: "though you were nothing but good works from the soles of your feet to the crown of your head, you would still not be righteous."[68] Adam and Eve's labor in the Garden was carried out simply to please God; it was not religiously meritorious labor considered a species of suffering to be credited to their account in the economy of salvation. True Christians give themselves to their neighbor's good as Christ gave himself to them.[69] Being a "little Christ" to others in gratitude for divine sacrifice is the commendable form of *imitatio Christi*, dramatically different from the chivalric understanding of following Christ as a warrior, as we have repeatedly encountered it.

Considering the influence of his ideas in the sixteenth-century world, Luther might seem to have clearer right than Clanvowe or Oldcastle to inscribe his name on the death certificate of chivalry. Yet the plain historical fact is that he soon had to come to terms with the nobles and the effective power of arms-bearers in a world filled with danger. It is difficult to imagine how he might have done otherwise. The necessity was especially clear after his dramatic appearance before the imperial Diet at Worms when his rescue from determined enemies depended upon powerful laymen in armor. It became yet clearer as his ideas of a purely religious liberty helped to spark peasant war, as rebels violently pursued a much more social and economic goal of liberty than Luther's theology intended. The force of the nobles was needed to restore social order, and Luther blessed them as they completed the harsh and bloody task. His younger colleague and intellectual successor in Germany, Philip Melanchthon, is often identified with strong desires to maintain social order against rising fears of anarchy and with an equal impulse to provide intellectual and religious stability insured by a properly authoritative and rigorously trained pastorate.[70] In the religious warfare that embroiled Europe for decades, the reformers could not afford the luxury of questioning the heroic forces that preserved them.

Heroic Asceticism, Religious Atonement, and State Power

We can be thankful that scholars have abandoned a simplistic picture of the sudden emergence of the European state in the sixteenth or even seventeenth century, sweeping away the feudalism that had provided the sole organizing schema for benighted medieval people. State-building was a real process in the Middle Ages, with significant results solidly documented in massive archival deposits and classic analytical works.[71] In Western Europe, medieval states had begun to emerge by the twelfth century and, of course, some could claim even earlier roots in Carolingian institutions; an off-shore version in Anglo-Saxon England showed special vigor.[72] Medieval achievement in turn provided a foundation on which later efforts would build. Although nascent states struggled in the fourteenth and fifteenth centuries with the drain and devastation of war, with demographic and economic crises, and with acute problems of public order, they survived and bequeathed durable ideas and structures. Sixteenth-century achievements scarcely represent creation ex nihilo, but rather a significant new phase of growth in a process of long standing.

In sixteenth-century Europe a conjuncture of socioeconomic conditions, new educational and religious ideas, and remarkable political actors amplified the directive power of monarchs and their administrations. Since chivalry had always balanced cooperation and tension in its relationship with the overarching power of kingship, any significant increase in royal power would necessarily affect the vitality of ideals by which knights lived.

Capsule career biographies of two early sixteenth-century knights can provide a sense of the changing relationship between chivalry and the state— or at least the sovereign as agent of the common good. Substantial accounts of both men were written in the homeland of chivalry in the early sixteenth century. Louis, Seigneur de la Tremouille, and Pierre Terrail, known as le Chevalier Bayard, are idealized by their humanistic biographers; their accounts thus provide fascinating insights into the ideal warrior in this age. In both cases, the hero is viewed in relationship to the power of kings.[73]

Life of Louis La Tremouille

Jean Bouchet, an intimate member of the household of his subject, La Tremouille, published a "Panegyric du chevalier sans reproche, ou memoires de la tremouille" in 1527, two years after Louis La Tremouille met his death in battle.[74] Its opening pages recall many a chivalric romance: In the manner of a Lancelot, La Tremouille has, we learn, a body finely formed for knightly action, and like any hero of romance, he is drawn from early years to vigorous, martial activities.[75] A new dimension, however, also appears almost at once: the king summons Louis for service at the royal court when he is only twelve years old, precipitating a series of dramatic scenes in the family.[76] Though his father argues for delaying a year, the lad is pictured delivering a lengthy and mature speech which makes a case for going at once to the king's side. At its core he asserts that "the royal court is the school of all respectability, where one encounters the good men who instruct in living the civilized life and the means of acquiring not only worldly wealth but imperishable treasures of honor."[77] Both Louis's father and mother voice their fears of the king's anti-Burgundian inclinations. The determined young Louis is not convinced. When he starts off for the king's court without their permission, he is swiftly brought home and lectured on the troubled state of the realm, his own tender age, and the dangerous falseness of court life. While Louis debates with his parents, citing among much else the early age at which Alexander the Great began his conquests, a missive from the king closes the family discussion. Louis is to appear at court at the end of his thirteenth year.[78]

It is love rather than honor that first touches him there, and he is entangled for a time in a complex triangle involving a friend and that man's wife. But after twenty interesting pages, with "the woman forgotten (la dame oubliée)," he returns to the serious business of succeeding at court by seeking from the king a return of family lands.[79] Significantly, it is the king (by now the young Charles VIII) who later chooses a wife for him.[80] Above all, La Tremouille launches the military career in the service of the king that will become the focus of his life as recorded by Bouchet. The account proceeds as much by battlefield speeches as by detailed narratives of combat.[81]

When he is twenty-seven years old, the first of many commands is bestowed, and La Tremouille becomes lieutenant general of the forces of Charles VIII for war in Brittany. The appointment comes, we learn, "from his boldness, prudence, hard work, and good conduct, and from many fine deeds of arms done by him in encounters and sallies performed at the siege of Nantes as well as sieges and attacks on many towns, castles, and fortified places in Brittany."[82] He accepts the assignment "tres-voluntiers" and sets to work "for the profit of the king and realm and to gain honor in this assignment."[83] The combination of royal service and the acquisition of honor will provide the leitmotif of Bouchet's story, and it will be strongly intermixed with religious valorization that his hero gained in such good service. These themes emerge unmistakably as French armies sweep through the Alps passes to conduct the Wars of Italy.

Even before the scene shifts dramatically south of the Alps, however, a speech to his troops by La Tremouille on a Breton battlefield sounds the message of loyal service to the crown and scepter of France; such service will be the cure for civil war, unnatural rebellion, injustice, and loss of nobility. Victory means service to king and country, glory and praise for all; defeat means destruction of country, homes, families, and wives, with endless shame covering all.[84] Rather than live in shame they must be ready to die in a good fight and in a just war, serving the king, who is significantly termed the foundation of honor.[85]

If this message is advanced repeatedly, it registers most powerfully and bonds with religious valorization most fully in the terrible aftermath of Louis's loss of his only son in battle.[86] Fighting against the Swiss at Marignan, this young son, the prince of Thalemont, is carried from the battlefield having suffered sixty-two wounds. He could have no hope of recovery. Yet, as Jean Bouchet presents his deathbed scene, if the prince regrets dying in the flower of youth (lacking even time to do full penance for his sins), he sees God's grace in being allowed to die "in service to the king and public weal."[87] Confessed and given last rites, he dies thirty-six hours after receiving his terrible wounds. The king in person informed La Tremouille of his son's death. Louis's response to the king is elaborated as a model for the reader. Showing only the few tears he could not restrain by a stern spirit, the father responded that his sorrow was moderated by knowing that his son had departed "on a bed of honor, having died in your company at your service and in a just war," though he grants that it does seem against nature to leave a father without his son, rather than the reverse, and to lose a young man "just as he was beginning to acquire honor and the king's good will."[88] Yet he rejoices that after all those wounds—and he repeats that they were suffered in maintaining the public good and in a just war—there was time for confession and last rites. And La Tremouille assures the king of his continued support on campaign while his own life lasts.

With minor variations, this theme is emphasized by being replayed as the sad news is given to the mother of the dead prince, and then to his widow. A bishop informs the widow, assuring her that the prince is now praised in the glorious world beyond, having died "the most virtuous death possible to any prince or lord; on a bed of honor in a justifiable battle in a licit war, not fleeing, but fighting and suffering sixty-two wounds in the royal company and service, admired by all the fighting men and in the grace of God, well-confessed and a good Christian."[89] Wishing to console her further, he assured her that the deadly multiple wounds came from honorable lance-thrusts, not from cannon shot.[90] Without these grisly details, La Tremouille's announcement to his wife by letter made the same large points about sacrifice to God, about prowess and service to the crown in licit warfare.[91] Both women became ill and soon died after receiving the news, enacting their own form of sacrifice.

La Tremouille, who remarried and kept fighting for the king and royal causes, died in the manner he had so resolutely approved in his son. At the disastrous battle of Pavia in 1525, he was wounded in the face and had his horse shot from under him. Remounted, he reached the king only to be shot dead at his side. His biographer intones the formula of loyalty, reflecting that La Tremoiuille "had often said that he wanted to die nowhere but on a bed of honor, that is, at the king's service in a just war."[92] His body was returned to France for burial in the collegiate church he had founded. He was shown the "honors customarily given in funeral rites for counts, princes, knights, and licit leaders in war, as he had well merited, as much for his honorable and correct life as for his noble acts and deeds."[93] Bouchet further assures readers that although he had been richly rewarded with offices and lands, all his lord's wages and pensions, and indeed all his revenue, had been spent in the service of the king and the public good.[94] La Tremouille had amply earned the title of *chevalier sans reproche*, the blameless knight.[95]

La Tremouille's virtues certainly never suffer in the telling of his life by Jean Bouchet. A second knight who likewise won so elevated a title in the early sixteenth century, Pierre Terrail, the Chevalier Bayard, becomes even more a model of virtue in the pages of the biography by the humanist Symphorien Champier.[96] Even if, as most readers might conclude, the book presents a glowing ideal for sixteenth-century chivalry rather than an actual man, its message is as important as it is clear, redoubling the theme of Jean Bouchet.[97]

Life of the Chevalier Bayard

Almost from the first page, in the dedicatory letter prefacing the volume, Champier praises the Chevalier Bayard both as "the mirror and model of all chivalry (le myrouer et exemple de toute chievalerie)" and for "the love he always had for the public good of the French nation (l'affection qu'il a eue tousjours au bien public de la nation de france)."[98] Even Bayard's war cry is significant. In the press of battle he shouts out not his family name or that of hereditary lands or title, but "France! France!"[99] If Champier strengthens this "national" theme through Bayard's chivalric career, he also strongly reinforces the religious dimension. The omnipotence and immanence of God (who seems to be French) moves out of the shadowy background of simple assumption (as in the life of La Tremouille) and takes the very foreground. The knight who serves the king serves his higher Lord as well, doing the divine will in a troubled world. That the wills of the Lord King and the Lord God might ever stand at odds never enters Champier's mind, or at least not his book.

A few pages set up Bayard's early life as he moves upward in the hierarchy of courts. After getting his start as a page in the household of the duke of Savoy, he soon entered the royal court of Charles VIII, where he earned from the king's own lips the nickname of "Spur (picque)" for his ability to tame horses.[100] Unlike La Tremouille, he showed no interest in women and maintained a determined focus on warfare. Champier says he wanted never to be linked or subordinated to women and needed no immortality through his posterity; he simply wanted like an angel to ascend to the skies.[101]

As soon as Champier has brought Bayard to the age when he can become a fighting man, he presents a series of three martial episodes, each receiving its own chapter or two. All three serve to document Bayard's personal prowess functioning as an agency of God's will. In the first of these encounters, a French company is attacked by a Spanish company and Bayard fights more like a lion than a man; in fact, he takes great pleasure in the combat.[102] Even the celebrated Aragonese champion named Alonzo Soto Majore surrenders. Bayard graciously allows him to return home in order to raise a ransom. The crucial twist quickly appears: with freedom secured, the Spaniard falsely claims he had suffered bad treatment when he should have been an honorable captive in Bayard's hands. No reader can doubt that the man will die for spreading this untruth. Champier's heading to the following chapter pointedly announces that when Bayard fought on foot against this Spanish champion "he killed him by the will of God."[103] Bayard had given Soto Majore the chance to correct his dishonoring lie before insisting on personal combat. He then generously agreed to fight on foot as his opponent insisted, despite his known superior skill as a horseman. He even agreed to fight while ill and recovering from a fever. These may be accurate details, but suspicion lingers that Champier is underscoring the divine will in effecting Bayard's victory.[104] Champier even gives Bayard a speech lamenting that two Christians should have to fight; the great knight patiently explains that it is necessary only because he must defend his honor and must give an instructive example that no Christian should falsely impute evil to his brother, as a true Christian knight.[105] Even when Alonzo has been laid flat on the ground by a devastating slash, Bayard sermonizes him; the liar must renounce his sinful claim and seek divine mercy. But it is too late. The man has bled to death. A weeping Bayard is pictured praying God to forgive the noble and chivalrous sinner and praying that God will forgive him as well, since he only wanted to save his honor. In remembrance of Christ who pardoned those who crucified him, Bayard himself pardons Alonzo.[106] The role Champier gives him is that of noble agent of divine will, killing reluctantly to restore just order in a world disordered by sin.[107]

A second combat, involving thirteen Frenchmen against thirteen Spaniards, carries the theme forward.[108] The Spanish ask for the combat, seeking revenge for the loss of their champion; but again they appear as agents of dishonor and sin. In the fight they deliberately kill eleven of the French mounts "against all that is honorable in chivalry and war."[109] Bayard loudly assures them that their act is useless, for "all victory comes from above and not from men." Champier even insists that he pedantically shouted citations to the Book of Judges, to actions of Gideon, Sampson, and Debora, "and many others," to drive home his point. Since the Spanish horses will not charge across a field littered with dead of their own kind, Bayard informs his enemies that the evidence is plain that God opposes them. Continuing his battlefield sermon, he exhorts them as fellow Christians to acknowledge their sin in killing harmless animals; "better it would have been to sell them and give the money to God's poor."[110] Of course, the thirteen Spaniards are soon routed by Bayard and a faithful companion, and even the eleven dismounted and captured Frenchmen are restored to freedom.

In the third encounter, the Chevalier Bayard plays Horatio at the bridge, though Champier surprisingly makes comparisons only to Hector, Pompey, and the good Christian knight Roland.[111] Bayard holds back two hundred Spanish soldiers—leaving some of them floating in the river—until help reaches him. Champier must struggle to recognize the divine will in this fight, but he succeeds. The Spanish are guilty of a battlefield ruse (vostre cautelle contre le vouloir de dieu) and have offended divine wisdom (Rien ne vault prudence humaine, que on appelle cautelle, contre de dieu la sapience).[112] He strengthens the point by having some Spaniards themselves declare that "God always keeps the bodies and honor of those men who do good and it would have been wrong had he been made a prisoner because he has a reputation as the knight beyond shame as he well demonstrated in the fight with Lord Alonzo."[113]

Clearly a humanist model-maker is at work here. Champier, rather than the Chevalier Bayard, would be inclined to shout biblical citations at an enemy in the height of battle or to preach to him primly about selling good war mounts for poor relief.[114] The drive to press an ideology leads Champier to present or invent an ideal, even as it leads him to find invariable Spanish sin and consistent French virtue. This very ideological drive, of course, remains the point for our inquiry. Bayard's prowess links with God's will and supports the most Christian king of France who always acts in accord with divine will.[115]

In these incidents the king remains in the background, though it is always his cause that is upheld. This emphasis on personal virtue in great knights appears again at the end of the book. After giving accounts of four worthy fellow knights from Bayard's own province of Dauphiné, Champier compares Bayard to a series of Greek, Roman, Hebrew, and Christian heroes, in each case to Bayard's advantage.[116] Throughout the rest of the book Champier, confident of having established Bayard's personal virtue, broadens his vision and stresses the king's wars, especially the Wars of Italy. Bayard the knight enforcing God's will appears painted in primary colors at the beginning and end of the account; in the bulk of the book his biographer adds the royalist tones: he shows Bayard as the servant of the crown and the upholder of the public good of the realm.

As the French campaigns in Italy begin, once again Champier emphasizes that Bayard rose from a sick bed to do his duty. He reports the very words the great knight spoke to him, dismissing Champier's civilian cautions: "in an emergency one must not fail his prince for anything, and it would be better to die with him than to die here shamefully."[117] Active in the campaigns in Italy, he is in the thick of the fighting and is soon wounded. Yet he again struggles out of the bed in which he is recovering to rejoin the king when needed.[118] Wounded and captured, he is eventually ransomed by the king, albeit with distressing delay.[119] In the midst of the renewed campaigning, Francis I asks Bayard to make him a knight. "Sire, one who is crowned, sworn, and anointed with oil from heaven," Bayard responds significantly, "and is the king of so noble a realm, and is the first son of the church, is already a knight above all others."[120] When the king insists, Bayard draws his sword and knights his sovereign. He then joyfully declares that his sword should be kept as a relic and used in battle only against infidels. After two celebratory somersaults he replaces the blade and the ceremony is complete.[121] Francis soon returned the favor by making him a Knight of the royal Order of Saint Michael.[122]

Bayard's sword was soon drawn again in what proved to be his last fight.[123] Narrowly escaping capture as he defended an unfortified village, Bayard was shot and mortally wounded.[124] Carried to a grove, he made his confession and his will.[125] His only regret in dying, he said, was that he could no longer serve the king his sovereign and had to abandon the great royal affairs, which made him sorry and regretful. His prayer was that after his death the king would have such servants as he had wanted to be.[126] Soon after uttering these royalist pieties he died. Champier says that the man whose firearm killed Bayard was disconsolate when he learned what heroic target his bullet had struck, that he swore never to fire another hacquebut, cursed its inventor for a device that killed the best knight in the world, and promised to retire to a monastery.[127] Champier is no man for half measures.

These two texts leave no doubt about their message. The minimal compromise required of noble warriors was that they now work within a frame of lowered independence, that they recognize something at least becoming the state—the realm, the common good under the sovereign—as the proper beneficiary of their hard labors and the rightful conduit through which sacred honor came to them. Moreover, the sovereign as virtual head of religion in the realm (whatever formal statements were made regarding the papacy) stood in effect as mediator between the warriors and God—as leading clerics, theologians, and even the pope had never quite managed to do. The shell of chivalry remained polished and intact; yet its inner workings have changed dramatically. The old quasi-independent professionalism and individual acquisition of honor now had to be channeled through the state. Equally important, the warrior could no longer achieve salvation by his independent accumulation of ascetic merit, won sword in hand. The old direct relationship between the knight and the divine was gone: the monarch was acclaimed as necessary broker and in his service great knights won spiritual rewards.

Chivalric Ideology and the Tudor Monarchy

If the written lives of La Tremouille and Bayard are filled with what Symphorien Champier called "ceste impetuosité Galicque,"[128] it was a quality bonded inseparably to royal service and religious valorization. Could anything similar appear in the damp isles across the Channel?[129] We have already encountered the young Henry VIII self-consciously playing the role of his chivalrous predecessor Henry V, with the bulk of the English aristocracy in

tow, banners waving and trumpets sounding for an invasion of France. Showing characteristic prudence, his daughter Elizabeth I strove for a more moder-
ate balance between honor and obedience, encouraging a spirit of continued
chivalry within her realm or at least within her court (and occasionally on
inexpensive forays outside the realm), so long as the sovereign was recognized
as repository and dispenser of honor. The jousting she sponsored to celebrate
the anniversary of her accession provides a case in point. Even though she
could not join in the sport and spectacle as her father had done, at least in
his youth, chivalry was to serve royalty and she was the arbiter of honor.
As she informed assembled troops in the famous review at Tilbury during
the crisis of the Spanish Armada, she would herself "be your general, judge,
and rewarder of every one of your virtues in the field."[130] That the Earl of
Essex should personally knight many of his followers on expeditions to Cadiz
and in Ireland truly upset Elizabeth's sense of the properly royalist order of
things. She was aware, as Aristotle had written, that "honour is felt to depend
more on those who confer than on him who receives it."[131] The principle
implies a degree of control that might raise eyebrows and hackles among the
military elite. Sir Philip Sidney insisted on fighting a duel with a man who
had impugned his honor, but when Elizabeth intervened to prevent it, he
reluctantly had to subordinate his honor to her sovereignty. After he died on
the battlefield at Zutphen (in 1586), a contemporary wrote—in words that
would have pleased our French biographers of La Tremouille and Bayard—of
Sidney's "manly woundes receiued in seruice of his Prince / in the open fielde,
in Martiall Maner, the honorablest death that could be desired and best be-
seeming a Christian Knight."[132]

Many lords could not easily accept such a point of view. In a court said to
be divided between *militia* and *togati*, Lord Willoughby de Eresby pointedly
asserted that "he was none of the reptilia," suggesting that he would never
crawl lizard-like at the approaching wave of what the Tudor historian Samuel
Daniel termed "the Ocean of all-drowning Sov'renty."[133] Robert Devereux,
Earl of Essex, famously did more than assert. After a career that included
much field service and Bayard-like challenges to enemy champions, he forcefully claimed his rights in a botched act of rebellion that brought him to
the scaffold. There he humbly voiced the official line that royal sovereignty
trumped chivalric independence. His contemporaries wavered between admiration and horror over his actions. Some had expected Essex to be the new
Protestant knight and crusader. Samuel Daniel, who had lamented that the
present age was "not of that virilitie as the former," wrote a play that seemed

to debate whether chivalry came by royal grant or through innate virtue; he thought it prudent to offer to withdraw the play when criticized by Cecil.[134]

This close relationship and tension between a chivalric sense of independence and royal claims to control animated much in Tudor culture. Some scholars have found that political and cultural ideals important both to the crown and its powerful subjects were built into the very brick and stone of major works of architecture. Simon Thurley reads the Tudor style of the great palace of Hampton Court, for example, as a program of "chivalric eclecticism."[135] The tension was undoubtedly written into works of literature—both those that have become admired classic texts and works now masked in obscurity.[136]

The humbler works, though of infinitely lower aesthetic value, may make the point more clearly. Strenuous efforts to fit chivalry and royal sovereignty into the same frame of thought appear in Samuel Daniel's *Civil Wars*, written at the end of the Tudor era (1595–1623?). Though a work that may now be all but forgotten, as a sweeping narrative of late medieval aristocratic quarrels over the English throne and the arrival of the Tudors it is especially revealing.[137] The old chivalric ethos of independent prowess appeals powerfully to Daniel. He wants honor to stem from danger bravely met in battle: "For, vile is honor, and a title vaine, / the which, true worth and danger do not gaine."[138] One side of his thought is immovably conservative. He devotes seven pages to a jeremiad against innovations such as "Artillerie, th'infernall instrument / New-brought from hell, to scourge imortalitie," along with other devilish inventions (including the printing press).[139] Two ringing lines given to Hotspur in the Fourth Book sing out the heroic creed concisely: "What? Haue we hands, and shall we seruille bee? / Why were swords made? But, to preserue men free."[140] Only a few pages later, however, he speaks of "that especial right of kings; the Sword," and laments that Hotspur's cause was personal ambition and not the protection and defense of his country.[141] Earlier, he admiringly shows how a deposed and imprisoned Richard II still plays the knight in his death scene; the king seizes a sword from one of his assailants and slays four of "These shameful beastes" with his "quicke and ready hand" before succumbing.[142] Daniel will not give the title of knight to the "caitiff" who finally cuts Richard down:

> To giue impietie this reuerent stile?
> Title of honour, worth, and virtues right,
> Should not be giuen to a wretch so vile.[143]

Knighthood and king-killing are incompatible. And as much as Daniel loves heroic deeds of prowess, he cannot stomach them in the cause of civil strife.[144] In fact, a leitmotif in Daniel's account is his horror of civil war rending the kingdom; this steady theme grows out of his belief in a sound monarchy as guarantor of necessary social and political order. In the civil strife of the battle of St. Albans, he admonishes that "who did best, hath but dishonour won," and the battle of Taunton he declared the "greatest day of ruine" for England.[145] Richard McCoy justly argues that laboring under such deep-seated ambivalence, Daniel's great project could only falter and lie unfinished.[146]

Pragmatic treatises redouble the message of literary works. Sir Humphrey Gilbert's proposal for what amounted to a new royal university in the capital shows new ideas amid echoes of the medieval. *Queene Elizabethe's Achademy*, the book Gilbert presented to the queen about 1570, argued for a model education for royal wards and, by extension, for young noblemen in general; though it did not move the queen to found his school, the plan is revealing.[147] He believes the youthful members of the elite are "estranged from all serviceable virtues to their prince and Cowntrey"[148] and asserts they need a broader education than the narrow "schole leareninges" provided by Oxford and Cambridge or by the hunting and hawking of country gentlemen.[149] Though he wants noble youths to have the use of a comprehensive scholarly library and be taught Greek and Latin grammar, he emphasizes learning in English in a wide range of pragmatic subjects, including mathematics for artillery and fortification, and law for their own affairs and for their governing roles as sheriffs and justices of the peace. If this educational plan truly sounds new, the older tradition also surfaces in a call for learning the joust, riding at the ring, and mastering heraldry, no less than mounted pistol practice and the firing of hacqbuts, marching, map-making, and the use of cannon. In fact, Gilbert assures Elizabeth in his closing argument that the center will be "an Achademy of Philosophie and Chiualrie" or even, a few lines later, "a most noble Achademy of Chiuallric policy and philosophie."[150] He has already pointedly assured his sovereign that in his institution "all the best sorte shalbe trained vp in the knowledge of gods word (which is the onely fowndacion of true obedience to the prince)."[151]

The issues that so troubled Samuel Daniel and animated Humphrey Gilbert were hardly settled in their lifetimes. The case stands rather that they are being debated and are moving in a significant direction in late Tudor days. Elements of the heroic ideal near the heart of chivalric thinking expired—or were transformed—slowly, but their final rituals seem to have taken place under royal patronage.[152] Is it not interesting that genuine tilting might often in the Tudor period be termed "Jousts Royal"?[153] The handwriting was on the wall, but perhaps under Tudor monarchs sufficient clarity for the line to be filled on the death certificate of chivalry was still in process. Chivalric ideology drew strength from an intertwined set of ideals that could not be severed all at once. It was a Jacobean author, Thomas Milles, who wrote a resolute defense of honor resting within the sovereign's gift, in his treatise titled "The Catalogue of Honour, or Treasury of True Nobility, Peculiar to Great Britain" (1610). He concluded that "our Kinges (who onely and alone, do in their kingdome bear the absolute rule and sway) are with us efficient causes of all POLITICAL NOBILITY."[154]

Emphasizing a *respublica* governed by citizen/administrators, the new learning gradually undermined surviving defenses of chivalry that lasted beyond traditional ending points for the medieval era. As in so many sieges, the process was slow. Vigorous praise of *virtu*, of heroic militarism—even of chivalry—in the beloved classical past, complicated matters. The great soul of Erasmus might long for peace, but the shadow of Turkish advance moved even him; Symphorien Champier, writing of the Chevalier Bayard, had fewer scruples about war and violence.

Conclusion

Can any cause be entered on the death certificate of chivalric ideology? Prudent legal counsel might suggest adding an appendix to that document, replete with scholarly qualifications (what medieval counsel would term a schedule sewn to the main parchment). The negative results have seemed easiest to discern. As a complex set of ideas and practices, chivalry cannot be hurried off the stage like a stiffening corpse. Its life did not suddenly end in a flash and smoke produced by black powder. Changes in military organization, the size, training, and equipping of armies, especially in relation to the growth of state power, are more subtle and complex; these changes still generate debate. Yet much scholarship doubts that even organizational improvements in the military can claim the role of prime mover. What is more, most scholars look as late as the seventeenth century for cumulative effects of processes emerging over generations, if not centuries. If military revolution seems less likely than military evolution, the change constitutes an important accomplice, but is unlikely to sustain a solitary murder charge.

Powerfully shifting currents in ideas may likewise have their charge reduced to acting as accessories rather than prime suspects. In the abstract, reforming ideas of religion and the new scholarship—when irenic and anti-heroic—were too radical, too disruptive of social discipline, order, and hierarchy, for any elite to subscribe to them or implement them fully, certainly not in an age of struggles between religious groups that finally took their appeals to arms. If not primary, this role as accessories was far from unimportant. New ideas may be necessary for the radical transformation of old ideas; and the process moves all the more swiftly if the newcomers are associated with effective power.

The chivalric code could finally be transformed (and not killed outright) only as sovereign governmental power increased, blessed by religion in both Protestant and Roman Catholic lands, and praised lavishly by practitioners of the new learning.[155] What shifted so significantly was the agency that mediated between heroic deeds and merit, between divine will and armed power. This pivotal role came into the hands of sovereigns. Royal administrations garnered a function long claimed by the church universal, and within their more limited areas of responsibility they achieved a more generous measure of success. The states under construction would become effective managers of sheer military power; warriors followed their dictates and absorbed their ideas and propaganda with less independence and reformulation than we saw them exercise in their relationship with the church.[156] Sovereigns enforced their claim to define and dispense blessings for valorous service. It came to be the sovereign who bestows honor on the deserving—a logical extension of capacity for rulers who had long been judging disputes and claims of the elite, taxing their wealth, and working to define and limit the legitimacy of their violence within the realm. Over centuries, sovereign lords had gradually succeeded in asserting divine approval for their growing role. Warriors who had accepted this insertion of royal authority into society now found it difficult to claim an independent basis for honor, personally choosing the causes, actions, and venues in which to perform their acts of prowess, confident (as was Geoffroi de Charny) that through shining deeds they would forever inscribe their honor within the lasting memory of a body of international professionals. Royal valorization of the heroic might still ultimately work through the hands of loyal churchmen, with their voices raised in blessing;

but royal authority to call upon this blessing was in as little doubt as the ultimate beneficiary. Virtual national churches under increasing lay control had emerged from the Late Middle Ages, even before the church universal fractured repeatedly across much of Europe.[157] Clerical dreams on the scale of Gregory VII or Innocent III—visions of directing ideal warriors within an ideal religious European society–had evaporated. By the early sixteenth century a single church no longer spoke for all of Western Europe and could no longer assert final claims on the use of armed force; in national or regional churches the sword was in effect directed by princes and sovereigns rather than ecclesiastics, and even in Catholic countries the directive voice of Rome was much muted by the voice of each sovereign. Warfare against the heads of these states by those living within them had (by a process long in preparation) become treason and, upon failure, was recognized even by the rebels as sinful.[158] The sovereign who awarded honor to individuals stood as head of the collective body that received divine blessing or suffered divine wrath. Few readers of the biographies of Louis La Tremouille or the Chevalier Bayard could doubt that even before religious war had hit stride, a crusading character had been infused into the accounts of their fighting for the righteous and most Christian king of France.

The warriors still enjoyed a special path to heavenly bliss, but it now passed through gateways prominently bearing royal insignia. Of necessity, the clerics (Protestant or Catholic) accepted the change and in most realms even loyally eased the new pattern into life, praying for those agents and blessing those actions that favored royal sovereignty under the watchful and approving eye of God (who was Protestant or Catholic as the case demanded). The death certificate of chivalry was issued—quietly and in properly oblique language—as a state document under the sovereign's seal. But it also carried innumerable signatures of humanist scholars and royalist clerics who served as willing and obedient witnesses and who helped to give the process legitimacy through their fervent blessing.

NOTES

CHAPTER 1. VIOLENT KNIGHTS, HOLY KNIGHTS

1. The story of this book, could it be fully known, was likely complex. The illumination was painted about the middle of the thirteenth century (1255–65) in a style that suggests links to the chronicler Matthew Paris and to artists at the royal court of Henry III. Obviously the book was written and painted for a discriminating customer of means, possibly an English Dominican of some standing. Our illustration may well have been taken from a previous book, parts of which are now missing. Yet this bilateral painting, along with two companion illuminations on the remaining sides of the bifolium—one showing a Dominican friar kneeling before Christ and the other an angel—well announces the interests governing the choice of contents. Several years after encountering this illustration, I discovered the wide-ranging and convincing discussion of these illustrations within the entire Harleian manuscript by the distinguished art historian Michael Evans, "An Illustrated Fragment of Peraldus's *Summa* of Vice." Evans discusses the theological ideas involved and also provides black-and-white photographs of the central miniature and the flanking illuminations on the opening and final sides of the bifolium. He extensively discusses the Christus/miles image, which will be analyzed as a general theme in Chapter 6 below.

2. See Dondaine, "Guillaume Peyraut, vie et oeuvres." Peraldus wrote this treatise in two parts c. 1236 and c. 1248. He may have studied at Paris but was not a university scholar. His concern for practical, pastoral theology shows at least similar interests to those in the circle of Peter the Chanter. At the Dominican house in Lyons, Étienne de Bourbon (a member of the circle of Peter, whose miracle stories will appear often in this book) was his fellow friar. This work by Peraldus was widely disseminated and was considered helpful in preparing sermons. A group of scholars in the U.S. and Canada, under the general direction of Siegfried Wenzel (University of Pennsylvania) is at work on Peraldus's *Summa de vitiis*.

3. The line appears frequently in medieval treatises, e.g., Alan of Lille's sermon *Ad Milites*, PL 210 col. 186. Biblical references throughout the text are drawn from the Vulgate, with English translations from the King James Version. Wherever a text is quoted in Latin and in English translation without mention of an English source, the translation is my own.

4. Ramon Llull, *Libre que es de l'ordre de cavalleria*; for the Old French translation see *Livre de l'ordre de chevalerie*.

5. Kennedy, *Lancelot do Lac: The Non-Cyclic Old French Romance*, 143–46, provides the symbolic meanings given by the Lady of the Lake to the young Lancelot in their famous conversation on ideal chivalry.

6. For this *scutum fidei*, see the discussion in Evans, "An Illustrated Fragment."

7. 2 Timothy 2:5: "nam et qui certat in agone non coronatur nisi legitime certaverit." The sentiment certainly continued in later medieval writing. Thomas à Kempis wrote: "Be thou therefore ready for the fight if thou wilt have the victory. Without striving thou canst not win the crown of patience; if thou wilt not suffer thou refusest to be crowned. But if thou desirest to be crowned, strive manfully, endure patiently. Without labour thou drawest not near to rest, nor without fighting comest thou to victory." *The Imitation of Christ*, 3.19.4. My thanks to Edward Wierenga for pointing me to both references.

8. Matthew 5:3–9: the meek in the illumination inherit *regnum* rather than *terram*, as in the Vulgate. In general, compare the Sermon on the Plain in Luke 6:20–23.

9. Southern, *Western Society and the Church*, 41.

10. Classic accounts appear in Southern, *Western Society and the Church*, and Vauchez, *The Laity in the Middle Ages*.

11. I investigate this theme in a forthcoming article.

12. Bertran, *The Poems of the Troubadour Bertran de Born*.

13. See *laisse* 57 in Bertrand de Bar-sur-Aube, *The Song of Girart of Vienne*.

14. Line 257 in Benson, *King Arthur's Death*.

15. This medieval tension is clearly part of a very old story. Arduous service, bravely undertaken, has seemed in most ages to merit special benefits from divinity. Our paradox is unique neither to medieval society nor to the medieval Christian religion that animated it. Eileen Power wrote of the "primal instinct which leads man to drag his god into his battles" in her splendid introduction to Herolt, *Miracles of the Blessed Virgin Mary*, xxii. But the medieval evidence provides a classic case in a formative era of European history. Unlike modern soldiers who leave peacetime occupations for temporary service in military or naval forces, knights were professional warriors who defined their status and place in the world by their right to bear and use arms.

16. The fundamental starting point is Erdmann, *The Origin of the Idea of Crusade*, originally published in German in 1935.

17. Marcus Bull, *Knightly Piety*, examines one region, the Limousin and Gascony, in the period of the First Crusade. His perspective differs somewhat from that presented in this book.

18. As I have argued elsewhere (*Chivalry and Violence*, 273–97), chivalric ideas, never monolithic, were themselves subject to debate. Yet, as with the elements in a mass, we need to think of substance and accidents. In other words, while debate swirled around specific questions of chivalric action, a core of ideas justifying the profession lasted.

19. Keen, *Chivalry*; Flori, *L'idéologie du glaive*; Erdmann, *Origins of the Idea of Crusade*.

20. See the comment of Clifford Geertz, "Religion as a Cultural System," 4: "The

notion that religion tunes human actions to an envisaged cosmic order and projects images of cosmic order onto the plane of human experience is hardly novel. But it is hardly investigated either, so that we have very little idea of how, in empirical terms, this particular miracle is accomplished."

21. I have argued this point throughout my studies of chivalry; see especially *Chivalry and Violence*, 30–41, and "Literature as the Key to Chivalric Ideology." This issue will be considered again, below, in Chapter 6. For a contrary view, see Nicholson, *Love, War, and the Grail*. I agree with Nicholson's point that knights may have written more of chivalric literature than we have previously imagined.

22. Leyser, "Warfare in the Western European Middle Ages."

23. For a recent discussion, see Bachrach, *Religion and the Conduct of War*.

24. Busby, *Raoul de Hodenc, Le Roman des eles*, 117 (French), 175 (translation); Shinners and Dohar, eds., *Pastors and the Care of Souls*, 197–98 print, "Blessing for the sword of a new knight." He is to fight God's enemies, defend Holy Church, etc., of course. With sword girded on, he is sprinkled with holy water and told to go in the name of the Lord. Printed from Collins, *Manuale ad Usum Percelebris Ecclesiae Sarisburiensis*, 69–70.

25. Gerald of Wales, *The Autobiography of Giraldus Cambrensis*, 47.

26. Baldwin kept relics of Thomas in his chapel after the martyrdom. Lambert of Ardres, *The History of the Counts of Guines and Lords of Ardres*, 110, 121.

27. Quoted in Knowles, "Archbishop Thomas Becket: A Character Study," 197.

28. McNab, "Obligations of the Church in English Society."

29. Hallam, "Monasteries as 'War Memorials'," 48.

30. Leyser, "Warfare in the Western European Middle Ages," 201.

31. The relationship between what is holy and what is physical provides a general example. Men and women whose holy lives and outlook stood as far as is humanly possible from the merely bodily and physical in life were—after death—revered by the faithful as physical objects; the remains of their bodies and even their possessions were piously venerated. See Finucane, *Miracles and Pilgrims*.

32. Considerable insight into the monastic view in the age when chivalry was just coming into being appears in Certain, *Les Miracles de Saint Benoit*, especially books 4, 5, 6, and 7. Some of these stories are discussed in Rollason, "The Miracles of St. Benedict."

33. William of Malmesbury, *Historia Novella*, 58–59.

34. Ralph of Niger worried that the shedding of human blood was in no way a fitting atonement for sin. See his "De re militari et triplici via peregrinationis," cited in Flahiff, "Deus Non Vult," 182.

35. The issue is debated. See Throop, *Criticism of the Crusade*; for the problems addressed by a specific preacher see Brett, *Humbert of Romans*, 167–94. For a critique of increasing negativity, see Siberry, *Criticism of Crusading*.

36. Quoting from a contemporary biography, "The Life of Leo IX," printed in Robinson, *The Papal Reform of the Eleventh Century*, 149.

37. Ibid., 151.

38. Cowdrey, "Pope Gregory VII and the Bearing of Arms," 23.

39. Ibid.

40. Ibid., 25.

41. Cowdrey, *Pope Gregory VII*, 650.

42. Ibid., 652.

43. Quoted in Erdmann, *Origin of the Idea of Crusade*, 154.

44. Bernard of Clairvaux, *In Praise of the New Knighthood*, 37; Latin in *Sancti Bernardi Opera* 3:216. Using the classic clerical word play, he refers to merely secular knighthood as "non . . . militiae, sed malitiae." He assured the Templars—and later those involved in the Second Crusade—that they fought with no danger to their souls. In addition to his *De Laude*, see letter 391, in *Letters of St. Bernard*, 460–63, especially 462.

45. Robert of Flamborough, *Liber Poenitentialis* (1208–13); see especially 184–85, 226–28. Rising momentarily to the vitriolic level of St. Bernard, he declared that knights who gave up the emblematic warrior belt (militiae cingulum), presumably to enter a monastery, but went back into worldly knighthood "truly returned to their own vomit (vero ad propriam vomitum sunt relapse)" (271).

46. Alan of Lille, *Textes inédits*, 16–17, n. 30. For use in *exempla* see BL Additional 18351 late 14C, *Exemplorum secundum ordinem alphabeti*, f. 39, and a story of Étienne de Bourbon in *Anecdotes historiques*, 370–71.

47. Alan of Lille, *The Art of Preaching*, 146; this text translates PL 210 cols. 109–95. Alan's general tirades against vanity and empty worldly honor run directly counter to central chivalric values. Sections of this work bear such telling titles as "On Despising the World," "On Despising Yourself," and "Against Pride."

48. Ibid., 150; PL 210 col. 186: "Ad hoc specialiter instituiti sunt milites, ut patriam suam defendant, et ut repellant ab Ecclesia violentorum injuries."

49. Ibid., 149–50; PL 210 col. 186: "sed jam milites facti sunt praedarii duces aliorum, facti sunt abigeri; nec jam exercent militiam, sed rapinam, et sub specie militis, assumunt crudelitatem praedonis: nec tam militant in hostes; quam grassantur in pauperes; et quos debent tueri clypeo militaris muniminis, persequuntur gladio feritatis. Jam suam prostituunt militiam, militant ut lucrentur; arma capiunt ut praedentur. Jam non sunt milites, sed fures et raptores; non defensores, sed invasores. In viscera matris Ecclesiae acuunt gladios, et vim quam debent in hostes expendere, expendunt in suos; hostes autem suos (aut torpore dejecti, aut timore perterriti) desistunt invadere, et in Christi famulos imbelles, cogunt gladios desaevire."

50. Ibid., 24: PL 210 col. 115: "Ubi vanitas nisi in honoribus qui ad hoc homini favent ut dejiciant, ad hoc erigunt ut destruant? Ad hoc suspendunt ut gravius impellant; in quibus est vanitas vanitatum, quia importabile onus in honore, phasticus honor in onere, et in eis omnia vanitas cum funditus." Reading this statement alongside a few pages of the works of Geoffroi de Charny or Sir Thomas Malory will make the incompatibility of ideas obvious.

51. La Bigne, ed., *Maxima bibliotheca vetervm patrvm*, 25, 495.

52. See the following BL examples: Arundel 506 f. 5, Arundel 22283 f. 14b col 2, Harley 273 f. 137b col. 2, Harley 2391 f. 221, Harley 2385 f. 65 col. 2, Harley 1288 f. 54, Additional 11284 f. 78b, Additional 18351 f. 12b col. 2, Additional 18347 f. 117, Additional 17336 f. 8, Burney 361 f. 154 col. 2. Versions of the story also appear in Banks, *An Alphabet*

of Tales, 337, Wenzel, *Fasciculus Morum*, 124–25, and Robert Mannyng, *Handlyng Synne*, 96–99. Alan Frantzen has found modern equivalents in the battlefield lore of the First World War: *Bloody Good: Chivalry, Sacrifice, and the Great War*. This tale evidently touched knights: it appears in the book of advice the Chevalier de la Tour Landry wrote for the instruction of his daughters in the fourteenth century: Offord, ed., *The Book of the Knight of the Tower*, 237.

53. Rolle, *The Contra Amatores Mundi*, 96, 181: "Non audaces tales dixeris, qui dum aliorum scindunt tunicam, mala morte premiuntur. Micantibus armis, phaleratis equis ad bella properant, et priusquam percuciant interius moriuntur. Dum corda transverberant hominum, penetrantur et ipsi interius iaculis demoniorum. Dicamus eis, ubi est deus vester? . . . Non utique deus noster, quia illud quod plus amant sibi deum constituerunt. Alii feacerunt sibi deum superbam vanitatem seu vanam dignitatem, pro qua se extollunt, aspera paciuntur, penurias habent, vulnerant et vulnerantur, occidunt et occiduntur." Even more than the rich invective, what is striking in this passage is its explicit denial that the suffering and hardships of knighthood serve the knights in a meritorious capacity, a theme of central interest throughout this book. Significantly, Rolle thinks it worthwhile to negate such a powerful idea. Far from gaining merit by their hard lives, a claim he obviously knows the knights make, they are, Rolle insists, damning themselves in the empty search for glory and honor.

54. One of the arguments advanced in Kaeuper, *Chivalry and Violence* (129–60) holds that chivalry involved the veritable worship of prowess as a demigod.

55. All this evidence and especially that from literary works will, of course, raise the question of prescription and description, discussed in Kaeuper, *Chivalry and Violence*, passim. The long prayers in *chansons de geste*, for example, surely represent didactic clerical effort rather than statement of knightly belief. On these prayers in general see Koch, *An Analysis of the Long Prayers in Old French Literature*, and Labande, "Le Credo Épique."

56. Duffy, *Stripping of the Altars*, 302.

57. Ibid., 303.

58. The story attributes this information to the Dean of Langres himself, who appeared after death to his bishop. BL Additional 21147 f. 24

59. The anonymous fourteenth-century *Pricke of Conscience*, ed. Morris says that suffering for one day in purgatory is worse than one year's earthly penance: "Swa es þe payn þar a day to se / Als mykel als here a yhere may be": bk. 4, lines 2756–57, p. 75.

60. Robert Mannyng, *Handlyng Synne*, line 3284.

61. Étienne de Bourbon., *Anecdotes historiques*, 29–30.

62. Power, Introduction to Herolt, *Miracles of the Blessed Virgin Mary*, xii.

63. See the helpful discussion in Baldwin, *Masters, Princes, and Merchants*, 206–27.

64. Herolt, *Miracles of the Blessed Virgin*, 103–4.

65. Sommer, *Vulgate Version of the Arthurian Romances*, 2: 234, lines 16–17: "couroucese sespee."

66. The tension is seen often in Middle English literature, e.g., Benson, ed., *Stanzaic Morte Arthure*, passim. The knightly were often prone, of course, to see no contradiction.

In *laisse* 158 of the Old French *Girart de Vienne*, ed. Emden, Oliver proclaims his trust rests in God and in his own flashing arms.

67. See, for example, Marcus Bull's estimate, summarized near the end of his *Knightly Piety*, 286.

68. Defense of their *ordo* is considered in Chapter 8.

69. For the early part of the period under survey, see Bull, *Knightly Piety*; for the Later Middle Ages, see the brief case studies in Contamine, *La noblesse au royaume de France*, 245–59.

70. See, e.g., Jordan Fantosme's chronicle, written 1174–75, which often links treason with service of the devil, and shows the knights constantly in touch with God, praying, thanking him and his Mother, and the like: *Jordan Fantosme's Chronicle*, 36–37, 42–43, 56–57.

71. As Bernier is told by his mother in *Raoul de Cambrai*, serve your overlord and God will be your reward. See Kay, ed., *Raoul de Cambrai, laisse* 68.

72. The topic of *ordines* will be examined in Chapter 7.

73. Even if the prohibition was considered to apply to murder rather than killing in general, the worry might persist. Indeed, might not any ambiguity here intensify personal reflection?

74. Bitterling, ed., *Of Shrift and Penance*, 66.

75. For Charny's views, see Kaeuper and Kennedy, *Book of Chivalry*, 178–81. Of course, he never stints in his praise of honor and severely castigates those who are cowardly, unwilling to risk all in the quest of honor. See Kaeuper, *Chivalry and Violence*, 124–31. The knightly belief in prowess as the center of chivalry is discussed in ibid., 129–60.

76. God is characterized as the Sovereign Avenger (souvrains vengieres) in Paris and Ulrich, *Merlin*, 31.

77. See the thoughtful work of Timothy Gorringe, *God's Just Vengeance*.

78. Frantzen, *Bloody Good*, especially 47–48. The *History of the Albigensian Crusade* by Peter of les Vaux-de-Cernay provides good examples of how the cross could be used to inspire violence. At the siege of Lavaur in 1211 the crusaders set a cross atop a wooden fortification erected near the castle under assault. When shot from the defenders' engines break one of its arms, Peter darkly assures his readers that "the Cross avenged the injuries it had suffered as will be shown later." *History of the Albigensian Crusade*, 115. Early in his narrative Peter has referred to God as "the Lord of Vengeance (dominus ultionum)." Ibid., 35; idem, *Petri Vallium Sarnaii monachi Hystoria albigensis*, i: 60. The clerical author of the chronicle of the Lisbon Crusade of 1147 tells of elevating a piece of the true cross to crusaders about to assault the city: David, *The Conquest of Lisbon*, 154–59. The crusaders in the Holy Land famously wheeled fragments of the true cross within a cumbersome carriage into battle and though they lost them to the Muslims at the Horns of Hattin in 1187, pieces subsequently appear on many crusading battlefields; see the comment by Ailes in Ambroise, *The History of the Holy War*, 2: 3.

79. The *History of the Albigensian Crusade* again provides a good example. At the

siege of Toulouse in 1218 Count Simon de Montfort, having witnessed the elevation of the host in a mass sung in his tent, proclaims "Let us go and if needs must die for Him who deigned to die for us." Peter of les Vaux-de-Cernay, *History of the Albigensian Crusade*, 276; for the Latin, *Petri Vallium Sarnaii monachi Hystoria albigensis*, vol. 3, par. 609.

80. Brandin, *Chanson d'Aspremont*; see *laisse* 235 and the beginning of 236.

81. Mullally, *The Deeds of the Normans in Ireland*, 102. It continues, "Strike, barons, without delay, in the name of Jesus, son of Mary! Strike noble knights (Al nun ihesu le fiz marie; / Ferez, chevaliers gentils)" (lines 1922–26). An earlier fight had left a thousand foemen beaten, killed, wounded, or captured "Par force e par uertu / Que lur fist le bon jhesu," 108. This text was earlier edited by Orpen as *The Song of Dermot and the Earl*.

82. Newth, *Aymeri of Narbonne*, 25; Demaison, ed., *Aymeri de Narbonne*, 2:33: "Que Damedex qui pardon fist Longis, / Te doint vitoire contra tes enemis!" The sentiment is repeated; see Newth, 88, Demaison, 118.

83. Sommer, *Vulgate Version*, 1: 80–81; Chase, "History of the Holy Grail," in Lacy, *Lancelot-Grail*, 1: 51–52.

84. Round, *Calendar of Documents Preserved in France*, no. 701.

85. He wrote that the foundation was "ad Deum propitiatio pro effusione tanti sanguinis Christiani"; William of Newburg, *The History of English Affairs*, i: 40. The motive for a foundation might, of course, be thanksgiving for victory: see, for example Boffa, *Warfare in Medieval Brabant*,168, a late thirteenth-century example.

86. Slack, *Crusade Charters 1138–1270*, 102–3.

87. Ibid., no. 24.

88. Orderic Vitalis, *Ecclesiastical History of Orderic Vitalis*, 4: 80–81, entire speech at 80–95. Significantly, the speech praises Norman prowess under God's beneficent hand.

89. Their literature often shows warriors communing in their own fashion with three blades of grass just before the opposing sides joined battle. E.g., Kay, *Raoul de Cambrai*, *laisse* 120. The bishops who blessed crusaders as the opposing forces took position just before the decisive battle of Muret in 1213 were repeatedly requested to renew assurances of divine favor and of heavenly reward to those who would perish. See Peter of les Vaux-de-Cernay, *History of the Albigensian Crusade*, 209–10; for the Latin, *Hystoria Albigensis*, 2: sections 461–62. David Bachrach gives many examples, *Religion and the Conduct of War*, passim.

90. See the comment of Walter Map, *De Nugis Curialium*, 416–17: Bonitas non nisi bonum, probitas utriumque facit," translated in James, Brooke, and Mynors as "goodness makes a man only good, prowess makes him either."

91. Douglas, *English Historical Documents*, 2: 316; Latin in Stubbs, *Chronicles and Memorials of the Reigns of Stephen, Henry II, and Richard I*, 3: 151 ff.

92. Vauchez, *The Laity in the Middle Ages*, 56–57.

93. Discussed in the chronicle by Peter of les Vaux-de-Cernay, *History of the Albigensian Crusade*, 58–59; Latin in *Hystoria Albigensis*, section 106.

94. Discussed, with many sources cited and quoted, in. Baker, "Meed and the Economics of Chivalry in Piers Plowman," in *Inscribing the Hundred Years' War*. Modern

scholars debate the degree of criticism of war and chivalric violence in the contemporary poem "Les Voeux du Heron." See in this same volume the essays "Warmongering in Les Voeux du Heron," by Norris Lacy, and "Inscribing the Body with Meaning: Chivalric Culture and the Norms of Violence in The Vows of the Heron," by Patricia DeMarco.

95. Newman, *The Cartulary and Charters of Notre-Dame of Homblieres*, no. 84, 163–64.

96. Caesarius of Heisterbach, *Dialogue on Miracles*, 1: 49; *Dialogus Miraculorum*, 1: 45–46.

97. Holden, Gregory, and Crouch, *History of William Marshal*, vol. 2, lines 18231–51.

98. See Poole, *Domesday Book to Magna Carta*, 486 n. 2.

99. Caesarius of Heisterbach, *Dialogue on Miracles*, 2: 103–4. In this case the worried knight was finally comforted by the Blessed Virgin, whom he had always revered.

100. Caesarius of Heisterbach, *Dialogue on Miracles*, 2: 290–91; *Dialogus Miraculorum*, 2: 316–17.

101. Thomas of Cantimpré tells an elaborate tale of this sort, *Bonum universale de apibus*, 2: 491–93. It is retold as a more concise sermon *exemplum* in BL Harley 2316 f. 10b.

102. Kay, *Raoul de Cambrai*.

103. Rosenberg, *Lancelot-Grail*, 2: 254; Micha, *Lancelot*, 1: 61.

104. Kay, *Raoul de Cambrai, laisse* 283: "Baron . . . por Deu, concilliés moi. / Pichiés ai fais dont je grant paor ai, / maint home aim ors dont je sui em esfrpo— / Raoul ocis, certes, ce poise moi. / Dusqu' a Saint Gile vuel aler demanois; / projerai le que placidis soit por moi / vers Damredieu qui sires est et rois."

105. Hahn, *Sir Gawain: Eleven Romances and Tales,* "Awntyrs off Arthur," lines 261–312. The Middle English quotation reads, " 'How shal we fare' quod the freke, 'that fonden to fight, / And thus defoulen the folke on fele kinges londes, / And riches over reymes withouten eny right, / Wynnen worship in were thorgh wightnesse of hondes?' "

106. Rosenberg, *Lancelot-Grail*, 2: 271, Micha, *Lancelot*, 1: 152: "mais Nostre Sire ne garde mie a la cortoisie del monde,kar cil qui est buens al monde est mals a Dieu."

107. Alan of Lille, *The Art of Preaching*, 52. PL 210 col. 131: "Quod hominibus altum est, abomination est apud Deum."

108. Examples of pious death on the Mount of Olives in BL Additional 33956 f. 41, Additional 27336 f. 67, Arundel 231 f. 16; stories of dying piously in battle for the faith in Jacques de Vitry: *The Exempla of Jacques de Vitry*, 172; Caesarius of Heisterbach, *Dialogue on Miracles*, 2: 259; *Dialogus Miraculorum*, 2: 291. There is also a story of Étienne de Bourbon in *Anecdotes historiques*, 92.

109. Willingness to die at the close of a day in which great prowess has been demonstrated appears in Micha, *Lancelot*, 6: 103–4, and Kennedy, *Lancelot do Lac*, 1: 414.

110. Robert Mannyng, *Handlyng Synne*, lines 466–68: "Þat he ne may sytte hys hors above, / Þat perauenture yn al hys lyue / Shal he neure aftyr þryue."

111.Hudson, *Four Middle English Romances*, 203, lines 4615–18.

112. Mills, *Lybeaus Desconus,*, 75.

113. Malory, *Works*, 156.

114. Evans, *Unconquered Knight*, 146.

115. Quoted in Cowdrey, *Pope Gregory VII*, 627.

116. Paris, *Chronica majora*, 3: 290–91, discussed by Cazel, in "Religious Motivation in the Biography of Hubert de Burgh," 109–10.

117. This source and the crusade are discussed in detail in Chapter 4.

118. David, *The Conquest of Lisbon*, 134–35.

119. Ibid.: "Quidam vero hoc interpretantes aiebant gentem illam ferocem et indomitam, alieni cupidam, licet tunc sub specie peregrinationis et religionis, sitim sanguinis humani nondum deposuisse."

120. Ibid., 120–21.

121. Ibid., 152–53.

122. "Haec itaque repugnantia, si quando indultum est indulgere quieti, sapientis viri, audaciam sopiebat," *RHC* III Occ., 605–6, discussed in Bull, *Knightly Piety*, 3–4. Urban's sermon and the difficulty of knowing exactly what was promised are discussed in Chapter 4.

123. Jean Leclercq discusses and prints this short Latin treatise, "Un document sur les debuts des Templiers." The date places it just a few years before the order received official standing with a Latin rule. Malcolm Barber and Keith Bate print the letter in English in *The Templars*, 54–59.

124. Leclercq, "Un document," 94: "audiuimus quasdam uestrum a quibusdam minus discretis perturbari, quasi profession uestra, qua uitam uestram ad portanda arma contra inimicos fidei et pacis pro defensione christianorum dedicastis, quasi, inquam, illa profession uel inlicita sit uel perniosa, id est uel peccatum uel maioris profectionis impedimentum."

125. All quotations in this paragraph are taken from ibid., 94–96.

126. Ibid., 96–98.

127. David Bachrach finds similar doubt and a desire for assurance of divine favor on the part of early crusaders. *Religion and the Conduct of War*, 149–50.

128. Crouch, "The Troubled Deathbeds of Henry I's Servants," 24; he notes that they were especially anxious before battle and on their deathbeds.

129. Shaw, *Joinville and Villehardouin: Chronicles of the Crusades*, 235; Joinville, *Histoire de Saint Louis*, 152: "Sire, je te pri que il te preingne pitié de moi, et m'ostes de ces guerres entre crestiens, là où j'ai vescu grant piesce; et m'otroies que je puisse mourir en ton servise, par quoy je puisse avoir ton regne de paradis."

130. Lemaitre, "Les miracles de saint Martial," 106–7; discussed in Goodich, *Violence and Miracles*, 135–46.

131. Evans, *Unconquered Knight*, 180–81. For the original Spanish see Carriazo, *El Victorial*, 272–73. The author comments that these folk are "cristianos católicos, e non son contraries a la feé de Jesucristo."

132. It was an economy of precise calculations. Those who venerated the vial of Christ's blood brought by Henry III to England, for example, were given remission from penances imposed on them for precisely six years and 116 days. Paris, *Chronicles*, 120.

CHAPTER 2. TWO MODEL KNIGHT/AUTHORS AS GUIDES

1. Fowler, *The King's Lieutenant: Henry of Grosmont, First Duke of Lancaster*, 71, 78. He notes the military service of Lancaster in Scotland and Prussia as well as France, and his frequenting of tournaments, 103–10, 162. Rogers, *The Wars of Edward III*, 141–42 prints documents on the truce. For Charny's military career in France and on crusade, see Kaeuper and Kennedy, *Book of Chivalry*, 3–18.

2. There were perhaps contradictions in Lancaster's piety, as appeared when he conducted a great raid out of Bordeaux into the Poitou in 1346. Despite Lancaster's intense personal piety, his raid involved much arson and bloodshed, and inflicted significant damage on churches. Hearing the reports, Pope Clement VI was moved to write to Lancaster urging restraints to prevent the continued destruction of churches and the robbing of ecclesiastics. The case in point was the Benedictine house of Saint-Jean-d'Angely, which Lancaster's troops had systematically looted, expelled its monks, and held them for ransom. They had likewise robbed other churches of religious ornaments, books, chalices, vestments, silver vases, and relics. See the discussion in Fowler, *King's Lieutenant*, 68, and sources cited there. On Lancaster's piety in general, see ibid., 187–96. Lancaster received the sacred thorn from the King of France: Fowler, ibid., 109. For Charny and the Shroud, see Kaeuper and Kennedy, *Book of Chivalry*, 39–41.

3. For Lancaster's foundation see Fowler, *King's Lieutenant*, 187–92; for Charny's, see Kaeuper and Kennedy, *Book of Chivalry*, 38.

4. This tendency appears in their emphasis on the discipline of chivalry, their prohibition of soft living, even their strictures on dress. Perhaps the knightly preference for strictly observant religious orders shows this frame of mind well before the era of our two knight-authors, from Cistercians in the twelfth century to Minims and Carthusians in the fifteenth century. Jeremy Catto comments on the line connecting Henry of Lancaster to Loyola and the New Model Army in "Religion and English Nobility in the Later Fourteenth Century," 52–54. Charny provides equally rich evidence.

5. Printed in Henry, Duke of Lancaster, *Le Livre de seyntz medicines*, ed. Arnould; discussed in Arnould, "Henry of Lancaster and His *Livres des Seintes Medicines*," reprinted as a separate piece, and idem, *Étude sur le Livre des saintes médecines du Duc Henri de Lancastre*. Cf. Tavormina, "Henry of Lancaster, *The Book of Holy Medicines*," which discusses the text and translates a small portion of it; and Legge, *Anglo-Norman Literature and Its Background*, 216–20. Cf. Ackerman, "The Traditional Background of Henry of Lancaster's *Livre*," 114–18.

6. See *Oxford Dictionary of National Biography* (*DNB*) entries for Thomas and his medieval descendants, all in military careers. His *DNB* entry labels Thomas "a noted warrior."

7. Two other shields are now unrecognizable. See Arnould, *Étude*, lxvi–lxvii.

8. Lancaster *Livre de seyntz medicines*, 64–84.

9. Arnould, *Étude*, lxxvii.

10. Cf. Legge's comments in *Anglo-Norman Literature*, 219, that his writing may have been an "imposition."

11. Pantin, *The English Church in the Fourteenth Century*, 231.

12. Fowler, *King's Lieutenant*, 195

13. Arnould's Introduction to Lancaster, *Livre de seyntz medicines*, viii, ix.

14. Lancaster, for example, accuses himself of being the "cheitif et malveis traitre, q'est la principale cause de la vileyne mort de son bon seignur" (5).

15. Lancaster, *Livre de seyntz medicines*, 178–79: "C'est une beiser qe jeo beise touz les jours a la Messe en signifiance de pees entre Nostre Seignur, luylo tresdouz Jesus, et moi, d'un mortel guerre qe sourdy entre luy et moi du primer qe jeo unqes fiu de age qejeo poai peccher. Car depuis ne feust unqes si mult trespetit noun qe jeo ne l'ai guerroie et sovent durement coroucee par le vile orde pecche mortel en qoi jeo siu mys tantl de terme, et me siu tenuz a la partie adverse contre mon droit seignour et contre mon homage qe jeo fisez en baptisme; et la siu jeo droitmal-veis traitre faux et desloials, et de tant pire come de moustrer si grant signe de pees tant come le fait et la volente estoient si contraires a pees et a bone acorde; et, coment qe a la foie un manere de soeffrance de guerre ad estee prise entre nous, come quant j'ai estee confes de mes pecchez et deusse receivoir le precious corps, Nostre Seignur, adonqes un poy duroient les trieves, mes ceo ne servoit pas longement qe rumpees ne feussente par moi contre bons promesses, et nepurgant tout dis beisaijeo en signe d'amour, la ou nul ne feust."

16. Ibid., 4: "jeo . . . vous prie, Sire, pur l'amour de cele en qi vous preistes nostre semblaunce, qe vous me pardonetz mes pecchés et voillietz, trecher Sire, qe desormes jeo vous puisse en alcunes choses tresembler si avaunt comme un si cheitif viande al verm poet resembler a si noble Roi comme le Roi de cel, de la terre, et de la meer de quantqe en eux sount. Et si j'ai, tresdouz Sires, pur vous en cest siecle ascune persecucioun de corps, d'avoir ou d'amys, ou en altre manere qele qe soit, jeo vous prie, tresdouz Sire, qe jeo le puisse prendre a gree pur l'amour de vous; et la ou vous, Sire de si bon gree soeffristes tauntz de peynes pur moi en ce siecle, jeo vous prie, Sire, qe jeo vous puisse resemblet en taunt qe jeo puisse trover en moun dur coer de soeffrir pur vous de bone volunté anguises, travailles, peynes, tiels comme il vous plerra, et nient soulement pur guerdoun avoir ne pur contrepeser a les mauz qe j'ai fait, mes tout entierement pur l'amour de vous, ensi comme vous feistes, Sire, pur l'amour de moi." The sinner as worm or food for worms is a venerable theme. In a chapter of his *Ars Predicandi* entitled "On Despising Oneself," Alan of Lille urges preachers to lead their hearers into thinking, "ego sum vermis (I am a worm)": PL 210 col. 115.

17. Determined by scanning the text and carrying out word searches electronically.

18. As Mitchel Merback notes, "Mary's emotional suffering as an eyewitness to her son's spectacular torture-execution was seen by medieval authors to rival, or even to surpass, the physical agonies endured by Christ, since it grew naturally out of a perfect maternal love." *The Thief, the Cross, and the Wheel*, 151.

19. Lancaster, *Livre de seyntz medicines*, 234. What counts is their "grandes peynes et tourmentz q'elle soeffri . . . et le martirement de touz les seintez martirs."

20. See discussion in Chapter 6 with reference to the "feudal" terminology of St. Anselm.

21. Lancaster, *Livre de seyntz medicines*, 178–79.

22. Ibid., 73; cf. 80, where he has left God's service for that of the devil.

23. Ibid., 116.

24. Ibid., 191: "jeo vous en prie, Sire, . . . qe jeo peusse si soeffrir toutes peynes et dolours pacientement pur l'amour de vous, douz Sires, a vous quiter une partie de ceo qe jeo vous doie de les tresoutrageousement greves peynes et vileynes qe vous soeffrestes, douz Sires, si debonairement pur moy cheitif."

25. Ibid., 197: "qe jeo puisse conoistre qe par un petite peyne cy endurer jeo soi quites de toutes les grandes peynes d'enfern. Ceo serroit une bon marchandise, quant pur une poy de tribulacions, qe n'est riens a soeffrir, de ceo mounde, l'en poet eschaper les peynes d'enfern qe sont si grandes et sanz desport; et tout ne poet homme plus par ceo gaigner de bonement soeffrir vostre envoie de persecucions qe par ceo avoit allegeance de peynes de purgatorie." Lancaster could easily have heard such language in crusade sermons or read them in chronicles or collections of moral tales. The chronicle of the crusade of Richard I frankly states that crusaders "had allowed themselves to be dispossessed that they might buy the love of God, for there can be no better bargain than [to gain] the love of the Heavenly King (E enguagier lor heritages / U perdu toz lor aages; / Se s'en laisserent deschater / Por lamor de Deu achater, / Que mieldre marcheiz ne pot ester / Que de l'amor le rei celestre)": Ambroise, *The History of the Holy War: Ambroise's Estoire de la guerre sainte*, vol. 1, lines 359–64; vol. 2, 35. Model sermons composed by several writers in the early thirteenth century stressed the great rewards from God for the supposedly light sufferings of going on crusade. See the following passages in Maier, *Crusade Propaganda*, 114–15, 118–19, James of Vitry, who even states that the Lord makes a "good bargain (bonum forum)"; 164–65, Eudes of Châteauroux; 188–89, 200–201, 208–9, Gilbert of Tournai, who, in the first entry cited, says the Lord "offers a very good business (optimum facit forum)" and in the final entry cited says the Lord "makes good business (modo bonum forum facit)."

26. Lancaster, *Livre des seyntz medicines*, 124.

27. Ibid., 165.

28. Ibid., 198. See Chapter 6 for discussion of parallels between Christ and his knights.

29. Ibid., 9, 61.

30. Ibid., 138.

31. Chapter 6 examines knightly *imitatio Christi*.

32. Only rarely did medieval writers recognize the danger of suggesting a form of penance without specifying the need for contrition. A conversation put into the mouth of a knight and bishop during the Albigensian Crusade has a doubting knight say "it amazes me that you clerics give absolution where there is no repentance." Arnold, bishop of Nîmes, responds that "it grieves me that you should doubt that any man alive, even one utterly condemned, is fully shriven, as long as he has fought these men." Shirley, *Song of the Cathar Wars*, 94–95; Martin-Chabot, *Chanson de la croisade albigeoise*, 2: 144: " 'Foucautz' so ditz l'ivesques, 'greu m'es car vos doptatz. / Que totz om calques sia, neis si era dampnatz, / Sol c'ab lor se combata, es totz penedensatz.' "

33. Dual language text and historical study appear in Kaeuper and Kennedy, *Book of*

Chivalry. Page numbers refer to facing pages in this edition. In only slightly less explicit terms, ideas we find in Lancaster and especially in Charny appear in the treatise a contemporary French knight, the Chevalier de la Tour Landry, wrote for his daughters, *Livre pour l'enseignement de ses filles.* He explicitly mentions Geoffroi de Charny and Marshal Boucicaut as standards of chivalry. For Caxton's translation see La Tour Landry, *The Book of the Knight of the Tower.*

34. See, for example, *Livre de chevalerie,* section 21, line 8; section 44, line 40 (122–23; 196–97).

35. Such denunciations also appeared in sermons. Alan of Lille in his *Art of Preaching,* denounced sloth, delicate foods, soft beds, loquaciousness, unwillingness to keep watch—the very vices Charny decried. See PL 210 col. 126.

36. Lancaster's gout: Fowler, *King's Lieutenant,* 194; Charny's view: *Livre de chevalerie,* 122–23. The Chevalier de la Tour could convert this duet into a trio. He writes that the good knight who seeks the great goal of worship (in Caxton's translation), "Payneth hym self and suffreth many grete trauuaylles as cold hete and hongre and putteth his body in to grete Ieopardy and aduenture to deye or lyue for to gete worship and good Renommee and maketh his body feble and wery by many vyages / also in many bat 많ylles and assautes / and by many other grete peryls / And as he hath suffred payne and trauail ynough / he is put and enhaunced in to grete honour / And grete yeftes ben thenne gyuen to hym / and grete wonder and merueylle it is of the grete worship and grete renommee that men beren unto hym." La Tour Landry, *The Book of the Knight of the Tower,* 151.

37. Charny, *Livre de chevalerie,* 121–22. As noted in Chapter 1, Charny obviously knows that the prowess of knights can be used badly. Tension over this central knightly quality appears regularly in most chivalric literature. The body of thought that knights accepted as their own tries to ignore this tension as fully as possible, preferring to think of prowess simply as a virtue and a gift of God.

38. Ibid., 90–91: "Car vraiment nulz ne peut aler en telx lointains voiages que le corps ne soit en peril maintes foiz. Et pour ce devons nous telz gens d'armes honorer qui a grant mise et a grant travail et en grant peril se mettent en aler." The Chevalier de la Tour, his thoughts turning to the glorious days of his youth, fondly remembers two model knights as "brethren and good knyþts in arms. . . . for euer they vyaged & neuer rested tylle they came in place where they might essaye and preue the strengthe of theyr bodyes for to gete worship and good renomme. And so moche they dyd by theyr valyaunce that at the last they were renommed ouer al as charny and bouchykault were in their tyme." La Tour Landry, *Book of the Knight of the Tower* (Caxton), 151.

39. Charny, *Livre de chevalerie,* 116, 119.

40. The spiritualized language of clerics could easily support this very physical and this-worldly contest. Alan of Lille urges Christians to be armed for the battle of life, not to fear boldness because of death, and the like. See PL 210 cols. 126, 134, 155. What is surely the pure knightly prayer is intoned in a chronicle of the Albigensian crusade: " 'Ah, Lord God of glory, by your most holy law,' said each man to himself, 'keep us from shame, do not let us be disgraced!' " Shirley, *Song of the Cathar Wars,* 54; Martin-Chabot, *Chanson de la croisade albigeoise,* 1: 234: " 'Oi, sire Dieus de Gloria!, per ta santisma lei / Garda'ns de

dezonor', so ditz cascuns per sei, / 'Que no siam auni!'" In the Middle English romance *Amis and Amiloun*, a character prays that God preserve him from shame even though he knows he fights in a wrong cause: Foster, *Amis and Amiloun*, 35.

41. Charny, *Livre de chevalerie*, 86–87.

42. Ibid., 90–91.

43. Ibid., 108–9.

44. Ibid., 110–11: "ont aquiz par leurs grans peines, travaulx et paours et perilz de corps et perte de leurs amis mors que ilz ont veu mourir en plusieurs bonnes places ou ilz ont esté, dont ilz ont eu mesaises et courroux en leur cuer souvent."

45. Lancaster, *Livre de seyntz medicines*, 4.

46. Charny, *Livre de chevalerie*, 110–11.

47. Ibid., 112–13.

48. Ibid., 194–95: "Et se ainsi le voulez faire bien continuelment et souvent, travaillez vous, armez vous, combatez vous, ainsi comme vous devrez, alez partout et par mer et par terre et en pluseurs pays, sanz doubter nulz perilz ne sanz espargne de voz chetiz corps, dont vous ne devez tenir nul compte, fors que de l'ame et vivre honoreement."

49. Ibid., 132–33. Cf. 86–87, where Charny explains that knights want to continue in tournaments "because of the success God has granted them in it."

50. Ibid., 134–35: "Et se vous avez renomee d'estre bons homs d'arames, et don't vous soiez enhauciez et honorez et vous l'aiez desservi par vostre grant travaille, peril et hardiesce, et Nostre Sires vous a fait telle grace qu'il vous ait ce laissié faire don't vous avez tele renommee, ycilz biens ne sont mie biens de fortune, mais sont biens qui par raison doivent durer."

51. Again, the Chevalier de la Tour agrees: "the good and auncyent knyghtes . . . thanked god that had gyue them grace to kepe and hold them clenely / whereby they were sette before the other and worshipped ouer al." La Tour Landry, *The Book of the Knight of the Tower*, 154.

52. The Chevalier de la Tour Landry similarly links meritorious suffering and disciplined knightly work in benefits he holds out to his daughters if they, in the manner he thinks appropriate to their sex, work to preserve honor as the knights do. Each must "thynk how thus doynge she geteth the loue of god and of her lord / of theyr frendes and of the world And the sauement of her sowle / whereof the world preyseth her and god also" (152). Context helps to support this reading of combined spiritual and earthly reward, for this story comes in the midst of several *exempla* in which women's sexual asceticism has been highly praised. The Chevalier's mind is clearly focused on bodily discipline as a high value in the eyes both of God and right-thinking society. Writing a few pages later of martyrs for love, he states "For yf they had suffred for the loue of god whiche suffered soo moch for them the tenthe parte of the payne and dolour which they dyd suffre for the fowle delyte of theyr stynkynge lecherye / they should haue hadde mercy and grete guerdon in the other world" (162). He laments that evil women are no longer burned, stoned, immured, or beheaded, nor do they have their throats slit, but consoles himself that at least "they lese therfore theyr worship and theyre estate/ the loue of god and of

theyre lordes and of theyre frendes and world also" (156). Once again worldly honor and God's love stand together. As in Charny's book, securing honor and saving the soul tend to move on parallel lines or even to merge.

53. Charny, *Livre de chevalerie*, 166–67.

54. Ibid., 174–77: "N'est ce mie comparasons d'assez souffrir comme en l'ordre de chevalerie. Que qui voudroit considerer les paines, travaux, douleurs, mesaises, grans paours, perilz, froisseures bleceures que li bon chevalier, qui l'ordre de chevalerie maintiennent ainsi comme il doivent, ont a souffrir et sueffrent mainte foiz, il n'est nulle religion ou l'en en sueffre tant comme font cil bon chevalier qui les faiz d'armes vont querant justement."

55. Ibid., 176–77. Compare Henry of Lancaster's confession that accounts of battles cause him fear of death and shame, and that he fears sudden death without a chance to make confession; see *Livre de seyntz medicines*, 9, 61.

56. Charny, *Livre de chevalerie*, 176–77.

57. Ibid.

58. Lancaster, *Livre de seyntz medicines*, 12.

59. Charny, *Livre de chevalerie*, 164–65.

60. Lancaster, *Livre de seyntz medicines*, passim, where references to the dolorous pains of hell, the unending prison of hell, etc, appear scores of times. Charny's more allusive reference to the "grant penitence" endured by the unworthy in this world and the next appears at 178–81 of his *Livre de chevalerie*.

61. See Flahiff, "Deus Non Vult," 267.

62. Bynum, *Holy Feast, Holy Fast*.

63. James, *Varieties of Religious Experience*, 243–44.

64. A good source for the constant reference to the toil and suffering of knightly life in a chivalric biography is the life of Don Pero Niño, told by his standard-bearer: Evans, *The Unconquered Knight*, 33–34, 38, 44, 82, 114, 131, 159, 176, 195.

65. *Chanson de Roland*, laisse 174: "Pur ses pechez Deu en puroffrid lo guant."

66. Carl Erdmann, *The Origin of the Idea of Crusade*, 19: "The moral precepts that accompanied [the migrating Germans] from their pagan past were completely oriented to war, focussing on heroism, famous deeds on the part of the leader, loyalty on the part of the followers, revenge for those killed, courage unto death, contempt for a comfortable life at home."

67. Lancaster, *Livre de seyntz medicines*, 73.

68. Charny, *Livre de chevalerie*, 176–81.

69. The tradition was venerable by the time of Lancaster and Charny. Even the uncompromisingly pious Simon de Montfort, the much lauded knight or athlete of Christ who guided the early phase of the Albigensian Crusade, was unyielding to clerical authority "when it conflicted with his ambitions or with his own sense of what was his due," as Sibly and Sibly note: Peter of les Vaux-de-Cernay, *History of the Albigensian Crusade*, 297.

70. Fowler, *King's Lieutenant*, 104–5.

71. *Calendar of Patent Rolls*, 1343–45, 196.

72. Fowler, *King's Lieutenant*, 78: He confesses to sinning in these activities, but the wrong is lechery, which he would still follow if he still had his youthful vigor, not the activities per se.

73. Livre de seyntz medicines, 138.

74. See the famous comment of William Marchal in Holden, Gregory, and Crouch, *Histoire*, lines 18480–18502.

75. Charny speaks to the issues directly at 164–67 of his *Livre de chevalerie*; Lancaster's view is diffused throughout his *Livre de seyntz medicines*, which assumes a framework of meritorious suffering in righteous warfare that mirrors that of Christ himself.

76. Lancaster, *Livre de seyntz medicines*, 77.

77. A modern theological stance recalling these knightly views appears in works of the famed Franz Bibfelt. See Marty and Brauer, *The Unresolved Paradox: Studies in the Theology of Franz Bibfeldt*. I owe this reference to Robert Wennerstrom and George Utech.

78. I accept the arguments of Jean Flori and Maurice Keen that the twelfth century is the formative period of chivalric growth, without denying that earlier precedents could be cited for elements that enter the great fusion of forces creating chivalry.

CHAPTER 3. THE RELIGIOUS CONTEXT FOR CHIVALRIC IDEOLOGY

1. Broad discussions appear in Southern, *Western Society and the Church*, 44–53, 100–170, 240–300; Vauchez, *The Laity in the Middle Ages*; Constable, *The Reformation of the Twelfth Century*; Cowdrey, *Pope Gregory VII*; Robinson, *Papal Reform of the Eleventh Century*. Yael Katzir stresses changes in the wake of failure on the second crusade: "The Second Crusade and the Redefinition of *Ecclesia*, *Christianitas*, the Papal Coercive Power."

2. This point of view finds support in Vauchez, *The Laity*, 98.

3. See Alexander Murray, "Confession Before 1215," 77. Murray thinks the theologians of Laon found a particularly receptive audience in England while on tour with relics to assist the rebuilding of their cathedral. David Crouch would agree that a flourishing penitential culture existed in England: "Troubled Deathbeds of Henry I's Servants."

4. See Bornstein's introduction to Vauchez, *The Laity*, xii. Part 1 of Vauchez's book speaks generally to these themes. In the process, these theologians would draw on older traditions of thought actively considered within monastic walls—about the variety of talents given by divine plan to humans, the place and value of labor in a religious life, the relative merit of the active and contemplative life, even the role of individual, private confession in cleansing sin.

5. Baldwin, *Masters, Princes, and Merchants: The Social Views of Peter the Chanter and His Circle*.

6. Ibid., 56–57. As Baldwin points out, at first the terminology of *ordines* was limited

in this circle to religious orders. Other terms served to distinguish lay social/professional groups. It is of interest that Peter the Chanter came from a family of knights and from a region of France that had suffered ravaging during the hostilities between kings of England and France; see 3–4, 205.

7. For a classic account, see Vauchez, *The Laity in the Middle Ages*.

8. How their independence shaped their ideology will be examined in Chapter 4; the knightly *ordo* is the subject of Chapter 7.

9. Of course the laity most involved were themselves among the elite in the broadest sense; they could claim at least some privilege, and ranged from great lords through knights, gentry and substantial local landowners, and from wealthy urban merchants to successful craftsmen.

10. Were a new term of art needed to characterize their stance I would borrow a splendid word learned from my grandfather. A heroically stubborn and self-confident person might be charged with "indegoddampendence." This term could concisely characterize knightly attitudes if we amend it to "selectively pious indegoddampendence."

11. Geertz, "Religion as a Cultural System," 18.

12. Auerbach, *Literary Language and Its Public*, 67. The tradition is, of course, even older. Mircea Eliade, *The Myth of the Eternal Return*, 95–102 (cited in Constable, *Three Studies*, 146) says the redemptive power of suffering was a normal aspect of ancient Mediterranean and Mesopotamian religions.

13. Auerbach, *Literary Language and Its Public*, 67–69.

14. Bernard of Clairvaux, *In Praise of the New Knighthood*, 65; idem, *Sancti Bernardi Opera* 3: 229: "nescio quid sentitur, ubi mortuus requievit, quam ubi vivens conversatus est, atque amplius movet ad pietatem mortis quam vitae recordatio."

15. Bernard, *In Praise of the New Knighthood*, 34; *Sancti Bernardi Opera*, 3: 215: "Nam si beati qui in Domino moriuntur, non multo magis qui pro Domino moriuntur?"

16. Rubenson, "Christian Asceticism," 54.

17. Kieckhefer, *Unquiet Souls*, 89, quoted in Merback, *The Thief, the Cross, and the Wheel*, 150.

18. Sara Hamilton, "Penance in the Age of Gregorian Reform," 62–63.

19. Vauchez, *The Laity in the Middle Ages*, 122.

20. Jacques de Vitry, *Exempla*, 164–65.

21. Rubin, "Choosing Death? Experiences of Martyrdom in Late Medieval Europe," and Geary, *Furta Sacra*, cited there.

22. See Constable, *Three Studies*, 149. Mid-twelfth-century crusaders on the expedition to take Lisbon were told they were being "reborn of a new baptism of repentance (novo penitentie renati baptismate)"; David, *The Conquest of Lisbon*, 72–73.

23. Quoted in Latin and translation in Auerbach, *Literary Language and Its Public*, 70. The Latin reads: "Enim vero non sentiet sua, dum illius [Christi] vulnera intuebitur. Stat martyr tripudians et triumphans, toto licet lacero corpore; et rimante latera ferro, non modo fortiter, sed et alacriter sacrum e carne sua circumspicit ebullire cruorem. Ubi ergo tunc anima martyris? Nempe in tuto. . . . in viscera Jesu, vulneribus nimirum patentibus ad introeundum. . . . Neque hoc facit stupor, sed amor."

24. Rolle, *Contra Amatores Mundi*, 76–77, 158–59: "Est igitur affirmandum quod inimicorum persecucio utilis et necessaria nobis esse ostenditur, nequando non habentes persecutorem nec coronam mereamur. Utique nisi pugnemus, non vincimus; nec coronabimur nisi vincamus. Armantur ergo milites, coronantur victores, devicti occiduntur. Dum pugnant, in mundo morantur; dum vincunt, in celo collocantur; et dum vincuntur, in baratro detruduntur."

25. Gerald of Wales, *The Jewel of the Church*, 146. The *Fasciculus Morum*, edited by Siegfried Wenzel, 136–37, cites the Book of Proverbs: "Coronoberis si sustinueris pacienter." It is worth recalling that the British Library Harley manuscript illumination with which this book began quotes the Pauline injunction that conquering and winning a crown require fighting; the illustrator pictured such a crown descending from heaven in the hands of an angel to rest on the ideal knight.

26. Some scholars have even argued that enthusiastic lay piety may have focused on ethical and ascetic ideas as much as on magico-religious rites. See Kaelber, *Schools of Asceticism*.

27. Quoted in Kieckhefer, *Unquiet Souls*, 109.

28. Merback, *The Thief, the Cross and the Wheel*, 97–99, 129, 149–50, 152.

29. Cohen, "Towards a History of European Physical Sensibility: Pain in the Later Middle Ages," 52–53. Cohen has also published "The Animated Pain of the Body." Cf. Mowbray, "The Development of Ideas About Pain and Suffering in the Works of Thirteenth-Century Masters of Theology at Paris, c. 1230–c. 1300." Mowbray opens his interesting study with the statement, "The importance which theologians attached to painful means of redemption from sin was, it seems, immense" (1). He elaborates what he terms the development of a "theology of voluntary suffering" (103). Scott Pincikowski has written an important study of the role of pain in German chivalric literature: *Bodies in Pain: Suffering in the Works of Hartmann von Aue*. P. S. Lewis wrote broadly of later medieval France, "Essentially it was upon pain that one dwelt in the later middle ages; upon the dolour of the Passion, upon the dolour of man." *Later Medieval France*, 17.

30. The significant issue of knightly imitation of Christ is taken up in Chapter 6.

31. Peter of les Vaux-de-Cernay, *The History of the Albigensian Crusade*, 62–63.

32. Cohen, "Pain in the Later Middle Ages," 69. Common consciousness does not equal common practice, of course.

33. Caroline Bynum, for example, provides some striking evidence in *Holy Feast, Holy Fast* passim, and especially 199–201.

34. Étienne de Bourbon, *Anecdotes historiques*, 30. See Foster, *Three Purgatory Poems*, for three highly descriptive Middle English accounts of journeys through purgatory.

35. BL Royal 7 D I, f. 138b.

36. BL Additional 11579 f. 6b. Motive was sometimes important. This same manuscript declares that a hermit witnessed the pains of a couple who kept themselves from sin while alive merely to avoid these punishments (f. 9). Similarly, a dead Franciscan was allowed to return to give testimony from purgatory: he has been suffering in the dread otherworld only long enough to chant a De Profundis and a prayer, but he announced he

would prefer to do earthly penance for the vast span of time extending from creation to Doomsday: BL Royal 12 E I, f. 157.

37. BL Arundel 231, vol. II, f. 6b.

38. Jacques de Vitry, *Exempla*, 38, 188–89.

39. BL Additional 15833 f. 141b.

40. BL Harley 3244 f. 84; also in BL Egerton 1117 f. 187b.

41. Jacques de Vitry, *Exempla*, 57: "Idcirco filios meos coram me adduci feci ut, excitato affectu ad ipsos, cum majori angustia mentis pro Christo relinquam illos, et ita magis merear apud Dominum." A departing crusader with his family on shore also appears in Banks, *Alphabet of Tales*, 334–35. For knights there were distinctly practical limits, of course. A story repeated often tells of a crusader (sometimes specifically a Templar) who fasts on bread and water to increase his merit. He is, of course, so weak that he is put to shame in battle. In one telling, a comrade addresses him contemptuously as Sir Bread and Water and warns that he has rescued him twice when unhorsed; he will not do so a third time. Meritorious suffering through rigorous fighting is penance enough.

42. Morris, *Pricke of Conscience*, bk. 4, p. 97, lines 3542–43: "And, if he it thole noght grotchand, / In-stede of penance it sal hym stand."

43. Caesar of Heisterbach, *Dialogue of Miracles*, 2: 255–56, *Dialogus Miraculorum*, 2: 288.

44. The story appears in several medieval collections: BL Cotton, Cleopatra C X f. 135b; BL Additional 33956 f. 75b col. 2; BL Royal 20 B xiv, f. 160 col. 2. Cf. Dexter, "Miracula Sanctae Virginis Mariae," 33–34. An interesting parallel in imaginative literature features a knight whose right hand is fixed to the hilt of his own sword which is thrust through the palm of his left hand and cannot be removed; Micha, *Lancelot, Roman en prose*, 2: 177–82.

45. What follows comes from Thomas of Cantimpré, *Bonum universale de apibus*, II, Li, 3, 386–88. The value of Thomas as a historical source is discussed in Alexander Murray, "Confession as a historical source in the thirteenth century," 286–322.

46. Thomas of Cantimpré, II, Li, 5, 388–89.

47. "O vtinam tormentum istud quod respectu scelerum meorum paruum sustinui, reiterare semel, iterum, ac tertio liceret mihi miserrimo, et in eo diutiis cruciari." The idea of being penitentially crucified is, of course, worth noting. Thomas uses this language more than once. See, for example, II, Li, 3, 386 where after an evil life a knight becomes a hermit and thus crucifies himself.

48. Ibid., II, Li, 5, 388–89.

49. Ibid., II, Liii, 23, 419–20.

50. Ibid. The saint is Christina the Astonishing, whose *vita* Thomas wrote.

CHAPTER 4. INDEPENDENCE IN KNIGHTLY PIETY

1. That there are some exceptions can cause no surprise. A major case is Froissart, whose chronicles seem simply to accept the validity of knightly life and combat as a given,

needing no justification; any paradox or tension between the grand lives lived by warriors and the principles of their religion hardly enters his mind.

2. A tendency that persists despite the balanced view presented by Sidney Painter, Maurice Keen, and Jean Flori. I fully agree with Matthew Strickland that "Resistance by the knighthood to clerical interference in matters deemed the preserve of warriors was . . . far from incompatible with profound expressions of Christian belief." See his *War and Chivalry*, 74, and the comments at 96–97.

3. Excellent surveys of tournament appear in Barker, *Tournament in England*; Barker and Barber, *Tournaments, Jousts, Chivalry and Pageants*; and Crouch, *Tournament*.

4. Caesarius of Heisterbach, *Dialogue on Miracles*, 2: 303–4; *Dialogus Miraculorum*, 2: 327–28.

5. The noted preacher Jacques de Vitry claimed that he convinced a knight of the sinfulness of tournament by proving to him the sport was indeed stained by every one of the seven deadly sins: *Exempla*, 62–64, 193. Walter Map focused on one deadly sin, pride: *Master Walter Map's Book*, 100–101. Attacks on tournament continued forcefully into the later middle ages in preaching manuals such as Johannes de Brom-yard, *Summa Praedicantium*. For an example in collected moral tales, see BL Arundel 506 f. 73.

6. Thomas of Cantimpré, *Bonum universale de apibus*. This highly useful book never received a modern scholarly edition and remains relatively unknown.

7. His book provides a series of anti-tournament *exempla*, 364–73. The seal-of-confessional issue troubled medieval folk. In BL Additional 27336 f. 73, judgment falls on a priest who reveals a knight's confession that he committed murder. Called before his king, the knight tells the truth and is forgiven. The king cuts the tongue from the priest and blinds him.

8. What follows draws on Thomas of Cantimpré, *Bonum universale de apibus*, II, Li, 3, 366–68. Thomas is discussed in Murray, "Confession as a Historical Source in the Thirteenth Century," 286–83.

9. Toads frequently appear in *exempla* and convey a sense of disgust and dread. Usurers were likely to be troubled by them in life or, especially, after death: see BL Royal 7di f. 129, BL Additional 18364 f. 43b; even a knight's wife tangles with a toad when her husband oppresses poor folk to buy her an expensive wimple: BL Additional 27336 f. 70. A toad can even represent the devil, as in the Middle English *Gesta Romanorum*: Her-rtage, *Early English Versions of the Gesta Romanorum*, 6: the identification "þe tode is þe devil" appears there twice. Thanks to Alan Lupack for this reference.

10. Clerical ambiguity could occasionally, of course, present a more favorable side. In a famous miracle story, the Blessed Virgin jousts for her unusually devoted knight in a tournament: see BL Arundel 406 f. 23, BL Additional 33956 f. 75b col. 2, BL Additional 32248 f. 3, BL Additional 11284 f. 35. The majority of clerical utterance, however, was stoutly anti-tournament.

11. St. Bernard famously complained in a letter to Abbot Suger that even crusaders could not be weaned away from "those accursed tournaments." *Letters of St. Bernard of Clairvaux*, Letter 405.

12. For the discussion of tournament in Johannes de Bromyard, *Summa Praedican-tium* (arranged by alphabetical topic); see the section on *Ludus*.

13. Erdmann, *Origins of the Idea of Crusade*, 343–44. Cf. Lea, *A History of Auricular Confession and Indulgences*, 60: "there was a widespread popular belief that plenary in-dulgences were *a culpa et a poena*." On all such issues the essays of James Brundage are insightful; see his *Crusades, Holy War, and Canon Law*.

14. Brundage, "The Hierarchy of Violence in Twelfth- and Thirteenth-Century Canonists," 677. Caroline Smith argues that even those preaching crusade sermons used deliberately unspecific language, suggesting benefits without precise canonical content: *Crusading in the Age of Joinville*.

15. Brandin, *Chanson d'Aspremont*, *laisse* 236, line 4309: "sans boce regehir."

16. William of Tudela, *Song of the Cathar Wars*, 14. An anonymous antipapal con-tinuator pictures a crusader doubting the effectiveness of forgiveness through fighting, achieved without repentance, but this seems likely to be an anti-crusade propaganda thrust (94–95).

17. Peter of les Vaux-de-Cernay, *The History of the Albigensian Crusade*, 137. The Latin reads, "promittentes firmissime quod, si in tam glorioso certamine pro fide occumberent christiana, remissionem adepti omnium peccatorum, statim gloria et honore coronati, mercedem reciperent sui certaminis et laboris" (*Historia Albigeoise*, 269).

18. Peter of les Vaux-de-Cernay, *History of the Albigensian Crusade*, 42. The Latin in *Hystoria Albigensis*, 74: "scientes remissionem omnium peccaminum a Deo et Ejus vicario universis indultam qui, orthodoxe fidei zelo succensi, ad opus se accingerent hujusmodi pietatis, dummodo contriti essent pariter et confessi. Quid plura? Publicatur ista indul-gentia in Francia, armat se multitudo magna fidelium signo crucis."

19. *History of the Albigensian Crusade*, 209–10; Peter's text says the knights wanted the assurances stated repeatedly.

20. Even so thoughtful an ecclesiastic as Humbert of Romans in his mid-thirteenth-century preaching exaggerated the power of crusade indulgences: see Brett, *Humbert of Romans, His Life and Views of Thirteenth-Century Society*, 172, and the sources he cites there. Brett emphasized how much more difficult it became to win crusading converts after the failures of both crusades of the saintly Louis IX (167–94).

21. See Tyerman, *Fighting for Christendom*, 27–30, 39, 110, 113–15, 126, 129; idem, *England and the Crusades, 1095–1588*, 8–9, 13, 15, 21, 162–63. To spread his message, Urban and others conducted a preaching tour after the meeting at Clermont. Elements of this crusading ideology had appeared in a series of statements made by earlier popes in pre-ceding decades. See, e.g., discussion in Bull, *Knightly Piety*, 2–3. Cowdrey points out that in statements of Gregory VII one can find the basic dichotomy between sinful violence of quotidian secular warfare and the blessed violence carried out at the behest of clerics. "Pope Gregory VII and the Bearing of Arms," 26.

22. See also Riley-Smith, *The First Crusade and the Idea of Crusading*, 1, 13, 15, 31; idem, *The Crusades, Idea and Reality*, 10; Brundage, *Medieval Canon Law and the Cru-sader*, 31–33; Tyerman, *England and the Crusades*, 17, 21, 154; idem, *Fighting for Christen-dom*, 27–30, 32, 42, 126, 129; Asbridge, *The First Crusade*, 32–35, 46–49; Porter, "Preacher

of the First Crusade?"; Cole, *The Preaching of the Crusades to the Holy Land*, x, 2–3, 5, 8–36; Cowdrey, *Popes, Monks, and Crusaders*, 177–88, 285–311; idem, *The Crusades and Latin Monasticism*, 59–61, 76, 81, 83, 721–726, 739. Marcus Bull's *Knightly Piety* has convincingly argued that local religious centers and figures, largely monastic, played an especially formative role in generating the first crusade. His argument makes our scholarly uncertainties over Urban's exact words less troubling and emphasizes the goal of recovering a broad set of ideas at work motivating knights to take the cross.

23. Bachrach, *Religion and the Conduct of War*; France, "Holy War and Holy Men."

24. The older view appears in Douglas, *William the Conqueror*, 187–88, and Erdmann, *Origin of the Idea of Crusade*, 154–55, 188–89. For doubts, see Bates, *Normandy Before 1066*, 189, 202.

25. See discussion in Chapter 8.

26. Only a fragment of the letter survives; it is printed in translation from manuscript in Bull, *Knightly Piety*, 73.

27. See, e.g., Wolf, *Deeds of Count Roger of Calabria and Sicily*, 110–11.

28. Cowdrey, "Pope Gregory VII's 'Crusading' Plans of 1074."

29. Powell, *Anatomy of a Crusade*; Lower, *The Barons' Crusade*.

30. Luke 9:23: "Si quis vult post me venire abneget se ipsum et tollat crucem suam cotidie et sequatur me," quoted in Maier, *Crusade Propaganda*, 59; Eudes of Châteauroux, "Sermon 4, 5" quoted in Maier, *Crusade Propaganda*, 164–65, 170–71.

31. Maier, *Crusade Propaganda*, 21–23: "in ista autem exponunt se morti, et hoc in casibus multis."

32. Ibid., 204–5. This language of labor will be examined more closely in Chapter 7.

33. Ibid., 60–61, 68.

34. Ibid., 86–87. "Hunc enim Deus Pater signavit, cuius carni crux clavis ferreis affixa est, que molli filo affigitur palliis vestries."

35. Ibid., 138–39: "omni periculo et labori se exponat." The issue of chivalric labor is significant and will be addressed in Chapter 7.

36. Ibid., 146–47: "hodie melius et expressius confitentur Christum esse suum dominum quam milites?. . . . Ipse enim velut aves nobiles ad vocationem Domini veniunt, faciunt ei exercitum et equitationem."

37. Fulcher of Chartres, *Historia Hierosolymitana A History of the Expedition to Jerusalem*, 66. The Latin (135) reads, "Praesentibus dico, absentibus mando, Christus autem imperat. Cunctis autem illuc euntibus, si aut gradiendo aut transfretando, sive contra paganos dimicando, vitam morte praepeditam finierint, remissio peccatorum praesens aderit. Quod ituris adnuo, dono isto investitus a Deo."

38. RHC Occ 3: 729: "Arripite igitur viam hanc in remissionem peccatorum vestrorum, securi de immarcescibili gloria regni coelorum."

39. Maier, *Crusade Propaganda*, 194–95.

40. William of Malmesbury, *Gesta regum anglorum*, 598–601: "Parui laboris in Turchos compendio retribuetur vobis perpetuae salutis statio. . . . Horum laborum erit causa

caritas ut, precepto Dominico ammoniti, animas pro fratribus ponatis; caritatis stipendium erit Dei gratia; Dei gratiam sequetur vita aeterna."

41. Ibid., 692–93, 606–7.

42. Ibid., 602–5: "Esto ergo ut sit semita itinerantium arcta, plena mortibus, suspecta periculis; sed haec eadem uos amissam ducet ad patriam; per multas nimirum tribulationes oportet nos introire in regnum Dei. Spectate ergo animo, si prensi fueritis cruces, spectate catenas, quaecumque postremo possunt tormenta infligi; operimini profidei uestrae robore horrenda suplitia, ut, si necesse fuerit, dampno corporum agatis animarum remedium. Mortemne timetis, uiri fortissimi, fortitudine et audatia prestantes? Nichil certe in uos poterit comminisci humana nequitia quo superna pensetur floria; non enim sunt condignae passiones huius temporis, ad futuram gloriam quae reuelabitur in nobis. . . . .Per mortem ergo liberae animae vel oblectantur gaudiis, spe meliora presumentes, vel fruuntur suplitiis, nichil peius timentes."

43. Maier, *Crusade Propaganda*, 98–99: "remissionem cunctorum scilicet peccatorum quantum ad penam et culpam et insuper vitam eternam."

44. Ibid.

45. Ibid., 112–13: "crucesignati qui vere contriti et confessi ad Dei servitium accinguntur, dum in Christi servitio moriuntur, vere martires reputantur, liberati a peccatis venialibus simul et mortalibus, ab omni penitentia sibi injuncta, absoluti a pena peccatorum in hoc seculo, a pena purgatorii in alio, securi a tormentis gehenne, gloria et honore coronandi in eterna beatitudine."

46. Ibid., 116–17; 208–9. Peter of les Vaux-de-Cernay likewise made this point in his chronicle; see *The History of the Albigensian Crusade*, 37, 60. For St. Bernard's statement, see *Letters of St. Bernard*, 461.

47. Maier, *Crusade Propaganda*, 97.

48. Nicholson, *Chronicle of the Third Crusade*, 257.

49. Jacques de Vitry, *Exempla*, 57, 188. Crusade sermons by Jacques de Vitry and Gilbert of Tournai explicitly recognize this willingness to be parted from "one's spouse, children, relatives and birthplace for the service of Christ alone (uxorem, filios, consanguineos et natale solum pro Christi servitio relinquere)"; quoted from Vitry's sermon in Maier, *Crusade Propaganda*, 112–13. Cf. Banks, *Alphabet of Tales*, 334–35. Gilbert tells almost the same *exemplum*, picturing a knight calling for his small sons as he leaves "so that by exciting my feelings towards them, I would leave them behind for Christ's sake with greater anguish of the mind, so that I would count for more with God (ut excitato affectu ad eos cum majori angustia mentis reliquam eos pro Christo et ita magis merear apud Deum)": Maier, *Crusade Propaganda*, 202–3. Nicholson, *Chronicle of the Third Crusade*, 150 pictures the tears and groans as crusaders depart. William Chester Jordan notes an entire set of departure rituals in "The Rituals of War: Departure for Crusade in Thirteenth-Century France." These rituals closely draw on practices preceding departure on pilgrimage.

50. Caesarius of Heisterbach, *Dialogue on Miracles*, 2: 259; *Dialogus Miraculorum*, 2: 291.

51. Étienne de Bourbon, *Anecdotes historiques*, 92.

52. BL Royal 7 D i f. 90, BL Arundel 52 f. 113b (told here of Thomas of Marle).

53. BL Arundel 52 f. 113b. For a similar story in a chronicle, see Shaw, *Chronicles of the Crusades*, 299; Joinville, *Histoire de Saint Louis*, 226. The idea that all crusaders suffer as martyrs, not merely those who die, appears clearly in Nicholson, *Chronicle of the Third Crusade*, 279–80.

54. Nicholson, 379.

55. Text in Maier, *Crusade Propaganda*, 186–87.

56. Morris, "Crusading Propaganda," 95.

57. Maier, *Crusade Propaganda*, 164–65: "quasi alter latro pendens in cruce absolvitur in momento."

58. Paris, *Chronicles*, 205, 276.

59. Maier, *Crusade Propaganda*, 84–85.

60. Ibid., 128–29.

61. Caesarius of Heisterbach, *Dialogue on Miracles*, 2: 47; *Dialogus Miraculorum*, 2: 119.

62. BL Additional 11284 f. 22.

63. Maier, *Crusade Propaganda*, 112–13: "nullo modo dubitetis quod non solum vobis ad remissionem peccatorum et eterne vite premium valet hec peregrinatio sed etiam uxoribus, filiis, parentibus, tam vivis quam defunctis, multum proderit quidquid boni feceritis in hac via pro ipsis."

64. Ibid., 164–65: "caros suos qui sunt in purgatorio iuvari potest, si crucem et peregrinationem assumpserit pro eis."

65. Paris, *Chronicles*, 244, 259.

66. Ibid., 158.

67. Nicholson, *Chronicle of the Third Crusade*, 362.

68. BL Additional 27909 B f. 11. In a Middle English romance the knights are told to show their best prowess; they may shortly come before God! See Conlee, ed., *Prose Merlin*, 48–49. Some crusaders took an understandably different view of enemy bolts. A man wearing a parchment on his chest with God's name upon it is struck by a crossbow bolt that pierces his armor but is stopped by the holy name on sheepskin. Nicholson, *Chronicle of the Third Crusade*, 104.

69. Levine, ed., *Deeds of God Through the Franks*, 43; the entire passage reads, "Indebita hactenus bella gessistis; in mutuas caedes vesana aliquotiens tela, solius cupiditatis ac superbiae causa, torsistis: ex quo perpetuos interitus et certa damnationis exitia meruistis. Nunc vobis bella proponimus quae in se habent gloriosum martyrii munus, quibus restat praesentis et aeternae laudis titulus." RHC Occ 4: 138.

70. Fulcher, *A History of the Expedition to Jerusalem*, 66–67; the entire Latin passage (136–37) reads, "Procedant, inquit, contra infideles ad pugnam iam incipi dignam et trophaeo explendam, qui abusive privatum certamen contra fideles etiam consuescebant distendere quondam. Nunc fiant Christi milites, qui dudum exstiterunt raptores; nunc iure contra barbaros pugnent, qui olim adversus fratres et consanguineos dimicabant; nunc aeterna praemia nanciscantur, qui dudum pro solidis paucis mercennarii

fuerunt. Pro honore duplici laborent, qui ad detrimentum, corporis et animae se fatigabant."

71. William of Malmesbury, *Gesta Regum Anglorum*, 590–99; "Fuerit auiditatis nimiae quod fraters uestros, illo magno et eodem pretio emptos, ut quisque poterat illaqueantes contumeliose pecuniis emunxistis. Nunc uobis, inter ista peccatorum naufragia constitutis, portus placidae quietis aperitur, nisi negligitis."

72. Maier, *Crusade Propaganda*, 88–89: "Non reputantes vere Christi milites qui aliquid panicellum, quod vulgari Gallico 'pannuncel' apellatur; de armis eius non habent."

73. Ibid. 172–75: "Non recte ergo crucem accipiunt qui aliena rapiunt et ea que debent non solvunt; et melius est homini ut 'nudus Christum nudum sequatur' quam . . . sequatur diabolum. . . . Non enim vult Dominus ut de rapina vel furto vel de re aliena ei serviatur."

74. *Laisse* 168 in Bertrand de Bar-sur-Aube, *Girart de Vienne*, and idem, *Song of Girart of Vienne*. I have somewhat modified Newth's translation. The French reads: "Franc chevalier, ennor vos est creüe! Ceste bataille ne soit plus meintenue; / gardez que plus ne soit par vos ferue, / car Damedeu la vos a deesfandue. / Mes en Espagne, sor la gent mescreüe, / soit vostre force prove et conneüe; / la sera bien vo proece veüe / por l'amour Deu conquerre."

75. Prestwich, *Edward I*, 395: "Both sides accepted an offer of arbitration from the pope, Boniface VIII, though the French insisted that he act in his private, not his public, capacity." Strayer, *The Reign of Philip the Fair*, 323: "In 1298 Boniface VIII persuaded Philip and Edward to let him arbitrate the quarrel as a private person, not as pope."

76. As always, I use crusade here in its common usage and do not wish to enter debates over modern designations of what constituted a "true" crusade.

77. It was written by an eyewitness to the events of 1147 but seems to have been reworked several decades later, as argued by Jonathan Phillips, "Ideas of Crusade and Holy War in *De Expugnatione Lyxbonensi*."

78. Constable, "The Second Crusade as Seen by Contemporaries," 221.

79. Livermore, "The 'Conquest of Lisbon' and Its Author."

80. Phillips, "Ideas of Crusade," passim.

81. Ibid., 126.

82. David, *Expugnatione*, 60–61: "Auanti illic penitentes, quanti peccata et negligentias cum luctu confitentes et genitu, peregrinationis sue conversionem utcumque inceptam, inundatione lacrimarum diluentes, in ara cordis contriti." The specific issue was the diversion of their crusade to Lisbon on the way to Jerusalem.

83. As was done in the case of a letter of exhortation sent by St. Bernard, in Latin, to the nobles and people of Bohemia. Bernard expected the bishop of Moravia, whom he characterized as a learned and holy man, to explain the contents. Bernard, *Letters*, Letter 392, p. 464.

84. Maier, *Crusade Propaganda*, 3–4, notes that though sermons in general and crusade sermons in particular are often mentioned in chronicles, seldom do such accounts give details about content. Cf. 18 n. 4 and sources there. Like so much of what was

presented to crusaders, this sermon has a strongly penitential and redemptive character. See the general discussion, 52, and Phillips, "Ideas of Crusade," passim.

85. David, *Expugnatione*, 70–72: "constat profecto omnes honorum dignitates, ut eternum a Deo consequerentur premium, felici peregrinatione commutasse! Blandos uxorum affectus, inter ubera lactentium pia oscula, adultorum magis dilecta pignora, parentum et amicorum affectanda solatia, soli natalis tantum dulci remanente sed torquente memoria, Christum sequuti reliquere."

86. See Maier, *Crusade Propaganda*, 57–59, 59.

87. David, *Expugnatione*, 72–73: "per tot terrarum et marium pericula et longi itineris dispendia."

88. Ibid. On the theme of new baptism, see Constable, *Three Studies*, 149.

89. Maier, *Crusade Propaganda*, 64–67; cf. the views of Jacques de Vitry, 84–85. Note that knights who become monks convert; knights who become crusaders convert temporarily. The idea of knights suffering as penance in their own order involves no conversion, but this does link them with broad movements toward religious life in the world, so typical of later medieval piety.

90. David, *Expugnatione*, 78–79: "nam iure hoc evenit ut quis que ob tutelam sui corporis fecerit iure fecisse arbitretur."

91. Ibid.

92. Ibid., 82–83.

93. Ibid., 85.

94. Even if it was written up for this very purpose later, it shows the continuing influence of a powerful set of ideas.

95. David, *Expugnatione*, 90–99: "Ecce nubes nostra devicit! Ecce nobiscum Deus!"

96. Constable, "The Second Crusade as Seen by Contemporaries," 222.

97. David, *Expugnatione*, 152–53: "O medicinam omnibus consulentem, tumentia comprimentem, tabescentia reficientem, superflua resecantem, necessaria custodientem, perdita reparantem, depravata corrigentem!"

98. Ibid. The Latin phrases are "Christum sequuti, exules spontanei, qui pauperiem voluntariam suscepistis," and "quia inchoantibus promittitur sed perseverantibus premium donataur."

99. Ibid., 154–55.

100. Ibid., 156–57; "si quem hoc insignitum mori contigerit, sibi vitam tolli non credimus, sed in melius mutari non ambigimus. Hic ergo vivere gloria est, et mori lucrum." There may be here an echo of the Pauline formula that "for me to live is Christ, to die is gain."

101. Ibid., 158–59: "Sique demum cum magna voce Dei postulantes auxilium . . . machinam contra murum appropinquavere."

102. Ibid., 106–7: "Normannorum genus quis nesciat usu continuatae virtutis laborem recusare nullum?—quorum scilicet in summa asperitate semper durata militia, nec in adversitate cito subvertitur, nec in prosperitate, tot difficultatibus exercitata, segni

valet otio subici, nam semper otii vitia discutere negotiis didicit. . . . Audite, fratres, et recolite corrigendo mores vestros."

103. Ibid., 106–7: "de piaculo violate societatis taceam, vos ubique terrarum infames et ignominiosi venietis."

104. Ibid., 112–13.

105. Ibid., 120–21: "ambitionem vestram rectitudinis zelum dicentes, pro virtutibus vitia mentimini." The chronicler may be using the Muslims here to express suppressed Christian self-doubts. A similar passage appears in the chronicle of Matthew Paris, relating to the crusade of Louis IX in Egypt. The sultan is made to say: "What rash insanity incites them to attack us in the hopes of disinheriting us, who have inhabited this most noble country since the flood? Surely they do not want us to believe in their Christ against our will? Who can be converted or believe, unwillingly?" Paris, *Chronicles*, 246.

106. The composition and intent of the text are closely discussed in Caroline Smith, *Crusading in the Age of Joinville*, 47–74. See also two essays in Yvonne Bellenger and Danielle Quéruelle, eds., *Les Champenois et la croisade*: Philippe Ménard, "L'esprit de la croisade chez Joinville" (131–47), and Armand Strubel, "Joinville, historien de la croisade?" (14–56). Danielle Quéruel edited another set of essays on Joinville in *Jean de Joinville: de la Champagne aux royaumes d'outre-mer*; and Jean Doufournet and Laurence Harf present another set of essays in *Le prince et son historien: la vie de Saint Louis de Joinville*.

107. Shaw, *Joinville and Villehardouin: Chronicles of the Crusades*, 329; Joinville, *Histoire de Saint Louis*, ed. Wailly, 279: "que peu sont de gens qui regardent au sauvement de lour ames ne à l'onnour de lour cors."

108. Philippe Contamine notes, in "Joinville, acteur et spectateur de la querre d'outremer" (42), that "Pour l'étude de la mentalité et des motivations des chevaliers, l'apport de Joinville est exceptionnel." He likewise notes (43) another tension: that between *la gloire* and the obedience owed to a chief and the need for military discipline.

109. As noted also by Jean-Pierre Perrot, "Le 'péché' de Joinville: é criteur du souvenir et imaginaire hagiographique," 196–98. He notes the use of the idea of *passio*, drawn from the rhetoric of martyrdom.

110. Shaw, 265; Wailly, 170.

111. Shaw, 216; Wailly, 88.

112. Shaw, 181; Wailly, 30.

113. Shaw, 247, Wailly, 140: "nous fist demander se c'estoit voirs que nous créiens en un Dieu qui avoit estei pris pour nous, navrez et mors pour nous, et au tiers jour rescscitez."

114. Shaw, 247; Wailly,140: "Et lors nous dist que nous ne nous deviens pas desconforter, se nous aviens soufertes ces persecucions pour li; 'car encore dist-il, n'estes-vous pas mort pour li, ainsi comme il fu mors pour vous'. . ." As usual, Joinville simply tells what he saw, without answering any of the many questions this ancient's appearance and speech raise.

115. Wailly, 2 (my translation).

116. Shaw, 163–64; Wailly, 2–3: "Et de ce me semble-il que on ne li fist mie assez,

quant on ne le mist ou nombre des martirs, pour les grans peinnes que il soffri ou pelerinaige de la croiz, parl'espace de six anz que je fu en sa compaignie, et pour ce meismement
que il ensui Nostre-Signour ou fait de la croiz. Car se Diex morut en la croiz, aussi fist-il;
car croissiez estoit il quant il morut a Thunes."

117. Shaw, 167; Wailly 7: "aussi come Diex morut pour l'amour que il avoit en son
peuple, mist-il son cors en avanture par plusours foiz pour l'amour que il avoit à son
peuple; et s'en fust bien soufers, se il vousist."

118. Shaw, 191; Wailly, 47.

119. Shaw, 295; Wailly, 217.

120. Shaw, 195; Wailly, 53: "ainsi alai à Blehecourt et a Saint-Urbain, et autres cors
sains qui là sont. Et onques retourner mes yex vers Joinville, pour ce que le cuers ne me at-
tendrisist dou biel chastel que je lessoie et de mes dous enfans." Cf. Nicholson, *Third Crusade*, 150, for an entire paragraph of description of the misery. The departure scene was a
standard of crusade writing; see Smith, *Crusading in the Age of Joinville*, 60, 65–66.

121. Shaw, 196; Wailly, 55: "car l'on se dort le soir là où on ne sait se l'on se trouvera
ou font de la mer au matin."

122. See especially the scene of the armed landing, and that on the causeway: Shaw,
204, 222; Wailly, 68, 95–96.

123. Shaw, 239, 240, 252–53; Wailly, 126, 128, 148.

124. Shirley, *Cathar Wars*, 54; Martin-Chabot, *Chanson de la croisade albigeoise*,
1: 234.

125. Caroline Smith notes the interplay between clerical and secular modes in *Crusading in the Age of Joinville*, passim. Conceptions of martyrdom provide a good case in
point: see ibid., 90–108, 139–49.

126. Shaw, 219; Wailly, 92.

127. Shaw, 293; Wailly, 214.

128. The English crusader William Longespee actually did leave Louis's service,
over a charge by French lords that he had acquired booty illicitly. See Paris, *Chronicles*,
228–29. This chronicler pictures the saintly king groaning that such quarrels would destroy the crusaders. The actual departure of Philip II of France from the Third Crusade
is well known.

129. Shaw, 346; Wailly, 306: "A ce respondi-je que, tandis comme je avoie estei ou
servise Dieu et le roy outre-mer, et puis que je en reving, li serjant au roy de France et le
roy de Navarre m'avoient destruite ma gent et apovroiez; si que il ne seroit jamais heure
que je et il n'en vausis-sent piz. Et lour disoie ainsi, que se je en vouloie ouvrer au grei
Dieu, que je demourroie ci pour mon peuple aidier et deffendre; car se je metoie mon
cors en l'aventure dou pelerinaige de la croiz, là où je veoie tout cler que ce seroit au mal
et au doumaige de ma gent, j'en courouceroie Dieu, qui mist son cors pour son peuple
sauver. Je entendi que tuit cil firent pechié mortel qui li loerent l'alee."

130. Joinville's self-assurance is all the more striking in being directed at a pious
king. The royal closeness to orders of friars and reliance on them as agents of reform in
the kingdom is stressed in William Chester Jordan's study, *Louis IX and the Challenge of
the Crusade*, 53–55, 63, 185.

131. The author of the *Chronicle of the Third Crusade* (ed. Nicholson, 76) refers to the bishop of Beauvais, "more devoted to battles than books," as a man who could have equaled Turpin if he could have found a Charlemagne. Cf. 96, where an archdeacon of Colchester is said to wear a double laurel wreath of feats of arms and learning; and 119, where Hubert Walter, bishop of Salisbury, is praised as a worthy knight and pastor.

132. Shaw, 261–62; Wailly, 164: "se hasta d'aler avec Dieu, et feri des esperons, et assembla aus Turs touz seus, qui à lour espées l'occistrent et le mistrent en la compaingnie Dieu, ou nombre des martirs."

133. Shaw, 230; Wailly, 109: "Vez-ci le prestre mon signour de Joinville, qui a les huit Sarrazins desconfiz." In 1171, during the Anglo-Norman invasion of Ireland, a monk named Nicholas "in a religious habit" is much praised for having killed an enemy leader with an arrow. Mullally, *The Deeds of the Normans in Ireland*, lines 1128–33.

134. Shaw, 298; Wailly, 223: "Ne troublés pas vostre conscience quant li patriarches ne vous absout; car il a tort, et vous avés droit; et je vous absoil en non dou Pere et dou Fil et dou Saint-Esperit. Alons à aus!"

135. Shaw, 243; Wailly, 132.

136. Studied by Jean Flori in "*Pur eshalcier sainte crestiënté*: Croisade, guerre sainte, et guerre juste dans les anciennes chansons de geste française." See also Smith, *Crusading in the Age of Joinville*, passim. For a general case for the independence of *chanson de geste* with regard to claims championed by the Gregorian papacy, see Kaeuper, *Chivalry and Violence*, 231–53.

137. Flori, "*Pur eshalcier sainte crestiënté*," 185.

138. Strickland, *War and Chivalry*, 34.

CHAPTER 5. KNIGHTLY IDEOLOGY DEVELOPED AND DISSEMINATED

1. Jean Flori entitled his biography of Richard *Richard Coeur de Lion, le roi cheavalier.*

2. Books providing important analysis of the origins of chivalric ethos include Keen, *Chivalry*; Flori, *L'Essor de la chevalerie*; Jaeger, *The Origins of Courtliness: Civilizing Trends and the Formation of Courtly Ideals*; Strickland, *War and Chivalry*; and Crouch, *The Birth of Nobility: Constructing Aristocracy in England and France*. That I have learned from these books on many points and disagreed with them on other points will be evident.

3. The evidence defies full citation. In addition to the examples given below, see the dozens of texts reproduced in the collection "Textes de Français Ancien" on the ARTFL website, http://www.lib.uchicago.edu/efts/ARTFL/projects/TLA/. Dana Sample conducted an electronic search for me, using a range of Old French terms relating to suffering. The results were impressive and voluminous.

4. Brandin, *La Chanson d'Aspremont*, lines 6102–6: " 'Baron, or del sofrir. / Se ci morés, tot esters martir; / Avec les sains vos fera Dex server, / En paradis coroner et florir: / Illuec arés trestot desir.' "

5. Suard, *Chanson de Guillaume, laisse* 43.

6. Ibid., *laisse* 44. The quotation appears at lines 545–48: "Car saint Estephne ne les alters martirs / ne furent mieldres que serrunt tut icil / Qui en Larchamp serrunt pur Deu ocis!"

7. Ibid., *laisse* 69.

8. Ibid., *laisse* 72.

9. Ibid., *laisse* 107: "Trop par es enfess e de petit eé, / Si purreies ne traviller ne pener, / La nuit veiller ne de jur juner, / La grant bataille suffrir n'endurer." Translation is by Lynette Muir in Glanville Price, *William, Count of Orange: Four Old French Epics*. Cf. Tusseau, ed., *La Prise d'Orange*, *laisse* 2.

10. Kay, *Raoul de Cambrai*, lines 470–71.

11. Kelly, "Love in the Perlesvaus: Sinful Passion or Redemptive Force?" 9; cf. his *Haut Livre du Graal: Perlesvaus, A Structural Study*, 157–80. The opening paragraph of the *Perlesvaus* refers to the truth established by writing and by the witness of knights "comme il voldrent soffrir paine e travail de la loi Jhesu Crist essaucier."

12. Quotations from Bryant, trans., *Perlesvaus* 237–38; French in Nitze and Jenkins, eds., *Perlesvaus*, 367 and 369.

13. Pauphilet, *Queste del Saint Graal*, 124; Lacy, *Lancelot-Grail*, 4: 40.

14. Matarasso, *Quest of the Holy Grail*, 65–66; Pauphilet, *Queste del Saint Graal*, 40: "se Diex plaist, l'onor de chevalerie sera en lui bien sauve; car por peine qu'il li coviegne a soffrir ne remaindra il mie." Knights on the Grail quest are said to suffer "les granz peines et les granz travauz"; Pauphilet, *Queste*, 235. More than once this text reminds its readers that Christ had suffered for his knights: e.g., Pauphilet, *Queste*, 84.

15. Lacy, *Lancelot-Grail*, 4: 191–93; Paris and Ulrich, *Merlin*, 1: 233–42.

16. Lacy, *Lancelot-Grail*, 2: 130; Kennedy, *Lancelot do Lac*, 306. He is bleeding from the mouth; he thinks he will die without confession; he faints, and is thought to be dead.

17. Lacy, *Lancelot-Grail*, 4:198; Roussineau, *La Suite du roman de Merlin*, 1: 113: "Cele bataille sans faille, qui tant fu crueus et felenesse, comment cha a eure de tierce et dura dusques a eure de viespres. Et se li rois Loth ne fust si tres bon chevaliers comme il estoit, si houme eussent esté plus tost desconfi qui il ne furent. Mais il tous seus soustenoit le fais de la bataille par deviers soi que tout cil qui l'esgardoient se sainnoient a mierveilles qe il puet endurer la moitié de chou que il souffroit. Il enpren doit si toutes les proueches et tous le caus a faire."

18. Lacy, *Lancelot-Grail*, 1: 51; Sommer, ed., *Vulgate Version*, 1: 80–81.

19. Lacy, *Lancelot-Grail*, 5: 186; Bogdanow, ed., *Version post-Vulgate*, 2: 455.

20. Holden, Gregory, and Crouch, *History of William Marshal*, lines 48–51.

21. Ibid., lines 10110–12.

22. Brault, *La Chanson de Roland*, lines 1010–14.

23. *History of William Marshal*. lines 280–83, 2175–82, 7208–15, 8870–76, 9475–86, 9498–9502.

24. I*bid.*, lines 1488–93, 4912–16.

25. Ibid., lines 704–8, 1764–66, 1864–68, 14455–63.

26. Hopkins, *Sinful Knights: A Study of Middle English Penitential Romance*, 3.

27. Benson, *King Arthur's Death*, lines 1850–52, 1855–60: "In the front of the firth, as the way forthes, / Fifty thousand of folk was felled at ones. / There was at the assemblee certain knightes / Some wounded soon upon sere halves. / . . . They sheerd in the sheltron shelded knightes / Shalkes they shot through shrinkand mailes; / Through brenyes browden brestes they thirled, / Bracers burnisht bristes in sonder / Blasons bloody and blonkes they hewen, / With brandes of brown steel, brankand steeds!"

28. Ibid., lines 2781–83: "All the flesh of the flank he flappes in sonder / That all the filth of the freke and fele of his guttes / Followes his fole foot when he forth rides!" and 3234–45: "There lions full lothly licked their tuskes / All for lapping of blood of my lele knightes!"

29. Conlee, *Prose Merlin*, lines 88–89, my emphasis.

30. Ibid., 154: the king swears, "so helpe me God, yef I might fynde a yonge bachelor that were a worthi man of armes that might wele endure peyne and travayle to meyntene my werre, to hym wolde I yeve my doughter." Likewise, we might note that the term martyrdom (martirdom, borrowed from the Old French noun *martire*) appears in this text; phrases such as "soche martirdom and soche slaughter of men and of horse" appear, for example, at 144. The usage has come to mean merely slaughter or great suffering. Though derived from Christian usage, it carries no explicit religious meaning. Saracens are martyred, as in Conlee, *Prose Merlin*, 127, 135–36, 145.

31. Lydgate, *Troy Book*, line 1156.

32. *Laisse* 236 in Brandin, *Chanson d'Aspremont*, and Newth, *Song of Aspremont*. The French reads: "Or me faites oïr, / Je suis uns om qui ne vos doi mentir: / Ki or ira sor Sarrasins ferir / Et le martire volra por Deu sofrir, / De xli fera paradis ovrir; / La nos fera coroner et florir / Et a sa destre nos fera seïr / Tes vos pechiés, sans bocce regechir, / Vuel hui sor moi de par Deu receuillir; / La penitence sera del bien ferir."

33. Bertrand de Bar-sur-Aube, *Song of Girart de Vienne*, trans. Newth, lines 6871–83; Yeandle, *Girart de Vienne*, lines 6876–84: "'Seignor baron, a moi entendez ça. / Je sui es leu de Deu qui tot forma, / Et de seint Pere que a Rome estora, / A cui pooir des pecheors donna / De pardoner qanque il mes fet a. / Qui sor paiens ore aler en voudra, / Avec le roi qui France a garder a, / De ses pechiez trestoz quites sera, / En l'annor Deu qui le mont estora.' / Dient François: 'Come haut pardon ci a.'"

34. *Laisse* 168 in Newth and Yeandle: "en Espagne sor la gent mescreüe / Soit vostre force prove et conneüe. / La sera bien vo proece veüe / Por l'amor Deu conquerre."

35. Newth, *Song of Aspremont*, and Brandin, *Chanson d'Aspremont*, lines 3969–71: "Je n'irai par ma foi. / Armes ai bones et ceval a mon qoi; / Jo nel la'rai que grans cols n'i employ / Et rendrai Deu tot ce que je li doi; / M'armes et mon cors quitement li otroi,'" Joinville narrates a historical case of a crusader who fears loss of honor if he goes for much needed help: *Histoire de Saint Louis*, ed. Wailly, 93–95; Shaw, trans., *Chronicles of the Crusades: Joinville and Villehardouin*, 220–21.

36. *Laisses* 420–23 in Newth and Brandin. In both cases the problem is solved by Archbishop Turpin, who volunteers to act as messenger and later as standard bearer. For the second service he extracts from the pope permission to act as both cleric and knight.

37. Ibid., lines 3960–61: "Ains serai hui em paradis flori / O les aposteles honorés et servi."

38. *Laisse* 46.

39. Ambroise, *The Crusade of Richard Lion-Heart*, lines 3131–42, 12216–22. See the comments of Jacques de Vitry in Maier, *Crusade Propaganda*, 112–13. The sermons Maier prints show repeatedly that crusading is itself a species of conversion and do not insist on salvific death sustained while on crusade.

40. Romances also valorize the knightly *ordo*, itself religiously based. This, too, will be considered shortly.

41. Schmidt and Jacobs, *Middle English Romances*, 6.

42. For Frappier's many insights see his *Autour du Graal* and *Chrétien de Troyes et le myth du Graal*. At page 156 in the latter, Frappier says Perceval is to represent "chevalerie très pieuse vivant dans le siècle." My thanks to Raymond Cormier for this reference. Frappier even sees the sinner Lancelot moving through grace to the highest Christian virtues in *La Mort le Roi Artu*; see his *Étude sur La Mort le Roi Artu*, 218–58.

43. Looking ahead to a topic explored closely in Chapter 7, it is worth noting here that all three linked sets of ideas were encompassed within the concept of a divinely ordained chivalric *ordo*. By elevating and defending this idea of an *ordo* of *bellatores*, one writer after another in effect awarded spiritual merit to knighthood in general: the knightly *ordo*, approved in highest heaven after all, was not composed of crusaders only. Whenever we encounter glorification and defense of a sanctified knightly *ordo* we can read it as a shorthand representation for the sets of linked ideas that generated and diffused a chivalric ideology.

44. "The Life of Pope Leo IX," in Robinson, *The Papal Reform of the Eleventh Century*, 149, 151.

45. Suger, *Deeds of Louis the Fat*, 37, and *Vie de Louis VI le Gros*, 30: "Thomam de Marna optinuisse, hominem perditissimum, Deo et hominibus infestum." Suger asserts clerical control when he assures his readers that Louis had at his coronation given up the sword of secular knighthood to take on the ecclesiastical sword used to punish evildoers, but here is another distinction destined to fade in chivalric ideology.

46. *Deeds of Louis the Fat*, 80, 94; *Vie de Louis VI le Gros*, 120: "impios pie trucidant."

47. Benton, *Self and Society in Medieval France*, 204–6. The conservative Guibert of Nogent is scathing about Bishop Godfrey's assertion that royalist forces at Laon will merit the kingdom of heaven if they die in the fight.

48. *Deeds of Louis the Fat*, 129; *Vie de Louis VI le Gros*, 222: "tanquam Saracenos."

49. Quoted and briefly discussed in Douglas, *English Historical Documents*, 2: 314. For the original Latin passage see Howlett, *Chronicles and Memorials of the Reigns of Stephen, Henry II, and Richard I*, 3: 151 ff.

50. Brundage, *Medieval Canon Law and the Crusader*, 193, says that in the thirteenth century the combination of pilgrimage and holy war inherent in crusade shifted from primary emphasis on pilgrimage to emphasis on holy war, which dominated for the rest

of the Middle Ages. In his view, we can only with great difficulty call crusades in Europe against Christians pilgrimages, but they are holy wars.

51. Moore, *Pope Innocent III*, 41–42.

52. Ibid., 66–67.

53. PL 221 cols. 780–82, quotation from col. 781. The enormities committed by Markward's force are described in lurid language: "Deposuit siquidem, sicut quondam, diruere muros urbium redigere civitates in villas, captivare nobiles, torquere ac mutilare potentes, spoliare divites, pauperes flagellare, trucidare coram patribus filios et adulterare conjuges ante viros, per vim violare virgins et gladio perimere repugnantes" (col. 780).

54. Ambroise, *History of the Holy War*, 1: line 1432, translated by Ailes in 2: 51; the French reads, "Peors sarazins ne velt querre."

55. See the useful generalizations made by Sibly and Sibly at the conclusion of their edition of Peter of les Vaux-de-Cernay's *History of the Albigensian Crusade*, 313–20. Cf. Strayer, *The Albigensian Crusades*, passim. Some crusaders—the elder Simon de Montfort a famous example—argued against diversion of the crusade and left the expedition to Zara, going instead directly to the Holy Land to fulfill their vows.

56. Shirley, *The Song of the Cathar Wars*, 89; Martin-Chabot, *Chanson de la croisade albigeoise*, 2: 118: " 'Senhors, de part de Dieu e del comte'n somo: / Cel que fara'l mur sec ne re I metra del so. / Que de Dieu e del conte n'ara bon gazerdo, / E desobre mas ordes aura salvacio.' Trastug essensescridan: 'Tuit anem al perdo!' "

57. See the argument of Michael Lower in *The Barons' Crusade: A Call to Arms and Its Consequences*.

58. Newth, *Aymeri of Narbonne*, 124; Demaison, *Aymeri de Narbonne*, 2: 167.

59. Foulet and Uitti, *Le chevalier de la charette*, line 2147: "Qui sont pires que les Sarrasins."

60. Lecoy, *Le Roman de la Rose*, 1: 206, lines 6723–28: "Mes, que cist dex plus net e tiegne, / de Mainfrai wel qu'il te soviegne, / de Henri et de Corradin, / qui firent pis que Sarradin / de conmencier bataille amere / contre Sainte Iglise, leur mere."

61. See Peter of les Vaux-de-Cernay, *The History of the Albigensian Crusade*, 37, 73, 198, respectively; idem, *Petri Vallium Sarnaii monachi Hystoria albigensis*. The final reference to a slaughter at Beziers comes from Shirley, *Song of the Cathar Wars*, 21; cf. 32 for a reference to the southerners' hatred of the French and Lombards as "worse than Saracens."

62. Deschamps, *Oeuvres complètes de Eustache Deschamps*, 3: 140, lines 33–34 of a chançon on the "Révolte des Maillotins à Paris" in 1381: "Car pis ont fait que ne font Sarrazins: / Saint Germain ont assailli les sotars."

63. Coopland, *Le Songe du Veiel Pelerin*, 1: 531: "il se puet dire selon la foy crestienne qu'ilz sont pires devant Dieu que Sarrazins. Et certainement se puet dire moralment que en la guerre des mescreans encontre les Crestiens, les mescreans ne sont pas si cruelx envers les Crestiens, et de l'eglise, des nobles, et du peuple comme sont les dessusdiz pillars."

64. Ermengard in some translations.

65. *Chanson d'Aspremont*, lines 1447–50.

66. Kay, *Raoul de Cambrai, laisse* 67.

67. Langlois, *Couronnement de Louis*; Hoggan, trans., *Crowning of Louis*, in Price, *William, Count of Orange: Four Old French Epics*.

68. Langlois, line 1408.

69. Langlois, lines 2089–90; Hoggan, 42.

70. Langlois, lines 2018–19; Hoggan, 42.

71. Langlois, lines 1408, 2018–19, 2089–90.

72. A *chanson* extolling the deeds of William's father, *Aymeri de Narbonne*, comments on this very point, stating that William's hard life of honorable fighting had earned God's love. See Newth, *Aymeri of Narbonne*, 142; and Demaison, *Aymeri de Narbonne*, 1: 189–90.

73. Geoffrey of Monmouth: *Historia Regum Britannie*, vol. 1; see also the mid-thirteenth-century Latin paraphrase written in Brittany, ibid., 5: 231–33. Wace: Weiss, *Wace's Roman de Brut*; see 292–327 for the invasion and battle. Lawman's description of the forces and battle comes at lines 12651–67 and 13635–41 in Brook and Leslie, *Lazaman: Brut*; he is even more explicit, denouncing the enemies of the Britons as followers of Mahound, hated of God, etc.

74. Wright, *Historia*, 1, and 5: 238–47. Weiss, *Wace*, 327–29; Brook and Leslie, *Lazamon: Brut*, lines 14104–19.

75. For what follows, see Bryant, *Merlin and the Grail*, 165–66, 169. The emperor compounds his wrong by marrying a beautiful Saracen princess.

76. As we will see below, this valorization continues in the *Alliterative Morte Arthure* and in Malory.

77. Benson, ed., Foster, rev., *King Arthur's Death*. That Arthur's goals may later grow dangerously grandiose is a theme, pressed very forcefully in essays collected in Göller, *The Alliterative Morte Arthure: A Reassessment of the Poem*. For a recent review of the considerable scholarship on this poem, see DeMarco, "An Arthur for the Riccardian Age: Crown, Nobility and the Alliterative Morte Arthure."

78. Bensen and Foster, *King Arthur's Death*, lines 569–623.

79. Ibid., lines 3802–5.

80. Ibid., lines 3988–94.

81. Ibid., lines 4087–90.

82. Malory, *Works*, 707–8.

83. Kelly, "Love in the Perlesvaus," 3.

84. Ibid., 9.

85. See Chapter 2.

86. Lacy, *Lancelot-Grail*, 4: 73, Sommer, *Vulgate Version*, 6: 165: "Et por lor grant desloialte auoient il si torne chaus de cest chastel quil estoient pior de sarasins. ne ne faisoient rien que contre dieu ne fust et contre sainte eglize . . . tant de honte que se ce fuissent sarasin."

87. Ibid. Of course, there is a stick as well as a carrot in this text. The mass of

unregenerate knights fail in the quest and must listen to condemnations of sexual laxity through homilies on virginity; they must get pride regularly ground out of their bodies in hard experiences that they come to understand only when one of the small army of hermits patiently explains matters.

88. Sommer, *Vulgate Version* 3: 60; Lacy, *Lancelot-Grail*, 2: 32; Kennedy, *Lancelot do Lac*, 72: "Et si nous sera honours au siecle et preus as armes se nous i mourons por els. Car por son lige signor deliurer de mort droit len mettre son cors en abandon sans contredit. Et qui en muert il est autresi sauf com sil moroit sor les sarasins qui sont anemi nostre signor ihesu crist."

89. Kennedy, *Lancelot do Lac*, 476; Lacy, *Lancelot-Grail*, 2: 199; Sommer, *Vulgate Version*, 3: 359: "nest cil qui destruit ceste vie sans forfeit pire que sarazins et se ie aloie outré meir sour les destruiseors de la crestiente il me seroit a bien iugie. Car puis que ie sui crestiens ie doi ester vengieres a mon pooir de la mort ihesu crist don't irai ie mon fil vengier qui crestiens est/ si li aiderai encontre cels qui sont en lieu de mescreans."

90. Holt, *Magna Carta*, 263, 364.

91. Moore, *Innocent III*, 251, citing Cheney and Semple, *Selected Letters of Innocent III*, 221, letter 85. Yet not long after, in a rapidly changing situation, Guala, the papal legate in England, made a form of holy war out of the fight of English royalists against the French invaders under Prince Louis. These blessed royalists wore white crusading crosses; they were absolved by clerics before battle and described their recruits as converts; see Clanchy, *England and Its Rulers*, 144–45.

92. Holden, Gregory, and Crouch, eds., *History of William Marshal,* line 16139.

93. Ibid., lines 16150–51.

94. Ibid., line 16181.

95. Ibid., lines 16190–91.

96. Ibid., line 16197.

97. Ibid., lines 16227–32: "Les assolt en remission / De lors pecchez e en pardon, / De trestoz icels que il firent / Puis icele ure qu'il nasquirent, / Si qu'il en fussent quitement / Salvé al jor del jugement."

98. Ibid., line 16233.

99. Ibid., lines 16292–98: "Dex qui ses buens veit e descuevre, / Nos met ui en son paradis; / De ce sui je certeins e fis; / E se nos lé vencons, sanz fable, / Nos avrons enor pardurable / Conquise a trestoz nose ages, / A nos e a toz nos lignages."

100. Ibid., lines 16312–13: "Come proz e comme leials / E comme sages chevaliers."

101. Ibid., lines 16378–400.

102. Ibid., line 16628.

103. Ibid., lines 17313–18.

104. Ibid., line 17328.

105. Ibid., line 17509.

106. Maurice Keen discusses this general phenomenon in "War, Peace, and Chivalry," in his collected essays, *Nobles, Knights, and Men-at-Arms in the Middle Ages*, 9–20.

CHAPTER 6. THE HERO AND THE SUFFERING SERVANT

1. See the overview in Marx, *The Devil's Rights and the Redemption.*

2. Southern, *Saint Anselm: A Portrait in a Landscape,* 215. He discusses this theory in general at 207–11.

3. See Southern's thoughtful discussion, ibid., 197–227.

4. Anselm, "Cur Deus Homo," in *S. Anselmi Opera Omnia* 2: 42–133; idem, *Complete Philosophical and Theological Treatises of Anselm of Canterbury,* 295–389. Cf. Southern, *Saint Anselm,* 197–227, 279; John Bossy, *Christianity in the West,* 3–6; and Woolf, "Doctrinal Influences on the Dream of the Rood." The study of Dániel Deme, *The Christology of Anselm of Canterbury,* is primarily concerned with the continuing theological relevance of Anselm's Christology in the modern world.

5. Quotation is from Southern, *Saint Anselm,* 223.

6. Anselm, "Cur Deus Homo," 2, c. 6.

7. Southern, *Saint Anselm,* 201.

8. Ibid., 224–25.

9. Ibid.

10. Shaw, *Joinville and Villehardouin: Chronicles of the Crusades,* 169; Joinville, *Histoire de Saint Louis,* ed. Wailly, 14: "Vraiement . . . c'est bien respondu, que ceste response que vous avez faite, cest escripte en cest livre que je tieing en ma main." Lea Shopkow noticed this evidence in *History and Community: Norman Historical Writing in the Eleventh and Twelfth Centuries,* 213–14.

11. Rubin, *Corpus Christi: The Eucharist in Late Medieval Culture,* 302.

12. Ibid., 303. Even St. Bernard of Clairvaux in his *De Laude Novae Militiae* (*Opera,* 3:229; *In Praise of the New Knighthood,* 154), mused about the contemporary identification with Christ's suffering more than with his life or teachings. In his chapter meditating on the Holy Sepulcher he confessed puzzlement over greater pious devotion to places where Christ's dead body rested than to places where he lived and taught. This passage is quoted in Chapter 3 note 14. And *In Praise of the New Knighthood,* 156: "For if he had not suffered physically, he would not have paid the debt, and if he had not died willingly his death would have been without merit."

13. David Aers in Aers and Staley, *The Powers of the Holy,* 23; cf. 16 ff.

14. Southern, *Saint Anselm,* 210–11; Clanchy, *Abelard, A Medieval Life,* 282–83. Abelard and his followers, for example, saw in the incarnation of Christ not legal redemption but a great act of love that humans should emulate. Christ gave humans "an example by word and deed of enduring until death."

15. We will see similar choices available to advocates of knighthood in cases of *ordines* and labor in Chapter 7 and confession and penance in Chapter 8.

16. Maier, *Crusade Propaganda,* 112–13.

17. Ross, *Middle English Sermons,* 39: "suffred so peynfull dethe for vs vpon þe Crosse for to delyvere vs from þe peynes of hell and owte of þe dewels poure."

18. Ibid., 37: "I seye euery man was gette in bateyll þrough þe myghtfull dethe þat Crist suffred on þe Rode Tree."

19. Henry, duke of Lancaster, *Livre de seyntz medicines*, 138.

20. Ibid., 95.

21. Ibid., 179.

22. Ibid., 80.

23. Ibid., 6. Cf. the language of battles against sin, the devil, and death at 162.

24. Étienne de Bourbon, *Anecdotes historiques*, 87.

25. Of course, images of Christ as warrior were much older, as that magnificent Anglo-Saxon poem *The Dream of the Rood* establishes. In this eighth-century text, Christ "the young warrior . . . / stripped himself; climbed the high gallows, / Gallantly before the throng, resolved to loose Man's bonds" (lines 39–41). See Woolf, "Doctrinal Influences on the Dream of the Rood." Our interest, however, must focus on High and Late Medieval works. There is an unusual Christ-knight story from c. 1400 in John Mirk, *Mirk's Festial*, ed. Erbe, 119–20. Christ appears as a knight who frees a lion (faithful) bound to a tree. Then leaves to go home (heaven), and the lion tries to follow, but drowns (pains of death).

26. Bennett, *Poetry of the Passion*, 65–66, quoting the Latin text.

27. The image is old. Even Gregory VII used the standard formula: as Christ laid down his life for men, so they should lay down their lives for their brethren. Cited and briefly discussed in Cowdrey, "The Spirituality of Pope Gregory VII," 3.

28. Brandin, *Chanson d'Aspremont*, lines 4772–77; my translation slightly modifies that of Newth, *Song of Aspremont*: "'Dex,' dist Gerars, 'par ton saintime non, / Ja ving jo, Sire, por toi en Aspremon. / De tant franc home ai faite noreçon, / Don't je vos fis ier matin livrisson; / Ne vos sai traire de ce alter sermon: / Por nos morustes et nos por vos moron'." Cf. lines 7659–61, where the message is repeated in a sermon by the pope: "Quint Dex por nos la mort en endura / Et il por nos ocire se laissa, / Faisons por lui ce qu'il fist por nos ja / Molt iert garis qui por luii i morra."

29. Suard, *Chanson de Guillaume*, lines 813–16: "Sainte Marie, mere genitriz, / Si verreiement cum Deus portas a fiz, / Garisez mei, pur ta sainte merci, / Que ne mocient cist felon Sarazin." Translation is by Lynette Muir, "Capture of Orange," in Price, *William of Orange: Four Old French Epics*.

30. Suard, lines 818–24; trans. Muir. The French reads: "Mult pensai ore que fols et que brixs, / que mun cors quidai de la mort garir, / quant Dampnedeu meismes nel fist, / que pur nus mort en sainte croiz soffri / par nuis raindre de noz mortels enemis. / Respit de mort, sire, ne te dei jo rover, / car a fei meisme ne la voilsis pardoner." The pope sweetens his message, as Duke Girart had earlier, by promising thoroughly earthly wealth to those who survive.

31. Suard, lines 310–14: "Et jo raft vus de Deu le rei fort, / et en cel esperit qu'il out en sun cors / pur pecchurs quant il suffri la mort, / ne vus faldrai pur destresce de mun cors" (translation by Muir).

32. Geoffrey of Monmouth, *Historia Regum Britannie*, ed. Wright, 5: 182–85 (facing pages, Latin text and English translation). Once again a text recalls the painted manuscript image with which this book began.

33. Ambroise, *The Crusade of Richard Lion-Heart*, lines 1186–92; cf. lines 1223–28.

34. Bryant, *High Book of the Grail: Perlesvaus*, 238; Nitze and Jenkins, *Le Haut Livre du Graal: Perlesvaus*, 368: "il n'est nul si bele chevalerie come cele est que l'on fait por la loi Deu essaucier, e por lui se doit l'on miex pener que por toz les autres; autresi com il mist son cors en paine e en travaill e en exill por nos, si doit chascuns le sien metre por lui."

35. Lupack, *Three Middle English Charlemagne Romances*, "Siege of Milan," lines 697–708: "Criste for the sufferde mare dere, / Sore wondede with a spere, / And werede a crown of thorne: And now thou dare noughte in the felde / For hym luke undir thy schelde, / I tell thi saul for lorne. Men will deme aftir thi day / How falsely thou forsuke thi laye / And calle the Kynge of Skornne."

36. Shaw, *Joinville*, 167, Wailly, *Histoire*, 7: "aussi comme Diex morut pour l'amour que il avoit en son peuple, mist-il son cors en avanture par plusieurs fois pour l'amour que il avoit à son peuple."

37. Shaw, 163; Wailly, 2–3. The *History of the Holy Grail* argues that "the good . . . will undertake to suffer the difficult burden of earthly exploits of chivalry in order to learn about the marvels of the Holy Grail and the lance." Chase, in Lacy, *Lancelot-Grail*, 1:51; Hucher, *Le Saint Graal*, 2:311: "pour les grans peinnes que il souffri ou pelerinage de la croiz, par l'espace de six anz que je fu en sa compaignie, et pour ce meismement que il ensui Nostre-Signour au fait de la croiz. Car se Diex morut en la croiz, aussi fist-il, car crosiez estoit-il quant il mourut à Thunes."

38. At the opening of Chapter 7 we will see the knight Owen putting himself into *avanture* in entering purgatory.

39. Shaw, 247; Wailly, 182, 184. The story of Louis on crusade is filled with meritorious suffering: his mother considers him a dead man as soon as he takes the cross (Shaw, 191; Wailly, 47); Joinville suffers from leaving his home and his children behind (Shaw, 195; Wailly, 53); Joinville is troubled by fears of sea travel (Shaw, 196; Wailly, 54–55); in fact, trials and tribulations are frequently emphasized (as in Shaw, 216, 240, 262, 265, 267–68); at one point Joinville is pointedly told by a papal legate that their suffering on crusade contrasts sharply with luxurious conditions at the papal court (Shaw, 317; Wailly, 257). Yet deliberately seeking martyrdom is not accepted, as when the crusaders ignore a baker's advice to let themselves be killed by their Saracen captors and thus earn martyrdom (Shaw, 243; Wailly, 132). The king personally carried hods used to build a fortification, however, wishing like all the rest to earn the indulgence promised (Shaw, 295; Wailly, 217).

40. Discussed in Catto, "Religious Change Under Henry V," 107–9. It is interesting that the new services at this time also included offices of the Five Wounds, the Crown of Thorns, and the Compassion of the Virgin, all obviously stressing righteous suffering. Religious foundations at Sheen and Syon similarly emphasized rigorous austerity.

41. General works: Le May, *The Allegory of the Christ-Knight in English Literature*; Waldron, "Langland's Originality: The Christ-Knight and the Harrowing of Hell," and sources there. See Woolf, "The Theme of Christ the Lover-Knight in Medieval English Literature."

42. Tolkien, *Ancrene Riwle, Ancrene Wisse*; see 198ff. Abundant citations to the voluminous literature on this text appear in Millett, *Annotated Bibliography of Old and Middle*

English Literature, vol. 2, *Ancrene Wisse, The Katherine Group, and the Wooing Group*. My references were taken before I had access to Hasenfratz, *Ancrene Wisse*.

43. Tolkien,*Ancrene Riwle, Ancrene Wisse,* 182: "nis he a cang cniht þe secheð reste I þe feht & eise in þe place?"

44. Ibid., 182–83.

45. Ibid., 199: "and scheawede þuruh knihtschipe þet he was luue-wurde."

46. Ibid., "He dude him ine turnement hefde uor his leofmannes luuve, his schelde ine uihte, ase kene kniht."

47. It also gives the first use of Middle English words for tournament and chivalry, as Bennett noted in *Poetry of the Passion*, 64.

48. Le May, *Allegory of the Christ-Knight*, 22. Cf. Innes-Parker, "The Lady and the King."

49. Le May, *Allegory of the Christ-Knight*, 22..

50. Text printed by Jubinal and Wright and discussed below.

51. As characterized by Legge, *Anglo-Norman Literature*, 271.

52. Ibid., 219.

53. Bryant, *High Book of the Grail: Perlesvaus*, 160; Nitze and Jenkins, *Haut Livre*, 249: "Il se traient atant arrier, et oent la dedenz mener la plus grant joie que nus oïst onques, et entendent que le pleseur dient la dedenz que cil est enuz par cui il ierent sauvé en ii. manieres sauvé des vies, et sauvé des ames, se De xli lesse conquerre le chevalier qui porte l'esperit du deable."

54. Bryant, *High Book of the Grail: Perlesvaus*, 161; Nitze and Jenkins, *Haut Livre*, 250: "que tot cil du chastel et d'autres chastiaz don't cil estoit garde, q'il tendroient la Viez Loi tresque a icele eure que li Bons Chevaliers seroit venuz' et por ce distrent il eu chastel tantost com il vint, que cil estoit venuz par qui lor ames seroient sauvees et lor mort respitiee; car il corurent tantost com it fu venuz au batesme, et creürent la Trinitéfermement, et tindrent la Novele Loi."

55. Lacy, *Lancelot-Grail*, 4: 5; Sommer, *Vulgate Version*, 6: 7–8.

56. Using Asher's translation in Lacy, *Lancelot-Grail*, 4: 190–91; Paris and Ulrich, *Merlin: Roman en Prose*, 1: 231–32.

57. Paul Meyer prints this in "Notice et extraits du MS 8336 de la Bibliothèque du Sir Thomas Phillipps a Cheltenham," quotation at 530–31.

58. The next line pictures Christ as a knight acting on behalf of love.

59. See the discussion of "Saint Patrick's Purgatory" in Chapter 7 for another example of blended categories of expression.

60. It was first printed in Jubinal, *Novel recueil de contes*, 2: 309, and then by Thomas Wright, as an appendix to his edition of Peter of Langtoft, *Chronicle of Pierre Langtoft*, Appendix 2, 426–36.

61. Peter of Langtoft, *Chronicle* Appendix 2: 426–27: "Tant fu de pruesce son noun renome, / Qe sa chevalerie de tyrant fut doté."

62. Ibid., 428–29.

63. Ibid., 430–31.

64. Ibid., 432–35.

65. Ibid., 436–37

66. Paris, *Matthæi Parisiensis, Chronica Majora* , 4: 593.

67. Henry, Duke of Lancaster, *Le livre de seyntz medicines*, 138; Piers Plowman, B Text Passus 19.

68. "And þanne should Ihesus juste þere-fore bi juggement of armes, / Whether shulde fonge þe fruit þe fende or hymselue."

69. "Iusted in ierusalem a joye to vs alle."

70. "wole juste in piers armes, / In his helme & in his haberioun humana natura."

71. References to both are provided in Gaffney, "The Allegory of the Christ-Knight in Piers Plowman."

72. BL Harley 219 f. 33, an early fifteenth-century book presenting Cheriton's tales from the thirteenth century.

73. See Wenzel, *Preachers, Poets and the Early English Lyric*, 234 n. 68.

74. "Tres persone Trinitatis possunt vocari milites rotunde tabule, quia omnes sunt equales virtutis et potencie." The text continues, "Legitur in gestis arturi quod habuit milites nobiles de tabula rotunda et quando congregabantur simul, singuli super parietem castelli pendebant sua scuta. Et si quis scutum alicuius tangebat, possessor scuti cum tangente pugnabat."

75. Warner, "Jesus the Jouster: The Christ-Knight and Medieval Theories of the Atonement in Piers Plowman and the 'Round Table' Sermons," 136–38. The Latin reads, "Ideo Filium oportebat descendere et defendere scutum et pugnare cum diabolo."

76. Plentiful references in Le May, *Christ-Knight*; Gaffney, "Allegory"; Warner, "Jesus the Jouster"; Woolf, "Christ the Lover-Knight"; and Wenzel, *Preachers*, 233–38 (which quotes some remarkable examples).

77. Ross, *Middle English Sermons*, 37–39. A hermit meets an unarmed knight (an indication of human nature, not divine power) going to fight a giant to free prisoners he holds. The knight's coat of arms has a black bier (his suffering), white lily (his lady), and five roses (wounds). He wins humankind in battle.

78. Offord, *The Book of the Knight of the Tower Translated by William Caxton*, 14: "As the swete Ihesu Cryst dyd whiche faught for the pyte of vs / and of all the humayn lygnage."

79. Ibid., 141: "And thus for pyte and Fraunchyse fought the gentyll knyght / and receyued v / mortalle woundes As the swete ihesu Cryst dyd whiche faught for the pyte of vs / and of al the humayn lygnage / For grete pyte he hadde to see them goo and falle in the tenebres of helle / wherfore he suffred and susteyned alone the bataylle moche hard and cruell on the tree of the holy Crosse / And was his sherte broken and perced in fyue places that is to wete the fyue dolorous woundes whiche he receyued of his debonayr and free wylle / in his dere body for the pyte that he had of vs."

CHAPTER 7. KNIGHTHOOD AND THE NEW LAY THEOLOGY: *ORDINES*
AND LABOR

1. *Recueil des historiens des Gaules et de la France*, 14: 245–46. All quotations in the following discussion are drawn from these pages.

2. The text states this is done "ad certificandam notitiam literis tradimus."

3. The Mauvoisin family were lords of Rosny on the Seine. A family tree appears in Power, *The Norman Frontier in the Twelfth and Early Thirteenth Centuries*, appendix 20.

4. The monks report, "quotidie et penè totâ die de monachatu loquebatur devotissimè."

5. The monastic ideal for knighthood appears in a highly visual *exemplum* purveyed by Caesarius of Heisterbach. The knight Walewan rode fully armed down the central aisle at the monastery of Hemmerode, to the altar devoted to the Blessed Virgin, and there took off his worldly armor to become a soldier of Christ: Caesarius, *Dialogue on Miracles*, ed. Scott and Bland, vol. 1, ch. 37, 49; idem, *Dialogus Miraculorum*, ed. Strange, 45. Monastic ambiguity over knighthood appears clearly in two stories told by the worldly cleric Walter Map later in the century. In one, a former knight extracts permission to leave the cloister at Cluny and win back lands taken from his son before returning to the life he had vowed to follow. In the second story, another knight leaves Cluny, promising not to fight personally, but becomes involved, is mortally wounded while unarmored, and—confessing to his squire—plans a fearsome penance of torment in hell lasting until judgment day. Map, *De Nugis Curialium*, ed. James, rev. Brooke; cf. the older translation by Tupper and Ogle, *Master Walter Map's Book*, 22–25, 215–18. Stories about knights often do not distinguish hell and purgatory: this knight obviously had hopes of heaven after he had been purged in hell until judgment day..

6. For the Latin text see Easting, *St. Patrick's Purgatory*. An English translation of the *Tractatus* is given in Pontfarcy and Picard, *St. Patrick's Purgatory*. For the popular Old French translation of Marie de France, see Curley, *Saint Patrick's Purgatory*. The Middle English text "Sir Owain" appears in Foster, *Three Purgatory Poems*, On the date of the *Tractatus*, see the sources in Easting, *St. Patrick's Purgatory*, lxxxiv, n. 1; his useful list of sources appears in ibid., n. 2, and xviii, n. 1.

7. In the process the story speaks powerfully to ideas of penance as well, introducing the topic to be examined closely in Chapter 8.

8. List of sources in Curley, *Saint Patrick's Purgatory*, 2–3.

9. The translation of Marie de France will be discussed below. D. D. R. Owen discusses both Anglo-Norman and Old French versions in *The Vision of Hell*, 37–47, 64–66. For the Middle English text, see Foster, *Three Purgatory Poems*, which prints "Sir Owain," 109–79. The introduction provides a good overview of issues and scholarship.

10. BL Egerton 1117 f. 182b, a collection of thirteenth-century religious tales.

11. Curley, *Saint Patrick's Purgatory*, l.

12. As perceptively noted by Yolande de Pontfarcy, in Pontfarcy and Picard, *Saint Patrick's Purgatory*, 31, 37. Michael J. Curley emphasized the role of Marie de France in putting the story into the context of contemporary romance; see his *Saint Patrick's*

Purgatory, 1–2, 23–24. He presents the Old French text and English translation on facing pages.

13. Lines 173, 178–80, in Foster, *Three Purgatory Poems*: "Wel muchel he couthe of batayle, / And swathe sinful he was saunfayle / Ogain his Creatour."

14. Lines 513–14. All citations of the poem by Marie are taken from Curley, *Saint Patrick's Purgatory*.

15. Easting, *St. Patrick's Purgatory*, 146.

16. Pontfarcy and Picard, 53.

17. Lines 530–36: "Sire eveskes, n'en vueil nïent / legierement espeneïr / ne tel penitence sufrir; / trop ai forfait a mun seignur / e offendu mun creatur. / Pur ceo eslirai, pr licence, / tute la plus grief penitence." D. D. R. Owen notes that the story gained popularity among nobles and the site was later visited by knights and nobles from many lands: *Vision of Hell*, 45.

18. Line 553.

19. Lines 555–57: "que nun fera: / ja altre habit n'en recevra, / fors tel cum il aveit eü."

20. Line 543.

21. The Latin: "aut viriliter agere ex necessitate compelleris aut pro inertia, quod absit, et anima et corpore peribis."

22. Lines 649–50: "ne redutent mie a sufrirpeine e turment pur Deu plaisir."

23. Easting, *St. Patrick's Purgatory*, 128.

24. See Ephesians 6:13–17.

25. Lines 879–80.

26. Easting, *St. Patrick's Purgatory*, 128.

27. Lines 1927–31: "E li reis li a respondu, / chevaliers seit, si cum il fu; / ço li loa il a tenir, / en ço poeit Deu bien servir. / Si fist il bien tute sa vie."

28. Lines 1971–76: "Issi remest od Gilebert / li chevaliers e bien le sert. / Mais ne voleit changier sun estre, / moignes ne convers ne volt estre: / en nun de chevalier morra, / ja altre habit n'en recevra."

29. Trifunctionalism is useful in the modern world to hard-pressed teachers of Western Civilization courses—as it was to me in *Chivalry and Violence*. The classic work, which has generated much response, is Duby, *The Three Orders*. For a highly perceptive and critical response, see Brown, "Georges Duby and the Three Orders."

30. A fourteenth-century sermon in Middle English describes hell as a place lacking *ordines*. See Knight, *Wimbledon's Sermon*, 66.

31. See Chenu, *Nature, Man, and Society in the Twelfth Century*, 223–27; he notes that *ordo* was originally a classical term, without a sacred sense, but that—a common development for ideals in Christian society—the term was sacralized, joining *status*, 223–26. So pervasive was the concept that even animals could be seen in their respective orders. In the *Quest of the Holy Grail* (though in a scene obviously drawn from Chrétien's *Conte du Graal*), Perceval chooses to aid a lion fighting with a serpent, "por ce que plus est naturel beste et de plus gentil ordre que le serpenz." Pauphilet, *Quest del Saint Graal*, 94. The author of the *Moniage Guillaume* even speaks of an order of thieves: Cloetta, *Moniage Guillaume, Première rédation*, line 546.

32. Erdmann, *Origin of the Idea of Crusade*, 17.

33. Giles Constable, *Three Studies*, 249–360 in general; 301 gives examples.

34. Bynum, "Revisiting the Twelfth-Century Individual," 91.

35. Ibid., 94–95.

36. Michaud-Quantin, *Sommes de casuistique et manuels de confession au moyen âge*, 43.

37. Kaeuper and Kennedy, *Book of Chivalry*, 164–83.

38. See classic works such as *Faire croire: modalités de la diffusion et de la réception des messages religieux du XIIe au XVe siècle*; Bynum, *Jesus as Mother*; Le Goff, *Pour un autre Moyen Âge*.

39. PL 172, 862–70. Honorius could take a decidedly dim view of *milites*; see PL 172, 1148.

40. See Le Goff, Schmitt, and Bremond, *L'Exemplum*, 150–53.

41. Cited in Hoven, *Work in Ancient and Medieval Thought*, 226.

42. See Brett, *Humbert of Romans*. Sermo LXXIX (ad maiores), cited in Hoven, *Work in Ancient and Medieval Thought*, 224 n. 117. Some preachers may even praise the peasantry as practicing, by their hard daily work, penitential virtues, and becoming no less than "martyrs of the Lord, offering their bodies as a living sacrifice to God"— as Claude Carozzi characterized sermons on agriculturalists, quoted in Hoven, *Work*, 236.

43. The themes of heroic and meritorious suffering have been developed in the previous chapter. Of course, suffering and renunciation by peasants would scarcely be considered heroic by High Medieval intellectuals. Yet suffering possessed such potency that the hard lives of even lowly villagers drew the attention of some clerics. See Hoven, *Work*, 237; *Faire Croire*, 15. Cf. Jacques de Vitry's "Sermo (LX) ad agricolas et vinitores et alios operatorios" in Pitra, "Semones Vulgares," 437.

44. Quoted in Ovitt, *Restoration of Perfection*, 151–52.

45. Gower, John. *Confessio Amantis*, lines 2338–39. My thanks to Russell Peck who supplied these references in Gower.

46. Lines 2342–44: "As the briddes to the flihte / Ben made, so the man is bore / To labour."

47. Line 2345.

48. Line 2452.

49. Hoven, *Work*; Ovitt, *Restoration of Perfection*.

50. Ovitt, *Restoration of Perfection*, 164–65.

51. Mirk, *Mirk's Festial*, 2: "he Þat syll scape Þe dome Þat he wyll come to at Þe second coming . . . must trauayl his body yn good workes, and gete his lyfe with swynke, and put away all ydlynes and slewth. For he Þat will not trauayle here with men, as Seynt Barnard sayth, he shall trauayle ay with Þe fendes of hell."

52. Evidence drawn from an electronic word-search of the many Old French texts in the collection "Textes de Français Ancien" on the ARTFL website conducted for me by Dana Sample.

53. Hoven, *Work*, 159–200.

54. Gower, *Confessio Amantis*, 2: 288, Latin verse number vii.

55. See Genesis 3:16–19.

56. Newth, *Song of Aspremont*, 15; Brandin, *Chanson d'Aspremont*, 17: "Et si fu fors de paradis chacié / Et estut querre cascun don't il vesquié."

57. Morawski, *Proverbes Français*, no. 376, 14: "Chevaliers sens espee, clers sens livre, menestrés sens outil ne pueent feire bonne besongne." The element of moral uncertainty appears in another maxim: "A knight rejoices in a short mass and a long dinner (Courte messe et long disner est la joye au chevalier)," no. 424, 16.

58. For a classic account, see the work of Carl Erdmann, who traces the slow change in ideas toward a more favorable view of knightly order and its work: *Origin of the Idea of Crusade*, 17, 80–82, 122–23, 135, 171–74, 263, 316.

59. Numerous examples cited in Kaeuper, *Chivalry and Violence*, passim.

60. Holden, Gregory, and Crouch, *History of William Marshal*, lines 16853–63.

61. E.g., "Bevis of Hamptoun," lines 810–14, 872–76, in Herzman, Drake, and Salisbury, *Four Romances of England*.

62. Mullally, *The Deeds of the Normans in Ireland*, lines 786–89, 1468–71, 1957–58, 2399–2402, 2482–84, 2978–81.

63. Even the hermit who planned to move his dwelling closer to the stream he used for water changed his mind when he sighted the hovering angel counting the steps required to fetch that water: Jacques de Vitry, *Exempla*, 38, 188–89.

64. Jacques le Goff, *Pour un autre Moyen Âge*, 172.

65. Suger, *Vie de Louis VI le Gros*, 176.

66. A belt made an order. Peter of Blois said Baldwin of Ford (who became archbishop of Canterbury and died on the Third Crusade) "girded himself with the belt of the army of Citeaux in the service of Christ." Peter of Blois, *Later Letters*, number 10, 53; cited in Constable, "The Place of the Crusader in Medieval Society," 381–82.

67. Leyser, "Early Medieval Canon Law and the Beginnings of Knighthood," 51 n. 1.

68. Leyser points to the dramatic increase in military activity in Europe, especially carried out by the Normans, as a significant force "for the formation of knighthood and the beginnings of an international knightly society," 68–70, quotation from 68. The dating of chivalry to the later twelfth century is especially emphasized in the works of Jean Flori, *Idéologie du glaive*, and *L'Essor de la chevalerie*. This is likewise the position of Maurice Keen, *Chivalry*, and David Crouch, *Birth of Nobility*.

69. Constable, *Three Studies*, 333. Guibert, discussed further below, finished his work in 1108 and touched it up in 1121.

70. Suger, *The Deeds of Louis the Fat*, 57.

71. See the clear discussion by Jean Flori, with abundant sources, in *L'Essor de la chevalerie*, 286–87.

72. Fitzneale, *Dialogus de Scaccario*, 117.

73. Cloetta, *Moniage Guillaume*, to be discussed below.

74. Chrétien de Troyes, *Conte du Graal*, line 1620. The phrase comes from Gornemant, the hero's instructor in chivalry.

75. Cited by Constable in *Three Studies*, 332, from Peter of Blois, Epistle 94, *Patres Ecclesiae Anglicanae: Petri Blesensis Opera Omnia*, 1: 328.

76. PL 210 col. 185, a part of his *Summa de arte praedicatoria* from 1184.

77. Étienne de Fougeres, *Le Livre des manières*, 13–14: "Sauver se pout bien en son ordre, / si l'en n'I trove que remordre. / S'a traïson se veult amordre / ne par engin pincier ne mordre, / sil deit l'en bien desordener, / tolir l'espee et grief penner, / les esperons escoleter / et d'entre chevalers geter"; my translation.

78. The numbers were determined by searching the digital version of the texts obtained from the editors and translators working under the general direction of Norris Lacy.

79. Keith Busby, *Raoul de Hodenc, Le roman des eles: The anonymous Ordene de chevalerie*.

80. Flori, *L'Essor de la chevalerie*, passim; Keen, *Chivalry*, 64–83.

81. Bynum, *Jesus as Mother*, 82–109.

82. Of course, the viewpoints of knighthood and clergy were by no means always directly opposed. Clerical authors wrote most of the propaganda on behalf of both *ordines*, as they had written both papal and imperial tracts in the great contest within the Empire. A number of them almost certainly wrote the vast body of *chanson de geste* and Arthurian romances which transmitted chivalric ideology. In stressing the important role of knighthood, even while hoping to guide and control it, they provided a rich store of imagery and vocabulary available to friends of knighthood who would use it imaginatively no less than selectively. Friendly authors could take the ironclad template of the most censorious commentary and snip, hammer, and reshape it for knightly life.

83. RS 21: 1, 119.

84. Gerald of Wales, *The Jewel of the Church*, trans. Hagen, 146; Latin in RS 21: 2, 190: "carnilibus desideriis viriliter resistentes, calore spiritus fontes libidinis exsiccate. Quanto nimirum lucta gravior, tanta corona major."

85. RS 21: 2, 194: "Scientes etiam quod aut Deus punit aut homo."

86. Hagen, *Jewel*, 153; Latin in RS 21: 2, 199: "Non enim est corona nisi fuerit difficilioris certaminis lucta."

87. Hagen, *Jewel*, 160; RS 21: 2, 208: "contra carnis tamen insultus fortiter dimicare debemus, et si conregnare volumus ut compatiamur eniti."

88. RS 21: 2, 268: "Item militia est hominis vita super terram et continuus est nobis cum hoste conflictus."

89. Hagen, *Jewel*, 202; RS 21: 2, 266–67: "Totum corpus suum Patri pro nobis victimam offerens, poenis, sputis, flagellis, vinculis, alapis, opprobriis, et ignominiso domum crucis patibulo gratis exposuit; sic nos, corpora nostra mundo propter ipsum crucifigentes, et abstinentiis, opprobriis, persecutionibus gratanter exponentes, divinis eidem obsequiis ex toto mancipemus."

90. Hagen, *Jewel*, 203; RS 21: 2, 268: "Delicatus es miles si sine certamine vis coronari, nec enim coronabitur quis nisi legitime certaverit."

91. Thomas de Cobham, *Summa confessorum*, quoted in Shinners and Dohar, *Pastors and the Care of Souls in Medieval England*, 9.

92. Shinners and Dohar, *Pastors and the Care of Souls*, 131–32.

93. Gregory VII thought that neither group could perform the labor of its vocation without sin: Cowdrey established that the view at the time of Gregory VII was that (like merchants) the knights would at least temporarily have to give up their professional labor if they wished to be reconciled with God. At the least, they could only use their arms under the close guidance of a bishop. See Cowdrey, "Pope Gregory VII and the Bearing of Arms"; Hamilton, "Penance in the Age of Gregorian Reform"; and Leyser, "Early Medieval Canon Law and the Beginnings of Knighthood." Cowdrey notes (25–26) that Gregory's view was cited frequently and was taken into both the *Decretum* of Gratian and Peter Lombard's influential *Sentences*.

94. Examples of various sites: BL Additional 32678 f. 80b, BL Additional 11284 f. 90b, BL Additional 16589 f. 91b col. 2, BL Additional 27336 f. 13b. Humbert of Romans in a treatise on sermon-giving notes that castles, supposedly the refuge of the defenseless, are often rather dens of thieves. La Bigne, *Maxima bibliotheca vetervm patrvm*, 494.

95. See Gerald of Wales in *The Autobiography of Giraldus Cambrensis*, 36.

96. See Benton, *Self and Society in Medieval France: The Memoirs of Abbot Guibert of Nogent*, 40.

97. Cited by Constable in *Three Studies*, 332, from Peter of Blois, Epistle 94, *Patres ecclesiae anglicanae*, 1: 328.

98. Étienne de Bourbon, *Anecdotes Historiques*, 371.

99. Ibid., 375.

100. Caesarius of Heisterbach, *Dialogus Miraculorum*, Chapter 48, 214: "Och fortem militem! Qui in bello diaboli non timuit gladios, in militia Christi timere debet pediculos?" Here the soldier of Christ is, of course, a monk.

101. Caesarius of Heisterbach, *Dialogue on Miracles* 1: 244; *Dialogus Miraculorum* 1: 214.

102. *Dialogue on Miracles*, 1: 280; *Dialogus Miraculorum*, 1: 245–46: "tales viri in saeculo tam delicati, oleribus inconditis, pisa et lente possunt uti."

103. Shinners and Dohar, *Pastors and the Care of Souls*, 139.

104. Suger, *The Deeds of Louis the Fat*, 50; *Vie de Louis VI Le Gros*, 58.

105. *The Deeds of Louis the Fat*, 63; *Vie de Louis VI Le Gros*, 86.

106. *The Deeds of Louis the Fat*, 51; Wright, ed., trans., *The Historical Works of Geraldus Cambrensis*, 160.

107. Compare the texts in Cloetta, *Les deux rédactions en vers du Moniage Guillaume, chansons de geste du XIIe siècle*,.In the first redaction, the concept of orders had appeared. Indeed, the text refers to an order of thieves (line 546). But William merely curses the monastic order, rather than engage in close debate (line 727).

108. "En penitance le martire suffrés." See ibid., second redaction, lines 472–75. Cf. lines 630–36.

109. Second redaction, lines 510–20: " 'Maistres,' dist il, 'vos ordenes est trop griés; / Sifais covens puisse prendre mal cief; / Qui l'estora Dieus doinst encombrier. / Assés vaut mieus ordene de chevalier: / Il se combatant as Turs et as paiens, / Por l'amor

Dieu se laissent martirier. / Et sovent sont en lor sane batisié / Pour aconquerre le regne droiturier. / Moine ne voelent fors que boire et mangier / Lire et canter et dormer et froncier."

110. Second redaction, lines 603, 637

111. Second redaction, lines 640–51.

112. Second redaction, lines 672–76.

113. Caesarius, *Dialogue on Miracles*, 2: 140–42; *Dialogus miraculorum*, 2: 193–95.

114. Caesarius's tale is all the more remarkable in that he surely had no doubts about the superiority of the clerical order. Yet he recognizes an opening for the virtue of direct knightly action. The tale is a useful reminder that clerical opinion could scarcely have been monolithic.

115. RS 21: 8, 207: "'Audaciter,' inquit, 'nos clerici ad arma et pericula provocare possunt, quoniam ipsi ictus in discrimine nullos suscipient, nec ulla quae vitare poterunt onerosa subibunt'."

116. BL Cotton, Cleopatra C xi f. 62, col. 2.

117. Ambroise, *The History of the Holy War*, 2: 53. The complex textual history is discussed in ibid., 1:1–23, and Nicholson, *Chronicle of the Third Crusade*, 1–17.

118. All the following quotations are taken from Paris, *Chronica Majora*, 4: 593.

119. Kaeuper and Kennedy, *Book of Chivalry*, 174–77: "Et ou sont les ordres qui tant pourroient souffrir?"

120. "Promisit etiam eis quod suae diocesis presbyteros singulos cum crucibus, et parochianis suis pariter cum illis, in bellum procedere faceret, et quod ipse cum suis bello interesse, Deo disponente, cogitabat." RS 82: 3, 161.

121. "Itaque, post acceptam privatam poenitentiam, illis pariter et omni populo archipraesul triduannum cum elemosinis indixit jejunium, ac deinde absolutionem, et benedictionem Dei et suam eis sollempniter tribuit" RS, ibid.

122. Richard of Hexham, *De gestis regis Stephani et de bello standardii*, in James Raine, *The Priory of Hexham*, Surtees Society 44, 46 (1864–65), 1: 87. Cited by Constable, *Three Studies*, 333. The text reads, "At illi ipsum remanere fecerunt, obsecrantes ut in orationibus, et elemosinis, vigiliis, et jejuniis, et in caeteris que ad Deum pertinent, pro eis intercedere satageret; ipsi vero pro ecclesia Dei et pro illo qui ejus minister erat, prout ipse eos adjuvare dignaretur, et, sicut illorum ordo exigebat, libenter contra hostes pugnarent."

123. Quoted in Prestwich, *Armies*, 170.

124. Caesarius of Heisterbach, *Dialogue*, 1: 388; *Dialogus*, 1: 325.

125. Nicholson, *Chronicle of the Third Crusade*, 254.

126. Lupack, *Three Middle English Charlemagne Romances*, lines 559–66: "Fye, preest, God gyfe the sorowe! / What doist thou armede in the feelde, / That sholdest saie thi matyns on morwe? / I hoped thou hadiste ben an emperoure, / Or a cheftayne of this ooste here, / Or some worthy conqueroure. / Go home and kepe thy qwere!"

127. Lancelot's own lineage is explained in the *Quest of the Holy Grail*: see Lacy, *Lancelot-Grail*, 4: 44–45; Sommer, *Vulgate Version*, 6: 96–98. Since Perceval's mother, Elaine, is descended from the line of Grail keepers, this later hero has a doubly blessed heritage.

128. For a good instance of a tenth worthy, see Guillaume de Machaut, *La Prise d'Alixandre: The Capture of Alexandria*, 20, 154, 191. John Lydgate in *Troy Book*, 339, equates Henry V of England to the Nine Worthies.

129. See, for example, the heroic, self-sacrificing death of old Sir Roger in the Middle English romance *Sir Tryamour*; his body is found to be uncorrupted in its grave: Hudson, *Four Middle English Romances*, 194.

130. The line of thought based on a succession of tables is not merely a literary conceit. The famous Round Table that still hangs in the hall of Winchester Castle may now be painted with a Tudor rose, but carbon 14 dating and dendrochronology show it was made by the mid-thirteenth century.

131. These might be thought of as "fourth tables" just as great knights were considered the "tenth worthy."

132. The arrangement God makes with Joseph is that no shame or loss will come to the people so long as the sacrament is carried out. See Bryant, *Merlin and the Grail*, 40.

133. Ibid., 92–93. The tradition continued into Middle English: Conlee, *Prose Merlin*, 52–53.

134. Bryant, *Merlin and the Grail*, 113.

135. For what follows, see ibid., 113, 118–20. He threatens to leave Arthur's service if his desire is denied.

136. Ibid., 120.

137. Ibid., 143.

138. Matarasso, *Quest*, 120; Sommer, *Vulgate Version*, 6: 72: "Car puis que vous en si haut degree estes montes vostre cuers me doit baissierpor paor ne por peril terrien. car cuers de cheualier doit ester si durs et si serres contra lanemi son signor que nule riens ne le puet flechir et sil est menes iusca paor il nest pas des urais cheualiers qui se laissent ochire en champains que la querele lor signor ne fust desraisnie bien et loiaument."

139. This close relationship is noted by Eileen Power in her introduction to Bland's translation of Herolt, *Miracles of the Blessed Virgin*, and by Benedicta Ward, *Miracles and the Medieval Mind*, 163. Particular localizations of her cult, such as that at Chartres, can yield stories of her favors to knights. See Jean Le Marchant, *Miracles de Notre-Dame de Chartres*, 41, 162–69. Of course, the Blessed Virgin had at times to restrain her vigorous chivalric friends, saving them from their worst excesses. In an attempted rape, the victim named Mary calls out to her namesake. At once the knight's strength fails him, his spirit withers, and the girl is saved: Herolt, *Miracles*, 45; also in Caesarius. In another revealing story, a rich and powerful knight fell into poverty through excessive largesse; he made a deal with the devil, exchanging his wife for wealth. As she is taken to be given over to the devil, his wife stops at a church to invoke the Virgin's aid. She falls asleep in prayer and the Virgin takes her place, confronting the devil. All turns out well: Thomas Wright, *A Selection of Latin Stories*, 31–33.

140. Gautier de Coincy, *Miracles de la Sainte Vierge*, 491–99: She leads the knight in this story to use loot to found a monastery, which he joins. When he dies before confession, the devils claim him as their own, but the Virgin secures help from her son and the knight is saved, to the great disgust of the demons.

141. Étienne de Bourbon, *Anecdotes historiques*, 109–10: he bows to her seven times daily and also says seven Paternosters. Cf. Herolt, *Miracles*, 96.

142. BL Harley 2851 f. 71; Banks, *Alphabet of Tales*, 370–72.

143. BL Additional 19909 f. 244 col. 2; BL Arimde 406 f. 23 col. 2 (although in this case the Blessed Virgin must be threatened by the knight's mother); Ward, *Miracles*, 163. Caesarius of Heisterbach tells one of many such tales and claims that the very chains, devoted to his monastic church, were still on view (*Dialogue of Miracles*, 1: 495–97; *Dialogus*, 2: 37–38).

144. Quoted in Power, introduction to Herolt, *Miracles*.

145. Caesarius of Heisterbach, *Dialogue of Miracles*, 1: 542; *Dialogus*, 2: 76.

146. *Bonum Universale*, bk. 2, 18: 246–47. A broadly similar story appears in BL Burney 361 f. 154b.

147. BL Additional 15833 f. 148b, from a fourteenth-century collection of religious tales. Later printed by Wynkyn de Worde, who piously increased the daily Aves to 150. Whiteford, *The Myracles of Oure Lady*, 47.

148. BL Additional 15833 f. 125.

149. BL Additional 15723 f. 78 from a late twelfth- or early thirteenth-century collection of stories of miracles of the virgin. Cf. BL Additional 32248 f. 4, and BL Arundel 506 f. 3 col. 2, first half of the fourteenth century. Wynkyn de Worde prints this, with some changes: Whiteford, *Myracles of Oure Lady*, 46–47.

150. BL Additional 18929 f. 83, BL Additional 32248 f. 5b.

151. BL Royal 20B f. 170 col. 2. Many similar stories could be cited.

152. Shaw, *Joinville*, 314; Wailly, *Histoire*, 328, where the three French passages read: "c'est li premiers autels qui onques fust fais en l'onnour de la Mere Dieu sur terre"; "Nostre Dame n'est ci, ainçois est en Egypte, pour aidier au roy de France et aus crestiens qui aujourd'ui ariveront en la terre, il à pié, contra la paennime à cheval"; and "Et soiés certeins qu'elle nous aida; et nous eust plus aidié se nous ne l'eussiens couroucie, et le et son Fil."

153. Caesarius, *Dialogue on Miracles*, 1: 510–12. *Dialogus*, 2: 49–57. Caesarius tries to edge around the thorny issue of the Blessed Virgin engaging in tournament, prohibited by church authority, by adding that knights commit double sin in the sport: showing both pride and disobedience. Jesus the Jouster in Langland's *Piers Plowman* is here joined by Saint Mary the Jouster. For retellings of the story, see BL Arundel 406 f. 23, BL Additional 33956 f. 75b col. 2, BL Additional 32248 f. 3, BL Additional 11284 f. 35. Sometimes the heavenly aid comes from God. See Map, *De Nugis Curialum*, 58–63. And we might recall the poem in which all three Persons of the Trinity are recognized as knights, any of which could be challenged to a joust by the devil.

154. See Power's comment in introduction to Herolt, *Miracles*, where she comments on the Virgin's help to very ordinary, sinful monks, nuns, and clerics.

155. Examples in Gautier de Coincy, *Miracles de la Sainte Vierge*, BL Additional 18364 f. 52; and Banks, *Alphabet of Tales*, 456–57.

156. There is a series of stories favoring knights and vilifying usurers in, for example, the *Exempla* of Jacques de Vitry, nos. 173, 175. Occasionally a miracle story even suggests

an active hostility between the Virgin and merchants. Jacques de Vitry says the relatives of an insane man—he applies the story to usurers—drag him before a statue of the Virgin and pray for his recovery. The attempt at healing quickly degenerates into a raucous family argument as the deranged man shouts at the image that he is saner than his relatives. Under pressure to adore the Virgin, he can only say, "I may adore thee, but I shall never love thee!" Jacques de Vitry, *Exempla*, 205.

157. BL Arundel 506 f. 27 col. 2.

158. Jacques de Vitry. *Exempla*, 206.

159. BL Harley 268 f. 29: "Tria sunt genera hominun que fecit deus: clericos, milites, et laborantes et quartus genus excogitavit diabolus, s[cilicet] burgenses et usurarios, qui non clerici quia nescierunt litteras, non sunt milites quia nesciunt arma portare, non sunt laborantes quia in labore humanum non sunt et diabolus eos laborabat. Item burgenses sunt inter hominess sicut busones inter apes qui nec mellificant nec frucaferant set apibus nocent. Similiter burgenses clericos opprimunt, milites exornant, laborantes excutiunt et quia die nullo serviunt otium tolunt et pluribus nocent. Propterea dicit salamon otiositas parit omne malum."

160. The council of 1179 had prohibited communion and burial in sacred ground for manifest usurers. Alms from them were to be refused. See Buckley, *Teachings on Usury*, 174.

161. Baldwin, *Masters, Princes, Merchants*, 296–311.

162. See his "Sermones vulgares," 344–442, cited in Constable, *Three Studies*, 330.

163. Jacques de Vitry, *Exempla*, 76, 206–7.

164. Quoted in Maier, *Crusade Propaganda*, 147–49. The Latin reads, "immo intendunt ad exheredandum eos qui vadunt" and "dominium semper remanebit penes nobiles, velint nolint feneratores qui eos devorarent."

165. Étienne de Bourbon, *Anecdotes historiques*, 124.

166. Jacques de Vitry, *Exempla*, 21, 156; BL Arundel 506 f. 41b; BL Harley 268 f. 43; BL Additional 18347 f. 116b.

167. Jacques de Vitry, *Exempla*, 73–74.

168. Ibid., 91, 221–22. There are many variants of this tale. See BL Harley 3244 for a knight who is exonerated for striking a blaspheming burgher. Sometimes the burger becomes a Jew, adding a new layer of prejudice: BL Additional 18929 f. 82b col. 2; in this case, the avenging knight has only one eye and fears he will be identified in court by this feature, but the Blessed Virgin restores his eye just in time.

169. BL Sloane 3102 f. 81b. Also in Étienne de Bourbon, *Anecdotes historiques*, 60.

170. Jacques de Vitry, *Exempla*, 203. These stories from Vitry come from a large store of anti-usury stories he tells.

171. BL Additional 16589 f. 93b col. 2. For more stories told against usurers, see, e.g., those in BL Royal 7D1 ff. 124–26.

172. BL Additional 33956 f. 41. In a later version the heart is even found to be quartered and bleeding; it bears an inscription in gold: "Jesus est amor meus." BL Harley 2391 f. 234.

173. Shirley, *Song of the Cathar Wars*, 100; Martin-Chabot, *Chanson de la croisade albigeoise*, 2: 168.

174. Benson, *King Arthur's Death: The Middle English Stanzaic Morte Arthur and Alliterative Morte Arthure*, 100. The scene comes in the *Stanzaic Morte Arthur*, by means of a vision appearing to Arthur in a dream.

CHAPTER 8. KNIGHTHOOD AND THE NEW LAY THEOLOGY: CONFESSION AND PENANCE

1. See discussions in Cowdrey, "Bishop Ermenfrid of Sion and the Penitential Ordinance Following the Battle of Hasting." Cowdrey provides the text. Cf. Verkamp, *The Moral Treatment of Returning Warriors*; and Bachrach, *Religion and the Conduct of War*, 102–4.

2. Hamilton, *Practice of Penance, 900–1060*, 190–96. David Bachrach discusses Carolingian ecclesiastical legislation and war in *Religion and the Conduct of War*, 32–64. Cf. Erdmann, *Origin of the Idea of Crusade*, 17–18. For an example of a forty-day fast for killing imposed "at the order of a legitimate prince," see Burchard of Worms in PL 140, 770D–771A, cited by Constable in "The Place of the Crusader in Medieval Society," 379. Burchard, however, imposed seven years of fasting for those who killed lacking this legitimacy.

3. Discussed in Bachrach, *Religion and the Conduct of War*, 103–4.

4. Ibid., 105.

5. Ibid., 103.

6. Jean-Charles Payen points out that in the eleventh century, penitence was not a recognized sacrament. "La Pénitence dans le contexte culturel des XIIe et XIIIe siècles," 401.

7. Recent work reviewing the field and arguing for changes appears in Mansfield, *The Humiliation of Sinners*; Hamilton, *The Practice of Penance*; and the essays in Cooper and Gregory, *Retribution, Repentance, and Reconciliation*, especially Hamilton, "Penance in the Age of Gregorian Reform." Classic older work appears in Lea, *A History of Auricular Confession and Indulgences*; Bossy, "The Social History of Confession in the Age of the Reformation"; Tentler, *Sin and Confession on the Eve of the Reformation*; Vogel, *Pécheur et pénitence au Moyen Âge* and *Les "Libri paenitentales"*; Hopkins, *The Sinful Knights: A Study of Middle English Penitential Romance*; and Murray, "Confession Before 1215."

8. The canons are printed in Tanner, *Decrees of the Ecumenical Councils*, 227–71.

9. Pierre Michaud-Quantin, *Sommes de casuistique et manuels de confession au moyen âge*, 9–11. Cf. Boyle, "The Fourth Lateran Council and Manuals of Popular Theology," in Heffernan, *The Popular Literature of Medieval England*. Boyle says, 31, "It is not too much to say that it was at the Fourth Lateran Council that the *cura animarum* came into its own for the first time ever." He sees a first wave of writing after the council aimed at educating priests, with a second wave in about 1260 directed more toward the penitents themselves

and often written in the vernacular. One of these, written by Guillaume Peyraut, is in the BL Harley 3244 manuscript, where it is introduced by the illustration used to open the present book. In this same modern volume of essays edited by Heffernan, see Shaw, "The Influence of Canonical and Episcopal Reform on Popular Books of Instruction." On the council itself and the events leading to it, see Foreville, *Latran I, II, III et Latran IV: Histoire des conciles oecuméniques*, 6: 237–320. David Bachrach notes Carolingian precedents for the High Medieval steps in *Religion and the Conduct of War*, 52.

10. Quoted in Lawrence, *The Friars*, 125.

11. St. Bernard had, for example, asserted that "priests, as ministers of the Word, must remain carefully solicitous toward erring hearts, using such moderation in the administering of the word of contrition and fear as will not frighten them away from the word of confession. They should open hearts in a way that does not close mouths"; *In Praise of the New Knighthood*, 78; Latin text in *Sancti Bernardi Opera*, 3: 237. The idea was, of course, much older still.

12. Studies of the history of penance are too numerous and contentious to be fully listed here. A good recent survey of the early period with many citations appears in Richard Price, "Informal Penance in Early Medieval Christendom," in Cooper and Gregory, *Retribution, Repentance, and Reconciliation*. Many issues await scholarly resolution: the local effectiveness of clerical legislation (perhaps especially that before the Lateran Council of 1215), the persistence of regional variations, the exact relationship of Carolingian ideals and practice to High Medieval legislation and social realities, even the relationship of High Medieval confessional measures to sweeping notions of individuality as a supposed key to modernity. A good survey of Carolingian penance appears in Rubellin, "Vision de la sociéte chrétienne à travers la confession et la penitence au IXe siècle." On continuities and discontinuities between Carolingian and High Medieval practice, for example, see Frantzen, *The Literature of Penance in Anglo-Saxon England*; Means, "The Frequency and Nature of Confession in the Early Middle Ages"; and Hamilton, *Practice of Penance*, 22–24. Berndt Hamm provides thoughtful comments on the transition between later medieval and early modern ideas in *The Reformation of Faith in the Context of Late Medieval Theology and Piety: Essays by Berndt Hamm*.

13. Some called penance a "laborious baptism." O'Loughlin, "Penitence and Pastoral Care," 95.

14. Löseth, *Robert le Diable*; Laskaya and Salisbury, *The Middle English Breton Lays* (for Sir Gowther); and Zupitza, *The Romance of Guy of Warwick*.

15.Tentler, *Sin and Confession on the Eve of the Reformation*, 14.

16. PL 1 1243, 1244, quoted and discussed in Hopkins, *Sinful Knights*, 36.

17. Gerald of Wales, *Jewel of the Church*, 150.

18. Quoted in *Faire croire: modalités de la diffusion et de la réception des messages religieux du XIIe au XVe siècle*, 145.

19. Le Goff, *The Birth of Purgatory*. Cf. Graham Robert Edwards, "Purgatory: 'Birth' or Evolution?"

20. Étienne de Bourbon, *Anecdotes historiques*, 30.

21. Robert Sweetman, "Thomas of Cantimpré, Mulieres Religiosae, and Purgatorial Piety," 610–11.

22. Bossy, *Christianity in the West*, 4–5.

23. Ibid., 50; general discussion 5–56.

24. Banks, *Alphabet of Tales*, 35. Another Middle English telling of the story in Furnival, *Handlyng Synne*, 57–56, specified that the dead knight's terrible pains result from his having stolen a cloth from a poor man. In the otherworld he is nearly crushed by its weight and is constantly burned by it: "Hyl ne mounteyne, erþe ne stone. / Vndyr heuene so heuy ys none. / No so hote fere ys yn no land / As hyt ys aboute me brennand," lines 2269–73. The dead man hopes to be freed by masses. But he rejects almost all priests named by his friend since they are "nat of clene lyffe." The text tells its tale, but explains that this attitude is not good theology.

25. Shinners and Dohar, *Pastors and the Care of Souls in Medieval England*, 137.

26. Étienne de Bourbon, *Anecdotes historiques*, 43.

27. Jacques de Vitry, *Exempla*, 52–53.

28. Banks, *Alphabet of Tales*, 270–71. Cf. BL Additional 11284 f. 446, in which a monk refuses to pray for a knight who is ill; BL Additional 27909B f. 6; BL Harley 3244 f. 82b, where a monk prays for a knight's continuing illness; and a similar story about a saint in BL Royal 7D f. 90.

29. Caesarius of Heisterbach, *Dialogue on Miracles*,1:278–79: *Dialogus Miraculorum*, I: 244–45.

30. BL Royal 7D i, f. 77.

31. BL Additional 33956 f. 47.

32. Cf. BL Additional 18364 f. 17b. BL Royal 7d i f. 82 presents a more uplifting case in which a pilgrimage to the Holy Land is imposed. Here the robber knight, obediently setting out, falls and breaks his neck outside the hermit's cell, but is forgiven by an understanding God.

33. BL Additional 6716 f. 39 col. 2. The writer says the story was told to canons at Kenilworth by the knight himself during the siege of the castle in the reign of Henry III.

34. Robert of Flamborough, *Liber Poenitentialis*, 201: "Frater, in fine vitae tuae omnia debes exonmere."

35. It is likewise of interest that the sharply anticlerical "Dialogus inter militem et clericum" (evidently an early fourteenth-century Latin text translated by John Trevisa later in that century) contains a willing knightly admission of the clerical power of confession and penance: see Perry, *Dialogus Inter Militem et Clericum*, 11.

36. Crouch, "The Troubled Deathbeds of Henry I's Servants: Death, Confession, and Secular Conduct in the Twelfth Century," 27–29.

37. Baldwin, "From the Ordeal to Confession."

38. Later works could, of course, be cited. In the Middle English *Prose Merlin*, written in the mid-fifteenth century, the great knights Ban and Bors are said to have learned to confess and commune every eight days: Conlee, *Prose Merlin*, 219–20.

39. Baldwin, "From the Ordeal to Confession."

40. Catto, "Religion and the English Nobility in the Later Fourteenth Century," 50.

41. William of Newburgh, *The History of English Affairs*, 70–73.

42. Wenzel, *Fasciculus Morum* (a fourteenth-century text), 489.

43. Bitterling, *Of Shrift and Penance* (last decade of fourteenth century), 120.

44. In Berrtage, *The Early English Versions of the Gesta Romanorum*, 87–93, 91: "the turnement of penaunce wherthurugh we mow come to euerlastyng joy."

45. Numerous manuscript collections from the British Library which tell this story attribute the truce-making ploy to St. Bernard: BL Additional 1579 f. 118, BL Additional 18351 f. 11, BL Additional 27336 f. 60 b, BL Burney 361 f. 146b col. 2.

46. Caesarius of Heisterbach, *Dialogue on Miracles*, 1: 150–51; *Dialogus Miraculorum*, 1: 134–35. Even so learned a cleric as Jacques de Vitry could urge confession with a risky story of its quasi-magical powers. A squire in adultery with his lord's wife was being taken to the local demon who could reveal even secret sins. In desperation the lad popped into a local church en route; after the squire had confessed, the demon was blocked from telling all (divertit ab itinere ad villam promimam, ibique plene confessus est, et acepta a sacerdote penitentia et disciplina aspera valde). Thomas Wright, *A Selection of Latin Stories*, 33–41.

47. Lacy, *Lancelot-Grail*, 3: 190. Micha, ed., *Lancelot*, 4: 322–23.

48. Caesarius of Heisterbach, *Dialogue on Miracles*, 1: 64–67; *Dialogus Miraculorum*, 1: 58–61.

49. Mirk, *Mirk's Festial*, 2: "trauayle his body yn good werkes, and gete his lyfe wyth swynke, and put away all ydylnes and slewth. For he þat will not trauayle here wyth men, as Seynt Barnard sayth, he schall trauavly ay wyth þe fende of hell. . . . For ryght as a knyght scheweth þe wondys þat he haþe yn batayle, yn moche comendyng to hym; ryght so all þe synnes þat a man hath schryuen him of, and taken hys penans for, schull be þer yschewet yn moch honowre to hym, and moche confucyon to þe fende."

50. Lacy, *Lancelot-Grail*, 4: 233; Paris and Ulrich, *Merlin: Roman en prose*, 2:95–98.

51. Lacy, *Lancelot-Grail*, 4: 61; Sommer, *Vulgate Version*, 6: 138: "diex biaz dols peres ihesu crist en qui seruice ie mestoie mis ne mie si dignement comme ie deusse aies merci de moi. Et absoules moi en tel manniere que ceste dolors que mes cors souffera ia pour bien faire que ce soit penitence et assouagemens a lame de moi si uoirement comme ie por bien et por aumosne le fis."

52. Malory, *Works*, 535

53. Lancelot apparently does not consider his considerable knightly labors to have counted as penance; they were all, of course, done to win the love of the queen, rather than the grateful forgiveness of God.

54. Lacy, *Lancelot-Grail*, 5: 46; Sommer, *Die Abenteur Gawains Ywains und Le Marholts mit den drei Jungfrauen*, 121.

55. A good description with illustrations is given in Nichols, "The Etiquette of Pre-Reformation Confession in East Anglia." Andrew Harris alerted me to other images he found within the *Roman de la Rose*. The on-line search engine ArtStore can be used to locate such images.

56. The circle of Peter the Chanter stressed the importance of shame. See John

Baldwin, "From the Ordeal to Confession"; Baldwin (204) quotes Gerbert's *Continuation* of Chrétien's *Perceval* to the effect that "Shame is the penance." Cf. the comment in Bériou, "Autour de latran IV (1215): la naissance de la confession moderne et sa diffusion." Andrew Jotischky notes that Jacques de Vitry insisted that this blushing with shame and sense of embarrassing humility were "the most important part of penance": "Penance and Reconciliation in the Crusader States," 75–77.

57. Thomas of Cantimpré and Caesar of Heisterbach, for example, casually mention stories told to them by fellow friars.

58. BL Additional 27336 f. 73b. The ruler is specified as Enzzelina da Romano, who died in 1259. The idea of a seal on the confessor's lips was as old as the mid-twelfth century. Discussed in Murray, "Confession as a Historical Source in the Thirteenth Century," 281–86.

59. That such a practice may have happened is at least suggested by a late medieval synod (from Breslau in 1446) ordering priests to confess folk as they entered and not to prefer the rich. See Duggan, "Fear and Confession on the Eve of the Reformation," 163. He notes further that many at this time were not confessing to local parish priests, especially for serious sins, 165–67. William Dohar, on the other hand, thinks most lay folk thought confession could be made only to their priest and were much troubled by the depletion of their ranks after the Black Death: "'Since the Pestilential Time.' Pastoral Care in the Later Middle Ages," 181. Social differences might well produce a difference in attitude, of course.

60. Questions are drawn from the *Liber Poenitentialis* of Robert of Flamborough (1208–13), 134, 185, 226–27; *Summa Poenitentia* of Raymond de Peñaforte (1224–26), quoted in Peter Biller's introduction to Biller and Minnis, *Handling Sin*, 17; and from the mid-fourteenth century *Memoriale Presbitorum*, in Michael Haren, *Sin and Society in Fourteenth-Century England: A Study of the Memoriale Presbitorum*, 119–24.

61. BL Birney 361 f. 150b. C. H. Lawrence notes the benefit of confessing at least to a friar, rather than to a local parish priest: "the ministry of a friar offered a welcome channel of escape from the embarrassment and discouragement of having to confess to his local parish priest, who knew too much about him and who might be personally hostile or perhaps simply uneducated and ignorant." *The Friars*, 125.

62. "Quant aux simples chapellenies, établies dans l'église paroissiale ou dans le château du seigneur, elles sont innombrables." He adds that "l'on trouve des Cordeliers, des Jacobins, des carmes, des augustins dans l'entourage de maints nobles don't ils peuplaient les hôtels comme chapelains, aumôniers ou confesseurs." Contamine, *La noblesse au royaume de France de Philippe le Bel à Louis XII*, 257–58.

63. Catto, "Religion and the English Nobility in the Later Fourteenth Century." In an article on English nobility and religion, J. A. F. Pollard notes that some English knights suspected of Lollardy were willing to seek papal license for private confessors and portable altars: "Knightly Piety and the Margins of Lollardy," 106.

64. *Chansons de geste*, written before private chapels were frequent, picture confession only to fellow knights (and then only when dying of grievous wounds) or to ecclesiastics

of high status. The hero Vivien makes his confession to Guillaume d'Orange in the *Song of Aliscans*, *laisses* 28, 29. Vivien recounts all the sins he can remember. Yet he worries most that he has broken a chivalric vow never to give ground to pagans in a fight. Lacking priests before a major fight, knights are often pictured taking a sort of self-administered lay communion with three blades of grass. A good case appears in *laisse* 120 of Kay, *Raoul de Cambrai*.

65. The hero of the Middle English romance *Bevis of Hampton* confesses to the patriarch in Constantinople: see Herzman, Drake, and Salisbury, *Four Romances of England*, 253.

66. Caesarius of Heisterbach, *Dialogue on Miracles*, 1: 95, *Dialogus Miraculorum*, 1: 86–87.

67. Lacy, *Lancelot-Grail*, 5: 177; Bogdanow, *Version post-Vulgate* 2: 302.

68. John, Abbot of Ford, *Vita Wulfrici Haselbergiae*. It is worth remembering that the Latin noun *lorica* can denote either a hauberk or the robe of a penitent. Each hero fights in his own way.

69. Zupitza, *The Romance of Guy of Warwick*. Good discussions in Andrea Hopkins, *The Sinful Knights*, 20–31, 70–118, and Crane, *Insular Romance*, passim.

70. The advice strikingly parallels that of the bishop to the knight Owen in *Saint Patrick's Purgatory*, discussed in Chapter 7. In that tale, too, heroic penance is chosen instead.

71. *Guy of Warwick* 404, reading the version in the Auchinleck MS: "Þat ich haue wiþ mi bodi wrou3t / Wiþ mi bodi it schal bea brou3t / To bote me of þat bale" (literally, to remedy me of that disaster).

72. Quoted in Andrea Hopkins, *Sinful Knights*, 124: "turnement of penaunce, wherthurugh we mow come to euerlastyng joy."

73. Lacy, *Lancelot-Grail*, 5:159; Bogdanow, *Version post-Vulgate*, 2: 227: "E ben sabede dom Boorz, que se vos fosedes o milhor cavaleiro que nunca no mundo ouve, a vosa cavallaria nom vos faria senam mal, ataa que fosedes bem menfestado e que ouvessedes reccebudo o Corpus Domini."

74. BL Arundel 506 f. 27 col. 2.

75. Lacy, *Lancelot-Grail*, 5: 310–11; for the original, which has been recovered from the Portuguese, see Piel, *A Demando do Santo Graal*, 471–72.

76. Lacy, *Lancelot-Grail*, 1: 145; Eugene Hucher, *Le Saint Graal*, 3: 226.

77. Lacy, *Lancelot-Grail*, 4: 10.

78. Ibid., 5: 174; Bogdanow, *Version post-Vulgate*, 2: 280–93. The romances of the entire cycle are replete with assertions of the need for knightly confession, the perils of dying without confession, and sometimes even a requirement of true (or good or full) confession. For example, a worried Arthur, under severe attack by Galehaut, is advised by a wise man (who combines political sense with good theology) to gather his noblest men and wisest clerics in his chapel and confess his sins to them, carefully according his heart and his tongue in the process, "for the confession is no good if the heart does not repent what the tongue confesses (car la confessions n'est preus, se le cuers n'est repentans de chou que la langue regehist)." Lacy, *Lancelot-Grail*, 2: 120; Micha, *Lancelot*, 8: 14. Cf. Kennedy, *Lancelot do Lac*, 284. *The History of the Holy Grail* declares that

confession is the whitest and highest thing that exists: *Lancelot-Grail*, 1: 27; Hucher, *Le Saint Graal*, 2: 191.

79. Lacy, *Lancelot-Grail* 2: 276; Micha, *Lancelot*, 1: 156: "Ha, Diex, confession. Kar ore est mestier!"

80. Benson, *King Arthur's Death*, lines 4312–15: "Do call me a confessor with Crist in his armes; / I will be housled in haste what hap so betides."

81. Malory, *Works*, 553. The hair shirt had figured in thirteenth-century French sources; see Lacy, *Lancelot-Grail*, 4: 42, and Sommer, *Vulgate Version*, 6: 92–93; *Lancelot-Grail* 5: 177, and Bogdanow, *Version post-Vulgate*, 302–6.

82. His willing acceptance of a beating appears in Lacy, *Lancelot-Grail*, 4: 42; Sommer, *Vulgate Version*, 6: 92–93.

83. Lacy, *Lancelot-Grail*, 4: 53, 58; Sommer, *Vulgate Version*, 6: 18–20, 130.

84. *Livre de seyntz medicines*, 169: "la satisfaction faire de corps et de biens solonc la disposicione de mon prestre."

85. What follows draws on Robert de Boron: Bryant, *Merlin and the Grail*, 129–31.

86. Ibid., 130–32.

87. Ibid., 146–56.

88. Ibid., 153–54.

89. An impression confirmed by electronic search of scanned text.

90. E.g., Étienne de Bourbon, *Anecdotes historiques*, 68, 143–44: "quidam miles fagiciosus . . . nollet facere penitenciam aliquam." This very phrase is picked up in collections of moral tales: see BL Additional 15833 148b–150.

91. Étienne de Bourbon, *Anecdotes historiques*, 68. In a retelling, the cleric is simply a bishop; but the knight again insists he will do no penance. See BL Royal 7d i., f. 63. The gift of a ring with admonition to think on death appears as a theme in several *exempla*. Only through his wife's influence is another knight brought to confess his homicides to a bishop. Though he refuses to go to Rome on pilgrimage, as the bishop has ordered, he does maintain an all-night vigil in the church although demons trouble him greatly, falsely appearing in the form of those he knows to try to dissuade him: *Anecdotes historiques*, 46–49. Another version appears in BL Additional 27336 f. 37b; this is printed in Jubinal, *Contes*, 1: 352.

92. Étienne de Bourbon, *Anecdotes historiques*, 143–44.

93. Entering without hindrance, he still went mad within the church, but was healed three days later at the spot where an injured statue of the child Jesus had bled copiously. Gerald of Wales, *Jewel of the Church*, 80–81.

94. Caesarius, *Dialogue on Miracles*, 2: 279; *Dialogus Miraculorum*, 2: 306–7.

95. *Dialogue on Miracles*, 1: 35–36; *Dialogus Miraculorum*, 1: 32–34.

96. BL Additional 27336 f. 57b.

97. Bryant, *The High Book of the Grail: Perlesvaus*, 144, 147.

98. Dialogue of Miracles, 2:258; *Dialogus Miraculorum*, 2: 289–90.

99. BL Additional 18347 f. 131.

100. Peter of les Vaux-de-Cernay, *History of the Albigensian Crusade*, passim.

101. BL Royal 5A viii f. 149. The story appears also in Étienne de Bourbon, *Anecdotes*

historiques, 104, printed there from a sermon story of Étienne de Bourbon. In this case it is told as a historical incident that supposedly took place in 1225.

102. BL Royal 20B xiv f. 170 col. 2.

103. Gautier de Coincy, *Les Miracles de la Sainte Vierge*, 494–99. In another extreme case the heavenly court recognizes that no time for confession existed: Pitiless enemies give one knight no time for confession, chopping him mercilessly to pieces, despite his pleas; he has been formally devoted to Christ and the Virgin, however, and despite his own wickedness and over bitter complaints of the demons claiming him, he is saved; upon the heart of his dead body is found the inscription, "animam meam commendo virginis filio (I commend my soul to the Virgin's son)." The inscription tells all. BL Arundel 406 f. 26b.

104. See BL Additional 18364 f. 60b.

105. Map, *De Nugis Curialium*, 314–41, 319.

106. BL Additional 18347 f. 116b. A similar story appears in BL Additional 27336 f. 37b.

107. Map, *Master Walter Map's Book*, 85.

108. Lecoy, *Le Chevalier au barissel*. The tale had a large readership or audience: Lecoy consulted four texts in Paris and a fragment in Oxford; five short versions of this story condensed into *exempla* are preserved in manuscript books collecting such stories, now in the British Library, though they differ in details. These BL mss. are cited in ibid., xviii. Cf. Payen, "Structures et sens du 'Chevalier au Barisel'," and Madeleine Le Merrer-False, "Contribution à une étude du 'Chevalier au Barisel."

109. Lecoy, line 101: "Plorer? fait il, est ce gabois?"

110. The French is "vous plourés et je rirai, / ke ja certes n'i plouerai."

111. Ibid., line 113: "Confesser, fait il, cent diable."

112. See Branch 7 of the *Roman de Reynard*, e.g., Roques, *Roman de Renart*. Cf. Jacques de Vitry, *Exempla*, 125: falsely confessing and then hurrying back to one's sin is called Reynard's confession in France: "peccata confituntur, sed statim capilli crescere incipiunt, quia statim ad peccata redeunt, et ita sacerdotibus illudunt. Hec est confession vulpis, que solet in Francia appellari confessio renardi."

113. Lecoy, *Le Chevalier au barissel*, line 136: "Tels confesse chiet a un soufflé," My thanks to Helen Swift who saved me from a more crude rendering of this vigorous expression.

114. Ibid., lines 161–62: "plus irous / ke ciens dervés ne leus warrous."

115. Ibid., lines 169–70: "Por coi, li prïerai, / quant je por lui riens ne ferai?"

116. Taking him by the hand may parallel seizing the reins of a knight's horse in combat as a formal gesture of capture. We have already noted the parallel in *exempla* in which a priest, or sometimes St. Bernard himself, convinces a knight to make successively more binding forms of truce and peace with God.

117. Ibid., lines 284–85: "Pres va que je ne vous ochi, / s'en seroit le siecles delivers."

118. His oath is of the style in romance, or parody: he will not rest day or night, nor wash his face, nor shave, nor trim his nails, and he will travel without money or bread or dough on his person until he has succeeded; see line 468 and the following discussion.

119. Ibid., line 501: "Por Dieu, voir, ne le faic jou mie"

120. Ibid., line 544.

121. Ibid., line 560.

122. Ibid., lines 780–81: "Te penitence riens ne set, / car tu l'as fait sans repentance / et sains amour et sains pitance."

123. Ibid., line 888.

124. Could the author imagine his returning to his castle and carrying on a knightly life?

CHAPTER 9. WRITING THE DEATH CERTIFICATE FOR CHIVALRIC IDEOLOGY

1. As repeatedly argued in this book, a lay framework does not imply rigid secularity or irreligion; that chivalric ideas borrowed heavily from religious themes, terminology, and practice is fundamental to the arguments presented here.

2. Hall, *Weapons and Warfare in Renaissance Europe*. Even cannon that could be brought onto the battlefield long failed to cause change on any remarkable scale. Siege artillery probably had more effect for a relatively short time, yet defense quickly recovered by adapting new forms of fortification. Ironically, by bringing sieges of towns and castles much more swiftly to a successful conclusion, the larger guns capable of turning a gate-house into rubble or reducing a traditional stout stone wall helped to bring about a golden age of open field encounters in which traditional heavy cavalry could flourish.

3. From the later fifteenth century into the early decades of the sixteenth century, French men-at-arms must have happily believed that they were still carrying out roles that Geoffroi de Charny would have understood and approved. Such is surely the attitude of the sixteenth-century French knights whose careers are examined below.

4. For studies and comment by medievalists, see Prestwich, *Armies and Warfare in the Middle Ages: The English Experience*, especially 334–46; DeVries, *Guns and Men in Medieval Europe, 1200–1500*, chaps. 8–18; Rogers, "The Military Revolutions of the Hundred Years War." On military professionalism, see the essays collected by Trim, *The Chivalric Ethos and the Development of Military Professionalism*; on Renaissance France, see Potter, "Chivalry and Professionalism in the French Armies of the Renaissance," in the volume edited by Trim. Potter notes (152) that heavily armored cavalrymen were in fact losing out to lighter cavalry and pistol-firing *reiters* but also comments on the revival of chivalric values in the Italian wars (154). Classic contributions to the general debate include Roberts, "The Military Revolution, 1560–1660"; Clark, *War and Society in the Seventeenth Century*; Parker, "The 'Military Revolution' 1550–1660—A Myth?"; idem, *The Military Revolution: Military Innovation and the Rise of the West, 1500–1800*; Black, *A Military Revolution? Military Change and European Society 1550–1800*; idem, *European Warfare, 1660–1815*; Parrot, "Strategy and Tactics in the Thirty Years' War: The 'Military Revolution'."; Lynn, *Giant of the Grand Siècle: The French Army, 1610–1715*; idem, "The Trace Italienne and the Growth of Armies: The French Case"; Downing, *The Military Revolution and Political Change in Early Modern Europe*; Rogers, "The Military

Revolutions of the Hundred Years War"; Hall and DeVries, "Essay Review: The 'Military Revolution' Revisited."

5. The notion of a long series of significant military changes from the fourteenth century into the eighteenth century has gained many distinguished supporters. Rogers, "Military Revolutions," 241–78; Lynn, *Giant of the Grand Siècle*, 4–5; Prestwich, *Armies and Warfare*, 334–46; Black, *Military Revolution?* 94. Clifford Rogers has proposed what he terms "punctuated equilibrium" in the broad course of military history (borrowing the term from biological science). The process implies a centuries-long series of occasional and sudden changes within a given field; cumulative change over time effects what a single cause could not. Changes in institutional culture and mentalité may have developed full force only in the seventeenth century rather than the sixteenth, let alone the later fifteenth. If these arguments stand, the major changes under debate made their effects felt after chivalry was surely dead (except for surface continuations and later revivals of the corpse in quite different form); not even stoutly entrenched medievalists would extend the active life of chivalry so far. Yet more cautionary is scholarly debate about the very direction of causation in the linkage of chivalry and the state. An undoubted increase in the size of armies, some scholars argue, may have resulted from state growth as much as it caused that growth. If this argument is accepted, military changes per se obviously loom less large as independent forces in analysis of broad change at the end of the Middle Ages. And some scholars even argue that finding the leadership for large armies need not have edged out the chivalrous. Michael Mallet has perceptively questioned whether a decline of chivalry is a necessary precursor or accompaniment to increasing military professionalism; Trim likewise concludes that chivalry and military professionalism "are not necessarily dichotomous," at least before the seventeenth century. See Mallet, "Condottieri and Captains in Renaissance Italy," in Trim, *Chivalric Ethos*. Trim's comment appears ibid., 3, 28–29. The broad issue of state-building and military change is debated in Parker, *Military Revolution*; Roberts, "Military Revolution"; Lynn, "Recalculating French Army Growth"; Tilly, *Coercion, Capital, and European States*; Downing, *Military Revolution and Political Change*; and Rasler and Thompson, *War and State Making*. If, as Arthur Ferguson claims, "it is fortunately no longer necessary to protest the once greatly exaggerated accounts of chivalry's death," he has done much toward securing that good end. Of course, he is referring to elements of chivalry that persist up to the present in our culture. See his *Chivalric Tradition in Renaissance England*, 11. Philippe Contamine provides interesting comments on continuity in his introduction to a collection of essays he edited, *War and Competition Between States*.

6. Ferguson, for example, states that "humanism . . . presented the English ruling classes for the first time with an alternative source of secular values": *Chivalric Tradition* 13. Cf. his interesting chapter on Tudor humanism, ibid., 55–65.

7. Scarisbrick, *Henry VIII*, 22; Baker-Smith, " 'Inglorious Glory': 1513 and the Humanist Attack on Chivalry"; Anglo, *The Great Tournament Roll of Westminster*, vol. 1, introduction. On the issue of "pacifism," see Musto, "Just Wars and Evil Empires: Erasmus and the Turks."

8. As in Anglo, *Great Tournament Roll of Westminster*, membrane 36. For the Greenwich armories, see ibid., 14–15; for martial feats, 4–5. James IV of Scotland kept a similarly chivalric court: ibid., 9–11.

9. See Gunn, "The French Wars of Henry VIII," and "Chivalry and the Politics of the Early Tudor Court."

10. Vergil, *The Anglica Historia [of Polydore Vergil]*, ed. Hay, 197, quoted in Baker-Smith, "Inglorious Glory," 137.

11. Baker-Smith, "Inglorious Glory," 136.

12. Dominic Baker-Smith notes that Erasmus thought of chivalry as "a cultural system devised to promote war and to disguise its true consequences under a veneer of glory." "Inglorious Glory," 131. The quotation from Erasmus appears in Phillips, *The "Adages" of Erasmus*, 313, cited in Baker-Smith, 139.

13. See Musto "Just Wars and Evil Empires: Erasmus and the Turks."

14. Baker-Smith, "Inglorious Glory," 136.

15. Phillips, *"Adages,"* 307, cited and discussed in Baker-Smith 134, 139.

16. Phillips, *"Adages,"* 318, 321, Baker-Smith, 139.

17. Phillips, *"Adages,"* 348–49, cited and quoted in Baker-Smith, 140. The famous verdict of Roger Asham (in *The Schoolmaster*, 1570)—would say of Malory's *Morte Darthur* "the whole pleasure of which booke standeth in two speciall poyntes, in open mans slaughter, and bold bawdrye."

18. Himelick, *The Enchiridion of Erasmus*. His caustic attacks on mere prowess, worldly honor, and reciprocal vengeance in the name of honor appear at 41, 136–37, 140–42, 149–51, 193.

19. Phillips, *"Adages,"* 336.

20. Baker-Smith, "Inglorious Glory," 140–41.

21. More, *Utopia*, 118.

22. Ibid.

23. Ibid., 120.

24. Ibid., 121.

25. About this same time, the humanist John Colet chose Good Friday as the timely day on which to preach a staunchly antiwar sermon. Ibid., 136–37. He sharply condemned those who would spoil the "mystical unity of the body of Christ by burying their swords in other Christian hearts." In the audience sat Henry VIII, whose response is not recorded. The three humanist thinkers form something of a group. Erasmus and More were in close contact and we know Colet's sermon only from Erasmus's later account of it.

26. The withering scorn all three humanists poured over the heroic ideal would certainly have won enthusiastic praise from that highly unusual knight of late fourteenth-century England, Sir John Clanvowe, discussed below. Yet he was essentially unusual.

27. The trend was evident in that early humanist John of Salisbury in the twelfth century.

28. Vale, *War and Chivalry*, and *The Princely Court*; Jaeger, *Origins of Courtliness*; Ferguson, *Indian Summer of English Chivalry*.

29. See Housley, *Religious Warfare in Europe, 1200–1536*. The Turkish enemy would prove useful, as the Saracens earlier had, as an evil to which enemies could be compared. See, e.g., Musto, "Just Wars and Evil Empires: Erasmus and the Turks."

30. Chapters 6, 7, and 8 above take this process within medieval centuries as their focus.

31. Humanist writers, as we will see, could stress that sixteenth-century French knights were loyally serving the *respublica*, and its chief, the king, with their swords.

32. As can be seen by reading through volumes of the *Statutes of the Realm* for England or the *Actes du Parlement* for France.

33. The term reflects Elyot's desire to give no license to the mere *plebs* or commoners by using the term commonwealth.

34. Elyot, *The Book Named the Governor*. All medievalists will insist, of course, that there are again precedents for classical virtues and sovereign power from several centuries earlier. The "new men" chosen as royal agents from modest social ranks were often decried in the twelfth century.

35. Potter, *History of France, 1460–1560*, 209.

36. As Margaret Aston and Colin Richmond say in their introduction to *Lollards and Reformers*, x, "we have learnt to see more clearly the dangers of our categories, to become more aware of the hazards of definition. The fourteenth century combined wide-ranging speculative criticism with lack of clarity about where orthodoxy ended and heresy began; the doubtful shared doubts with the devout." Cf. Larsen, "Are All Lollards Lollards?"

37. Cluniacs, Cistercians, and the several orders of mendicant friars in turn voiced their gratitude for patronage flowing from the chivalric at various social levels. Knightly families took a positive view of each new intercessor between sinful humanity and God. Though the proliferation of new orders ceased with a decision for closure taken at the Fourth Lateran Council of 1215, the newly lionized Carthusians and Minims of fifteenth-century France and England had sound reasons for gratitude to knightly donors.

38. Berndt Hamm makes the interesting suggestion that the "innovatory thrust of the Reformation consists above all in the fact that it breaks with the tensions and contradictions in the pluralism of the medieval Church." Hamm, *The Reformation of Faith in the Context of Late Medieval Theology and Piety*, 269.

39. Diarmaid Macculloch notes the launching of this major theme of Reformation history after the Imperial Diet of Speyer in 1526. *The Reformation*, 159–60, 266, 346. This principle is not suddenly new in the sixteenth century. Henry V was effective head of English church, as Jeremy Catto notes: "In all but name, more than a century before the title could be used, Henry V had begun to act as the supreme governor of the Church of England." "Religious Change Under Henry V," 115.

40. Printed in Scattergood, *The Works of Sir John Clanvowe*, 57–80. K. B. McFarlane complained that it is "dreary cant" but granted that its significance lies in its revelation of common Lollard ideas: *Lancastrian Kings and Lollard Knights*, 201–6, at 201.

41. McFarlane notes that if written by a monk or recluse, the work would excite little interest. But its author is a knight. *Lancastrian Kings and Lollard Knights*, 204.

42. "Byfore God alle virtue is worsshipe and alle synne is shame. And in þis world

it is euene þe revers, ffor þe world holt hem worshipful þat been greete werreyours and fiȝteres and þat distroyen and wynned manye loondis, and waasten and ȝeuen muche good to hem þat haan ynouȝ, and þat dispended oultrageously in mete, in dyrnke, in clooþing, in buyldyng and in lyuyng in eese, slouþe, and many ooþer synnes. And also þe world worsshipeþ hem muchel þat woln bee venged proudly and dispitously of euery wrong þat is seid or doon to hem. And of swyche folke men maken bookes and soonges and reeden and syngen of hem for to hoolde þe mynde of here deedes þe lengere here vpon earth, ffor þat is a þing þat worldely men desiren greetly þat here name myghte laste loonge after hem here vpon earth." Scattergood, *Works of Sir John Clanvowe*, 69.

43. Ibid., 70: "is alle synne shame and vnworsshipe. And also swiche folk that wolden fayne liuen meekeliche in þis world and ben out offe swich forseid riot, noise, and stryf, and lyuen symplely, and vsen to eten and drynken in mesure, and to clooþen hem meekely, and suffren paciently wroonges þat ooþere folke doon and seyn to hem, and hoolden hem apayed with lytel good of þis world, and desiren noo greet name of þis world, ne no pris ther of, swiche folke þe world scoorneth and hooldeþ them lolleris and loselis, foolis and shameful wrecches. But, sikerly, God holdeth hem moost wise and most worshipful."

44. Ibid.: "And alle þat he suffrede paciently. And Seynt Poul seith þat Crist suffrede for vs leeuynge vs ensaumple þat we schulden so doo folewynge hise traces. And, there-fore, folewe we hise traces and suffer we paciently þe scoornes of þe world as he dede, and þanne wole he ȝeuen vs grace to comen in by þe narrugh wey to the worsshipfulle blisse that he regneth inne."

45. Catto suggests this tract may be Clanvowe's confession, written just before his last crusade. "Religion and English Nobility in the Later Fourteenth Century," 53–54. Cf. his analysis in "Sir William Beauchamp Between Chivalry and Lollardy."

46. Scattergood, *Works of Sir John Clanvowe*, 9. Cf. Catto, "Fellows and Helpers: The Religious Identity of the Followers of Wyclif": "we paciently þe scoornes of þe world as he dede, and þanne wole he ȝeuen vs grace to comen in by þe narrugh wey to the worsshipfulle blisse that he regneth inne."

Catto suggests this tract may be Clanvowe's confession, written just before his last crusade. "Religion and English Nobility in the Later Fourteenth Century," 53–54. Cf. his analysis in "Sir William Beauchamp Between Chivalry and Lollardy."

wers of Wyclif."

47. Catto, "Religion and English Nobility," 53.

48. Wyclif seems, however, to have looked to the knights as agents of reform. Various scholars make this point; see the comment of Christina von Nolcken, "Richard Wyche, a Certain Knight, and the Beginning of the End," 136.

49. McFarlane, *Lancastrian Kings and Lollard Knights*.

50. These differing points of view appear in Hudson, *The Premature Reformation*; Rex, *The Lollards*; Haigh, *English Reformations: Religion, Politics and Society Under the Tudors*; Duffy, *The Stripping of the Altars*; and Scarisbrick, *The Reformation and the English People*.

51. See the views of Aston, "Were the Lollards a Sect?"; Ann Hudson, *Premature Reformation*, 168–73; Catto, "Fellows and Helpers"; and Rex, *The Lollards*, vii–viii and, on Lollard knights and gentry (whose importance he minimizes), 62–63, 71.

52. McFarlane, *Lancastrian Kings and Lollard Knights*, 220–26. He notes the early ecclesiastical toleration (prior to the Oldcastle rising) and suggests some complicity of view among higher churchmen.

53. J. A. F. Pollard points out that in his will Sir Brian Stapelton used the phrase "mon chautiffe corps," the very term found in Henry of Lancaster and, slightly different, in Geoffroi de Charny. See "Knightly Piety and the Margins of Lollardy," 99. Catto suggests this "penitential rhetoric" was to be found in wills by Henry V and Archbishop Arundel and thus "cannot be a peculiarity of the small circle of Lollard knights." "Religion and the English Nobility," 51.

54. Catto, "Religion and the English Nobility," 54.

55. Aston terms proposed seizure of church lands "the richest bait to hook or hold a Lollard knight" in "Lollardy and Sedition," in Aston and Richmond, *Lollards and Reformers*, 21. Cf. the insightful introduction by Aston and Richmond to the volume of essays, *Lollardy and the Gentry in the Later Middle Ages*, 1–27, and in ibid., J. A. F. Thompson, "Knightly Piety and the Margins of Lollardy."

56. Hudson, *Selections*, 24, 28: "þe tende conclusion is þat manslaute be batayle or pretense lawe of rythwysnesse for temporal cause or spiritual withouten special reuelaciun is expres contrarious to þe newe testament, þeqwiche is a lawe of grace and ful of mercy. Þis conclusion is opinly prouid be exsample of Cristis preching here in erthe, þe qwiche most taute for to loue and to haue mercyon his enemys and nout for to slen hem. Þe reason is of þis for the more partye þere men fythte, aftir e firste strok, charite is ibroke' and quose deyth out of charite goth þe heye weye to helle. And ouer þis we knowe wel þat no clerk can fynde be scripture or be resun lawful punschement of deth for on dedly synne and nout for anoþer. But þe lawe of mercy þat is þe newe testament, forbad al manisslaute: *in evangelio dictum est antiquis, Non occides*. Þe correlary is: it is an holy robbing of þe pore puple qwanne lordis purchase indulgencis *a pena et a culpa* to hem þat helpith to his oste, and gaderith to slen þe cristene men in fer londis for gode temperel, as we haue seen. And geten miche maugre of þe King of Pes; for be mekenesse and suffraunce oure beleue was multiplied, and fythteres and mansleeris Iesu Cryst hatith and manasit. *Qui gladio percutit, gladio peribit*."

57. Wright, *Political Poems and Songs*, quoted in Wilks, "Wyclif and the Great Persecution,"62.

58. See especially the account of Powell, *Kingship, Law, and Society*, 141–67, and McFarlane, *John Wyclif*, 171–97. Paul Strohm argues that the revolt was stage-managed by the crown for its own purposes in *England's Empty Throne*. Cf. Rex, *Lollards*, 84–87. Jeremy Catto terms the actual fight that defeated Oldcastle's men "a pathetic skirmish." "Religious Change Under Henry V," 97

59. Pollard, "Knightly Piety and the Margins of Lollardy," 109.

60. Emphasized in Powell, *Kingship, Law, and Society*, 166–67.

61. The phrase "wir hier ritterlich ringen" appears in a 1524 text from Luther used

repeatedly by J. S. Bach: for example, in the closing chorale from his cantata "Wer mich liebet" (BWV 59) and the motet "Der Geist hilft unsrer Schwachheit auf" (226).

62. Richard II's first wife was Anne of Bohemia. Cf. Catto, "Sir William Beauchamp Between Chivalry and Lollardy," 42: Bohemian scholars visit manors of Sir William Beauchamp in 1407 and 1408 in search of Wycliffite texts.

63. Excellent discussion of the conflicts that emerged appear in Housley, *Religious Warfare in Europe, 1400–1536*.

64. Hamm, *The Reformation of Faith in the Context of Late Medieval Theology and Piety*, passim, especially 263.

65. As emphasized by David Bagghi, "Luther and the Sacramentality of Penance."

66. Denis Crouzet, however, has written that Luther's ideas directly contradicted those of the model chevalier Bayard. See his *Symphorien Champier. La vie du preulx Chevalier Bayard*, 68–72.

67. Luther, *Christian Liberty* (Lambert/Grimm), 21.

68. Ibid., 16

69. Ibid., 30.

70. See, e.g., Hill, *The Loci Communes of Philip Melanchthon*.

71. Any scholar who has worked in the Public Records Office in London (with its tons of surviving parchment records) or the substantial manuscript collections of the Archives National in Paris, has a personal recognition of the results of this process. J. R. Strayer wrote a classic, concise history of state formation, *On the Medieval Origins of the Modern State*. The seven-volume series edited by William Blockmans and Jean-Philippe Genet, *The Origins of the Modern State in Europe, Thirteenth to Eighteenth Centuries*, analyzes the emergence of the state from the late medieval through the early modern era thematically. Many of the scholars writing in these volumes show considerable interest in twelfth- and thirteenth-century developments. Note also, for example, the conclusion of Antonio Padoa-Schioppa in his edited collection, *Legislation and Justice*, 338, stressing the long duration of European state-formation, and the chapter by Hilde de Ridder-Symoens, "Training and Professionalization," in Reinhard, *Power Elites and Statebuilding*. See also Tilly, *Coercion, Capital, and European States, AD 990–1990*; and Ertman, *Birth of the Leviathan*.

72. James Campbell has demonstrated this point with special force: see his *Anglo-Saxon State*.

73. If, as D. J. B. Trim has wisely cautioned, there is no single timeline or inevitable pattern for these changes across Europe (*Chivalric Ethos*, 24–26, 24 n. 93), the shifting pattern in France retains much interest. He notes that by the mid-seventeenth century, the nobles were, in fact, serving as members of an officer corps to the great benefit of state power. See the essays in that volume for a range of case studies.

74. Printed in Petitot, *Collection complète des mémoires relatifs à l'histoire de France*, 14: 323–556.

75. Ibid., 349–50. David Potter notes that these opening pages show a fusion of chivalric romance with classical myth: "Chivalry and Professionalism," 157.

76. As a Burgundian, young Louis would be useful to the king, Louis XI.

77. Petitot, *Collection*, 356: "la court du Roy, où est l'escolle de toute honnesteté, et où se tiennent les gens de bien soubz lesquelz on aprend à civillement vivre, et la forme d'acquerir non seulement les mondaines richesses, mais les incorruptibles tresors de honneur." By contrast, Charny had simply urged his aspiring knights to find good men at arms wherever there was military action: Kaeuper and Kennedy, *Livre de chevalerie*, 90–93. The centrality of the monarch within the growing state is stressed by the contributors to Allan Ellenius, *Iconography, Propaganda, and Legitimation.*

78. Petitot, *Collection*, 352–63.

79. Ibid., 385–92.

80. Ibid., 393–99.

81. Interesting contrasts appear when this text is set alongside the story of Guillaume d'Orange told in the twelfth-century *Couronnement de Louis.* Both heroes serve their king. But Louis La Tremouille draws honor from his sovereign in a text filled with speeches about honor linked to royalty. William props up a feeble king by his own valor, lovingly detailed.

82. Petitot, *Collection*, 402–3: "de sa hardiesse, prudence, diligence et bonne conduicte, et de plusieurs beaulx faiz d'arjmes par luy faiz es rencontres et saillies qu'on avoit fait au siege de Nantes et aussi es sieges et assaulx de plusieururs villes, chasteaux et fortes places de Bretraigne."

83. Ibid., 403: "pour le prouffit du Roy et du royaume, et acquerir honneur en sa charge."

84. Ibid., 405–6.

85. Ibid., 407: "Trop mieulx nous vault mourir en juste bataille, guerre premise, et au service du Roy, qui est le lict d'honneur que vivre en reproche."

86. This event and its consequences occupy pages 499–524.

87. Ibid., 499: "de mourir au service du Roy et de la chose publique."

88. Ibid., 501: the first statement reads, "au lict d'honneur decedé en vostre compaignée, à vostre service et en juste querelle"; the second reads, "et il commanceoit acquerir honneur et vostre grace."

89. Ibid., 506–7: "la plus honneste mort que mourut onc prince ou seigneur; c'est au lict d'honneru, en bataille premise pour juste querelle, non en fuyant, mais en bataillant, et navré de soixante deux playes, en la compaignée et au service du Roy, bien exxtime de toute la gendarmerie, et en la grace de Dieu, car luy bien confessé est decedé vray crestien."

90. Ibid., 509.

91. Ibid., 511–13.

92. Ibid., 551–53, quotation at 553: "disoit souvent ne vouloir mourir aillerus que au lict d'honneur, c'est à dire au service du Roy en juste guerre."

93. Ibid., 554: Les honneurs qu'on acciystyné faire en obseques de contes, princes, chevaliers et chiefz de guerre, luy furent baillz, comme bien le meritant, tant pour son honorable et droicte vie que pour ses nobles faictz et gestes."

94. Ibid., 555: "Il despendoit non seulement ses gages et pensions, mais aussi tout son revenue, au serviced du Roy et de la chose publique, et non ailleurs."

95. Ibid.

96. Champier, *Les gestes ensemble la vie du preulx Chevalier Bayard*, ed. Denis Crouzet.

97. Bayard was admired long after the sixteenth century, of course. Frederick the Great even founded an honorific order named for this remarkable "chevalier sans peur et sans reproche." See Schieder, *Friedrich der Grosse*, 51. My thanks to Dorinda Outram for this reference.

98. Champier, *Les gestes ensemble*, 108.

99. Ibid., passim. Charny had regularly called out his family name as war cry: Kaeuper and Kennedy, *The Chivalry of Geoffroi de Charny*, 4, 198.

100. Champier, *Les gestes ensemble*, 129–32. The early career of William Marshal comes to mind.

101. Ibid., 233.

102. Ibid., 136: "Sa hardiesse n'estoit de home ançoys de lyon. . . . Il prenoist grant plaisir au combast."

103. Ibid., 137: "lequel il occist par la volunté de dieu." Crouzet discusses this fight at 22–30 in Champier, *Les gestes ensemble*.

104. This might reflect the poet of the *Song of Roland* who emphasizes the unimpressive size of the champion Thierry who will overcome the massive but evil Pinabel, judicial champion of the traitor Ganelon.

105. Champier, *Les gestes ensemble*, 142: "à ceste cause, comme deffendeur et saulvant mon honneur, et pour donner example à tous chrestien ne imposer crime sur son frere chrestien . . . comme chrestien chevalier de vérité."

106. Ibid., 143–44.

107. Ibid.: see Crouzet's Introduction and 144.

108. Ibid., 145–49. Crouzet discusses this fight at 31–33.

109. Ibid., 146: "contre tout honneur de chevalerie et de la guerre."

110. Ibid., 148: "car toute victoyre vient du ciel et non des homes." The second quotation reads, "je vous exhorte comme freres chrestiens de recongnoistre vostre peché et la faulte d'avoir tués ces beaulx chevaulx qui ne vous avoient riens offence. . . . Il eust esté meilleur les vendre et donner l'argent aulx pouvres de dieu."

111. Ibid., 149–54. Crouzet's discussion of this combat comes at 33.

112. Ibid., 153.

113. Ibid., 154: "que dieu garde tousjours les gens de bien et leur honneur, et que ce eust esté dommaige s'il eust esté prisonnier, pour ce qu'il a le bruyt d'estre chevalier sans reproche et bien le demonstra au combat du seigneur Alonce."

114. We may likewise question who is actually speaking when Bayard later announces how hard it is for a warrior within Christian law to follow arms and die rich, and who says a man must follow God and make do with simply enough: "c'est moult difficile en la loy chrestienne suyvir les armes et mourir riche: c'est assés vivre selon Dieu et avoir souffisance." Ibid., 170.

115. Crouzet emphasizes the religious system of the text above any other ideological lines of thought.

116. Champier, *Les gestes ensemble*, 211–34.

117. Ibid., 156: "à la necessité on ne doibt laisser pour aulcune chose son prince, et mieulx aimeroys mourir avecques luy que de mourir ycy à honte."

118. Ibid., 172.

119. Ibid., 181–83.

120. Ibid., 195: "Sire, celluy qu'est courroné, sacréé et oing de l'uyle envoyé de ciel, et est roy d'ung si noble reaulme, le premier filz de l'esglise, est chevalier sur tous aultres chevaliers."

121. Ibid., 196.

122. Ibid., 201.

123. The battle took place around the Sesia River at the end of April, 1524. See Hall, *Weapons and Warfare*, 180.

124. He was apparently shot at short range by a hacquebutier, a man firing a large-bore "hacquebut a croc," a gun heavy enough to require a rest to steady its barrel. Bert Hall describes this weapon as "the 'elephant gun' of sixteenth century shoulder arms." See Hall, *Weapons and Warfare*, 176–77.

125. Crouzet stresses that the tree beneath which Champier's hero is laid represents the cross of Christ, an image both of sorrow and triumph. In fact, Crouzet finds much Christological symbolism in Champier's biography. In the eschatological fears of the early sixteenth century, Champier sees Bayard's triumphs as victories over mere mortals elevated into dread collective enemies: see Crouzet's discussion, *Les gestes ensemble*, 17–22, 63.

126. Ibid., 209: "n'ay aulcune desplaisance ny regret à mourir, fors que je ne puis faire service aulcum pour l'advenir au roy mon souverain et qu'il le me fault delaisser à ses grandz affaires, don't je suys trèsdolent et desplaisant. Je prie dieu le souverain que, après mon trespass, il ave telz serviteurs que je vouldroye ester."

127. Ibid., 210.

128. Ibid., 167.

129. Ferguson provides useful information and analysis in *Chivalric Tradition*, 45–55.

130. Quoted in McCoy, *Rites of Knighthood*, 51.

131. See McCoy's comments on the Essex knightings, *Rites of Knighthood*, 87, 96, and quoting Aristotle's *Nichomachean Ethics*, 12.

132. Quoted in McCoy, *Rites of Knighthood*, 76.

133. Daniel, *The Civil Wars*, 240; cf. McCoy, *Rites of Knighthood*, 12, 115.

134. McCoy, *Rites of Knighthood*, 108, 122–24.

135. Thurley, *Hampton Court: A Social and Architectural History*, 99–105. "The style was about creating, or possibly in Henry's mind recreating, a chivalric setting for the human magnificence of the Tudor court" (99). If its origins lay in the Burgundian court, Thurley thinks the Tudors made their architecture national. By the 1580s, the style was being copied by non-royal great builders in an age of chivalric resurgence—"a society obsessed by the idea of chivalry"— and national pride (103). Self-conscious chivalric

elements in the architecture include asymmetrical façades and backward-looking great halls with roof louvers for escape of smoke from the central hearth. I owe this reference to Dale Hoak.

136. As only one of many possible examples, we could consider the elaborate chivalric symbolism in Sir Philip Sidney's unfinished "New Arcadia." Clare R. Kinney argues that Sidney's words "do not so much celebrate chivalric rituals as place them within a larger design that invites their demystification." See her "Chivalry Unmasked: Courtly Spectacle and the Abuses of Romance in Sidney's 'New Arcadia'." Ferguson comments in *Chivalric Tradition* on Sidney, 113–18 and on Spencer, 118–23.

137. Daniel, *Civil Wars*. Daniel, McCoy argues, cannot find the proper balance between heroic prowess and stable state power in an age of repeated civil wars. *Rites of Knighthood*, 103. It is interesting that Sidney's "New Arcadia" likewise remained unfinished. See McCoy's comments, 136–37.

138. Daniel, *Civil Wars*, 228.

139. Ibid., 213–19.

140. Ibid., 163.

141. Ibid., 166–67.

142. Ibid., 148.

143. Ibid., 144–45.

144. Even his much-admired Henry V does not escape Daniel's ambivalence. See 178–79, 181. Much as he loves prowess, shades of doubt fall even on this virtue. See stanzas 37–40, p. 187.

145. Ibid., 266–67. Such a civil strife is "A Warre that doth the face of Warre deforme," 235. Yet the bright side is that "These Lords who thus against their Kings draw swords, / Taught Kings to come how to be more than Lords," 240.

146. McCoy, *The Rites of Knighthood*, 103

147. Furnivale, *Queene Elizabethes Achademy*, 1–13. The estimated costs (3,000 pounds annually) may have deterred the queen. Gilbert's assertion that his plan would make young nobles "for some what" who are at present "god for nothinge" cannot have won him copious aristocratic support.

148. Ibid., 1.

149. Ibid., 10–11.

150. Ibid., 13.

151. Ibid., 11. This is to avoid their being "corrupted with papistrie."

152. See the argument of Mervyn James, "English Politics and the Concept of Honour, 1485–1642," in his collected essays, *Society, Politics, and Culture*, 332–74. Steven Gunn comments on the contrasting situation in Germany and provides sources in "Chivalry and the Politics of the Early Tudor Court," 124–25.

153. As noted by Anglo in *The Great Tournament Roll of Westminster*, 81.

154. Milles, *Catalogue of Honour*, 74. Cf. his peroration on the Order of the Garter as the great combination of chivalry, religion, and royal court at 89–90.

155. To use an image I developed in *Chivalry and Violence*, in the complex cooperation

and conflict among *royauté*, *clergie*, and *chevalerie*, the forces associated with kingship (or *souverainité*) have triumphed with the support of *clergie* both in the sense of the clerical caste and of learning in general.

156. The difference registers even if we think of crusaders and the church.

157. See, for example, the clear and concise analysis of David Potter, *A History of France 1460–1560*, 219–31. Cf. the attempt to reform "l'Église gallicane toute entière" in meetings at Tours in 1493: Godet, "Consultation de Tours pour la réforme de l'église de France, 175–96. Jeremy Catto says that "In all but name, more than a century before the title could be used, Henry V had begun to act as supreme governor of the Church of England." "Religious Change Under Henry V," 115.

158. Bellamy, *The Law of Treason in England in the Later Middle Ages* and *The Tudor Law of Treason*; Cutler, *The Law of Treason and Treason Trials in Later Medieval France*.

BIBLIOGRAPHY

Ackerman, Robert W. "The Traditional Background of Henry of Lancaster's *Livre*." *L'Esprit créateur* 2 (1962).

Aers, David, and Lynn Staley. *The Powers of the Holy: Religion, Politics, and Gender in Late Medieval England*. University Park: Pennsylvania State University Press, 1996.

Alan of Lille. *The Art of Preaching*. Trans. Gillian R. Evans. Kalamazoo, Mich.: Cistercian Publications, 1981.

———. *Alain de Lille: textes inédits*. Ed. Marie-Thérèse d'Alverny. Paris: J. Vrin, 1965.

Ambroise. *The Crusade of Richard Lion-Heart*. Trans. and ed. Merton Jerome Hubert and John La Monte. New York: Columbia University Press, 1941.

———. *The History of the Holy War: Ambroise's Estoire de la Guerre Sainte*. 2 vols. Ed. Marianne Ailes and Malcolm Barber. Rochester, N.Y.: Boydell, 2003.

Anglo, Sydney, ed. *The Great Tournament Roll of Westminster*. 2 vols. Oxford: Clarendon Press, 1968.

Anselm of Canterbury. *Complete Philosophical and Theological Treatises of Anselm of Canterbury*. Trans. Jasper Hopkins and Herbert Richardson. Minneapolis: A.J. Banning, 2000.

———. *S. Anselmi Cantuariensis archiepiscopi Opera Omnia*. Ed. Franciscus S. Schmitt. 6 vols. Stuttgart-Bad Cannstatt: Frommann, 1968.

Arnould, E. J. *Étude sur le Livre des saintes médecines du Duc Henri de Lancastre*. Paris: M. Didier, 1948.

———. "Henry of Lancaster and His *Livre des seintes medicines*." *Bulletin of the John Rylands Library* 21 (1937).

Asbridge, Thomas. *The First Crusade: A New History*. New York: Oxford University Press, 2004.

Aston, Margaret. *The Premature Reformation: Wycliffite Texts and Lollard History*. Oxford: Oxford University Press, 1988.

———. "Were the Lollards a Sect?" In *The Medieval Church: Universities, Heresy, and the Religious Life: Essays in Honour of Gordon Leff*, ed. Peter Biller and Barie Dobson, 163–91. Woodstock: Boydell, 1999.

Aston, Margaret, and Colin Richmond. *Lollards and Reformers: Images and Literacy in Late Medieval Religion*. London: Hambledon, 1984.

————, eds. *Lollardy and the Gentry in the Later Middle Ages*. New York: St. Martin's, 1997.

Auerbach, Eric. *Literary Language and Its Public in Late Latin Antiquity and in the Middle Ages*. New York: Pantheon, 1965.

Bachrach, David. *Religion and the Conduct of War, 300–1215*. Rochester, N.Y.: Boydell, 2003.

Bagghi, David. "Luther and the Sacramentality of Penance." In *Retribution, Repentance, and Reconciliation*, ed. Kate Cooper and Jeremy Gregory, 119–27. Studies in Church History 40. Woodbridge: Boydell and Brewer for Ecclesiastical History Society, 2004.

Baker, Denise N. "Meed and the Economics of Chivalry in Piers Plowman." In *Inscribing the Hundred Years' War in French and English Cultures*, ed. Baker, 55–72. Albany: State University of New York Press, 2000.

Baker-Smith, Dominic. "'Inglorious Glory': 1513 and the Humanist Attack on Chivalry." In *Chivalry in the Renaissance*, ed. Sydney Anglo, 129–44. Rochester, N.Y.: Boydell, 1990.

Baldwin, John. "From the Ordeal to Confession." In *Handling Sin: Confession in the Middle Ages*, ed. Peter Biller and A. J. Minnis, 191–211. Woodbridge: York Medieval Press, 1998.

————. *Masters, Princes, and Merchants: The Social Views of Peter the Chanter and His Circle*. Princeton, N.J.: Princeton University Press, 1970.

Banks, Mary Macleod. *An Alphabet of Tales: An English 15th-Century Translation of the Alphabetum Narrationum of Étienne de Besançon*. London: K. Paul, Trench for Early English Text Society, 1904–5.

Barber, Malcolm, and Keith Bate. *The Templars: Selected Sources*. Manchester: Manchester University Press, 2002.

Barker, Juliet. *Tournament in England, 1100–1400*. Woodbridge: Boydell, 1985.

Barker, Juliet, and Richard Barber. *Tournaments, Jousts, Chivalry and Pageants in the Middle Ages*. New York: Weidenfeld & Nicolson, 1989.

Bates, David. *Normandy Before 1066*. New York: Longman, 1982.

Bellamy, J. G. *The Law of Treason in England in the Later Middle Ages*. Cambridge: Cambridge University Press, 1970.

————. *The Tudor Law of Treason: An Introduction*. London: Routledge, 1979.

Bellenger, Yvonne, and Danielle Quéruelle, eds. *Les Champenois et la croisade: Actes des Quatrièmes Journées Rémoises, 27–28 novembre 1987*. Paris: Aux amateurs de livres, 1989.

Bennett, J. A. W. *Poetry of the Passion: Studies in Twelve Centuries of English Verse*. New York: Oxford University Press, 1982.

Benson, Larry, ed. and trans. *King Arthur's Death: The Middle English Stanzaic Morte Arthur and Alliterative Morte Arthure*. Rev. Edward E. Foster. Kalamazoo, Mich.: Medieval Institute Publications, 1994.

Benton, John, ed. *Self and Society in Medieval France: The Memoirs of Abbot Guibert of Nogent*. New York: Harper & Row, 1970.

Bériou, Nicole. "Autour de latran IV (1215): la naissance de la confession moderne et sa diffusion." In *Pratiques de la confession*, ed. Groupe de la Bussière, 73–92. Paris: Cerf, 1983.

Bernard of Clairvaux. *In Praise of the New Knighthood: A Treatise on the Knights Templar and the Holy Places of Jerusalem*. Trans. Conrad Greenia. Kalamazoo, Mich.: Cistercian Publications, 2000.

———. *The Letters of St. Bernard of Clairvaux*. Ed. and trans. Bruno Scott James. Kalamazoo, Mich.: Cistercian Publications, 1998.

———. *Sancti Bernardi Opera*. Vol. 3. Ed. Jean Leclercq and H. M. Rochais. Rome: Editiones Cistercienses, 1963.

Bertran de Born. *The Poems of the Troubadour Bertran de Born*. Ed. William D. Paden, Tilde Sankovitch, and Patricia H. Stablein. Berkeley: University of California Press, 1986.

Bertrand de Bar-sur-Aube. *The Song of Girart of Vienne by Bertrand de Bar-sur-Aube: A Twelfth-Century Chanson de Geste*. Trans. Michael Newth. Tempe: Arizona Center for Medieval and Renaissance Studies, Arizona State University, 1999.

———. *Girart de Vienne*. Ed. Wolfgang van Emden. Paris: Société des Anciens Textes Français, 1977.

Biller, Peter, and A. J. Minnis. *Handling Sin: Confession in the Middle Ages*. Woodbridge: York Medieval Press, 1998.

Bitterling, Klaus, ed. *Of Shrifte and Penance: The ME Prose Translation of Le manuel des pechés*. Heidelberg: C. Winter, 1998.

Black, Jeremy. *European Warfare, 1660–1815*. New Haven, Conn.: Yale University Press, 1994.

———. *A Military Revolution? Military Change and European Society, 1550–1800*. Atlantic Highlands, N.J.: Humanities Press, 1991.

Boffa, Sergio. *Warfare in Medieval Brabant*. Rochester, N.Y.: Boydell, 2004.

Bogdanow, Fanni, ed. *La Version post-Vulgate de la Queste del Saint Graal et de la Mort Artu: troisième partie du Roman du Graal*. Paris: Société des Anciens Textes Français, 1991.

Bossy, John. *Christianity in the West, 1400–1700*. New York: Oxford University Press, 1985.

———. "The Social History of Confession in the Age of the Reformation." *Transactions of the Royal Historical Society* 5th ser. 25 (1975): 21–38.

Boyle, Leonard. "The Fourth Lateran Council and Manuals of Popular Theology." In *The Popular Literature of Medieval England*, ed. Thomas Heffernan, 30–43. Knoxville: University of Tennessee Press, 1985.

Brandin, Louis, ed. *La Chanson d'Aspremont*. Paris: Champion, 1970.

Brault, Gerald, ed. and trans. *La Chanson de Roland*. University Park: Pennsylvania State University Press, 1984.

Brett, Edward. *Humbert of Romans: His Life and Views of Thirteenth-Century Society*. Toronto: Institute for Mediaeval Studies, 1984.

Bromyard, Johannes de. *Summa Praedicantium*. Nurenberg: Anton Koberger, 1485.

Brook, G. L., and R. F. Leslie, eds. *Lazamon: Brut*. London: Oxford University Press for Early English Text Society, 1963.

Brown, Elizabeth A. R. "Georges Duby and the Three Orders." *Viator* 17 (1986): 51–64.

Brundage, James. *The Crusades, Holy War, and Canon Law*. Brookfield, Vt.: Gower, 1991.

———. "The Hierarchy of Violence in Twelfth- and Thirteenth-Century Canonists." *International History Review* 17 (1995): 670–81.

———. *Medieval Canon Law and the Crusader*. Madison: University of Wisconsin Press, 1969.

Bryant, Nigel, trans. *The High Book of the Grail: A Translation of the Thirteenth-Century Romance of Perlesvaus*. Totowa, N.J.: Rowman & Littlefield, 1978.

———. *Merlin and the Grail: Joseph of Arimathea, Merlin, Perceval: The Trilogy of Prose Romances Attributed to Robert de Boron*. Rochester, N.Y.: D.S. Brewer, 2001.

Buckley, Susan. *Teachings on Usury in Judaism, Christianity, and Islam*. Lewiston, N.Y.: Edwin Mellen, 2000.

Bull, Marcus. *Knightly Piety and the Lay Response to the First Crusade: The Limousin and Gascony, c. 970–c. 1130*. New York: Oxford University Press, 1993.

Busby, Keith. *Raoul de Hodenc, Le roman des eles: The Anonymous Ordene de chevalerie*. Philadelphia: Benjamins, 1983.

Bynum, Caroline Walker. *Holy Feast, Holy Fast: The Religious Significance of Food to Medieval Women*. Berkeley: University of California Press, 1987.

———. *Jesus as Mother: Studies in the Spirituality of the High Middle Ages*. Berkeley: University of California Press, 1982.

———. "Revisiting the Twelfth-Century Individual: The Inner Self and the Christian Community." In *Das Eigene und das Ganze: Zum Individuellen im mittelalterlichen Religiosentum*, ed. Gert Melville and Markus Schuerer, 57–85. Münster: LIT, 2002.

Caesarius of Heisterbach. *Dialogus Miraculorum*. Ed. Joseph Strange. Coloniae: Sumptibus J. M. Heberle, 1851. Reprint Ridgewood, N.J.: Gregg, 1966.

———. *The Dialogue on Miracles of Caesarius of Heisterbach*. Ed. and trans. H. von E. Scott and C. C. Swinton Bland. 2 vols. London: Routledge, 1929.

Calendar of the Patent Rolls. 1343–45.

Campbell, James. *The Anglo-Saxon State*. London: Hambledon, 2000.

Carriazo, Juan de Mata, ed. *El Victorial: Crónica de Don Pero Niña, Conde de Buelna, por su alf'eraz Gutierre Díez de Games*. Madrid: Espasa-Calpe, 1940.

Catto, Jeremy. "Fellows and Helpers: The Religious Identity of the Followers of Wyclif." In *The Medieval Church: Universities, Heresy, and the Religious Life*, ed. Peter Biller and Barie Dobson, 154–61. Woodbridge: Boydell, 1999.

———. "Religion and the English Nobility in the Later Fourteenth Century." In *History and Imagination: Essays in Honor of H. R. Trevor-Roper*, ed. Hugh Lloyd-Jones, Valerie Pearl, and Blair Worden, 43–55. New York: Oxford University Press, 1980.

———. "Religious Change Under Henry V." In *Henry V: The Practice of Kingship*, ed. G. L. Harriss, 97–115. New York: Oxford University Press, 1985.

———. "Sir William Beauchamp Between Chivalry and Lollardy." In *The Ideals and*

Practices of Knighthood, vol. 3, ed. Christopher Harper-Bill and Ruth Harvey, 39–48. Woodbridge: Boydell, 1990.

Cazel, Fred A., Jr. "Religious Motivation in the Biography of Hubert de Burgh."In *Religious Motivation: Biographical and Sociological Problems for the Church Historian*, ed. Derek Baker, 109–19. Studies in Church History 15. Oxford: Blackwell for Ecclesiastical History Society, 1978.

Certain, Eugène de. *Les Miracles de Saint Benoit*. 1863. Reprint New York: Johnson Reprints, 1968.

Champier, Symphorien. *Les gestes ensemble la vie du preulx Chevalier Bayard*. Ed. Denis Crouzet. Paris: Imprimerie Nationale, 1992.

Chase, Carol J., trans. The History of the Holy Grail. Vol. 1 of Lancelot-Grail: The Old French Arthurian Vulgate and Post-Vulgate in Translation, ed. Norris Lacy, 3–49. New York: Garland, 1993–95.

Cheney, C. R., and W. H. Semple. *Selected Letters of Pope Innocent III Concerning England (1198–1216)*. London: T. Nelson, 1953.

Chenu, M.-D. *Nature, Man, and Society in the Twelfth Century: Essays on New Theological Perspectives in the Latin West*. Chicago: University of Chicago Press, 1968.

Chrétien de Troyes. *Le Conte du Graal*. Trans. and ed. Pierre Kunstmann. Paris, BN fr. 794. Laboratoire de Français Ancien, Université d'Ottawa, Website, September 1998.

Clanchy, M. T. *Abelard: A Medieval Life*. Oxford: Blackwell, 1997.

———. *England and Its Rulers, 1066–1272*. Oxford: Blackwell, 1998.

Clark, George. *War and Society in the Seventeenth Century*. Cambridge: Cambridge University Press, 1958.

Cloetta, Wilhelm, ed. *Moniage Guillaume: Les deux rédactions en vers du Moniage Guillaume, chansons de geste du XIIe siècle*. Paris: Firmin-Didot, 1906.

Cohen, Esther. "The Animated Pain of the Body." *American Historical Review* 105 (2000): 36–68.

———. "Towards a History of European Physical Sensibility: Pain in the Later Middle Ages." *Science in Context* 8 (1995): 47–74.

Cole, Penny. *The Preaching of the Crusades to the Holy Land, 1095–1270*. Cambridge, Mass.: Medieval Academy of America, 1991.

Collins, A. Jeffries, ed. *Manuale ad Usum Percelebris Ecclesiae Sarisburiensis*. Henry Bradshaw Society 91. London: The Society, 1960.

Conlee, John, ed. *Prose Merlin*. Kalamazoo, Mich.: Medieval Institute Publications, 1998.

Constable, Giles. "The Place of the Crusader in Medieval Society." *Viator: Medieval and Renaissance Studies* 29 (1998): 377–403.

———. "The Second Crusade as Seen by Contemporaries." *Traditio* 9 (1953): 214–79.

———. *The Reformation of the Twelfth Century*. New York: Cambridge University Press, 1996.

———. *Three Studies in Medieval Religious and Social Thought*. New York: Cambridge University Press, 1995.

Contamine, Philippe. "Joinville, acteur et spectateur de la querre d'outremer." In *Le prince et son historien: la vie de Saint Louis de Joinville*, ed. Jean Doufournet and Laurence Harf. Paris: Champion, 1997.

―――. *La noblesse au royaume de France de Philippe le Bel à Louis XII*. Paris: Presses Universitaires de France, 1998.

―――. *War and Competition Between States*. Oxford: Oxford University Press, 2000.

Cooper, Kate, and Jeremy Gregory, eds. *Retribution, Repentance, and Reconciliation*. Studies in Church History 40. Woodbridge: Boydell and Brewer for Ecclesiastical History Society, 2004.

Coopland, George W., ed. *Le Songe du Vieil Pelerin*. 2 vols. Cambridge: Cambridge University Press, 1969.

Cowdrey, H. E. J. "Bishop Ermenfrid of Sion and the Penitential Ordinance Following the Battle of Hastings." *Journal of Ecclesiastical History* 20 (1969): 225–42.

―――. *The Crusades and Latin Monasticism, 11th–12th Centuries*. Brookfield, Vt.: Ashgate, 1999.

―――. *Pope Gregory VII*. New York: Oxford University Press, 1998.

―――. "Pope Gregory VII and the Bearing of Arms." In *Montjoie: Studies in Crusade History in Honour of Hans Eberhard Mayer*, ed. Benjamin Z. Kedar, Jonathan Riley-Smith, and Rudolf Hiestand, 21–35. Brookfield, Vt.: Variorum, 1997.

―――. "Pope Gregory VII's 'Crusading' Plans of 1074." In *Outremer: Studies in the History of the Crusading Kingdom of Jerusalem Presented to Joshua Prawer*, ed. Benjamin Kedar, H. E. Mayer, and R. C. Smail, 27–40. Jerusalem: Yad Izhak Ben-Zvi Institute, 1982.

―――. *Popes, Monks, and Crusaders*. London: Hambledon, 1984.

―――. "The Spirituality of Pope Gregory VII." In *The Mystical Tradition and the Carthusians*, ed. James Hogg, 1–22. Salzburg: Institut für Anglistik und Amerikanistik, Universität Salzburg, 1995.

Crane, Susan. *Insular Romance: Politics, Faith, and Culture in Anglo-Norman and Middle English Literature*. Berkeley: University of California Press, 1986.

Crouch, David. *The Birth of Nobility: Constructing Aristocracy in England and France: 900–1300*. New York: Pearson/Longman, 2005.

―――. *Tournament*. London: Hambledon, 2005.

―――. "The Troubled Deathbeds of Henry I's Servants: Death, Confession, and Secular Conduct in the Twelfth Century." *Albion* 34 (2002): 24–36.

Curley, Michael J. *Saint Patrick's Purgatory: A Poem by Marie de France*. Binghamton, N.Y.: Medieval and Renaissance Texts and Studies, 1993.

Cutler, S. H. *The Law of Treason and Treason Trials in Later Medieval France*. Cambridge: Cambridge University Press, 1981.

Daniel, Samuel. *Civil Wars*. Ed. Laurence Michel. New Haven, Conn.: Yale University Press, 1958.

David, Charles Wendell, ed. and trans. *De expugnatione Lyxbonensi--The Conquest of Lisbon*. New York: Columbia University Press, 1936, repr. 2000.

Demaison, Louis, ed. *Aymeri de Narbonne, chanson de geste*. Paris: Didot, 1887.

DeMarco, Patricia. "An Arthur for the Riccardian Age: Crown, Nobility, and the Alliterative Morte Arthure." *Speculum* 80 (2005): 464–93.

———. "Inscribing the Body with Meaning: Chivalric Culture and the Norms of Violence in The Vows of the Heron." In *Inscribing the Hundred Years' War in French and English Cultures*, ed. Denise N. Baker, 27–55. Albany: State University of New York Press, 2000.

Deme, Dániel. *The Christology of Anselm of Canterbury*. Aldershot: Ashgate, 2003.

Deschamps, Eustache. *Oeuvres complètes de Eustache Deschamps*. 2 vols. Ed. Le Marquis de Queux de Saint-Hillaire. Paris: Société des Anciens Textes Français, 1992.

DeVries, Kelly. *Guns and Men in Medieval Europe, 1200–1500: Studies in Military History and Technology*. Aldershot: Ashgate/Variorum, 2002.

Dexter, Elise F. "Miracula Sanctae Virginis Mariae." *University of Wisconsin Studies in the Social Sciences and History* 12 (1927): 1–61.

Dohar, William J. "'Since the Pestilential Time': Pastoral Care in the Later Middle Ages." In *A History of Pastoral Care*, ed. Gillian R. Evans, 169–200. New York: Cassell, 2000.

Dondaine, Antoine. "Guillaume Peyraut, vie et oeuvres." *Archivium fratrum praedicatorum* 18 (1948): 162–236.

Doufournet, Jean, and Laurence Harf. *Le prince et son historien: la vie de Saint Louis de Joinville*. Paris: Champion, 1997.

Douglas, David, ed. *English Historical Documents*. 12 vols. London: Eyre & Spottiswoode, 1953–.

———. *William the Conqueror: The Norman Impact upon England*. London: Eyre & Spottiswoode, 1964.

Downing, Brian M. *The Military Revolution and Political Change in Early Modern Europe: Origins of Democracy and Autocracy in Early Modern Europe*. Princeton, N.J.: Princeton University Press, 1992.

Duby, Georges. *The Three Orders: Feudal Society Imagined*. Trans. Arthur Goldhammer. Chicago: University of Chicago Press, 1980.

Duffy, Eamon. *The Stripping of the Altars: Traditional Religion in England, c.1400–c.1580*. New Haven, Conn.: Yale University Press, 1992.

Dufournet, Jean, and Andrée Méline, eds. *Le Roman de Renart*. 2 vols. Paris: Flammarion, 1985.

Duggan, Lawrence G. "Fear and Confession on the Eve of the Reformation." *Archiv für Reformationsgeschichte* 75 (1984): 153–75.

Easting, Robert. *St. Patrick's Purgatory: Two Versions of Owayne Miles and the Vision of William of Stranton Together with the Long Text of the Tractatus de purgatorio Sancti Patricii*. Oxford: Oxford University Press, 1991.

Edwards, Graham Robert. "Purgatory: 'Birth' or Evolution?" *Journal of Ecclesiastical History* 36 (1985): 634–36.

Eliade, Mircea. *The Myth of the Eternal Return*. Princeton, N.J.: Princeton University Press, 1955.

Ellenius, Allan, ed. *Iconography, Propaganda, and Legitimation*. Oxford: Clarendon Press, 1998.

Elyot, Thomas, Sir. *The Book Named the Governor*. Ed. S. E. Lehmberg. London: Dent, 1962.

Erdmann, Carl. *The Origin of the Idea of Crusade*. Princeton, N.J.: Princeton University Press, 1977.

Ertman, Thomas. *Birth of the Leviathan: Building States and Regimes in Medieval and Early Modern Europe*. Cambridge: Cambridge University Press, 1997.

Étienne de Bourbon. *Anecdotes historiques, légendes et apologues, tirés du recueil inédit d'Étienne de Bourbon, Dominicain du XIIIe siècle*. Ed. A. Lecoy de la Marche. Paris: Librairie Renouard, 1877.

Étienne de Fougeres. *Le Livre des manières*. Ed. R. Anthony Lodge. Geneva: Droz, 1979.

Evans, Joan, ed. and trans. *The Unconquered Knight: A Chronicle of the Deeds of Don Pero Niño, Count of Buelna*. Rochester, N.Y.: Boydell, 2004.

Evans, Michael. "An Illustrated Fragment of Peraldus's *Summa* of Vice: Harlian MS 3244." *Journal of the Warburg and Courtauld Institutes* 45 (1982): 14–68.

Faire croire: Modalités de la diffusion et de la réception des messages religieux du XIIe au XVe siècle. Rome: École française de Rome, 1981.

Fantosme, Jordan. *Jordan Fantosme's Chronicle*. Ed. and trans. R. C. Johnston. New York: Oxford University Press, 1981.

Ferguson, Arthur B. *The Chivalric Tradition in Renaissance England*. London: Associated University Presses, 1986.

———. *The Indian Summer of English Chivalry: Studies in the Decline and Transformation of Chivalric Idealism*. Durham, N.C.: Duke University Press, 1960.

Finucane, Ronald C. *Miracles and Pilgrims: Popular Beliefs in Medieval England*. New York: St. Martin's, 1995.

Fitzneale, Richard. *Dialogus de Scaccario*. Ed. Charles Johnson. New York: Oxford University Press, 1950.

Flahiff, George B. "'Deus Non Vult': A Critic of the Third Crusade." *Mediaeval Studies* 9–10 (1947).

Flori, Jean. *L'Essor de la chevalerie, XIe–XIIe siècles*. Geneva: Droz, 1986.

———. *L'Idéologie du glaive: Préhistoire de la Chevalerie*. Geneva: Droz, 1983.

———. "*Pur eshalcier sainte crestïenté*. Croisade, guerre sainte, et guerre juste dans les anciennes chansons de geste française." *Moyen Âge* 97 (1991): 171–87.

———. *Richard Coeur de Lion, le roi cheavalier*. Paris: Payot & Rivages, 1999.

Foreville, Raymonde. *Latran I, II, III et Latran IV*. Histoire des conciles oecuméniques 6. Paris: Éditions de l'Orante, 1965.

Foster, Edward, ed. *Amis and Amiloun, Robert of Cisyle, and Sir Amadace*. Kalamazoo, Mich.: Medieval Institute Publications, 1997.

———. *Three Purgatory Poems*. Kalamazoo, Mich.: Medieval Institute Publications, 2004.

Foulet, Alfred, and Karl D. Uitti, eds. *Le Chevalier de la charette*. Paris: Bordas, 1989.

Fowler, Kenneth. *The King's Lieutenant: Henry of Grosmont, First Duke of Lancaster, 1316–1361*. London: Elek, 1969.

France, John. "Holy War and Holy Men: Erdmann and the Lives of the Saints." In *The Experience of Crusading*, vol. 1, *Western Approaches*, ed. Marcus Bull and Norman Housley, 193–208. Cambridge: Cambridge University Press, 2003.

Frantzen, Alan J. *Bloody Good: Chivalry, Sacrifice, and the Great War*. Chicago: University of Chicago Press, 2004.

———. *The Literature of Penance in Anglo-Saxon England*. New Brunswick, N.J.: Rutgers University Press, 1983.

Frappier, Jean. *Autour du Graal*. Geneva: Droz, 1977.

———. *Chrétien de Troyes et le mythe du Graal*. Paris: Société d'édition d'enseignement supérieur, 1972.

———. *Étude sur La Mort le Roi Artu, roman du XIIIe siècle, dernière partie du Lancelot en prose*. Geneva: E. Droz, 1961.

———. *La Mort le Roi Artu; roman du XIIIe siècle*. Paris: Droz, 1964.

Fulcher of Chartres. *A History of the Expedition to Jerusalem, 1095–1127*. Ed. Harold S. Fink, trans. Frances Rita Ryan. Knoxville: University of Tennessee Press, 1969.

Furnivale, F. J., ed. *Queene Elizabethes Achademy: A booke of precedence, The ordering of a funerall, &c. Varying versions of The good wife, The Wise man, &c. Maxims, Lydgate's Order of fools, A poem on heraldry, Occleve On lord's Men*. Early English Text Society e.s. 8. London: N. Trübner for Early English Text Society, 1869, 1898.

Gaffney, Wilbur. "The Allegory of the Christ-Knight in Piers Plowman." *Proceedings of the Modern Language Association* 46 (1931): 155–68.

Gautier de Coincy. *Les miracles de la Sainte Vierge*. Paris: l'Abbé Poquet, 1857. Reprinted Geneva: Slatkin, 1972.

Geary, Patrick. *Furta Sacra: Thefts of Relics in the Central Middle Ages*. Princeton, N.J.: Princeton University Press, 1990.

Geertz, Clifford. "Religion as a Cultural System." In *Anthropological Approaches to the Study of Religion*, ed. Michael Banton, 1–46. London: Tavistock, 1966.

Geoffrey of Monmouth. *The Historia regum Britannie of Geoffrey of Monmouth*. Ed. Neil Wright. Vol. 1, *Bern, Burgerbibliothek, MS. 568*, vol. 5, *Gestum regum Britannie*. Cambridge: D.S. Brewer, 1985, 1991.

Geoffroi de Charny. *Le livre de chevalerie*. Trans. in Richard W. Kaeuper and Elspeth Huxley, *The Book of Chivalry of Geoffroi de Charny: Text, Context, and Translation*. Philadelphia: University of Pennsylvania Press, 1996.

Gerald of Wales. *The Autobiography of Giraldus Cambrensis*. Ed. and trans. Harold Edgeworth Butler. London: Cape, 1937.

———. *The Jewel of the Church*. Trans. John Hagen. Leiden: Brill, 1979.

Godet, Marcel. "Consultation de Tours pour la réforme de l'église de France." *Révue de l'histoire de l'Église de France* 9 (1911): 175–86, 333–48.

Goller, Karl-Heinz. *The Alliterative Morte Arthure: A Reassessment of the Poem*. Cambridge: D.S. Brewer, 1981.

Goodich, Michael. *Violence and Miracle in the Fourteenth Century: Private Grief and Public Salvation*. Chicago: University of Chicago Press, 1995.

Gorringe, Timothy. *God's Just Vengeance: Crime, Violence, and the Rhetoric of Salvation*. New York: Cambridge University Press, 1996.

Gower, John. *Confessio Amantis*. 3 vols. Ed. Russell A. Peck, trans. Andrew Galloway. Kalamazoo, Mich.: Medieval Institute Publications, 2006.

Guillaume de Machaut. *La Prise d'Alixandre: The Capture of Alexandria*. Trans. and ed. Janet Shirley and Peter Edbury. Aldershot: Ashgate, 2001.

Gunn, Steven. "Chivalry and the Politics of the Early Tudor Court." In *Chivalry in the Renaissance*, ed. Sydney Anglo, 107–28. Rochester, N.Y.: Boydell, 1990.

———. "The French Wars of Henry VIII." In *The Origins of Early Modern Europe*, ed. Jeremy Black, 28–51. Edinburgh: John Donald, 1987.

Hahn, Thomas, ed. *Sir Gawain: Eleven Romances and Tales*. Kalamazoo, Mich.: Medieval Institute Publications, 1995.

Haigh, Christopher. *English Reformations: Religion, Politics and Society Under the Tudors*. Oxford: Clarendon Press, 1993.

Hall, Bert S. *Weapons and Warfare in Renaissance Europe: Gunpowder, Technology, and Tactics*. Baltimore: Johns Hopkins University Press, 1997.

Hall, Bert S., and Kelly DeVries. "Essay Review: The 'Military Revolution' Revisited." *Technology and Culture* 31 (1990): 500–507.

Hallam, Elizabeth. "Monasteries as 'War Memorials.'" In *Church and War*, ed. W. J. Sheils. Studies in Church History 20. Oxford: Blackwell for Ecclesiastical History Society, 1983.

Hamilton, Sara. "Penance in the Age of Gregorian Reform." In *Retribution, Repentance, and Reconciliation*, ed. Kate Cooper and Jeremy Gregory, 47–73. Studies in Church History 40. Woodbridge: Boydell and Brewer for Ecclesiastical History Society, 2004.

———. *The Practice of Penance: 900–1050*. Rochester, N.Y.: Boydell, 2001.

Hamm, Berndt. *The Reformation of Faith in the Context of Late Medieval Theology and Piety: Essays by Berndt Hamm*. Ed. Robert J. Bast. Boston: Brill, 2004.

Haren, Michael. *Sin and Society in Fourteenth-Century England: A Study of the Memoriale Presbitorum*. New York: Oxford University Press, 2000.

Harriss, G. L., ed. *Henry V: The Practice of Kingship*. New York: Oxford University Press, 1985.

Hasenfratz, Robert, ed. *Ancrene Wisse*. Kalamazoo, Mich.: Medieval Institute Publications, 2000.

Heinz-Göller, Karl, ed. *The Alliterative Morte Arthure: A Reassessment of the Poem*. Cambridge: D.S. Brewer, 1981.

Henry, duke of Lancaster. *Le Livre de seyntz medicines: The Unpublished Devotional Treatise of Henry of Lancaster*. Ed. E. J. Arnould. Anglo-Norman Text Society 2. Oxford: Blackwell for Anglo-Norman Text Society, 1940.

Herolt, Johann. *Miracles of the Blessed Virgin Mary*. Ed. and trans. C. C. Swinton Bland, intro. Eileen Power. New York: Harcourt, Brace, 1928.

Herrtage, Sidney J. H., ed. *The Early English Versions of the Gesta Romanorum*. London: Trübner for Early English Text Society, 1879.

Herzman, Ronald B., Graham Drake, and Eve Salisbury. *Four Romances of England: King Horn, Havelok the Dane, Bevis of Hampton, Athelston*. Kalamazoo, Mich.: Medieval Institute Publications, 1999.

Hill, Charles Leander, ed. *The Loci Communes of Philip Melanchthon*. Boston: Meador, 1944.

Himelick, Raymond, trans. *The Enchiridion of Erasmus*. Bloomington: Indiana University Press, 1963.

Holden, A. J., S. Gregory, and David Crouch, eds. *History of William Marshal*. 2 vols. London: Anglo-Norman Text Society for Birkbeck College, 2002–6.

Holt, J. C. *Magna Carta*. Cambridge: Cambridge University Press, 1965.

Hopkins, Andrea. *The Sinful Knights: A Study of Middle English Penitential Romance*. New York: Oxford University Press, 1990.

Housley, Norman. *Religious Warfare in Europe, 1400–1536*. Oxford: Oxford University Press, 2002.

Hoven, Birgit van den. *Work in Ancient and Medieval Thought: Ancient Philosophers, Medieval Monks and Theologians, and Their Concept of Work, Occupations, and Technology*. Amsterdam: J.C. Gieben, 1996.

Howlett, Richard. *Chronicles of the Reigns of Stephen, Henry II, and Richard I*. 4 vols. RS 82. London: Longman, 1884–89.

Hucher, Eugène, ed. *Le Saint Graal: ou, Le Joseph d'Arimathie, première branche des Romans de la Table Ronde, pub. d'après des texts et des documents inédits*. 3 vols. Le Mans: Monnoyer, 1875.

Hudson, Anne, ed. *Selections from English Wycliffite Writings*. Cambridge: Cambridge University Press, 1978.

Hudson, Harriet, ed. *Four Middle English Romances: Sir Isumbras, Octavian, Sir Eglamour of Artois, Sir Tryamour*. Kalamazoo, Mich.: Medieval Institute Publications, 1996.

Innes-Parker, Catherine. "The Lady and the King: Ancrene Wisse's Parable of the Royal Wooing Re-Examined." *English Studies* 25 (1994): 509–22.

Jacques de Vitry. *The Exempla or Illustrative Stories from the Sermones Vulgares of Jacques de Vitry*. Ed. Thomas Frederick Crane. London: Folk-lore Society, 1890. Reprint New York: B. Franklin, 1971.

———. "Sermones vulgares." In *Analecta novissima, Spicilegii Solesmensis altera continuatio*, ed. J.-B. Pitra, 2: 344–442. Paris: Tusculanis, 1885–88.

Jaeger, C. Stephen. *Origins of Courtliness: Civilizing Trends and the Formation of Courtly Ideals, 939–1210*. Philadelphia: University of Pennsylvania Press, 1985.

James, Mervyn. *Society, Politics, and Culture: Studies in Early Modern England*. New York: Cambridge University Press, 1986.

James, William. *The Varieties of Religious Experience*. New York: Collier, 1961.

Joinville, Jean de. *Histoire de Saint Louis*. Ed. M. Natalis de Wailly. Paris: J. Renouard, 1868.

John, Abbot of Ford. *Vita Wulfrici Haselbergiae--Wulfric of Haselbury, by John, Abbott of Ford*. Ed. Maurice Bell. Somerset Record Society 47. London: Somerset Record Society, 1933.

Jordan, William Chester. *Louis IX and the Challenge of the Crusade*. Princeton, N.J.: Princeton University Press, 1979.

———. "The Rituals of War: Departure for Crusade in Thirteenth-Century France." In *The Book of Kings: Art, War, and the Morgan Library's Picture Bible*, ed. William Noel and Daniel Weiss, 98–105. Baltimore: Third Millennium, 2002.

Jotischky, Andrew. "Penance and Reconciliation in the Crusader States." In *Retribution, Repentance and Reconciliation*, ed. Kate Cooper and Jeremy Gregory, 74–83. Studies in Church History 40. Woodbridge: Boydell and Brewer for Ecclesiastical History Society, 2004.

Jubinal, Achille. *Novel recueil de contes*. 2 vols. Paris: Pannier, 1839–42.

Kaelber, Lutz. *Schools of Asceticism: Ideology and Organization in Medieval Religious Communities*. University Park: Pennsylvania State University Press, 1998.

Kaeuper, Richard W. *Chivalry and Violence in Medieval Europe*. New York: Oxford University Press, 1999.

———. "Literature as the Key to Chivalric Ideology." *Journal of Medieval Military History* 4 (2006).

Katzir, Yael. "The Second Crusade and the Redefinition of *Ecclesia, Christianitas*, the Papal Coercive Power." In *The Second Crusade and the Cistercians*, ed. Michael Gervers, 3–13. New York: St. Martin's, 1992.

Kay, Sarah, ed. and trans. *Raoul de Cambrai*. New York: Oxford University Press, 1992.

Keen, Maurice Hugh. *Chivalry*. New Haven, Conn.: Yale University Press, 1984.

———. "War, Peace, and Chivalry." In Keen, *Nobles, Knights, and Men-at-Arms in the Middle Ages*, 9–20. London: Hambledon, 1996.

Kelly, Thomas. *Le Haut Livre du Graal: Perlesvaus, a Structural Study*. Geneva: Droz, 1974.

———. "Love in the Perlesvaus: Sinful Passion or Redemptive Force?" *Romanic Review* 66 (1975): 1–12.

Kennedy, Elspeth, ed. *Lancelot do Lac: The Non-Cyclic Old French Romance*. New York: Oxford University Press, 1980.

Kieckhefer, Richard. *Unquiet Souls: Fourteenth-Century Saints and Their Religious Milieu*. Chicago: University of Chicago Press, 1984.

Kinney, Clare R. "Chivalry Unmasked: Courtly Spectacle and the Abuses of Romance in Sidney's 'New Arcadia'." *Studies in English Literature, 1500–1900* 35 (1995): 35–52.

Knight, I. I. K. *Wimbledon's Sermon: Redde Rationem Villicationis tue: A Middle English Sermon of the Fourteenth Century*. Duquesne Studies, Philological Series 9. Pittsburgh: Duquesne University Press, 1967.

Knowles, David. "Archbishop Thomas Becket: A Character Study." *Proceedings of the British Academy* 35 (1946): 197.

Koch, Sister M. P. *An Analysis of the Long Prayers in Old French Literature with Special Reference to the "Biblical-Creed-Narrative Prayers"*. Washington, D.C.: Catholic University of America Press, 1940.

Labande, E. R. "Le Credo Épique: à propos des prières dans les chansons de geste." In *Recueil de travaux offerts a Clovis Brunnel*, 62–80. Paris: École de Chartes, 1955.

La Bigne, Marguerin de, ed. *Maxima bibliotheca vetervm patrvm*. Lyons, 1677.

Lacy, Norris, ed. *Lancelot-Grail: The Old French Arthurian Vulgate and Post-Vulgate in Translation*. 5 vols. New York: Garland, 1993–96.

———. "Warmongering in Les Voeux du Heron." In *Inscribing the Hundred Years' War in French and English Cultures*, ed. Denise N. Baker, 17–27. Albany: State University of New York Press, 2000.

Lambert of Ardres. *The History of the Counts of Guines and Lords of Ardres*. Ed. Leah Shopkow. Philadelphia: University of Pennsylvania Press, 2001.

Lancaster. See Henry, duke of Lancaster.

Langlois, Ernest, ed. *Couronnement de Louis*. Paris: H. Champion, 1969.

Larsen, Andrew. "Are All Lollards Lollards?" In *Lollards and Their Influence in Late Medieval England*, ed. Fiona Somerset, Jill C. Evans, and Derek G. Pitard, 59–73. Rochester, N.Y.: Boydell, 2003.

Laskaya, Anne, and Eve Salisbury. *The Middle English Breton Lays*. Kalamazoo, Mich.: Medieval Institute Publications, 1995.

Lawrence, C. H. *The Friars: The Impact of the Early Mendicant Movement on Western Society*. New York: Longman, 1994.

Lea, Charles Henry. *A History of Auricular Confession and Indulgences in the Latin Church*. New York: Greenwood, 1968.

Leclercq, Jean, ed. "Un document sur les debuts des Templiers." In *Receuil d'études sur Saint Bernard* 2: 87–99. Rome: Apud Curiam Generalem Sacri Ordinis Cisterciensis, 1966.

Lecoy, Felix, ed. *Le Chevalier au barissel: Conte Pieux du XIIIe siècle*. Paris: H. Champion, 1955.

———, ed. *Le Roman de la Rose*. 3 vols. Paris: H. Champion, 1965.

Legge, M. Dominica. *Anglo-Norman Literature and Its Background*. Oxford: Clarendon Press, 1963.

Le Goff, Jacques. *The Birth of Purgatory*. Trans. Arthur Goldhammer. Chicago: University of Chicago Press, 1984.

———. *Pour un autre Moyen Âge: temps, travail et culture en occident: 18 essais*. Paris: Gallimard, 1979.

Le Goff, Jacques, J. C. Schmitt, and Claude Bremond. *L'Exemplum*. Turnhout: Brepols, 1982.

Lemaitre, Jean-Loup. "Les miracles de saint Martial accomplis lors de l'ostention de 1388." *Bulletin de la Société archéologique et historique du limousin* 102 (1975): 67–139.

Le May, Sister Marie de Lourdes. *The Allegory of the Christ-Knight in English Literature*. Washington, D.C.: Catholic University of America, 1932.

Le Merrer-False, Madeleine. "Contribution à une étude du Chevalier au Barisel." *Le Moyen Âge* 77 (1971): 263–75.

Levine, Robert. *The deeds of God through the Franks: a translation of Guibert de Nogent's Gesta Dei per Francos*. Woodbridge: Boydell Press, 1997.

Lewis, P. S. *Later Medieval France: The Polity.* New York: St. Martin's Press, 1968.

Leyser, Karl. "Early Medieval Canon Law and the Beginnings of Knighthood." In *Communications and Power in Medieval Europe: The Carolingian and Ottonian Centuries,* ed. Timothy Reuter, 51–71. London: Hambledon, 1994.

———. "Warfare in the Western European Middle Ages: The Moral Debate." In *Communications and Power,* ed. Reuter, 189–203.

Livermore, Harold. "The 'Conquest of Lisbon' and Its Author." *Portuguese Studies* 6 (1990): 1–16.

Llull, Ramon. *Libre que es de l'ordre de cavalleria.* In *Obres Essencials,* vol. 1, ed. Pere Bohigas. Barcelona: Editorial Selecta, 1957.

———. *Livre de l'ordre de chevalerie.* Ed. Vicenzo Minervini. Bari: Adriatica, 1971.

———. *Obres Essencials.* 2 vols. Barcelona, 1957–60.

Löseth, Eilert, ed. *Robert le Diable: Roman d'aventures.* Paris: Firmin Didot, 1903.

Lower, Michael. *The Barons' Crusade: A Call to Arms and Its Consequences.* Philadelphia: University of Pennsylvania Press, 2005.

Lupack, Alan, ed. *Three Middle English Charlemagne Romances.* Kalamazoo, Mich.: Medieval Institute Publications, 1990.

Luther, Martin. *Christian Liberty.* Trans. W. A. Lambert, rev. Harold J. Grimm. Philadelphia: Fortress Press, 1957.

Lydgate, John. *Troy Book: Selections.* Ed. Robert R. Edwards. Kalamazoo, Mich.: Medieval Institute Publications, 1998.

Lynn, John A. *Giant of the Grand Siècle: The French Army, 1610–1715.* Cambridge: Cambridge University Press, 1997.

———. "Recalculating French Army Growth During the Grand Siècle." *French Historical Studies* 18 (1994): 881–906.

———. "The Trace Italienne and the Growth of Armies: The French Case." *Journal of Military History* 55 (1991): 297–330.

Macculloch, Diarmaid. *The Reformation.* New York: Viking, 2004.

Maier, Christoph. *Crusade Propaganda and Ideology: Model Sermons for the Preaching of the Cross.* New York: Cambridge University Press, 2000.

Mallet, Michael. "Condottieri and Captains in Renaissance Italy." In *The Chivalric Ethos and the Development of Military Professionalism,* ed. D. J. B. Trim, 67–89. Leiden: Brill, 2003.

Malory. *Malory: Works.* Ed. Eugene Vinaver. Oxford: Clarendon Press, 1971.

Mansfield, Mary. *The Humiliation of Sinners: Public Penance in Thirteenth-Century France.* Ithaca, N.Y.: Cornell University Press, 1995.

Map, Walter. *De Nugis Curialium.* Ed. and trans. M. R. James, rev. C. N. L. Brooke and R. A. Mynors. New York: Oxford University Press, 1983.

———. *Master Walter Map's Book, De nugis curialium.* Trans. Frederick Tupper and Marbury Bladen Ogle. New York: Macmillan, 1924.

Marchant, Jean Le. *Miracles de Notre-Dame de Chartres.* Ed. Pierre Kunstmann. Ottawa: Éditions de l'Université d'Ottawa, 1973.

Martin-Chabot, Eugène, ed. *La Chanson de la croisade albigeoise*. Paris: Belles Lettres, 1972.

Marty, Martin E., and Jerald C. Brauer, eds. *The Unresolved Paradox: Studies in the Theology of Franz Bibfeldt*. Grand Rapids, Mich.: Eerdmans, 1994.

Marx, C. W. *The Devil's Rights and the Redemption in the Literature of Medieval England*. Cambridge: D.S. Brewer, 1995.

Matarasso, P. M. *The Quest of the Holy Grail*. Baltimore: Penguin, 1977.

McCoy, Richard. *Rites of Knighthood: The Literature and Politics of Elizabethan Chivalry*. Berkeley: University of California Press, 1989.

McFarlane, K. B. *John Wyclif and the Beginnings of English Nonconformity*. London: English University Press, 1966.

———. *Lancastrian Kings and Lollard Knights*. Oxford: Clarendon Press, 1972.

McNab, Bruce. "Obligations of the Church in English Society: Military Arrays of the Clergy, 1369–1418." In *Order and Innovation in the Middle Ages*, ed. William C. Jordan, Bruce McNab, and Teofilo F. Ruiz, 293–314. Princeton, N.J.: Princeton University Press, 1976.

Meens, Rob. "The Frequency and Nature of Confession in the Early Middle Ages." In *Handling Sin: Confession in the Middle Ages*, ed. Peter Biller and A. J. Minnis, 35–61. Rochester, N.Y.: York Medieval Press, 1998.

Ménard, Philippe. "L'esprit de la croisade chez Joinville." In *Les Champenois et la croisade: Actes des Quatrièmes Journées Rémoises, 27–28 novembre 1987*, ed. Yvonne Bellenger and Danielle Quéruel, 131–47. Paris: Aux amateurs de livres, 1989.

Merback, Mitchell. *The Thief, the Cross, and the Wheel*. Chicago: University of Chicago Press, 1999.

Meyer, Paul. "Notice et extraits du MS 8336 de la Bibliothèque du Sir Thomas Phillipps a Cheltenham." *Romania* 13 (1884): 497–541.

Micha, Alexandre, ed. *Lancelot: Roman en prose du 13e siècle*. Geneva: Droz, 1978.

Michaud-Quantin, Pierre. *Sommes de casuistique et manuels de confession au moyen âge*. Louvain: Nauwelets, 1962.

Milles, Thomas. *The Catalogue of Honour or Treasure of True Nobility*. London: William Iaggard, 1610.

Millett, Bella. *Annotated Bibliography of Old and Middle English Literature*. Vol. 2, *Ancrene Wisse, The Katherine Group, and the Wooing Group*. Cambridge: D.S. Brewer, 1996.

Mills, Maldwyn, ed. *Lybeaus desconus*. London: Oxford University Press for Early English Text Society, 1969.

Mirk, John. *Mirk's Festial: A Collection of Homilies by Johannes Mirkus (John Mirk)*. Ed. Theodore Erbe. London: K. Paul, Trench, Trübner, 1905.

Moore, John C. *Pope Innocent III: To Root Up and to Plant*. Boston: Brill, 2003.

Morawski, Joseph, ed. *Proverbes français antérieurs au XVe siècle*. Paris: É. Champion, 1925.

More, Thomas. *Utopia*. Ed. Edward Surtz. New Haven, Conn.: Yale University Press, 1964.

Morris, Colin. "Propaganda for War: The Dissemination of the Crusading Ideal in the Twelfth Century." In *Church and War*, ed. W. J. Sheils, 79–101. Studies in Church History 20. Oxford: Blackwell for Ecclesiastical History Society, 1983.

Morris, Richard, ed. *The Pricke of Conscience: A Northumbrian Poem*. Berlin: A. Asher for Philological Society, 1863.

Mowbray, Donald. "The Development of Ideas About Pain and Suffering in the Works of Thirteenth-Century Masters of Theology at Paris, c. 1230–c. 1300." Ph.D. dissertation, Bristol University, 1999.

Mullally, Evelyn, ed. and trans. *The Deeds of the Normans in Ireland*. Portland, Ore.: Four Courts, 2002.

Murray, Alexander. "Confession as a Historical Source in the Thirteenth Century." In *The Writing of History in the Middle Ages: Essays Presented to Richard William Southern*, ed. R. H. C. Davis and J. M. Wallace-Hadrill, 275–322. New York: Oxford University Press, 1981.

———. "Confession Before 1215." *Transactions of the Royal Historical Society* 6th ser. 3 (1992): 51–81.

Musto, Ronald. "Just Wars and Evil Empires: Erasmus and the Turks." In *Renaissance Society and Culture: Essays in Honor of Eugene F. Rice*, ed. John Monfasani and Ronald G. Musto, 197–216. New York: Italica Press, 1991.

Newman, William Mendel, ed. *The Cartulary and Charters of Notre-Dame of Homblières*. Cambridge, Mass.: Medieval Academy of America, 1990.

Newth, Michael, trans. *Aymeri of Narbonne: A French Epic Romance*. New York: Italica Press, 2005.

———, trans. *The Song of Aspremont: La Chanson d'Aspremont*. New York: Garland, 1989.

Nichols, Ann Eljenholm. "The Etiquette of Pre-Reformation Confession in East Anglia." *Sixteenth Century Journal* 17 (1986): 145–63.

Nicholson, Helen, ed. *Chronicle of the Third Crusade: A Translation of The Itinerarium Peregrinorum et Gesta Regis Ricardi*. Brookfield, Vt.: Ashgate, 1997.

———. *Love, War, and the Grail*. Leiden: Brill, 2001.

Nitze, William A., and T. Atkinson Jenkins, eds. *Le Haut Livre du Graal: Perlesvaus*. Chicago: University of Chicago Press, 1932.

Nolcken, Christina von. "Richard Wyche, a Certain Knight, and the Beginning of the End." In *Lollardy and the Gentry in the Later Middle Ages*, ed. Margaret Aston and Colin Richmond, 127–55. New York: St. Martin's, 1997.

La Tour Landry, Geoffroy de. *The Book of the Knight of the Tower. Translated by William Caxton*. Ed. M. Y. Offord. Oxford: Oxford University Press for Early English Text Society, 1971.

O'Loughlin, Thomas. "Penitence and Pastoral Care." In *A History of Pastoral Care*, ed. G. R. Evans, 93–111. London: Cassell, 2000.

Orderic Vitalis. *Ecclesiastical History of Orderic Vitalis*. 6 vols. Ed. and trans. Marjorie Chibnall. Oxford: Oxford University Press, 1969–80.

Orpen, Goddard Henry, ed., trans. *The Song of Dermot and the Earl*. Oxford: Clarendon Press, 1892.

Ovitt, George, Jr. *The Restoration of Perfection: Labor and Technology in Medieval Culture*. New Brunswick, N.J.: Rutgers University Press, 1987.

Owen, D. D. R. *The Vision of Hell: Infernal Journeys in Medieval French Literature*. New York: Barnes & Noble, 1970.

Padoa-Schioppa, Antonio, ed. *Legislation and Justice*. Oxford: Clarendon Press, 1997.

Pantin, W. A. *The English Church in the Fourteenth Century*. Cambridge: Cambridge University Press, 1955.

Paris, Gaston, and Jacob Ulrich, eds. *Merlin: Roman en prose du XIIIe siècle*. 2 vols. Paris: Firmin Didot, 1886.

Paris, Matthew. *Chronicles of Matthew Paris: Monastic Life in the Thirteenth Century*. Trans. Richard Vaughan. New York: St. Martin's, 1984.

———. *Matthæi Parisiensis, monachi Sancti Albani, Chronica majora*. Ed. Henry Richards Luard. 7 vols. RS 57. London: Longman, 1872–84.

Parker, Geoffrey. "The 'Military Revolution' 1550–1660—a Myth?" *Journal of Modern History* 48 (June 1976): 195–214.

———. *The Military Revolution: Military Innovation and the Rise of the West, 1500–1800*. 2nd ed. Cambridge: Cambridge University Press, 1996.

Parrot, David A. "Strategy and Tactics in the Thirty Years' War: The 'Military Revolution'." In *The Military Revolution Debate: Readings on the Military Transformation of Early Modern Europe*, ed. Clifford Rogers, 227–51. Boulder, Colo.: Westview Press, 1995.

Pauphilet, Albert. *Le Queste del Saint Graal: Roman du XIIIe siècle*. Paris: Champion, 1923, 1949.

Payen, Jean-Charles. "La pénitence dans le contexte culturel des XIIe et XIIIe siècles." *Revue des Sciences Philosophiques et Théologiques* 61 (1977): 399–428.

———. "Structures et sens du 'Chevalier au Barisel.'" *Moyen Âge* 77 (1971): 239–62.

Perrot, Jean-Pierre. "Le 'péché' de Joinville: écriteur du souvenir et imaginaire hagiographique." In *Le prince et son historien: la vie de Saint Louis de Joinville*, ed. Jean Doufournet and Laurence Harf, 196–98. Paris: Champion, 1997.

Perry, A. J., ed. *Dialogus inter Militem et Clericum: Richard FitzRalph's Sermon: "Defensio curatorum" and Methodius: "Þe bygynnyng of þe world and þe ende of worldes," by John Trevisa, vicar of Berkeley*. London: Oxford University Press / H. Milford for Early English Text Society, 1925.

Peter of Blois. *The Later Letters of Peter of Blois*. Ed. Elizabeth Revell. Oxford: Oxford University Press, 1993.

———. *Patres Ecclesiae Anglicanae: Petri Blesensis Bathoniensis Archidiaconi Opera Omnia: nunc Primum in Anglia Ope Codicum Manuscriptorum Editionumque Optimarum*. Ed. J. A. Giles. Oxford, 1847–88.

Peter of Langtoft. *The Chronicle of Pierre Langtoft, in French Verse from the Earliest Period to the Death of King Edward I*. Ed. Thomas Wright. RS 47. London: Longman, Green, Reader, and Dyer, 1866–68.

Peter of les Vaux-de-Cernay. *The History of the Albigensian Crusade: Peter of les Vaux-de-Cernay's Historia Albigensis*. Trans. W. A. Sibly and M. D. Sibly. Rochester, N.Y.: Boydell, 1998.

————. *Petri Vallium Sarnaii monachi Hystoria albigensis.* Ed. Pascal Guébin and Ernest Lyon. 3 vols. Paris: Champion, 1926–39.

Petitot, M., ed. *Collection complète des mémoires relatifs à l'histoire de France.* Vol. 14. Paris: Foucault, 1820.

Phillips, Jonathan. Introduction to *De Expugnatione Lyxbonensi,* ed. and trans. Charles Wendell David. New York: Columbia University Press, 2000.

————. "Ideas of Crusade and Holy War in *De Expugnatione Lyxbonensi* (The Conquest of Lisbon)." In *The Holy Land, Holy Lands, and Christian History,* ed. R. N. Swanson, 123–41. Studies in Church History 36. Rochester, N.Y.: Boydell, 2000.

Phillips, M. M. *The "Adages" of Erasmus: A Study with Translations.* Cambridge: Cambridge University Press, 1964.

Piel, Joseph-Maria, ed. *A Demando do Santo Graal.* Lisbon: Impr. Nacional-Casa da Moeda, 1988.

Pincikowski, Scott. *Bodies in Pain: Suffering in the Works of Hartmann von Aue.* New York: Routledge, 2002.

Pollard, J. A. F. "Knightly Piety and the Margins of Lollardy." In *Lollardy and the Gentry in the Later Middle Ages,* ed. Margaret Aston and Colin Richmond, 95–112. New York: St. Martin's, 1997.

Poole, Austin Lane. *From Domesday Book to Magna Carta, 1087–1216.* Oxford: Clarendon Press, 1955.

Pontfarcy, Yolande de, and Jean-Michael Picard, trans. *Saint Patrick's Purgatory: A Twelfth Century Tale of a Journey to the Other World.* Dublin: Four Courts Press, 1985.

Porter, J. M. B. "Preacher of the First Crusade? Robert of Arbrissel After the Council of Clermont." In *From Clermont to Jerusalem: The Crusades and Crusader Societies, 1095–1500,* 43–52. International Medieval Research 3. Turnhout: Brepols, 1995.

Potter, David. "Chivalry and Professionalism in the French Armies of the Renaissance." In *The Chivalric Ethos and the Development of Military Professionalism,* ed. D. J. B . Trim, 149–82. Leiden: Brill, 2003.

————. *A History of France, 1460–1560: The Emergence of a Nation State.* New York: St. Martin's Press, 1995.

Powell, Edward. *Kingship, Law, and Society: Criminal Justice in the Reign of Henry V.* New York: Oxford University Press, 1989.

Powell, James M. *Anatomy of a Crusade, 1213–1221.* Philadelphia: University of Pennsylvania Press, 1986.

Power, Daniel. *The Norman Frontier in the Twelfth and Early Thirteenth Centuries.* Cambridge: Cambridge University Press, 2004.

Prestwich, Michael. *Armies and Warfare in the Middle Ages: The English Experience.* New Haven, Conn.: Yale University Press, 1996.

————. *Edward I.* New Haven, Conn.: Yale University Press, 1997.

Price, Glanville, ed. *William, Count of Orange: Four Old French Epics.* Trans. Glanville Price, Lynette Muir, and David Hoggan. London: Rowman and Littlefield, 1975.

Price, Richard. "Informal Penance in Early Medieval Christendom." In *Retribution, Repentance, and Reconciliation,* ed. Kate Cooper and Jeremy Gregory, 29–38. Studies in Church History 40. Woodbridge: Boydell and Brewer for Ecclesiastical History Society, 2004.

Quéruel, Danielle, ed. *Jean de Joinville: de la Champagne aux royaumes d'outre-mer.* Langres: Dominique Guéniot, 1998.

Rasler, Karen, and William R. Thompson, *War and State Making: The Shaping of the Global Powers.* Boston: Unwin Hyman, 1989.

Rex, Richard. *The Lollards.* New York: Palgrave, 2002.

Ridder-Symoens, Hilde de. "Training and Professionalization." In *Power Elites and State Building*, ed. Wolfgang Reinhard. Oxford: Clarendon Press, 1996.

Riley-Smith, Jonathan. *The Crusades, Idea and Reality, 1095–1274.* London: E. Arnold, 1981.

——. *The First Crusade and the Idea of Crusading.* London: Athlone Press, 1986.

Robert Mannyng. *Handlyng Synne.* Ed. Idelle Sullens. Binghamton, N.Y.: Medieval and Renaissance Texts and Studies, 1983.

——. *Handlyng Synne.* Ed. Frederick J. Furnivall. London: J.B. Nichols and Sons, 1862.

Robert of Flamborough. *Liber Poenitentialis.* Ed. J. J. Francis Firth. Toronto: Pontifical Institute of Mediaeval Studies, 1971.

Roberts, Michael. "The Military Revolution, 1560–1660." In *The Military Revolution Debate: Readings on the Military Transformation of Early Modern Europe*, ed. Clifford Rogers, 13–37. Boulder, Colo.: Westview Press, 1995.

Robinson, I. S. *The Papal Reform of the Eleventh Century: Lives of Pope Leo IX and Pope Gregory VII.* New York: Manchester University Press, 2004.

Rogers, Clifford. "The Military Revolutions of the Hundred Years War." *Journal of Military History* 57 (1993): 241–78.

——. *The Military Revolution Debate: Readings on the Military Transformation of Early Modern Europe.* Boulder, Colo.: Westview Press, 1995.

——. *The Wars of Edward III.* Rochester, N.Y.: Boydell Press, 1999.

Rollason, D. W. "The Miracles of St. Benedict: A Window on Early Medieval France." In *Studies in Medieval History Presented to R. H. C. Davis*, ed. Henry Mayr-Harting and R. I. Moore, 73–90. London: Hambledon Press, 1985.

Rolle, Richard. *The Contra Amatores Mundi of Richard Rolle.* Ed. and trans. Paul F. Theiner. Berkeley: University of California Press, 1968.

Roques, Mario, ed. *Le Roman de Renart.* Paris: H. Champion, 1948.

Rosenberg, Samuel N., trans. *Lancelot, Part III.* In *Lancelot-Grail: The Old French Vulgate and Post-Vulgate in Translation*, vol. 2, ed. Norris Lacy. New York: Garland, 1993.

Ross, Woodburn O., ed. *Middle English Sermons.* London: Oxford University Press / H. Milford for Early English Text Society, 1940.

Round, J. H. *Calendar of Documents Preserved in France.* London: HMSO, 1899.

Roussineau, Gilles, ed. *La Suite du roman de Merlin.* 2 vols. Geneva: Droz, 1996.

Rubellin, Michel. "Vision de la sociéte chrétienne à travers la confession et la penitence au IXe siècle." In *Pratiques de la confession*, ed. Groupe de la Bussière, 53–70. Paris: Cerf, 1983.

Rubenson, Samuel. "Christian Asceticism." In *Asceticism*, ed. Vincent Wimbush and Richard Valentasis, 48–57. New York: Oxford University Press, 1998.

Rubin, Miri. "Choosing Death? Experiences of Martyrdom in Late Medieval Europe." In *Martyrs and Martyrologies*, ed. Diana Wood, 153–83. Studies in Church History 30. Oxford: Blackwell for Ecclesiastical History Society, 1993.

———. *Corpus Christi: The Eucharist in Late Medieval Culture*. Cambridge: Cambridge University Press, 1991.

Scarisbrick, J. J. *Henry VIII*. Berkeley: University of California Press, 1968.

———. *The Reformation and the English People*. Oxford: Blackwell, 1984.

Scattergood, V. J., ed. *The Works of Sir John Clanvowe*. Cambridge: D.S. Brewer, 1975.

Schieder, Theodor. *Friedrich der Grosse*. Ed. and trans. Sabina Berkeley and H. M. Scott. New York: Longman, 2000.

Schmidt, A. V. C., and Nicholas Jacobs. *Middle English Romances*. New York: Holmes & Meier, 1980.

Schnerb-Lievre, Marion, ed. *Le Songe du vergier*. Paris: CNRS, 1982.

Shaw, Judith. "The Influence of Canonical and Episcopal Reform on Popular Books of Instruction." In *The Popular Literature of Medieval England*, ed. Thomas Heffernan, 44–60. Knoxville: University of Tennessee Press, 1985.

Shaw, M. R. B., ed. and trans. *Joinville and Villehardouin: Chronicles of the Crusades*. Baltimore: Penguin, 1963.

Shinners, John, and William Dohar. *Pastors and the Care of Souls in Medieval England*. Notre Dame, Ind.: University of Notre Dame Press, 1998.

Shirley, Janet, ed. and trans. *Song of the Cathar Wars: A History of the Albigensian Crusade*. Brookfield, Vt.: Ashgate, 1996.

Shopkow, Leah. *History and Community: Norman Historical Writing in the Eleventh and Twelfth Centuries*. Washington, D.C.: Catholic University of America Press, 1997.

Siberry, Elizabeth. *Criticism of Crusading, 1095–1274*. Oxford: Clarendon Press, 1985.

Slack, Corliss Konwisser, ed., and Hugh Bernard Feiss, trans. *Crusade Charters 1138–1270*. Tempe: Arizona Center for Medieval and Renaissance Studies, 2001.

Smith, Caroline. *Crusading in the Age of Joinville*. Burlington, Vt.: Ashgate, 2006.

Sommer, H. Oskar. *Die Abenteur Gawains Ywains und Le Marholts mit den drei Frauen*. Zeitschrift für Romanische Philologie 47. Halle: Niemeyer, 1913.

———, ed. *The Vulgate Version of the Arthurian Romances, ed. from Manuscripts in the British Museum*. Washington, D.C.: Carnegie Institution, 1908–16.

Southern, R. W. *Saint Anselm: A Portrait in a Landscape*. Cambridge: Cambridge University Press, 1990.

———. *Western Society and the Church in the Middle Ages*. Harmondsworth: Penguin, 1970.

Strayer, J. R. *The Albigensian Crusades*. Ann Arbor: University of Michigan Press, 1992.

———. *On the Medieval Origins of the Modern State*. Princeton, N.J.: Princeton University Press, 1970.

———. *The Reign of Philip the Fair*. Princeton, N.J.: Princeton University Press, 1980.

Strickland, Matthew. *War and Chivalry: The Conduct and Perception of War in England and Normandy, 1066–1217*. New York: Cambridge University Press, 1996.

Strohm, Paul. *England's Empty Throne: Usurpation and the Language of Legitimation, 1399–1422*. New Haven, Conn.: Yale University Press, 1998.

Stubbs, William. *Chronicles and Memorials of Reign of Richard I*. 2 vols. RS 38. London: Longman, Green, Longman, Roberts, and Green, 1864–65.

Strubel, Armand. "Joinville, historien de la croisade?" In *Les Champenois et la croisade: Actes des Quatrièmes Journées Rémoises, 27–28 novembre 1987*, ed. Yvonne Bellenger and Danielle Quéruel, 14–56. Paris: Aux amateurs de livres, 1989.

Suard, François, ed. *Chanson de Guillaume*. Paris: Bordas, 1991.

Suger, Abbot. *The Deeds of Louis the Fat*. Ed. and trans. Richard Cusimano and John Moorhead. Washington, D.C.: Catholic University of America Press, 1992.

————. *Vie de Louis VI le Gros*. Ed. Henri Waquet. Paris: H. Champion, 1929.

Sweetman, Robert. "Thomas of Cantimpré, Mulieres Religiosae, and Purgatorial Piety: Hagiographical Vitae and the Beguine 'Voice.'" In *A Distinct Voice: Medieval Studies in Honor of Leonard E. Boyle*, ed. Jacqueline Brown and William P. Stoneman, 606–29. South Bend, Ind.: University of Notre Dame Press, 1997.

Tanner, Norman P., ed. *Decrees of the Ecumenical Councils*. Washington, D.C.: Georgetown University Press, 1990.

Tavormina, M. Teresa. "Henry of Lancaster, *The Book of Holy Medicines*." In *Cultures of Piety: Medieval English Devotional Literature in Translation*, ed. Anne Clark Bartlett and Thomas H. Bestul, 19–41. Ithaca, N.Y.: Cornell University Press, 1999.

Tentler, Thomas. *Sin and Confession on the Eve of the Reformation*. Princeton, N.J.: Princeton University Press, 1977.

Thomas à Kempis. *The Imitation of Christ*. London: Sheed and Ward, 1978.

Thomas of Cantimpré. *Bonum universale de apibus*. Ed. Georgius Colvenerius. Douai: Lusei, 1597.

Thomas de Chobham. *Summa Confessorum*. Ed. F. Broomfield. Louvain: Éditions Nauwelaerts, 1968.

Thompson, J. A. F. "Knightly Piety and the Margins of Lollardy." In *Lollardy and the Gentry in the Later Middle Ages*, ed. Margaret Aston and Colin Richmond. New York: St. Martin's Press, 1997.

Throop, Palmer A. *Criticism of the Crusade: A Study of Public Opinion and Crusade Propaganda*. Philadelphia: Porcupine Press, 1975.

Thurley, Simon. *Hampton Court: A Social and Architectural History*. New Haven, Conn.: Yale University Press, 2003.

Tilly, Charles. *Coercion, Capital, and European States, AD 990–1990*. Cambridge, Mass.: Blackwell, 1990.

Tolkien, J. R. R., ed. *The English Text of the Ancrene Riwle*. London: Oxford University Press for Early English Text Society, 1962.

Trim, D. J. B., ed. *The Chivalric Ethos and the Development of Military Professionalism*. Leiden: Brill, 2003.

Tuffrau, Paul, ed. *La legende de Guillaume d'Orange*. Paris: Édition d'art, 1947.

Tusseau, Jean Pierre. *La Prise d'Orange*. Paris: Klincksieck, 1972.

Tyerman, Christopher. *England and the Crusades, 1095–1588*. Chicago: University of Chicago Press, 1988.

———. *Fighting for Christendom: Holy Wars and the Crusades*. New York: Oxford University Press, 2004.

Vale, Malcolm. *The Princely Court: Medieval Courts and Culture in North-West Europe, 1270–1380*. Oxford: Oxford University Press, 2001.

———. *War and Chivalry: Warfare and Aristocratic Culture in England, France, and Burgundy at the End of the Middle Ages*. Athens: University of Georgia Press, 1981.

Vauchez, André. *The Laity in the Middle Ages: Religious Beliefs and Devotional Practices*. Notre Dame, Ind.: University of Notre Dame Press, 1993.

Vergil, Polydore. *The Anglica Historia*. Ed. Denys Hay. London: Royal Historical Society, 1950.

Verkamp, Bernard J. *The Moral Treatment of Returning Warriors in Early Medieval and Modern Times*. Scranton, Pa.: University of Scranton Press, 1993.

Vogel, Cyrille. *Les "Libri paenitentales"*. Turnhout: Brepols, 1978.

———. *Pécheur et pénitence au Moyen Âge*. Paris: Cerf, 1969.

Waldron, R. W. "Langland's Originality: The Christ-Knight and the Harrowing of Hell." In *Medieval English Religious and Ethical Literature: Essays in Honour of G. H. Russell*, ed. Gregory Kratzmann and James Simpson, 66–81. Cambridge: D.S. Brewer, 1986.

Ward, Benedicta. *Miracles and the Medieval Mind: Theory, Record, and Event, 1000–1215*. Philadelphia: University of Pennsylvania Press, 1982.

Warner, Lawrence. "Jesus the Jouster: The Christ-Knight and Medieval Theories of the Atonement in *Piers Plowman* and the 'Round Table' Sermons." *Yearbook of Langland Studies* 10 (1996): 129–43.

Weiss, Judith. *Wace's Roman de Brut: A History of the British*. Exeter: University of Exeter Press, 2002.

Wenzel, Siegfried. *Fasciculus Morum: A Fourteenth-Century Preacher's Handbook*. University Park: Pennsylvania State University Press, 1989.

———. *Preachers, Poets, and the Early English Lyric*. Princeton, N.J.: Princeton University Press, 1986.

Whiteford, Peter, ed. *The Myracles of Oure Lady*. Heidelberg: C. Winter, 1990.

Wilks, Michael. "Wyclif and the Great Persecution." In *Prophecy and Eschatology*, ed. Michael Wilks, 39–63. Studies in Church History Subsidia 10. Cambridge, Mass.: Blackwell for Ecclesiastical History Society, 1994.

William of Malmesbury. *Gesta regum anglorum*. Ed. and trans. R. A. B. Mynors, Rodney M. Thomson, and Michael Winterbottom. New York: Oxford University Press, 1998.

———. *Historia Novella: The Contemporary History*. Ed. Edmund King, trans. K. R. Potter. Oxford: Clarendon Press, 1998.

William of Newburgh. *The History of English Affairs*. Ed. and trans. P. G. Walsh and M. J. Kennedy. Warminster: Aris & Phillips, c.1988–c.2007.

William of Tudela, *The Song of Cathar Wars: a History of the Albigensian Crusade*. Ed. And trans. Janet Shirley. Aldershot: Ashgate.

Wolf, Kenneth Baxter, ed. and trans. *Deeds of Count Roger of Calabria and Sicily and of His Brother Duke Robert*. Ann Arbor: University of Michigan Press, 2005.

Woolf, Rosemary. "Doctrinal Influences on the Dream of the Rood." *Medium Aevum* 28 (1958): 137–53.

———. "The Theme of Christ the Lover-Knight in Medieval English Literature." *Review of English Studies* n.s. 13 (1962): 1–16.

Wright, Thomas. *The Historical Works of Geraldus Cambrensis*. London: George Bell, 1887.

———. *Political Poems and Songs: Relating to English History, Composed During the Period from the Accession of Edward III to That of Richard III*. London: Longman, Green, Longman, and Roberts, and Green, 1859–61.

———. *A Selection of Latin Stories, from Manuscripts of the Thirteenth and Fourteenth Centuries: A Contribution to the History of Fiction During the Middle Ages*. London: T. Richards for Percy Society, 1842.

Yeandle, Frederic G., ed. *Girart de Vienne, Chanson de Geste*. New York: Columbia University Press, 1930.

Zupitza, Julius. *The Romance of Guy of Warwick*. London: Oxford University Press for Early English Text Society, 1966.

INDEX

ACKNOWLEDGMENTS

Adequately thanking all who assisted me in writing this book would require a small companion volume; yet my genuine gratitude and a sense of justice require some acknowledgment of help, however general and inadequate. Through an imaginative program within my own academic department, a veritable *mesnie* of able undergraduate student research assistants (too numerous to mention by name) contributed time and talents and used their keen eyesight to supplement and correct my own vision, severely troubled by retinal disease. On this score, doctors of the medical variety earned more gratitude than I can express: my heartfelt thanks to Steven Rose and Paul Caito. Among undergraduate assistants special thanks must go to Christopher Guyol and Michael Egolf, who generously devoted a year after graduation to advancing this book in scores of ways; Sam Scrimshaw provided valuable information on and from Google word searches, among much else. Ben Tejblum likewise earned a medal.

All my current graduate students have functioned as junior colleagues; they have lived with the evolving book manuscript and provided constant and essential help, discussing ideas, finding and checking sources, proofreading my shambles of drafts. Hearty thanks to each of them for help that finally brought this project to conclusion: Paul Dingman, Daniel Franke, Christopher Guyol, Andrew Harris, Craig Nakashian, and Peter Sposato. Thanks also go to two graduate assistants from the Department of English at Rochester: Dana Symonds and Ryan Harper.

Librarians, as ever, proved themselves a special breed. Particular thanks to Alan Lupack (Director of Robbins Medieval Library, University of Rochester), Alan Unsworth (History Bibliographer, Rush Rhees Library, University of Rochester) and Pablo Alvarez (Rare Books and Manuscripts Librarian, Rush Rhees Library). In the Huntingtron Library in Pasadena, California, I owe much to the entire staff and I warmly recall the generous assistance of

Mary Robertson (Chief Curator of Manuscripts) and Suzi Krasnoo in Reader Services.

My year at the Huntington Library, in fact, launched this study, and I am most grateful to have held the R. Stanton Avery Distinguished Chair there for 1999–2000. Special thanks go to Roy Ritchie, Director, and all his staff in the Research Division at the Huntington for ceaseless efforts to make that year enjoyable as well as productive. The University of Rochester provided a year of leave that enabled me to accept this position. The Department of History in the California Institute of Technology gave me a one-term teaching position that proved valuable to my own thinking about my themes even as it helped to support my stay in Pasadena. John Mueller, at that time Director of the Wallis Institute at the University of Rochester, offered supplemental funding that was much appreciated, as was his constant interest in topics of shared scholarly concern. For the summer of 2002, I was able to explore and photograph the riches of books of *exempla* in the British Library thanks to a grant from the Penrose Fund of the American Philosophical Society. Invitations to deliver papers in conferences at the Max Planck Institut in Göttingen, Germany; the Research Center for the Study of Japanese History in Kyoto, Japan; the Five College Symposium in Amherst, Massachusetts; and the Medieval and Renaissance Center at the University of California, Los Angeles, provided splendid forums in which to try out initial ideas.

In a study reaching into historical corners that were new for me, I turned both to medieval and early modern scholars in history, literature, and religion. Within my own university, thanks go to Russell Peck and Thomas Hahn in the Department of English, to Alan Lupack in the Robbins Library, and to Curt Cadorette in the Department of Religion. Extramural thanks are due to Dale Hoak (College of William and Mary), David L. Potter (University of Kent), James B. Collins (Georgetown University), the late Elspeth Kennedy, Scott Waugh, and Teofilo Ruiz (UCLA), Helen Swift (St. Hilda's College, Oxford), Raymond Cormier (Longwood University), Norris J. Lacy (Pennsylvania State University), Kelly DeVries (Loyola College), and Cliff Rogers (U.S. Military Academy).

As ever, the University of Pennsylvania Press proved to be an ideal publisher, and I happily acknowledge the collegial and professional work of Jerry Singerman and his assistant Yumeko Kawano, the series editor, Ruth Mazo Karras,, the superhuman copy editor, Kathryn Krug, and the wise managing editor, Alison Anderson. Hearty thanks also go to the readers who commented perceptively on the book while it was a rough manuscript.

The dedication of this book records a sense of gratitude so overwhelming it should be sung, as indeed the statement quoted is, in the last act of Beethoven's incomparable *Fidelio*.